The Theory of Experiential Education

Karen Warren
Mitchell Sakofs
Jasper S. Hunt, Jr.
Editors

Association for Experiential Education
2885 Aurora Avenue #28
Boulder, Colorado 80303

KENDALL/HUNT PUBLISHING COMPANY
4050 Westmark Drive   Dubuque, Iowa 52004

Cover design by Mary Anne Pratt

Contents

Section IV: Social Foundations

Section V: Theory and Practice

Section VI: Ethics

Section VII: Research and Evaluation

Section VIII: Speeches and Perspectives

Introduction

Experiential educators have a keen interest in thinking about why they do what they do. This thinking has manifested itself in a fairly recent publication, the *Journal of Experiential Education*. Begun in the early 1970s, the *Journal* has been a steady source for putting ideas before the emerging profession of experiential education.

With very few exceptions, the articles in the *Journal* have been written by practitioners for practitioners. They have drawn on theoretical sources from philosophy, psychology, theology, political science, women's studies, minority studies, religion, and anthropology. What is unique about much of this writing by practitioners is the wide range of theoretical sources which have nurtured their thinking and the applicability of theory for a deeper understanding of practice.

In the early 1980s, the Association for Experiential Education had the wisdom and foresight to gather together some representative examples of writing which had appeared in the *Journal of Experiential Education*, and to publish these articles in book form. The result was the first edition of *The Theory of Experiential Education*, edited by Mitchell Sakofs and Richard Kraft. The first edition consisted of exact facsimiles of original articles glued together, with a book cover. That first edition provided a much-needed service for many years, and filled a gap between practitioners of experiential education and the world-at-large of education in general.

As the years have passed, it has become evident to many people that the theory book needed to be improved and updated. For one thing, the *Journal of Experiential Education* continued to be published, and a wide variety of articles and authors began to appear. The field of experiential education also began to expand and grow, with practitioners specializing in areas such as classroom teaching, psychological counseling and therapy, corporate training and development, concerns of women and people of color, physically and developmentally differently-abled programming, etc. As the *Journal* and practitioners evolved and developed, the theory book stayed as it was.

In this edition, we have had a twofold task before us. First, we have been very aware of the strong history of the theory book, and we have sought to preserve that written tradition as it emerged. There was some temptation to go back and improve earlier articles in terms of writing style, grammar, and punctuation. We elected to leave the original pieces as the various authors wrote them.

Our other task was to select articles that would reflect the ever-expanding scope of experiential education in various settings. We wanted the specialist to see a wider scope of experiential education and we wanted the generalist to realize the varieties of specialization.

Mainly, we have attempted to put together a book that will encourage readers to think about *why* they are doing *what* they are doing. It has become a generally accepted truth in experiential education that one must always combine action with reflection in order to have a full human experience. This book shows the reflection side of the experience of experiential educators. Reflection, when written down, becomes in some sense theory.

In addition, it seems appropriate that the book should look more like a professional publication. Therefore, all articles have been re-keyed and the physical layout of the book has been done with aesthetics and with readability for users in mind.

It is a tough job to select articles when most of the articles that have appeared in the *Journal of Experiential Education* over the years have been quite good and worth reprinting. We have tried to achieve a balance of perspectives on experiential education as it stands in 1994. This quest for balance necessitated the exclusion of some very good articles because of space and financial constraints. Errors of selection and omission lie with the editors, and in no way reflect on the writers in the *Journal of Experiential Education* who have taken the risk of putting thoughts down on paper for the public to read and judge. In many ways the very existence of this book is predicated on those writers who took the time to reflect and theorize about the practice of experiential education. To all of them we say, "thank you."

Karen Warren
Instructor
Outdoor Program and Recreation Athletics
Hampshire College
Amherst, Massachusetts, USA

Mitchell Sakofs
Director of Special Projects
Outward Bound National Headquarters
Garrison, New York, USA

Jasper Hunt
Professor
Experiential Education
Mankato State University
Mankato, Minnesota, USA

Section I

Philosophical Foundations

1

A Critical Look: The Philosophical Foundations of Experiential Education

April Crosby

I HAD PARTICIPATED IN EXPERIENTIAL LEARNING AS STUDENT AND AS TEACHER numerous times, but I was not officially introduced to the concept or to its many organized schools, camps, and activities until very recently. When I did become aware, I approached it in the way consistent with my training—skeptically. I found myself questioning all the assumptions and values of experiential education, and I found myself, as some advocates of experiential education would say we all are, unable to really look at it until I had put it into a context that means something to me. In my case this context was philosophical, and I began to look at experiential education as a philosophy of education that would include assumptions and value judgments. I investigated experiential education as a philosophy of education in a long line of such evolving philosophies, and I examined it in light of this line. I found it has a very interesting place in line.

Before I go on, I must make some ideas clear. It is important to see that a philosophy of education, or a theory of education, is based on more general beliefs than may appear in the theory. These are the preconceptions or underlying assumptions of a theory, and until they are seen to be the basis of a theory, and accepted, the theory is unfounded. Some are of the school of thought about experiential education that it is *activity*, not theory, and second, that nothing should be written about experiential education because it threatens its action orientation and tends to rigidify it. But even if you only "do" experiential education, there are presuppositions you are acting on. What I want to clarify here is that any theory (or action) of education is based on more general theories of epistemology, and those in turn are based on assumptions about metaphysics.

Epistemology is, roughly, the study of how and what we know. It deals with such questions as whether we know via our sense or our reason, or some combination of the two, and whether we know objects of reason (like higher mathematics, for which there is no action or experiential route) with more certainty than we may know things which we learn through our senses. We might think this because information we get from our senses is sometimes mistaken, as when an object in the far distance appears small when in fact it is large. Epistemology is also concerned with the objects of knowledge: can we know only things which we can tangibly experience, like rocks and tables, or can we know that a non-tangible object, like love, or perhaps God, exists? Some, of course, would say that we have equally reliable experience of God as we do of tables, but for others, this claim raises the question of what do we mean by "experience?" Epistemology is a field which examines many of the underlying assumptions which may be made by people working in the field of experiential education

Also, epistemology is concerned with such distinctions as that between "belief" and "knowledge." Do we say we *knew* the world was flat but now we *know* it is round? We might say we "know" the true things and "believe" the things which may be proven false, or the things which aren't available for proof, as some would say of the existence of God. The point I am trying to make here is how epistemology, or ideas about how we might learn about the world, is based on what we feel and think to be the case about that world, and hence, it is based on metaphysics.

Metaphysics is, roughly, the study of the way the world is. Aristotle said it is the study of things which don't change, for the most part. It is investigation into what is real; for instance, Why does time seem to speed up and slow down? The clock measures objective time while we feel it pass subjectively. Which is real? Is there objectivity at all? Should there be? Is it a handy concept for explaining things, or is it a troublesome ideal which gets in the way? What are the organizing principles in the world? Is history headed in a certain direction, toward a specific actualization toward which we progress, as Christians believe we are headed toward the Kingdom of God and Marxists believe we are headed toward a classless society? Or do we go in cycles of reincarnation, as the Hindus say? Are all of these merely subjective human constructs? Does the world change, or is the change an illusion? Is there ever novelty in the world? These are some of the issues in metaphysics, and clearly theories about how and what we learn about the world would have to entail certain things about that world itself. This is what I mean when I say that philosophy of education, or any activity in the field of education, is based on an epistemology, and therefore, on a metaphysic.

What I found when I did investigations about the philosophical underpinnings of experiential education is that those assumptions underlying experiential education are much more reliable than those underlying more traditional theories of education, and I want to explain what I mean by that. One thing it implies is that students educated according to these assumptions are better prepared to deal with the world than are students educated according to traditional epistemologies. I must say one more thing before going on, however: that is that I am aware that not all people who do experiential education agree on what experiential education is, or what a statement of its theory or values would be.|What I mean by experiential education is a very general belief: that learning will happen more effectively if the learner is as involved as possible, using as many of his faculties as possible, in the learning; and that this involvement is maximized if the student has something that matters to him at stake.\How you get the learner to have something at stake is another issue, and it is, I think, the most controversial question I've encountered in connection with experiential education, but I'm not concerned with it here.

Back to the philosophical underpinnings of experiential education. I want to cursorily review the history of the philosophy of education to show how I think experiential education and some of its philosophical assumptions developed, and why I think it is epistemologically sound.

HISTORY

An early theory of education was illustrated by the Sophists, who were teachers in ancient Greece. We think of them as flourishing prior to what we call the golden age of classical Greece, though they were still extant then. These men charged fees for their tutelage, and leading citizens of Athens would pay handsome sums to have their sons taught by them. The teaching consisted primarily of reciting opinions on profound subjects, and helping students to learn to recite these opinions equally persuasively. Students learned answers to questions such as "What is virtue?", "What is piety?", "What is the nature of the beautiful?", and others. We can call this theory the "pouring theory" of education, because the teachers had the learning which they could pour into the students as if they were vessels. Once the students had the learning, they too could recite definitions and theories on deep subjects.

We can see the epistemological and metaphysical assumptions of this educational practice even more easily if we look at another modern counterpoint: the way the catechism is taught in very orthodox Roman Catholic church schools. There, children are given books which pose questions and also give answers. The children learn to recite the specified answers and are said to know their catechism. According to this, we could know that God exists whether or not we have experienced Him, and we know that He, the utmost Reality, does not change. That's why these answers need not change, and why the method of teaching need not change. The children are learning about an unchanging reality, and those who know can tell those who don't yet know the truth about it. Because of the nature of the *object* of knowledge, in this case God (which is a metaphysical principle), the subjectivity of the learner is not relevant. What is true of God is simply true of Him, not true for me but not for you, or true in different ways.

The Sophists also thought that way about the objects of knowledge. Each knew the final word about things which did not need debate. A curious thing is that the Sophists disagreed among themselves, just as our religious leaders might also disagree about what they think is absolute. A father sent his sons to the Sophist with the most prestige, or to the Sophist who would make his son the most influential orator, or, if he were a thinking father, to the Sophist with whom he agreed. In any event, learners were the uninformed who could be filled up with knowledge as if it were soup and one could get it all.

This model of education changed radically with the teacher Socrates (470-399 B.C.) He taught by asking questions, not reciting answers, and he asked many questions of the Sophists which they couldn't answer because their opinions couldn't stand up under scrutiny. Socrates was asking about *their* underlying assumptions, and they frequently got confused. They were not used to discussion.

As a teacher, Socrates made two major methodological changes from the Sophists. First, he believed that the students had something to contribute to the learning, and he elicited that; second, he believed that the *process* of becoming educated was the important thing, rather than arriving at a final static state, and he practiced that. He taught by beginning where the students were and leading them, through discussion, to examine their own ideas. He taught that the educated person was the one who questions all through life; that learning is a lifestyle, and this style he called "tending the soul." These beliefs and practices sound much closer to those of experiential education than do those of the Sophists.

However, according to Plato, who recorded the conversations of Socrates, the true goal of this search for knowledge is knowledge of the Forms (or what we might call essences) and these were Objective Reality. According to Plato, dialectic discussion is the epistemological tool by which we can learn of The Forms, the metaphysical principles of Reality. Plato says in the *Republic* that this true knowledge of absolutes is not achievable by most of us because of our limited capacity to learn from dialectic. Most of us are doomed to forever mistake images and the sensible objects around us as the highest Reality. Any learning of which we are capable is gained by reflection on our own beliefs, and this is accomplished best by critical discussion with others. Plato also pointed out, accurately, that most of us are hesitant to have our beliefs and assumptions questioned and therefore, learning is usually painful.

Let's look at Plato's epistemological and metaphysical assumptions. Although few students would ever know them, Socrates tried to lead knowledge of the Forms, or absolutes. There was an essence or Form of virtue, and of beauty, and of other less profound things, each of which was a true, perfect, and unchanging model of that quality or Thing. The Forms existed, in some sense, and functioned as paradigms.

Why would he arrive at such an idea of absolutes? He saw that all we have available to us through experience are *particular* beautiful things, yet we say that one is more or less beautiful, as if we had some knowledge of an absolute standard of Beauty to which we compare all individual cases. Or, take the idea of a chair. We all know more or less what a chair is, but if you were asked to define it, would you include four legs? Bean bag chairs have no legs at all, and some chairs have three. Would you include that it is used for sitting? If I sit on a table, does that make it a chair? Perhaps you would specify that it has to be *intended* for sitting. Well, is a bicycle seat a chair? We can imagine someone stopping us by saying, "That's not a chair!" when we start to sit on something which might break. Plato saw that although not many of us can articulate what the essence of "chair" is, there *must* be one, because despite differing and changing definitions, we all know what a chair is.

The same is true of Virtue. We may think we know what it is until we are forced to define it. Most likely, even if we don't claim to be able to define it, we could recognize particular cases we would call acts of virtue, and cases we would say clearly are not. Plato watched people wrestle with these things and it made him propose that objective absolutes do exist, but we are just in very hazy touch with them. We can get closer to the metaphysical realities by the epistemological method of reflective and critical dialogue about our theories. This is accomplished in education by asking students to set forth their ideas which are then examined.

We may call the Socratic philosophy of education the "midwifery theory" because Socrates saw the role of the teacher as that of a midwife: helping give birth to the knowledge which is already within the student The teacher simply assists with delivery. The goal is persons who can continue to express and examine their own and others' ideas. Socrates saw such constant intellectual exercise as a way of life.

Philosophy of education went through another evolution with Aristotle, (384–322 B.C.). In metaphysics, Aristotle rejected Plato's theory of the Forms as Reality because he saw too many problems with trying to defend their existence. Besides, Aristotle's background was as a biologist and he saw the universe in terms of growth and change as a biologist would. Reality as unchanging Forms made no sense to him. He believed that the organizing metaphysical principle was one of change: the world can be explained in terms of things changing from what they *potentially* are to their state of being *actually* realized. For example, acorns always become oak trees, oak trees may become tables, that table may become firewood, or decay into the earth again, etc. Aristotle's Reality was one which took into account change, and the change is from potentiality to actuality. The actualization of a thing depends on its species. For example, the full actualization of a colt is a beautifully running horse because it is the highest function of a horse to run. The fully actualized human being, according to Aristotle, is the one who thinks most fully because thinking is the function of the human species, peculiar to it only.

At this point we can see how the metaphysical principles of potentiality, actuality, and the change from one to the next would influence education theory. Young men were taught to use the highest function of their species, their cognitive minds, in order to become fully realized humans. This led to obvious trouble with ethical questions. We can see that a man who is most highly developed *mentally* might not be what we think of as a *morally* developed man. Aristotle never solves this dilemma very satisfactorily, but he begins to answer with a distinction between "theoretical wisdom," which is the highest function of our minds, and "practical wisdom," which is the highest human potential in the social or moral realm. This is the distinction between "theoria" and praxis," and Aristotle seems to say that theoria is the higher goal for man.

We can see that by the end of Plato and Aristotle's time, Western intellectual thought had developed a twofold bifurcation: the distinction between Reality and the sensible world, and the distinction between theory and practice. In each case, there is an implied value judgment in favor of the former, but for neither philosopher was attainment of highest knowledge readily possible for man. Very few people could truly know the Forms, said Plato; and the life of pure theoria was not possible for man, said Aristotle. Hence, the search for knowledge in its true form was frustrating.

Western intellectual thought, and the philosophy of education with it, thus inherited a problem of the separation between:

Knowing Mind<————————————————>Knowable Mind
(subject)   (object)

The object of knowledge may be a substance like the Forms, for Plato; or a process like theoria, for Aristotle. The problem of epistemology and therefore, education, becomes: How do we get the knowing mind in touch with its object of knowledge, the world?

The answers to this question fell into two major categories. The Rationalists in the 16th century, led by Descartes in France, thought we could only know with certainty those things which we knew through Reason or thinking alone. This meant logic and mathematics were knowable, but the sensible world which we know through our senses was suspect; $2+2=4$ never changes, he thought, but sensual things do. The other epistemological school, led generally by the Scotsman Hume, said we could rely only on sense data, and that mental operations were only compilations and augmentations of what we gain through our senses. He thought, exactly contrary to Descartes, that knowledge gained through purely mental means was suspect, and it led to such unfounded hypotheses as "God." All knowledge must be based on what is empirically available to our senses. The debate between empiricism and rationalism is the most basic epistemological debate in philosophy, and depending where you stand on this issue, radically influences how you would think education is effectively conducted, and what its proper subjects are.

Let's examine for a minute the problems which would follow from adhering to either a strict rationalism or a strict empiricism. If we believe with Descartes that the information we gain through our senses is unreliable because it is sometimes misleading, then the only knowledge we can have reliably is that gained from using reason only. That limits us to abstract areas such as math and logic and theoretical subjects. We could not even have certain knowledge of our own bodies, as, after all, amputees often "feel" their nonexistent limbs. While the knowledge we *can* have may be objectively true, it is not very useful for functioning in this human world. If we can't trust our senses, how could we ever check our knowledge of the external world, or of each other? If I perceive that an object in a dim light is a dark blue, and I want to confirm it, so I ask you, the confirmation means little more than my original sense impression. The reason is that if I can't trust my senses, then I can't trust my ears to hear you correctly any more than I can trust my eyes to correctly see the blue. If our senses are unreliable, then checking like this is like buying another copy of the same newspaper to confirm a story. Hence, the predicament which follows from a strict rationalist epistemology is that each individual consciousness is forever locked into itself with no way to verify that the external world (and that includes other people) is really there. Knowledge is limited to fairly useless abstractions.

If, on the other hand, we believe with Hume that knowledge comes from empirical sense data, and all knowledge must be traced back to its empirical evidence for validation, then the mind and what it can know is severely limited in another direction. Hume says we cannot legitimately draw conclusions on the basis of sense data which are not themselves directly evidenced. "God" is not the only concept which immediately goes out the window as unfounded. "Causation" is another one. Hume points out that while we may be able to see billiard ball #1 hit billiard ball #2, and then we see billiard ball #2 move, we never in fact *see* the sensual impression which is "cause." All we *know* is that ball #2 always moves when ball #1 hits it (if ball #2 is not impeded) because that is all we *see*. When we jump to the conclusion that ball #1 *caused* ball #2 to move and from there to the conclusion that causation is an explanation of relationship between events, this is an unfounded mental move. "Causation" is merely a mental construct which is made on the basis of habit, not because there is legitimate evidence for the idea. Hence for the empiricists, our knowledge is grossly limited to what Hume called the "blooming, buzzing confusion" of sensual impressions, and any inferences about what causes them or relates them to each a other are baseless. We may know our own sense impressions, but we cannot know what it is out there that "causes" them, or orders them.

Before returning to the implications of all this for education, one more step in the history of epistemology must be discussed. This step is how the German philosopher Kant, in 1787, resolved the rationalist/empiricist debate. Reading Descartes and Hume, Kant saw an impasse. He realized that if we assume that the world is orderly, as both Plato did with his Forms and Aristotle did with his growth model, and if we assume that to gain knowledge of this order, the human mind must in some way find and match that objective order, then there was no way we could ever have knowledge. We would have to be outside our own minds to see if what we thought was right about the world was in fact the way the world was.

So Kant saw that the basic approach of expecting the mind to match the world was an impossible premise: it made knowledge impossible. He revolutionized the whole field by supposing instead that the source of order is not in the external world but in the human mind. That is, we order our world in the very process of perceiving it. We cannot use what we perceive unless it is ordered according to certain categories, e.g., space, time, and causation. Kant hypothesized that because of the structure of the human mind, we would never receive experience except as already organized by our active, structuring minds. For all we know, the "objective" world may be Hume's "blooming, buzzing confusion" but by the time it is available to us, it is not confused. The point is that any notion of what the objective world is like is of no interest to us and should not be taken as a goal of human knowledge because there is absolutely no way we can get in touch with it. We would have to be gods or at least some consciousness other than humans to see it. The only "objectivity" we can have is knowing that humans all order experience in some of the basic same ways because our minds have the basic same structure. Hence, according to Kant, I cannot imagine experience outside of time and space, and I can count on your not being able to either.

By seeing the mind as the active source of order, rather than some objective unchanging Reality as the order, Kant attempted to solve the problem of certainty. Certainty, Reality, objectivity, etc., all have less rigorous meanings, in a sense. They are reality-for-us, or objectivity-for-us, but that is good enough.

Thanks to Kant, Western thought got beyond this epistemological impasse. (There are lots of problems with Kant's work, but those are other issues.) His theory provides room for both reason and experience to function, and gets us out of the disastrous problem of how to get in touch with that which we want to know.

Years later the American, John Dewey (1859-1952) picked up the debate. We can say that he accepted Kant in that the mind is an active, ordering principle, and in that he accepted the world as we experience it rather than seeking some other Reality.

Dewey noted that not only theoretical problems followed from the split between Reality and the sensible world, and from the split between theoria and praxis, but problems of immediate human concern arose because of them also. One problem was that the emphasis on the intellectual or cognitive side of man (especially noted in Aristotle) alienated man from his immediate environment, and also from his emotional, affective self. The emphasis of the rationalists is overly cerebral. Dewey noted that the unavoidable concerns of human beings are not with some abstract and unattainable Reality, but with prosperity and adversity, success and failure, achievement and frustration, good and bad. In other words, humans are more concerned with questions of value than questions of Reality, and any adequate epistemological and educational theory ought to be geared toward knowing values, rather than toward theoretical abstractions.

Dewey saw that the need to achieve *certainty* led Western thought to theoretical constructs like those of Plato and Descartes, or to the epistemological impoverishment of Hume. Dewey saw clearly enough to see that the goal of certainty must be rejected as a starting point. Man is first and foremost an active and emotive being, said Dewey, and reflection and concern with knowing is secondary learned behavior. Furthermore, it is learned primarily as a result of uncertain or problematic situations.

Therefore, said Dewey, the metaphysical starting point should not be an abstraction, but experience itself: philosophy should investigate life as humans experience it, not as it might be. We find ourselves in continual transaction with the physical, psychological, mental, spiritual world, and philosophy should be a *systematic investigation into the nature of this experience.* Dewey's systematic investigation led him to see that experience is subject to a pattern: first, it has an immediate, felt, aesthetic quality. Experience is not, at first, reflective, and is not at first replete with the distinctions which reflection bestows upon it. Then, the distinctive qualities *evolve* from the indeterminate, inchoate: and experience *becomes* determinate and meaningful. Finally, experience is often felt to have a consummation, or what might now be called a closure. Dewey saw that the enemy of experience in this sense is not the intellect but the extremes of diffusion or rigidity, either of which would preclude the movement from the felt aesthetic immediacy to reflective meaningfulness. Human life, concluded Dewey, as felt, is a rhythmic movement from events of doubt and conflict to events of integrity and harmony. When humans face the world and want to know about it, the goal is not to find Reality, but to change the problematic to the integrated and consummated.

Starting with this notion of experience as the metaphysical category of what is, changes in epistemology followed. Gaining knowledge was the process of making determinate the indeterminate experience, and the method was the scientific method. The steps are:

1.   We find ourselves in a "felt difficulty" and this is the condition for inquiry.
2.   We articulate the problem for solution.

3.   We form a hypothesis for solution, and deduce the consequences of alternative solutions.

4.   We test the hypothesis: we confirm or disconfirm.

5.   We have knowledge: that which is warranted through inquiry, and it becomes incorporated as background for further inquiry.

Hence, "Reality" is not that which matches some abstract objective level of being, but that which gives meaning to inquiry, and that which is repeatedly meaningful in inquiry and experience. This method of inquiry is self-correcting, because if something is incorrect, it will make experience meaningless, not meaningful, and will be found out.

And "Truth" is not some abstract, objective reality, but rather "that which works" or "that which explains." Knowledge is primarily instrumental for action, not an end-in-itself.

And "Reason" is not an intuitive light which puts men in touch with certainty and truth, but rather, it is a disposition of conduct to foresee consequences of events, and to use what is foreseen in planning and conducting one's affairs.

And "Mind" refers to an instrumental method of directing change.

For Dewey, the point is to intentionally *use* experience in its dynamic form to divest experience of its indefinite and unintelligible nature, and to bring about consummations in life. The point is to make experience usable.

The difference that Dewey made in metaphysics was to start with the experienced world as reality and not to assume some objective Reality which would require God's vision to see. The difference that follows from this for epistemology is that the knowing tools we have, including pure reason and including empirical data from our senses, are both legitimate tools for knowing our world and functioning intelligently in it. The goal of learning is to know about the world as we experience it, and both theory and practice are components in the scientific method for achieving this knowledge.

All of this, which is Dewey's metaphysical and epistemological starting point in experience *as felt*, rather than as objective, leads to a very clear philosophy of education which is, I think, the foundation of what most people call experiential education. In Dewey's philosophy of education, the goal of education is not the right answer, for that might change. The goal is being able to understand and use our experience, and this is achieved by developing the thought processes with which we examine our experience. In this model, the teacher aids the student in developing an approach to his own experience by structuring the student's experience so that he may move from a challenge to a resolution. The educational process is based on the human experience of movement from difficulty to resolution. After resolution comes reflection on the movement so that what is learned may be generalized and used again.(

Early in this article, I said that the assumptions of experiential education are more reliable than those underlying more traditional theories. By "more reliable," I meant more helpful in understanding our world, and why I conclude this is by now, I hope, clear. In experiential education, the learner-involved-in-immediate-experience is the object of knowledge, and the activity in, and reflection on, that involvement are the means of knowing. Experiential education attempts to blur the distinction between cognitive and affective learning because experience does not come distinguished this way and is not lived this way.

The paradigm of experiential education, which I encountered in a model designed by Laura Joplin, has the following elements: challenge, support, "feedback," and "debrief." Dewey's theory of experience begins with a challenge: the "felt difficulty" which must be resolved. It includes support and "feedback" in that the attempts at resolution either work or don't work; they help in making meaning or they increase confusion. For Dewey, "debriefing" consists of reflection on the now-resolved difficulty, and is the process of integrating what was learned in a way which makes future experiences more intelligible.

Experiential educators may or may not be familiar with Dewey, or with Einstein, Heisenberg, Godel, and other thinkers whose hypotheses imply how misconceived is an educational process which aims at objectivity. What they do recognize is that education which teaches tools which can used regardless of whatever is currently called truth is the more lasting accomplishment. The assumptions of this orientation better fit the world as we know it, and would appear to still fit as that changes.

In looking at experiential education in this way, I was able to see that it is not unfounded, nor is it anti-intellectual as some critics charge and as some practitioners hope. The philosophy and practice of experiential education are developments which have a heritage, regardless of whether its advocates know, acknowledge, or value it. On the basis of this examination, one is able to see that experiential education "teachers" are subject to a misconception which faced the Sophists even 2,000 years ago: they thought they knew the truth, and that therefore people should behave accordingly.

2

On Defining Experiential Education

Laura Joplin

THE PREMISE OF THIS PAPER IS THAT ALL LEARNING IS EXPERIENTIAL. THIS MEANS that anytime a person learns, he must "experience" the subject—significantly identify with, seriously interact with, form a personal relationship with, etc. Many educational settings only partially promote learning. Those aspects which yield learning can be defined by an experiential model, whether intended or not. Much that is done under the guise of education does not involve learning. Likewise, though all learning is experiential, not all of it is deliberately planned or takes place through an educational institution or setting. This paper is designed to define or identify those aspects of education that are experiential, i.e., those portions of experiential learning which are deliberately planned. This paper includes two approaches to defining experiential education:

1) A five-stage model generalized from reviewing the processes and components of those programs calling themselves experiential;

2) A review of nine characteristics developed by comparing experiential and nonexperiential programs and describing the implicit and explicit assumptions in the experiential programs.

THE FIVE-STAGE MODEL

Beyond particular agency- and client-related tasks, experiential programs begin with two responsibilities for their program design: providing an experience for the learner, and facilitating the reflection on that experience. Experience alone is insufficient to be called experiential education, and it is the reflection process which turns experience into experiential education. The process is often called an "action-reflection" cycle. The process is generally referred to as cycle, ongoing and ever-building, with the later stages being dependent on the earlier stages. Most program descriptions and experiential educators hold these statements as "givens" in defining experiential education.

The five-stage model was developed to communicate an experiential action strategy to teachers as they planned their courses. The intent was to enable teachers to more deliberately design their courses and thus, increase the experiential nature of those designs.

Briefly stated, the five-stage model is organized around a central, hurricane-like cycle, which is illustrated, as challenging action. It is preceded by a focus and followed by a debrief. Encompassing all is the environment of support and feedback. The five stages are one complete cycle, where completion of the fifth stage is concurrent with commencing the first stage of the following cycle.

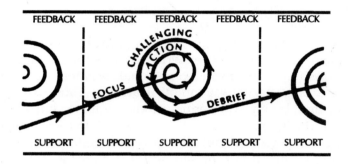

The model is both "maxi" and mini" in scope. A one-semester course could be viewed through the five stages of the model, and also have the limitless repetitions within the whole course. Following the initial premise that all learning is experiential, every time a person "learns," these five stages are involved in one way or another. Thus, interpretation of each of the stages for any one situation is very dependent upon the degree of "maxi" or "mini" that is under study. A flash of insight would be describable in these terms. However, the initial purpose of the model is to enable teachers to design courses and course components. Thus, the model is intentionally simple. For purposes of defining learning, the model is far from appropriate and should not be scrutinized for its relation to learning theory. Rather, the model should be viewed so that regardless of what mental processes and brain functions may be involved, these five stages remain the responsibility of the facilitator of learning.

FOCUS is the first stage of the cycle. Focus includes presenting the task and isolating the attention of the learner for concentration. It defines the subject of study and prepares the student for encountering the challenging action that is to follow. A good focusing stage is specific enough to orient the student, but not too specific so as to rule out unplanned learning. Most experiential programs expect and intend students to learn things that their fellow learners did not learn: it is the nature of individualized education. Focus facilitates that by helping the learner prepare for what he or she views as important. Focus also works to tell the student what the course and/or teacher holds as important and thus, explains the expectations placed on him.

The actions in the focus stage are dependent upon the activity to follow as well as the activity rating on the "maxi-mini" scale. Focus actions may include meeting as a group and having each member discuss his expectations, desires, or needs. It may also include having students use learning contracts. Reading an article relevant to the ensuing action is focusing, as well as the teacher's explanation for the next class activity. Focus can also be indirect, such as when a rock-climbing instructor opens a packsack and begins laying out an array of climbing paraphernalia.

ACTION is the hurricane stage of the model. This stage places the learner in a stressful or jeopardy-like situation where he is unable to avoid the problem presented, often in an unfamiliar environment requiring new skills or the use of new knowledge. Action may be physical, mental, emotional, spiritual, or of any other dimension. Action involves the student with the subject, occupying much of his attention and energy in sorting, ordering, analyzing, moving, struggling, emoting, embracing, etc. The action phase gives the learner great responsibility.

Different actions—such as wilderness experiences, environmental education, and internship programs—have often become confused or synonymous with experiential education. The design of the action component should not be confused with the educational approach being used. All of these, and many more, can be characterized by the same model or philosophy. Recent work in brain research promises the most complete description of action as it relates to the brain's operations. Leslie A. Hart, in _How the Brain Works_, has explained that the brain is innately active. The brain is "on" when it is actively choosing, ordering, making decisions, etc. The brain is not "on" when someone is attempting to pour information into it. Therefore, to design an action component for experiential programs, it is mandatory that the student and his brain be given responsibility in the learning process. Reading a book is a challenging action for an experiential program, IF it gets the student responsible for processing the information within it. The student can be given such responsibilities as choosing the book to read on a teacher-assigned topic; defining the reason for reading the book; searching for an answer to a problem in a book; using the book as a reference; or defending a personally held value position.

Another cross-reference for defining action is the use of "original sources." Watching a film of someone rock climbing is far different from climbing the rock oneself. Similarly, reading about business administration is much different from interning in a business office. A history class studying the United Nations might take the dramatic field trip and visit that august facility in New York. However, original sources for studying the United Nations could also be interviewing people about its current activities or reading newspaper clippings during a time of great debate on it. Textbooks are a supposedly efficient means of giving information to students. However, textbooks innately deny much responsibility to the student. The textbook author decides which source he will cite, what the correct references are, and the important points of the topic. All of this denies the student and his brain the opportunity and necessity of deciding, sorting, or actively pursuing information.

The overarching strategy which helps implement these ideas of original sources and a brain that is "on," is student responsibility. A student climbing a rock is allowed to succeed and fail on his own; indeed, he must do it on his own. In a classroom, a student must be given the freedom to fail. A teacher who leads the student through an assignment has not given the student the responsibility for that action phase. Increasing student responsibility does not mean leaving a student to struggle with a problem that is beyond his capacity or background preparation. The problem must be appropriate to the learner, and it is the teacher's responsibility to design it accordingly.

Using a student-responsibility schema requires great faith in the learner. Students often express great anger and resentment when first introduced into a responsibility-oriented experiential situation. Tricks to get teachers to assume their overly helpful habits will be tried by many students: students will often exclaim that they are unable to solve the problem. The teacher's only assurance in this situation is his own experience and faith that the student can master the task. The teacher needs to gain faith in the students as more capable than many educational situations accept. The stages of support and feedback in the model mediate the student's anxiety and the teacher's responses.

SUPPORT and FEEDBACK exist throughout the learning experience, maxi and mini. Adequate support enables the student to continue to try. Adequate feedback will ensure that the student has the necessary information to be able to move ahead.

Support provides security and caring in a manner that stimulates the learner to challenge himself and to experiment. Support demonstrates that the learner is not working alone but has human responsiveness that accepts personal risk taking. Support is implemented in many subtle and obvious ways. Support is demonstrating interest in the learner's situation and letting him know that help is available if needed. Having the group share individual frustrations will help each member see that his feelings are not unique. Support can be physical, verbal, or written.

Feedback provides information to the student about what he has been doing. It can include comments about how the student works, his manner of interactions, or the substance of his work. Feedback works best with an equalization of power between learner and facilitator. The teacher should distinguish between those ideas that the teacher holds as true, and those ideas that the teacher believes most professionals in the field hold as true. The areas given to student discretion should be made clear. Feedback is also more easily understood the more specific it is. Specific examples help clarify the meaning, especially those coming from mutually experienced activities.

The fifth stage in the model is *DEBRIEF.* Here, the learning is recognized, articulated, and evaluated. The teacher is responsible for seeing that the actions previously taken do not drift along unquestioned, unrealized, unintegrated, or unorganized. Debrief helps the student learn from experience. Debrief is a sorting and ordering of information, often involving personal perceptions and beliefs. In experiential learning—as opposed to experiential education—debrief may occur within the individual. However, in experiential education, debrief needs to be made public. It can be made public through group discussion, writing of themes or summary papers, sharing of personal journals, doing a class project, or a class presentation. It is the publicly verifiable articulation which makes experience and experiential learning capable of inclusion and acceptance by the educational institutions. The public nature of debrief also ensures that the learner's conclusions are verified and mirrored against a greater body of perception than his alone. The process of reflecting on the past often includes decisions about what needs to be done next or how it should have been done initially. The public nature of debrief helps turn these comments into focusing agents for the next five-stage cycle.

This five-stage model presents the general actions and responsibilities that a teacher maintains through experiential education. The nature of the actions chosen by a teacher at each stage of the model can be further clarified by looking at the overarching characteristics on experiential programs. The descriptors to be presented have one unifying parameter: they are based on an "involved" paradigm.

Experiential education is based on the assumption that all knowing must begin with the individual's relationship to the topic. The involved paradigm explains that everything is connected to everything else. Therefore, to learn, we must investigate those relations. Among other things, this necessitates including personal perceptions and values. The process of learning may involve being as objective as possible in any given situation. However, the innate subjectivity that characterizes all knowing must be recognized and accounted for in our learning systems. Following are nine characteristics which further clarify how this involved paradigm is characterized in educational settings.

8 - Nine Characteristics

- *Student based rather than teacher based.* Learning starts with the student's perceptions and current awareness. Much of typical course design attempts to start with an orderly format based on the teacher's ideas of the ideas of the textbook author or the school board. These starting points and the context organization may or may not be relevant to the learner. Experiential education starts with the student and goes at his pace of learning. It does necessitate some latitude given for including unplanned topics and not including all that might otherwise be covered. Though less teacher-decided material may be covered, more material may be learned because of the student-oriented process.

- *Personal not impersonal nature.* The learner as a feeling, valuing, perceiving being is stressed. Experiential education starts with the individual's relationship to the subject of study. How a student feels about a subject is valued along with the student's prowess or factual recall. The relationship of educational experiences to personal growth is allowed to be incorporated into the classroom. There are degrees of psychological change that are not appropriate to the classroom. However, the ordinary maturing process of a person often accompanies and affects increasing knowledge. Thus, the person who is learning is as important as the subject which is being studied.

- *Process and product orientation.* Experiential education stresses how a student arrives at an answer as well as how "right" that answer may be. The product of the study is valued within the context of the thought and work processes behind it. This is especially important in the evaluation process. Student evaluation is commonly a "products only" evaluation. Experiential educators also need to assess a student's ideas, developing processes, and work strategies. These are readily monitored by student journals. The process of idea investigation can be viewed by looking at the reasons a student chose a book, why it was finished instead of being put aside, and how the ideas within it relate to his problem of study.

- *Evaluation for internal and external reasons.* Much of educational evaluation is done for agents external to the student's learning experience, such as parents, school boards, entrance to other educational programs, etc. Evaluation in experiential education also includes evaluation as a learning experience. Evaluation is not something that is only "done to" the student. Students can be encouraged to develop self-evaluation skills and take part in the monitoring of their learning. Competence in evaluation skills can help a student become more of an independent, self-directed learner. Students participating in their own evaluation increase their responsibility.

5 ▪ *Holistic understanding and component analysis.* Experiential education includes both the explanation of phenomena through statistical equations and describing the variety and depth of the qualities of the subject. Narrative descriptions, interviews, personal reports, inventories, questionnaires, or group discussions can provide information. Representing the complexity of situations is stressed over the simple summation.

6 ▪ *Organized around experience.* Direct experience provides the substance from which learners develop personal meaning. Since the learning starts with the learner's experience, the subject organization must start there also. A problem or thematic approach can provide a strong organization for experiential education. Rather than building from the simple to the complex, experiential situations start with a complex experience and analyze it as the follow-up study. Enlisting student participation in choosing among a set of topics to be covered as well as the order of study, helps the teacher organize the course around the student's experience.

7 ▪ *Perception based rather than theory based.* Experiential learning emphasizes a student's ability to justify or explain a subject, rather than to recite an expert's testimony. His ability to articulate and argue his position in the light of conflicting theories, facts, and firsthand encounters will be the test and learning medium. Expert testimony is one source for investigating an idea. Experiential education stresses knowing the subject from the ground up, starting with the student's perception and moving to the expert testimony as verifier of views.

8 ▪ *Individual based rather than group based.* Experiential education stresses the individual's development in a self-referenced fashion. Group comparisons or norm ratings are useful as supplemental information. Norm-referenced grading can be a part of experiential education, especially for target audiences such as school systems and college entrance boards. However, the emphasis and goal within experiential education is toward monitoring the individual's growth and the development of self-awareness. Group identity and socialization skills are often involved in experiential programs. The emphasis is, however, on the individual's relationship and role within the group, and that person's awareness of group functioning and his part in it.

These nine characteristics and the five-stage model taken together can provide the stimulus and home base for a teacher's course-design endeavors. They are intrinsically individually based, for teachers as well as learners. How a teacher implements the ideas will depend on that person's characteristics, perceptions, and goals. The model necessitates that the teacher be a learner along with the student The model demands continual responsiveness that can only work when the teacher is an active perceiver and learner in the situation. Deliberate exploration of these ideas can help a teacher know himself, his goals for his students, and his ability to implement the type of experiential program that he desires.

3

Dewey's Philosophical Method and Its Influence on His Philosophy of Education

Jasper S. Hunt, Jr.

INTRODUCTION

THE THESIS OF THIS PAPER IS THAT JOHN DEWEY DEVELOPED A PHILOSOPHICAL method and that his philosophy of education presupposes this method. I want to show that: given his way of doing philosophy, it would have been impossible for Dewey to have espoused any other philosophy of education than the one he developed.

The paper will proceed by first outlining Dewey's method of philosophy. This will be done by focusing in on two fundamental ideas of his entire philosophy. These are Dewey's attack on any form of philosophical dualism and his category of experience. The final section of the paper will show how Dewey's philosophy of education comes directly from his basic philosophical method.

ATTACK ON DUALISM

As a young graduate student of philosophy at Johns Hopkins University from 1882-1884, Dewey was confronted by a philosophical corpus that seemed to draw its very lifeblood from philosophical dualism.

In epistemology, the lines were drawn between the rationalists and the empiricists. On the American philosophical scene, this contrast was made evident to Dewey by the diverse views of Chauncy Wright and Charles Peirce. Although both Wright and Peirce were empirical in their methods, they reached different positions, with Wright maintaining a rigid empiricism and Peirce becoming, eventually, more of a rationalist. Dewey was also confronted by William James, who termed himself a radical empiricist but who sought at the same time to defend religious sources of knowledge.

In metaphysics, the battle lines were established between the materialists and the idealists. On the one hand, Dewey was confronted by the philosophy of Ralph Waldo Emerson, who explicitly advocated an idealistic view of metaphysics. Dewey was also familiar with the work of Auguste Comte and his resulting rejection of metaphysics and adoption of materialism. Dewey quotes Bertrand Russell as an example of the attempt to create dualisms in metaphysics. Russell says that mathematics "finds a habitation eternally standing, where our ideals are fully satisfied and our best hopes are not thwarted."[1]

It should be pointed out here that Dewey was himself a metaphysical idealist as a young man. Morton White points out that Dewey turned toward Hegelian idealism as a reaction against British empiricism.[2] Indeed, Paul Conkin says that "Dewey had learned to hate the atomistic sensationalism of British empiricism."[3] But Dewey's exposure to the scientific thought of Chauncy Wright and Charles Peirce led him away from the dominant influence of idealism.

The ultimate dualism Dewey fought was the separation of the human from the natural. Dewey saw this separation as having disastrous results both in epistemology and in metaphysics. In epistemology, it resulted in either an empirical skepticism, which said that all man could know truly was his own sensations, or else a rigid scientism, which said that all man could know was the phenomenal world.

In metaphysics, dualism resulted in either a denigration of the world of being, in favor of the world of becoming, or the opposite. Dewey's main concern was that these dualisms resulted in an ontological fragmentation, that is, a fragmentation of being, with negative results in practical affairs. Dewey refers to the opposites in metaphysics as either total objectivism or else total subjectivism. He was critical of both, as evidenced by the following quote:

> But philosophical dualism is but a formulated recognition of an impasse in life; an impotence in interaction, inability to make effective transition, limitation of power to regulate and thereby to understand. Capricious pragmatism based on exaltation of personal desire; consolatory estheticism based on capacity for wringing

---

[1] John Dewey, *Experience and Nature* (LaSalle, 1925) p. 51. Henceforth referred to as E.N.

[2] Morton White, *Science and Sentiment in America: Philosophical Thought from Jonathan Edwards to John Dewey*. (New York, 1972) pp. 269-273.

[3] Paul K. Conkin, *Puritans and Pragmatists: Eight Eminent American Thinkers*. (Bloomington, 1968) p. 350.

contemplative enjoyment from even the tragedies of the outward spectacle; refugee idealism based on rendering thought omnipotent in the degree in which it is ineffective in concrete affairs; these forms of subjectivism register an acceptance of whatever obstacles at the time prevent the active participation of the self in the ongoing course of events.[4]

This quote shows the stress Dewey laid on the practically bad results of such philosophical dualism as subjectivism or objectivism. Indeed dualism, says Dewey, renders man "impotent."

Dewey refers to philosophical dualism by means of a technical term. He calls the attempt to create dualisms, both in epistemology and metaphysics, the "fallacy of selective emphasis."[5] This fallacy consists in the efforts of philosophers to take a particular aspect of knowledge or reality and to universalize it to a superior status of reality or knowledge. Dewey illustrates the fallacy of selective emphasis by entering into the metaphysical conflict between being and becoming. Dewey refers to the "precarious" and "stable" aspects of existence.[6] He argues that ever since the days of Heraclitus and Parmenides, metaphysics has tended to focus on either the world of the precarious or else of the stable at the expense of the reality of the other. Dewey rejects the idea that the world is either in a state of total flux or of total being. The fallacy of selective emphasis is also seen in epistemology by the old conflict between rational and empirical sources of knowledge. He refers to both epistemological systems as falling under the heading of the fallacy of selective emphasis.

The Category of Experience

Dewey was not content to simply criticize the prevailing tendency of philosophy to fall into the fallacy of selective emphasis and thereby create dualisms. Dewey saw his major philosophical task as dealing with this fundamental issue and, hopefully, solving it. Dewey does not attempt to solve the problems of dualism by entering into the old dialectical arguments directly. Indeed, he rejects the attempt to enter directly into the conflicts outlined above both in epistemology and in metaphysics. He says, "I know of no route by which dialectical argument can answer such objections. They arise from associations with words and cannot be dealt with argumentatively."[7]

---

[4]John Dewey, E.N. p. 198.

[5]John Dewey, E.N. p. 24.

[6]John Dewey, E.N. p. 37-66.

[7]John Dewey, E.N. p. 1.

Dewey's resolution to these problems rests in his analysis of experience. The word "experience" is a technical term for Dewey and contains within it the seeds of his entire philosophy. Evidence for this claim can be seen simply by reading the titles of three of his most influential works. These are *Art as Experience, Experience and Nature,* and *Experience and Education.*

It is with the category of experience that Dewey enters directly into the conflicts which he inherited philosophically. Dewey terms the method of basing philosophical inquiry upon experience as "empirical naturalism."[8] The empirical naturalist is attempting to make a bridge between the human and the natural, the rational and the empirical, and the material and the idealistic. Dewey wants empirical naturalism to render the old philosophical dualisms obsolete, rather than refute them directly. He simply abandons these terms and approaches philosophy from a new perspective—the perspective of experience.

It is at this point that a critical aspect of Dewey's philosophical method comes into play. In his analysis of experience as the base for philosophical method, Dewey distinguishes between two different but interconnected aspects of all experience. These are the "primary" and "secondary" parts of all experience. These two terms serve as the base by which Dewey later reconciles the dualisms in epistemology and metaphysics. They will also play a pivotal role in his philosophy of education.

Primary experience for Dewey refers to the immediate, tangible, and moving world which presents itself to the senses. Dewey refers to primary experience as "gross, macroscopic, crude."[9] When British empiricism refers to sensation as the basis for all knowledge, it is referring to the primary aspect of experience. Primary experience provides the raw materials from which knowledge can begin. When Dewey refers to his method as empirical naturalism, we see the primary aspect of experience at work. His method begins with the world of primary experience. It is explicitly empirical in its method in that it has as its starting point the world presented to the senses. But Dewey goes on to explain that primary experience is essentially "non cognitive."[10] Primary experience is the starting point in his method, but it is not the end point. It is not the stopping point because of its non-cognitive nature. Dewey does begin his entire method on the empirical immediacy presented to man.

Secondary experience (also called reflective experience) for Dewey refers to what happens after a primary experience is had. Reflective experience takes the "gross,

---

[8]John Dewey, E.N. p. 1.

[9]John Dewey, E.N. p. 6.

[10]John Dewey, E.N. p. 23.

macroscopic, and crude" materials furnished by primary experience and seeks to make them precise, microscopic, and refined. The work of reflective experience is to take the data provided by primary experience and order and arrange them. In effect, reflective experience is that part of all experience which temporarily removes itself from the immediacy of empiricism. Secondary experiences, says Dewey, "*explain* the primary objects, they enable us to grasp them with *understanding* instead of just having sense contact with them."[11]

Dewey illustrates the distinction between primary and secondary experience by looking at the work of the modern scientist. The scientist does not have a series of disconnected sensory experiences. He does not sit and stare steadily at his instruments. In short, the scientist does not rest content with primary experience. The scientist takes the data derived from primary experience and reflects upon them. He removes himself from the immediacy of primary experience and reflects upon the information conveyed by the primary experience. The ultimate goal of the secondary experience in science is to take the data and reflect upon them such a way as to be able to make predictive statements about future experiences in the form of the hypothesis.

The category of experience in empirical naturalism seeks to unite the primary and the secondary into a single unity. As Dewey says:

> What empirical method expects of philosophy is two things: First, that refined methods and products be traced back to their origins in primary experience, in all of its heterogeneity and fullness; so that the needs and problems out of which they arise and which they have to satisfy be acknowledged. Secondly, that the secondary methods and conclusions be brought back to the things of ordinary experience, all of their coarseness and crudity, for verification.[12]

In the opening section of this paper, I argued that the foundation of Dewey's method rested upon his rejection of philosophical dualism and his adaptation of experience as the base for empirical naturalism. I also pointed out that this method had implications both in epistemology and in metaphysics. In epistemology, I contrasted the positions of Chauncy Wright and Charles Peirce as immediate precursors of Dewey. Extrapolating from Dewey, we can see how both the fallacy of selective emphasis and the category of experience attempt an answer to the empiricism-versus-rationalism dialectic. In the primary aspect of experience, we see Dewey adopting empiricism and its method of basing knowledge on the senses and on the data provided by the senses. In the idea of reflective experience, we see Dewey making room for the method of rationalism. The fallacy of selective emphasis

---

[11]John Dewey, E.N. p. 7.

[12]John Dewey, E.N. p. 23.

refuses to focus exclusively upon the primary aspect of knowledge. It also refuses to focus exclusively upon the reflective, or rational, nature of knowledge. In short, by beginning from experience in the first place, Dewey avoids the dualisms, while at the same time allowing for the combined roles of empirical and rational knowledge.

There are obvious metaphysical implications in Dewey's epistemological method. I contrasted Ralph Waldo Emerson with Auguste Comte as representing idealism and materialism in the opening section of this paper. Dewey refers to metaphysics "as a statement of the generic traits manifested by existence of all kinds without regard to their differentiation into physical and mental."[13] Later, Dewey also says of metaphysics that "Qualitative individuality and constant relations, contingency and need, movement and arrest are common traits of all existence."[14] The point to be gained here is that metaphysics for Dewey is *not* an attempt to discover some aspect of being, either materialistic or idealistic, and then elevate that aspect to a status of the really real at the expense of the other aspects of reality. Dewey sides neither with Emerson nor with Comte in this matter. Rather, his answer to the really real question rests in his notion of the "generic traits manifested by existence" lying *within* experience. Again, the fallacy of selective emphasis comes into play and saves Dewey from metaphysical dualism. By beginning from experience as the basis for metaphysics, Dewey allows for the reality of both the material and the ideal as "generic" traits within experience. What is ultimately real for Dewey is experience.

PHILOSOPHY OF EDUCATION

Richard Bernstein has argued that the heart of Dewey's philosophical endeavor is to be found in his philosophy of education. Bernstein says that according to Dewey, "All philosophy can be conceived of as the philosophy of education."[15] In keeping with the thesis of this paper, that Dewey's philosophy of education presupposes his philosophical method, outlined above, I want to show how the method gives rise to his educational position.

Dewey's attack on dualism in philosophy in general can be seen clearly in his philosophy of education. The opening two sentences in *Experience and Education* make this evident: "Mankind likes to think in terms of extreme opposites. It is given to formulating its beliefs in terms of Either-Ors, between which it recognizes no

---

[13]John Dewey, E.N. p. 334.

[14]John Dewey, E.N. p. 334.

[15]Richard Bernstein, *John Dewey* in *Encyclopedia of Philosophy* (New York, 1967) pp. 383-384, Vol. 2

intermediate possibilities."[16] Dewey connects the epistemological dualism of empiricism and rationalism to educational problems. He says:

> Upon the philosophical side, these various dualisms culminate in a sharp demarcation of individual minds from the world, and hence from one another. While the connection of this philosophical position with educational procedure is not so obvious as is that of the points considered in the last three chapters, there are certain educational considerations which correspond to it.[17]

On the one hand Dewey was confronted by an educational philosophy that emphasized a purely rationalistic approach to learning. This school maintained that the main goal of education was to inculcate into students the received ideas and facts of the past.[18] This method of education laid great stress on the ability of the student to sit passively and to commit ideas to memory. It tended to devalue initiative and reward obedience and docility. Dewey contends that a philosophy of education which is based upon a purely rationalistic epistemology, necessarily presupposes a separation of the mind from the external world. This method saw the goal of education as purely cognitive and not connected or involved with the environment in which mind existed.[19] Methodologically, we see the rationalistic school of education taking the secondary, or reflective, aspect of experience and elevating it to an idolatrous position. That is, reflective experience was pursued in and for itself at the expense of primary, or empirical experience.

We can see that the opposite educational philosophy drawing from Dewey's method would be to elevate the primary aspect of experience to the sole end of education. This would involve taking the purely empirical element in experience and neglecting the reflective element. One of the most common criticisms of the so-called "progressive" education derived from Dewey, was, and is, that in reacting against the rationalistic elements so dominant in education, the progressives neglected the role of the reflective. Dewey himself explicitly rejects any idea that education should swing from a purely reflective, rationalistic position to a purely empirical, non-reflective mode.[20] Here he is being consistent with his fallacy of selective emphasis

---

[16]John Dewey, *Experience and Education* (New York, 1938) p. 17. Henceforth referred to as E.E.

[17]John Dewey, *Democracy and Education* (New York, 1926) p. 340. Henceforth referred to as D.E.

[18]John Dewey, E.E. p. 17.

[19]John Dewey, D.E. p. 377.

[20]John Dewey, E.E. pp. 20-21.

in avoiding creating any dualism in his reaction to the educational system he inherited.

Dewey's answer to educational dualism is drawn directly from his philosophical method. Just as metaphysics and epistemology must begin from experience rather than from dialectical bifurcations, so too must education begin from experience. Dewey rejects any idea that education must be completely based upon primary experience or upon secondary experience. Education, according to Dewey, must be based upon experience, period, which involves both the primary and the secondary. In describing the central role of experience in education, Dewey says:

> For one has only to call to mind what is sometimes treated in schools as acquisition of knowledge to realize how lacking it is in any fruitful connection with the ongoing experience of the students—how largely it seems to be believed that the mere appropriation of subject matter which happens to be in books contains knowledge. No matter how true what is learned to those who found it out and in whose experience it functioned, there is nothing which makes it knowledge to the pupils. It might as well be something about Mars or about some fanciful country unless it fructifies in the individual's own life.[21]

Dewey's rejection of philosophical dualism and his adaptation of experience as the basis of education give rise to a central idea in his philosophy of education—the idea of the experiential continuum. Dewey argues that the opposite of dualism is continuity. The educational dualisms which Dewey rejects include such things as the separation of mind and body, authority and freedom, experience and knowledge, and dozens of others. Dewey criticizes all of these dualities because they result in a lack of continuity within experience. By his idea of the experiential continuum within educational experience, Dewey hopes to stop duality before it ever gets started.

Dewey illustrates the need for an experiential continuum in education by contrasting the ideas of authority and freedom in education. The old educational methods which Dewey inherited put almost complete stress upon authority in education. This stress upon authority in education stemmed directly from the presuppositions of rationalism. That is, the student was to learn the ideas of the past which the teacher deemed important. This stress upon authority created a basic schizophrenia in education in a society which claimed to value freedom, democracy, self-direction, and personal responsibility. Dewey argues that the result was that the actual experience of the student under the yoke of education was in no way similar to the basic values espoused by the surrounding culture. Therefore, there was no continuity in the experience of the pupil. What was expected in school was docility, passiveness, and submission to authority. What was expected in the "real world"

---

[21]John Dewey, D.E. p. 389.

was aggressiveness, self-initiative, and a democratic response to authority.[22] Dewey argues that the ultimate goal of education is to make an experiential continuum where the *process* of education, that is *how* a student learns, is given equal footing with the *content* of education.[23]

Dewey wants to take the primary and reflective aspects of all experience and apply them to education. Dewey does not downplay the important role of subject matter, or reflective experience, in education (as superficial critics have claimed). He does want to get away from the obsessive preoccupation of traditional education with secondary experience. Just as Dewey looks to the work of the modern scientist as an example of his basic philosophical method, so too does he look at the education of the scientist as an example for his views on education. Dewey argues that the old methods of education are incompatible with the education of a good experimental scientist. For Dewey sees the good scientist as having cultivated a keen ability at questioning the world around him, rather than simply committing it to memory. I argued in the philosophical method section of this paper that the ultimate goal of knowledge for the scientist was the formulation of the hypothesis as predictive of future experiences. It can be seen here, drawing from the basic method, that education must stress other ideals than the old methods did in order to produce a good scientist. These ideals must include freedom, inquisitiveness, and experiential continuity, as well as the received materials from the past.

SUMMARY AND CONCLUSION

The goal of this paper was to outline Dewey's basic philosophical method, and then to connect it with his philosophy of education. The basic philosophical method was outlined, starting with Dewey's rejection of metaphysical and epistemological dualism and his adaptation of experience as the starting point for all philosophy. Two other technical terms in Dewey were introduced—the fallacy of selective emphasis, and the primary and secondary aspects of experience. The paper then connected Dewey's philosophy of education with his basic philosophical method. This was done by showing Dewey's rejection of traditional education's obsession with the secondary aspect of experience and the resulting stress upon docility and passivity in the educational process. Dewey's discussion of freedom versus authority in education was used to illustrate the effects of dualism in education. Finally, the important role of Dewey's idea of continuity in education was illustrated using both the freedom/authority example and the training of the experimental scientist.

---

[22]John Dewey, D.E. pp. 95-116.

[23]John Dewey, E.E. p. 20.

In conclusion, I want to argue that Dewey offers a coherent and sensible pedagogical theory. I will argue that Dewey's educational philosophy is as relevant today as it was in 1920. Dewey offers a source of inspiration to future and present educators who are confronted by timid and reactionary educators screaming for "back to the basics" and the elevation of a rationalistic principle of education to a supreme status. Dewey also offers a strong warning to those who, in their zeal for reform, would neglect the role of content in the educational process. One only need look at some products of innovative education who are very much "in touch with their feelings," but who cannot write a coherent sentence.

Dewey demands of professional philosophy the highest standards of the application of his theory. For those of us in the field of educational philosophy, Dewey reminds us that philosophy is not an isolated discipline, disconnected from the issues of everyday life. I am here reminded of the modern professor of ethics who is an expert at doing ethical analysis using modal operators, but who is rendered speechless when asked by a pregnant student if it would be ethical for her to seek an abortion. He is also warning us about the other modern ethics professor who spends long hours in the demonstration picket lines in support of a cause, but who is scared to death when confronted by convincing arguments that he may be less than totally right in his convictions.

In short, Dewey is demanding that philosophers and educators begin and end their work from the category of experience. As Dewey himself said:

> I remarked incidentally that the philosophy in question is, to paraphrase the saying of Lincoln about democracy, one of education of, by, and for experience. Not one of these words, *of, by* or *for*, names anything which is self-evident. Each of them is a challenge to discover and put into operation a principle or order and organization which follows from understanding what educational experience signifies.[24]

---

[24]John Dewey, E.E. p. 29.

4

Kurt Hahn and the Aims of Education

Thomas James

BIOGRAPHY OFFERS TWO VISIONS OF HUMAN GREATNESS. THE FIRST MOVES ALONG a line from youth to old age, the chronicle of events and entanglements through which people weave their lives into the collective history around them. The other springs from the invisible center within a life; it moves outward from a moment of self-discovery which knows no beginning and no end, suffusing one's whole existence, and others beyond it, with the meaning of experience.

In the first, the chronicle of a life, sequence is crucial. Time and place, the context of growth, an ability to capitalize on circumstance—these are the stuff of life histories when seen as linear progression. Victory comes in leaps and bounds of clever adaptation, the string of successes and compromises through which one creates for oneself a place in the world.

The second vision cares little for growth and adaptation. The center of a life comes all at once, as a gift. When it emerges, the center arranges everything else

of how society should be organized, and what people must do to maintain human decency in a world of conflict. No idyllic schoolmaster's life awaited him.

As the Nazis rose to power, the director of Salem School became an outspoken opponent. In 1932, a group of fascist storm troopers kicked a leftist activist to death before the eyes of his mother. Adolph Hitler immediately praised the action of his followers. Kurt Hahn wrote to the alumni of Salem, telling them to choose between Salem and Hitler. A man who knew Hahn at the time called it "the bravest deed in cold blood that I have ever witnessed." When he became the chief of state in 1933, Hitler imprisoned Hahn. Fortunately for the embattled educator, he still had friends in Britain who remembered his idealism and his hopes for friendship between the two nations. Prime Minister Ramsay MacDonald and others helped to arrange for Hahn's release and timely emigration to England in 1933.

Within a year of his arrival, Kurt Hahn started another institution, Gordonstoun, which became one of Britain's most distinguished progressive schools and served as a model for similar schools in other countries. In the following decades, Hahn's educational vision served as the moving spirit for new institutions and programs of world-wide renown: the Moray Badge and County Badge Schemes, and their successor, the Duke of Edinburgh Awards; Outward Bound; the Trevelyan Scholarships; and the United World Colleges.

Judging from the chronology, the sequence of accomplishments in the career of a prominent educator, one might be inclined to notice only the power and success of the man. A biography pursued along this vein would find no shortage of material to demonstrate the pattern of growth. Nor would it be difficult to show the man's brilliant capabilities of creative adaptation throughout his career. Hahn always had the resounding quote—often still quotable to this day—when the occasion demanded or seemed likely to respond to eloquence. He was, it could be argued, a discerning idealist; his dreams were driven as much by political acumen as by educational wisdom. Given his penchant for currying the favor of powerful men, it would even be tempting for the biographer to caricature Hahn's ponderous moralism as a relic of the last century, and expose the ambition behind his charisma as he operated in high places during some of the most anguished moments of a troubled century.

Such a chronicle would leave out something essential, an element without which Hahn's philosophy of education makes no sense at all. To imagine what might have been inside the schoolman, what drove his dreams, another kind of biography is needed. Where was Kurt Hahn's life center? When, and under what circumstances, did it emerge in recognizable form? How did its imperatives widen to become his whole life, then to drive others' dreams over the years? Without answers to these questions, the rest of the story virtually writes itself and can be told in a few insipid pages. To seek Hahn's center requires beginning the story all over again.

THE CENTER OF A LIFE

Kurt Hahn understood weakness better than strength. The goal of learning, in his view, was compensatory: to purify the destructive inclinations of the human personality, to redress the imbalances in modern ways of living, to develop each person's disabilities to their maximum potential, and to place new-found strength in service of those in need. Kurt Hahn was suspicious of presumed excellence; he paid scant attention to the glories of unsurpassed individual performance, whether it be on the playing fields at Eton or the examination ordeal of the German gymnasium. He understood, as few educators have so well, the tender fears of young people, their alienation before the rigors and rituals of adult power. He understood how wrong it was to vanquish them with that power to make them learn. This strategy would only deepen their confusion about the meaning of their lives, making them cynical, lacking in humanity, even if it strengthened them. Hahn's favorite story was the Good Samaritan, wherein the strong, those clearly in a position to help the most, failed to act. It was the outsider, the weak, the despised who taught what it means to be a civilized human being.

Where did Hahn learn this, and if he once felt it himself, how did he convert his own weakness into an enduring vision of education? We must look, I believe, to that most tumultuous time of life to see the emerging center. In late adolescence, on the threshold of higher education and adult life, Hahn felt the impact of three events that changed his life.

The first was an expedition, some days of fresh air and majestic surroundings on a walking tour of the Dolomite Alps. One can well imagine the exhilaration of a boy in his teens on such a rite of passage. Famed for their bold, other-worldly shapes, their awe-inspiring hues of light and shadow from sunrise to sunset, the Dolomites imprinted on Hahn an inextinguishable love of natural beauty. As an educator, he would always be devising ways to turn his classrooms out of doors, putting his students into motion and forcing his teachers to come to grips with the healing powers of direct experience.

Something else happened on this expedition. A second event added a specific passion to these other feelings, strong enough to organize his self-discovery into a lifelong vocation. Two English schoolboys who accompanied Hahn gave him a gift, a book called *Emlohstobba* by the German educator Hermann Lietz. The title of the book was the name of their school, Abbotsholme, spelled backwards. Lietz wrote rapturously of life inside that school, where he served as master of studies for a sabbatical year under the innovative headmaster, Cecil Reddie. When Lietz returned to Germany, he fathered the country school movement there, inspiring others to begin schools more healthful for young people than the prevailing system of the time.

For Hahn this book was a momentous gift. Along with the living example of the two students from Abbotsholme, who impressed him with their healthy love of life, and the sheer beauty of their alpine journey together, young Hahn must have felt in himself a new conviction of life's possibilities. Coming at a time when his own formal education was marching lockstep through the authoritarian, rigidly academic curriculum of the gymnasium, the alternative vision of a more humane and democratic school, capable of fostering more perfect human beings, seized his imagination with a force that can be judged only by abandoning strict chronology and looking ahead to the seventy indefatigable years of institution-building that lay in front of him.

It was not on that trip, however, that Hahn imagined the school he hoped to build. Two years later, the year of his graduation from the gymnasium, a third event completed his initiation. He suffered a life-threatening sunstroke that permanently changed his life. Never again would he have the freedom to trek or sail long, pleasurable distances out-of-doors. Nor was it certain, in the weeks following the accident, whether he would recover enough even to participate in normal functions of life. Depression set in, squelching his hopes. One would not be surprised if his boyhood dreams became cruel reminders of all that was not possible now. His life was a wash-out, a failure before it had really begun.

Here, and not in his later life of so many memorable accomplishments, the educational genius of the man is to be found. The center emerged as a discovery of who he really was inside, the gift of suddenly knowing what he had to do, and would do, when he bumped up against his own limitations. It was the scale of values, the plan of life, the desired future he asserted as his response to adversity.

Adversity came to Hahn in several forms, all of which must have seemed insuperable from his perspective in a darkened room as he recovered from his accident. The physical disability would always be present in his life. It would be necessary for him to wear a broad-brimmed hat to protect his head from the sunlight. Frail in the heat, he would have to flee northward to a cooler climate in the summers. Periodically, he would need to undergo major operations to relieve the fluid pressure within his head. All this he knew, or could well imagine, in those months of convalescence, but he also could not help but be conscious of other adversities that would dog his every effort to improve himself for the rest of his life. In his family, the other sons, considered more intelligent, received encouragement to go into business; plodding Kurt was marked for a less prestigious career, possibly as a teacher. He loved the classics and pushed himself hard in his attempts to master them, but alas, he did not shine as a student. Although he revered tradition, he would never know the life of a scholar. Even if he had been a much better student, his Jewish background would always limit his opportunities in a nation whose anti-Semitism was becoming increasingly strident with each passing decade.

In his darkened room, Kurt Hahn regenerated his spirit with a vision of what he could do with his life. He decided that he would someday start a school modeled on principles drawn from Plato's *Republic*, a school that would expand the wholesome influence he identified with Hermann Lietz and Cecil Reddie's Abbotsholme. How much of the vision came to him at that time and how much came later is not clear, but he grasped the essential outline. The school would harmonize the social and intellectual differences between its students by operating as a community of participation and active service. It would seek out the natural qualities of leadership, skill, and responsibility possessed by all in different ways when they see that they are truly needed. His school of the future would harmonize the wild and discordant personality of the adolescent by demonstrating this true need.

How could his vision be made believable to the alienated young? Closer to home, how could Kurt Hahn himself, in his debility and depression, bring himself to believe in a better life? Forced by the accident to reflect upon his own childhood, to seek out some deeper matrix of meaning to keep his spirits up, Hahn came face to face with his own youthful passion. He came to see that there exists in everyone a grand passion, an outlandish thirst for adventure, a desire to live boldly and vividly in the journey through life. This vision sprang forth as the most salient lesson of his lifelong pedagogy.

That was not all, however, and it was not enough. For now the Dolomites and the classics flowed together to become Hahn's vision of the good. Passion must not be treated lightly. Its deep springs in human nature must not be poisoned. Above all, it must not be misdirected and turned to inhumane ends. The grand passion of the young must be embraced in wholesome ways by adult power. It must be nurtured instead of deformed or punished. Its creative force must be harnessed to the quest for a good society, the aim of Plato's educational designs. To accomplish this purpose would require more than a school in the traditional sense. Hahn believed that some separation from the existing human world, into the intensity of a journey-quest, confronting challenges and transforming opportunities for service, could change the balance of power in young people. Then they would be more inclined to use their lives, back in the world from which they came, to bring the good society into being.

With the center in view, the chronology of Kurt Hahn's life takes on greater meaning. Expelled from the land of his birth, the schoolmaster continued his career in Britain, which became a second homeland for him. When he opened Gordonstoun in 1934, Hahn carried the Salem tradition to the new setting, and he brought staff and students with him. New features appeared, such as the addition of rescue training to the service program. And some of the old practices changed, or were presented differently, in response to the cultural milieu of the British Isles. All this, of course, is to be expected in transplanting the design of an institution from one place and time to another. Certainly the transition was made easier by the strong affinity of Hahn's thinking with the traditions of Abbotsholme and the English public schools. What stands out, nonetheless, is the fact that Hahn was able in so short a time to create a new institution which, like his first school, would become known around the world for its distinctive educational practices.

If Hahn had not been restless, if he had not felt driven toward wider applications of his principles beyond any school he might ever create, he would perhaps have settled down to a long career as the eccentric headmaster of a school favored by the English aristocracy. But he was not satisfied. He began to organize a constellation of other educational forms around Gordonstoun, using the school as a staging ground for programs through which he hoped to instruct the whole society around him in the first lessons of sound living and civic responsibility. The Moray Badge Scheme took form in 1936, followed quickly by the larger and better known County Badge a year later. Hahn and the allies he gathered around his educational vision experimented with short courses. They hoped to discover the combination of challenging experiences that might help young people discover new ways of organizing their lives and working with other people. In 1941, with Laurence Holt, Hahn started Outward Bound as a short course. Initially, the goal was to strengthen the will of young men so that they could prevail against adversity as Great Britain faced staggering losses at sea during World War II. After the program had demonstrated its effectiveness, it continued to expand during the post-war years, furnishing opportunities for personal and social growth to many people beyond the original clientele of boys and young men.

Chronology alone cannot account for Hahn's widening sphere of educational activity. Only by grasping how he continued to draw both from a sense of weakness and from the strong idealism at the center of his being, can we understand his intuitive leaps as he created new programs over the years. Hahn perceived clearly that schools as we know them are not equal to the urgent problems of social life in this century. Even the best schools probably damage as much as develop the volatile inner lives of young people. One reason for this unintended consequence is that schools represent only a partial solution to a much more pervasive problem. The problem of how to educate the whole person cannot be solved without learning how to civilize human communities, which in turn cannot be done without preparing the entire world society in the arts of living harmoniously at the highest levels of potential activity and understanding. Hahn's debt to Plato was his conviction that education must embrace all these aspects of human life.

Exiled to England, Kurt Hahn was restless at the center of his being. Carrying with him an unflinching impression of the expanding Third Reich and its effects on European civilization, he could never be satisfied with the auspicious beginning of a single school. Soon after his arrival, he began to write and speak in public, deploring the general lack of fitness among the British people. He urged his hosts to recognize the need for programs on a large scale that would combine individual training plans with group projects to build stronger civic consciousness. Out of such concerns he initiated the Moray and County Badge Schemes.

The latter quickly expanded and became further elaborated in many counties across the British Isles, spreading even to other countries in the British Commonwealth. The County Badge granted public recognition to young people who completed a planned course of challenges. They first adopted a training plan of physical conditioning and personal health habits. Then they undertook an arduous expedition requiring group decision making as well as individual effort. They also completed a project demanding new skills and craftsmanship. Finally, they engaged in service activities, experiencing the value of compassion through direct action on behalf of the community or specific people in need.

At the beginning of the war, the County Badge contained most of the essential features of the Outward Bound program as it would develop in future years. Indeed, the secretary and key promoter of the County Badge Experimental Committee, James Hogan, became the first warden of the first Outward Bound School at Aberdovey, in Wales. Yet there was a difference, and it was more than the residential setting and month-long sustained program of Outward Bound. Although both programs offered models for changing how individuals organize their lives, there was something more universal and enduring about Outward Bound.

Hahn had realized how close weakness and strength are in the most powerful forms of education. In his own day, he perceived clearly, while others did not, the subtle line that distinguishes compassionate service from destructive egotism. On the one hand, he feared the lack of will among those whose lives stood in the path of the advancing Third Reich. Hence his call for programs like the County Badge to build fitness and commit young people to civic ideals. But on the other hand, he recognized the affinity between his methods and those of the Nazis, one used for the good, the other for deadly ends.

There is an irony in this affinity, since Hahn was criticized by some in England for importing the paramilitary methods of the Hitler Youth. The irony is that the Hitler Youth movement did not discover the intensive methods of socialization they used to unleash the energies of the young. Rather, they borrowed from the leading educators of the day and applied the methods to their own goals. Hahn knew this well, for he had seen the Hitler Youth before he left Germany. Their leaders had adapted and twisted to demonic purposes the training plan of Salem.

Hahn had witnessed, therefore, the effects of reaching the whole person with the fascist plan of life instead of a Samaritan ethic. Hitler and his followers were reinforcing the passion of the young, giving them a spirit of adventure, introducing them to self-development and cooperation in the outdoors, then giving them meaningful opportunities to serve. Hahn recognized that there was no time for complacency. The weakness of the status quo must be acknowledged. All education must be made activist, or else the humane values upon which Western democracies were built would succumb to a determined usurper.

Not even in its desperate beginnings before the onslaught of the Third Reich did Outward Bound ever train young people for war, but it arose fully conscious of the challenge presented by the Hitler Youth, that nationwide mobilization of young people to serve the cause of world conquest and genocide. Never did anyone press Outward Bound toward becoming a preparation for violence. In this respect, it would always remain distinct from youth mobilizations under totalitarian regimes. Yet it is difficult to imagine how Outward Bound would ever have come into being if it had not been for Hahn's recognition of the weakness of democratic cultures before well-organized forms of authoritarian education that were appallingly efficient at stirring up the passions of the young for collective violence.

Through Outward Bound, Hahn hoped to foster a deeper intensity of commitment in the rite of passage from youth to adult life. He was intent on creating more dramatic challenges and victories for the young than were available in conventional forms of schooling. Advocating a more arduous quest than was present in the institutions around him, Hahn was working from a disability greater than his own, a collective predicament verging on catastrophe. In England during the German Blitzkrieg, it was by no means apocalyptic to argue that there would need to be a new education, reconstructed on a massive scale, to produce the compassionate army needed to preserve what was left of civilization at home. Hahn believed that an intensive program of training, expedition, reflection, and service could make a difference.

That belief survived beyond the exigencies of war, but Hahn's own direct role quickly receded once the philosophical values were in place to launch Outward Bound. While Hahn continued to influence Outward Bound, it soon took on a life of its own under the vigorous leadership of many people drawn to its idealism and hardy lifestyle over the years. Taking an image from Plato, Hahn likened himself to a midwife of educational projects as he sparked ideas for new endeavors and then left much of the development and maintenance to others. Outward Bound sea and mountain schools proliferated across several continents in the following decades. As it adapted itself to different cultures in later years, Outward Bound lost some of its wartime urgency, but it maintained a zest for adventure and Hahn's legacy of moral purpose.

Outward Bound has come to mean many things in different places and for the great variety of people who are drawn to it. But at its heart, in every time and place, is Hahn's own center, his conviction that it is possible, even in a relatively short time, to introduce greater balance and compassion into human lives by impelling people into experiences which show them they can rise above adversity and overcome their own defeatism. They can make more of their lives than they thought they could, and learn to serve others with their strength.

Hahn's post-war contributions include several other projects of which he considered himself more midwife than instigator. It would be most accurate to characterize him as the moving spirit, since his arts of persuasion were decisive in each case. The Trevelyan Scholarships, for example, provided funds for young people to attend Oxford and Cambridge, based on experiential as well as academic criteria: applicants were asked to complete a project of their own design, which would be reviewed by a selection panel. Shortly after a recurrence of his sunstroke in the early 1950s, Hahn helped to launch the Duke of Edinburgh Award, a program similar to the County Badge but more widely developed throughout the British Commonwealth. His crowning achievement after the war was the United World Colleges, which began with the founding of Atlantic College in 1962.

If Outward Bound's origins are to be found in the war, those of the United World Colleges appear in the desire to build institutions that will offer a living example of what it means to be at peace. Taking students from ages sixteen to nineteen, equivalent to the sixth form in England or the last two years before post-secondary education in the United States, these colleges bring together boys and girls from all over the world, from competing social and economic systems, from rival cultures and religions. The program fosters world citizenship, an interconnected leadership of people who have experienced a collective life of active dialogue and peacemaking service. The curriculum, like that of Gordonstoun, combines both academic and experiential challenges, but the institutions have developed in new directions under their diverse leadership, leaving some of Hahn's educational practices behind while preserving others. Kurt Hahn's original insight that such institutions were possible stands as perhaps the greatest legacy of his influence as they continue to thrive and expand in the 1980s.

Returning to Germany for his last days, Kurt Hahn died near Salem, in Hermannsberg, on December 14, 1974. The entry in Britain's Dictionary of National Biography calls him "headmaster and citizen of humanity." Hahn's educational influence persists under such organizations as the Round Square Conference, which comprises schools modeled on Salem and Gordonstoun. His genius in devising short-term, educational experiences has not stopped infusing energy and inspiration into the Outward Bound Trust, which oversees Outward Bound schools throughout the world. His love of peace flourishes in the United World Colleges, not to mention the many other institutions and individuals who continue to embody his ideals.

The man's center remains, beckoning like an adventure. Arise from weakness to teach about strength. Turn self-discovery into acts of compassion. Everywhere defend human decency.

Notes

The author would like to thank Charles P. Stetson for his support and encouragement during the preparation of this essay, an earlier draft of which was written to provide background for a scholarship sponsored by Stetson at the University of Bridgeport in Connecticut to honor the ideals of Kurt Hahn.

5

Wilderness as Healing Place

John Miles

For John Muir, wilderness was a restorative place, a place in which he could not only learn and grow but also restore his mental and physical well-being. He often wrote of this quality of wilderness experience. In the mountains, "cares will drop off like autumn leaves." In the "great fresh, unblighted, unredeemed wilderness" people will find hope. "The galling harness of civilization drops off, and the wounds heal ere we are aware." Muir himself seemed to have a physiological need for contact with wilderness. After he was married and responsible for the welfare of his family and their fruit ranch, he spent long periods away from wilderness. The demands of business and work took their toll, and he would seek restoration in the exploration of some wild place. He bid others to do the same:

> Go now and then for fresh life—if most of humanity must go through this town stage of development—just as divers hold their breath and come ever and anon to the surface to breathe. Go whether or not you have faith. Form parties, if you must be social, to go to the snow-flowers in winter, to the sunflowers in summer. Anyway, go up and away for life; be fleet! (Teale, 1954, p. 319)

Nearly a century has passed since Muir wrote these words, and in that time many people have followed his advice. In fact, during the latter half the twentieth century so many people have sought the benefits of contact with nature that Muir would be amazed and chagrined. Outdoor recreation has become an industry, and even the search for "healing" in wild places has become organized and institutionalized. Now we have "therapeutic recreation" and "stress-challenge adventure" programs to assist people in following Muir's advice. Wilderness as a

The article was originally published in the 1987 *Journal of Experiential Education*, 10(3), 4-10.

"healing place" has truly been recognized on a scale beyond anything that Muir imagined.

How Does Wilderness Contribute to Health?

Wilderness experience, many claim, can allow us to build the structure of our being on a healthy foundation and also allow reconstruction and restoration of a cracked or crumbling foundation. Many programs today use wilderness for therapeutic goals of one sort or another. Undoubtedly, both the experiences planned and facilitated by the program leaders and the environment itself contribute to the healing effect of wilderness experience. We are concerned here with how the wilderness environment contributes to improvement of health.

First, we should define what we mean by healing in this context. It is a broad and value-laden concept. As Webster defines it, to heal is "to make sound or whole"; it is "to cause an undesirable condition to be overcome"; "to make a person spiritually whole"; or "to restore to original integrity." Healing involves an improvement of the condition of our mind/body. We need healing when we suffer pain and a reduction of our ability to live well. When we speak of healing here, we are not referring to its usual meaning as applied to our physical selves but to a process involving physical, emotional, and even spiritual dimension. Healing usually involves all of these dimensions simultaneously. The wilderness engages the whole person and thus may be an environment ideally suited to the holistic healing that John Muir experienced and advocated to his fellows.

Psychological Benefits of Wilderness

There have been literary allusions to the restorative and therapeutic values of nature for centuries. This is valuable testimony, but is there any "hard" evidence that wild places contribute to healing? There is, it turns out, but not as much such evidence as we believers in the powers of wilderness experience would like. Two psychologists, Stephen Kaplan and Janet Frey Talbot, recently researched what we know about the psychological benefits of wilderness. Their review of the literature led to the less-than-startling conclusion that people find experiences in natural environments highly satisfying and that they highly value the benefits which they perceive themselves to derive from experiences there (Kaplan & Talbot, 1983, p. 166). The research literature trying to document the specifically therapeutic value of wilderness experience is generally flawed methodologically. It does indicate that programs like Outward Bound "can and do result in positive changes in the self-concepts, personalities, individual behaviors and social functioning of program participants" (Gibson, 1979, pp. 13, 2, 30).

Kaplan and Talbot set up their own elaborate study of the psychological effects of wilderness experience, trying to determine how wilderness affects people and what the effects are. In summary, they identified three benefits. These seem to come progressively, beginning with an increased awareness of relationship with the physical environment and an increasingly effortless attention to one's surroundings. Sometimes people find that daily life causes them to have difficulty concentrating, to experience mental work as unusually effortful, and to be irritable in the face of noise and distraction. These may all be symptoms of "a fatigued voluntary attention mechanism that has been pushed beyond its effective limits" (Kaplan & Talbot, 1983, p. 188). Wilderness seems to free people from this condition with a functional demand on attention and an interesting environment.

> The growing sense of enjoyment is likely to be a reflection of the decreased need to force oneself to attend. There is the discovery, in other words, that in addition to being comfortable and exciting it is also quite safe to attend to what one feels like attending to in the wilderness environment. (p. 193)

Later in the wilderness experience a second benefit appears. People experience an increase in self-confidence and a feeling of tranquility. They come to feel that they can deal with whatever challenges the environment may offer them. This is a profoundly satisfying and even surprising experience for people who have been struggling with their "normal" world. Kaplan and Talbot suggest that these benefits are in part attributable to the realization that one cannot control the wilderness environment:

> Although often not a conscious priority, the need for control nonetheless can be an important factor in the way an individual attempts to relate to an environment. Yet the assertion of individual control is incompatible with much of what wilderness offers and demands; rather than struggling to dominate a hostile environment, the participants come to perceive their surroundings as quite safe as long as one responds appropriately to environmental demands. Thus there is a tendency to abandon the implicit purpose of control because it is both unnecessary and impossible. (p. 194)

By relinquishing the illusion of control over the environment, people paradoxically acquire more internal control and can relax and pay more attention to their surroundings and to their inner selves.

Finally, Kaplan and Talbot noted a third benefit which they describe as contemplation. This is made possible by a high degree of compatibility among environmental patterns, the inclinations of the individual, and the actions required to feel comfortable in the environment. The daily round of activity back home is often anything but compatible. People are bombarded with diverse information and demands and are often unable to do what their environment requires of them as well as what they desire. They may experience frustration and tension and be entirely incapable of reflection on their situation.

Wilderness is very different. Kaplan and Talbot note:

> In wilderness what is interesting to perceive tends to be what one needs to know in order to act. For many people the purposes one carries into the wilderness also fit closely with the demands that the wilderness makes: What one intends to do is also what one must do in order to survive. (p. 191)

All of this compatibility can be liberating. It can allow reflection that can lead to discovery of a different self, a self less conflicted, more integrated, and more desirable. It can lead to a new intensity of contact with nature. "They feel a sense of union with something that is lasting, that is of enormous importance, and that is larger than they are" (p. 195). Thus they tap a spiritual dimension of the human experience that generations of writers have extolled.

At the end of their decade-long research, Kaplan and Talbot had to admit that there was much to learn about the benefits of wilderness experience, but they believed they had documented and described a set of significant psychological benefits. They raised more questions than they answered, but their work should be encouraging to those who, on the basis of personal experience, literary testimony, and intuition, have been taking people into the wilderness to heal and to grow. Kaplan and Talbot conclude with the observation that "we had not expected the wilderness experience to be quite so powerful or pervasive in its impact. And we were impressed by the durability of that residue in the human makeup that still resonates so strongly to these remote, uncivilized places" (p. 201). Their work suggests that wilderness experience can contribute to the healing of people overburdened by demands of the home environment, that it calms them and improves their ability to cope with the stresses of their normal round of activity.

WILDERNESS ENHANCES SELF-WORTH

Some sociologists suggest other ways in which wilderness experience contributes to healing. They describe two conditions from which many people suffer: anomie and alienation. A person with anomie is faced with myriad possibilities in life; he/she is bombarded by stimuli and moves rapidly through a set of unrelated experiences in a condition of separation from other people. Richard Mitchell notes that such a person is ". . . unsupported by significant others, free to choose from meaningless alternatives, without direction or purpose, bound by no constraint, guided by no path, comforted by no faith" (1983, p. 178).

In such a condition, this person fears the outcomes of his/her actions and is plagued by an uncertainty that renders routine and normal tasks very difficult. Such a person may feel desperately in need of stability, security, and certainty.

Alienation, on the other hand, may occur when someone finds the world too predictable. Mitchell summarizes the contributing factors:

> When people can predict their own behaviors on the basis of the social order in which they are situated, when they perceive their world as constrained by social forces, bound over by rule and regulation at every turn to the extent that personal creativity and spontaneity are stifled, when they know what they will and must do in a given situation regardless of their own interests, they experience alienation. (1983, p. 179)

The effect of this condition on someone is to feel powerless and indifferent, estranged and separate from self and others. Interest in the world lessens and he/she may become depressed, lethargic, and uninvolved. The alienated person comes to believe that effort cannot bring about the outcomes desired, so why bother?

We cautiously say that these two conditions are unhealthy, or at least they can contribute to a reduction of psychological and even physical well-being. Mitchell and others suggest that people suffering anomie and alienation need to balance their perception of their abilities with the responsibilities and possibilities available to them. They need to reduce the variability of stimuli when too much is present (anomie) and to increase it there is too little (alienation). In a social sense, notes Mitchell, people are moved to seek competence, a sense of personal worth.

> Competence grows from the process of recognizing one's abilities and applying them meaningfully and completely. Competence means assessing oneself as qualified, capable, fit, sufficient, adequate. Competence emerges when a person's talents, skills, and resources find useful application in meeting a commensurate challenge, problem, or difficulty. In sum, the competent individual's perceived abilities are roughly equal to their perceived responsibilities. (1983, p. 180)

Mitchell argues that certain activities provide ways for people to seek this competence and to break out of their anomie or alienation. Such activities (he explores mountaineering in considerable depth in this regard) allow people to enjoy a freedom and creativity that disrupt their emotional treadmill and open new possibilities for them. The anomie person will find a helpful measure of uncertainty. We may add to Mitchell's contention the argument that the wilderness environment in which many such activities occur contributes to the healing outcomes as well.

Central to the healing property of mountain experience, argues Mitchell is "flow." Mihaly Csikszentmihalyi has described this "flow":

> Flow refers to the holistic sensation present when we act with total involvement . . . . It is the state in which action follows upon action according to an internal/logic which seems to need no conscious intervention on our part. We experience it as a unified flowing from one moment to the next in which we are in control of our

actions, and in which there is little distinction between self and environment; between stimulus and response; or between past, present, and future. (p. 58)

This sounds remarkably similar to the "fascination" that Kaplan and Talbot earlier described, a condition in which attention flows effortlessly to whatever is being done. Mitchell, though, argues that it is the act of climbing that creates the flow experience, while Kaplan and Talbot suggest that the environment is the principle factor. The latter investigators did not study the action of mountaineering, and Mitchell studiously avoids discussion of environment as a contributing factor in flow. The question of the relative importance of action and environment in helping with problems such as anomie and alienation remains an open one.

WILDERNESS AND THE ABILITY TO LEARN

Many programs that use wilderness as a healing place seem to assume that the environment contributes to achievement of their goals and that certain activities do so better than others. Outward Bound schools usually use both the opportunity for flow that activities in the wilderness provide and the fascination effect of the wilderness environment. The combination of these factors may partly explain the power of the Outward Bound process.

This process is being used in many places to help young people who are in trouble, particularly delinquents. These are people who are usually unwilling to take responsibility for themselves and others; they resent the situations in which they find themselves and the necessity to work. They are often limited learners, unable or unwilling to collect new knowledge and apply it to their lives. Many lack confidence in themselves and resist the idea that anyone can be of help to them (Golins, 1978, p. 26). In acting out their resentment and frustration with their lot in life, these adolescents often find themselves in trouble with the law and in the court system. As part of their therapy, an increasing number of them are being provided an opportunity to participate in a wilderness-based adventure education program.

Golins has reviewed how such programs " . . . impel a delinquent to rearrange his destructive ways" (1978, p. 27). He notes how the outdoor environment contributes to this process through its "evocative" quality. The outdoors in general and the wilderness in particular are unfamiliar and captivating for most delinquent youths. It engages the participants' senses and increases receptivity to stimuli in their environment. Their chances for success seem to be increased because of their experiences. This may be because the needs and purposes of the moment (to be warm, to stay dry, to curtail hunger) are compatible with the demands of the environment, as Kaplan and Talbot observed. A person usually resistant to learning is made less so when the learning is necessary to solve basic problems of comfort and even survival.

Golins describes another way in which the outdoor environment is conducive to growth:

> The outdoors also presents itself in a very physical, straightforward way. There are mountains to climb, rivers to run, bogs to wade through. As an adolescent delinquent whose principal mode of expression is an action-oriented one and whose thinking process is mostly concrete, the possible activities in the outdoors fulfill his developmental capability. He just stands a better chance of excelling here. (1978, p. 27)

The environment may be unfamiliar, but the demand for action is familiar. Those who design the challenges of wilderness-based educational programs are very careful to present the opportunity for success. Usually the learner is presented with a progressively more difficult series of challenges, demonstrating the value of learning and the positive outcomes to be derived from applying what is learned. In the outdoors the feedback and reinforcement from successful application of something learned is immediate. Rewarded for learning, the delinquent goes on to the next challenge and the next learning experience.

Yet another way the outdoors may help delinquents is described by Golins. He notes that the "symbolic potential" of the outdoors is greater for the person who has difficulty conceptualizing and generalizing. He argues that if we subscribe to the theory that learning involves thinking about the meaning of experience, then the experiences in nature, by their power and simplicity and concreteness, are easier to generalize than learning experiences in the complex social contexts of normal life.

Consider, for instance, a young woman learning to rock climb. She must learn to depend on her belayer. She must communicate with her and must care for her in the sense that she must not knock any rocks down or otherwise endanger this person upon whom she is dependent. The problems she needs to solve are simple and straightforward. There is a beginning and end to the task at hand. The difficulties are easy to identify and define, as are the actions necessary to solve them. Tackling the rock pitch, the slanting jam crack, the "holdless" section, the climber takes the difficulties one at a time and works them out. She is in charge and, after the anxiety of the adventure recedes, feels a surge of confidence. "I did that!?" is often the comment, part surprised query, part triumphant exclamation.

From all of this the woman may generalize about problem solving, cooperation, communication, and the nature of dependency in certain social situations. The outdoor environment presents these concepts boldly so that they can hardly be missed. It places them in a pragmatic context that increases the likelihood that the learner will think about them in the larger framework of her life. "If these processes have served me here," she may reason, "then perhaps they will do so in my world in general." Golins thinks that such experiences help young people to learn to think conceptually and thereby deal more effectively with situations that have previously baffled and frustrated them.

WILDERNESS AS A METAPHOR FOR LIFE

Bacon, like Golins, has analyzed the Outward Bound process and how it works, and his thinking reveals yet another way in which wilderness contributes to healing in people who go there. Bacon's theory is that the Outward Bound experience can serve as a metaphor for the life of the participant, as a set of experiences that can clarify real-life situations and thereby help the learner contend with them. Most of the metaphorical power of the Outward Bound process, Bacon argues, comes from the conscious programming of the leader, but he also contends that an archetypal quality of the wilderness environment contributes to this power. He takes the foundation of his idea from the psychiatrist Carl Jung who suggested that there are some ways of organizing and understanding the works that are passed down in cultures and individuals from early human experience and that transcend culture to the point of being universal. Jung argued that these original patterns are produced in all of us and are a factor in how we perceive the world.

One such pattern of archetype is Sacred Space. This is a place pervaded by a sense of power, mystery, and awesomeness. Such places are not suitable for living, lacking the resources for day-to-day comfort and survival, and the seeker cannot stay there anyway for he/she has important work to do in the everyday world. If the seeker comes to the Sacred Space with full respect and a clean spirit, he/she may be empowered in a positive way. Bacon argues that wilderness is Sacred Space.

> Anyone who has spent much time in the wilderness can easily recognize the parallels between it and the archetype of Sacred Space. Wilderness is difficult to get to and difficult to travel through. One passes a series of tests in order to exist within it. It is unlike the normal world in hundreds of ways. Above all, it pervades one with a kind of religiosity or mysticism—one of the most compelling things about nature is that it seems to implicitly suggest the existence of order and meaning. (1983, p. 53)

In Bacon's view, wilderness as Sacred Space is useful to Outward Bound because implicit in this archetype is the concept of transformation and change. If Jung is correct and there is an archetype of Sacred Space within us, then when we go to such a place, especially in the context of programs like Outward Bound or Vision Quest, we accept the possibility that some kind of transformation may occur. This acceptance may not be conscious, but it is there and it makes change, growth, or healing possible.

A central principle of many psychotherapists is that a person does not change unless he/she wishes to change. Despite themselves, people cling to their problematical behaviors. Only when they become willing to change does healing become possible, as in the wilderness as Sacred Space. A young person in trouble with the law or plagued by emotional difficulties is given the opportunity by a judge or a physician to try something new, to go into the wilderness. If they choose to go, they accept, perhaps begrudgingly or even unconsciously, the possibility of change. The outcome is certainly not a sure one, but there is the potential for something new.

> There is little question that certain course experiences do involve the presence of one or more of these primordial patterns . . . the students covertly participate in age-old patterns of human development. Anyone who has taught an Outward Bound course is aware that the spirit of the course often seems to move beyond the capabilities of the human beings involved. It is in this sense that one can argue that the mountains do speak for themselves. (Bacon, 1983, p. 53)

Kaplan and Talbot, without reference to Jung's archetype idea, argue that wilderness is suggestive of a larger framework, of rich possibilities not considered before:

> The wilderness experience is "real" in some rather concrete ways, as well as in a somewhat more abstract sense. It is real not because it matches one's ways of the everyday world (which of course it does not do), but because it feels real because it matches some sort of intention of the way things ought to be, of the way things really are beneath the surface layers of culture and civilization. (1983, p. 190)

In a metaphorical way, the wilderness experience suggests the possibility of returning to the "real" world from this "other world" and finding coherence there. The wilderness traveler recognizes that daily life may not be as chaotic as previously experienced. There is, of course, no assurance that the possibility will be achieved, that the perception will be transferred back home. The transfer is possible, especially if part of the follow-up to the therapeutic wilderness experience of the "other world" fulfills the archetypal promise of Sacred Space. It is a change and holds out the possibilities of change to come. When this change helps a person to understand and cope with the world, it is a part of healing.

WILDERNESS AND PHYSICAL FITNESS

A final way in which wilderness may contribute to healing is by the physical demands that it makes upon people who travel there. Wilderness by definition is a place without the amenities of civilization. The wilderness traveler must negotiate rough trails or travel cross-country with no trail. All the conveniences and necessities of life must be carried, usually on one's back. Physical effort is needed to satisfy basic needs, as in erecting the tent, cooking dinner, or staying warm and dry in rain or snow. The ultimate wilderness adventure, like climbing a mountain or rafting a wild and rough river, can demand considerable physical stamina and skill.

So how might the physical demands of wilderness travel contribute to healing? First, and most obviously, the demands of wilderness activity, if faced over a considerable period of time (like the 3 weeks of the standard Outward Bound course), lead to physical conditioning and stamina. A fit body can do much to enhance self-image, and a positive self-image is a boost in confidence. An increase in confidence opens new possibilities of learning and growth.

Thomas Stich (1983) notes other ways that physical activity can be helpful in dealing with psychological difficulties. When a person gains control over his/her body, as must be done in wilderness travel, there may be corresponding gain in control in other areas. Perhaps there is also a metaphorical dimension. Traveling to a wilderness objective requires taking one step at a time, putting one foot in front of the other, pacing oneself. So it may be in daily life in a wide range of tasks. The way to the objective is not impatient rushing but steady effort. Alan Drengson has noted this quality of the physical act of wilderness walking. He calls the process "mindful walking" and points out that while one must be attentive to the physical act of walking, one can still look at the larger view and even achieve a meditative state. Meditation is an advanced state of psychological awareness and control, and wilderness walking certainly does not lead everyone automatically to that state. Some measure of the condition is often achieved, though, with beneficial effects.

Stich notes that physical exercise can cause self-expression and be an outlet for aggression and anxiety. All physical exercise provides these opportunities, including that involved in wilderness travel. Self-expression may come in many forms, as in the style in which one climbs a rock or the route one picks on a ski tour. Attacking the difficult pitch on a climb or the physically demanding long, heavy haul can be an outlet for aggression. Struggling with anxiety about bears or exposure or avalanches, pushing down the anxious upwelling while coping with the problem, then screaming with delight when the climb is done or the tricky avalanche slope passed—all provide an outlet for anxiety. The coping with anxiety is in part physical, moving beyond the threat to a position of safety. This is a concrete experience, one that cannot be denied. Back home a success (or failure) might be measured on some abstract scale, by someone sitting in judgment. The physical acting on a problem in the wilderness is real and undeniable. For a person who has often failed in society and thinks there can be no alternative, the physical, concrete experience of achievement in a wild place can be uplifting and restorative.

We can argue with confidence that wilderness has great potential to contribute to improvements in physical well-being. It cannot, of course, "cure" illness, but by its nature it can place demands on us that force us to call upon physical and emotional potential often unrealized. It can allow us to release pent-up energy and to feel our bodies, reminding ourselves that we have physical powers we may lose if we never use them. In short, the physical demands of wilderness places can perhaps motivate us to take better care of our own bodies; and such physical achievement can lead us to want more of the same and to initiate a regular physical fitness regime. In a world seemingly bent on taking the physical exertion out of every action, wilderness travel can give us a forceful reminder of what we are losing.

CONCLUSION

We have seen that wilderness environments can in many ways contribute to restoration of health. We have identified the qualities of such places that contribute to healing, as well as some of the problems where wilderness experiences can be especially helpful. Throughout our discussion, we have noted that our activities in wild places are as important to healthful outcomes as the physical qualities of the places. We cannot separate the program from the place. The particular ways that being in wilderness can contribute to health can be summarized as follows:

1. In wilderness, people experience increasing effortlessness in attending to their surroundings, which can be an antidote to the irritability and stress that comes with attention overload in daily life.

2. Recognition of limits regarding control of the wilderness environment can lead to reduction of the compulsion for control in other aspects of people's lives and to a more relaxed and comfortable posture generally.

3. Compatibility between environmental demands and individual inclination can contribute to personal integration and a sense of union with nature, which may lead to a sense of being at one with the universe, a highly desirable spiritual condition for many people.

4. Wilderness can be a place where people experience competence and consequently enhancement of self-worth. Thus, people can be helped to cope with the contrasting conditions of alienation and anomie.

5. Wilderness is a place with high potential to captivate and stimulate, to increase one's feeling of engagement with one's surroundings. This may improve a person's ability to learn.

6. The concreteness of challenges posed by wilderness experience allows delinquents who usually fail to meet abstract challenges to enjoy success and consequent enhancement of self-image and confidence.

7. The metaphorical potential for learning in wilderness is great and may allow insight into the challenges of life back home and how they can be better managed.

8.   The physical challenges of wilderness travel can enhance physical fitness and can also allow expression of frustration and anxiety, thereby reducing stress.

John Muir knew that his wilderness days restored his body, mind, and soul. He did not know how this restoration occurred, but the effect of his wilderness travels upon him was so great that he prescribed the experience to anyone with the means to go there. Today we still do not know exactly how and why nature has curative and restorative effects upon us, but as our modern lifestyle and development remove us farther from the natural world, we are consciously seeking the succor of wild places and researching the possibility that we need contact with nature to be fully functioning humans.

6

The Need for Something Different: Spirituality and Wilderness Adventure

L. Allison Stringer and Leo H. McAvoy

"I FELT SO PEACEFUL . . . WORDS CANNOT DESCRIBE THE FEELING . . . IT WAS spiritual."[1] These words, spoken by a participant on a wilderness adventure trip, are similar to those often used by participants in wilderness programs to describe their experiences. Tacit knowledge[2] and written personal accounts by philosophers, theologians, environmentalists, experiential educators, and outdoorspersons throughout history have suggested that wilderness adventure experiences offer the opportunity to explore the spiritual side of human existence.

It seems, however, that these spiritual experiences have been taken for granted as something that merely "happens" or something that people (perhaps unconsciously) generally seek. While there is a solid research literature on spirituality and related topics in the fields of psychology and religion, relatively little

---

[1]This is a journal entry of a wilderness trip participant from September 1987 and is used with permission. All of the other participant quotations are taken from personal interviews or journal entries during the summer and fall of 1987 and are used with permission.

[2]Tacit (intuitive) knowledge is that which one knows or understands based on experience and is not expressible by language. "Tacit knowledge includes a multitude of unexpressible associations which give rise to new meanings, new ideas, and new applications of the old" (Lincoln & Guba, 1985, p. 196).

research has been conducted in leisure and recreation to support the inclusion of spiritual goals in wilderness adventure programs.[3]

If spiritual experiences are to be a purposeful element of adventure programs, then there is a need to know more about spirituality in general, and specifically about spiritual experiences in the context of wilderness adventure activities. Therefore, the purpose of this study was to investigate whether the wilderness environment and wilderness adventure programs are conducive to spiritual development, and to investigate what the nature of such spiritual experiences might be.

SPIRITUALITY AND EXPERIENTIAL EDUCATION

The modern world provides many reasons for disillusionment and despair: a troubled economy, high crime rates, a ravaged environment, the drug crisis, child abuse, and war (to name a few). Traditional methods of finding meaning and purpose in the face of such horrors are no longer helpful for many people. Chenery (1984) argues that spiritual development or "centering" is an urgent need for children in today's world. She provides a detailed example of how camps could integrate this development into their programs, the key factors being time for contemplation and guided dialogues on spiritual issues. Fox (1983) suggests that spirituality—in his definition, a dependency on faith—should be the real core of experiential education (of which adventure programs are a part). He states:

> Our experiential education programs must introduce students not only to the abstract and theoretical reality of their spiritual center and dependency, but to its concrete reality, real people, real feelings, real decisions. (1983, p. 6)

In a more recent presentation of the concepts of Transpersonal Psychology, Brown (1989) notes that a primary reason many people seek the wilderness environment is to fulfill spiritual needs. Pendleton (1983) summarized the need for attention to a spiritual dimension in wilderness-based experiential education when she said:

---

[3]Relevant research related to spirituality found in the psychological, religious, and leisure literatures include the following: Maslow's (1968, 1970) theories of self-actualization and peak experiences: Csikszentmihalyi's (1975) concept of flow; James' (1902/1958) discussion of mystical experiences; Otto's (1950/1970) description of the sacred dimension of experience; Beck's (1988) "glow" theory; and Kaplan and Talbot's (1983) analysis of the relationship between wilderness experiences and spiritual meaning. For further information, please contact the authors.

Cut off from nature, we have lost a sense of a sacred reality, we reject spiritual value and neglect our own and others' spiritual needs . . . . Even in the field of experiential education, there has been too little effort made to allow the sacred to be reconciled with the physical reality of our experience. (p. 11)

All four of these writers—Chenery, Fox, Brown, and Pendleton—speak to the need for experiential educators to include a spiritual focus in their programs. There is a need to document and define the spiritual components of wilderness adventure experiences and to make recommendations for programs regarding these spiritual components.

DEFINITIONS

For the purpose of this study, *spiritual* and *spirituality* were taken in their broadest senses to include both religious and non-religious connotations.[4] The concept of spirituality has traditionally included an awareness of and fusion with a power or principle greater than the self. Spirituality has often been described as that which gives meaning and purpose to life. Beck (1986) has suggested that there are several qualities which characterize the spiritual person: awareness, breadth of outlook, a holistic outlook, integration, wonder, gratitude, hope, courage, energy, detachment, acceptance, love, and gentleness.

As with spirituality, *spiritual experience* has no one definition or source and is unique to each individual. Descriptions of spiritual experiences usually include evidence of both cognitive processes (active contemplation) and affective dimensions (feelings and emotions, such as peace, tranquility, joy, love, hope, awe, reverence, and inspiration). They are frequently described as involving a transcendence of self and/or surroundings and are most often perceived as having some degree (usually high) of emotional intensity.

William James (1902/1958), in the classic work *The Varieties of Religious Experience*, proposes that the mystical experience (which the authors believe is similar to, if not synonymous with, the spiritual experience) is marked by four characteristics. These are "ineffability," the inability to describe the experience in words (one must experience it directly); "noetic quality," the sense of the significance of the experience as insight into, or illumination and revelation of, greater truth; "transiency," the short duration of the experience (although experiences can build upon one another); and "passivity," the feeling of being "held" or "grasped" by a superior power during the

---

[4]The reader should note that these definitions were used for the purposes of designing the study only and were not imposed upon the participants. Rather, a crucial part of the study was to have participants define the terms in their own words.

experience (James, 1902/1958, pp. 292-293). These characteristics described by James form the basis for the authors' understanding of spirituality as used in designing this study.

DESCRIPTION OF THE STUDY

This study was designed to explore the spiritual dimension of wilderness experiences at a very basic level. Our specific research questions were as follows:

1.   What is the nature of the participants' wilderness adventure experiences physically, cognitively, and emotionally?

2.   How do the participants define the term "spiritual/ity?" Do these definitions differ in a wilderness environment as opposed to the participants' customary environments?

3.   Do the participants believe that they had spiritual experiences of some sort on their trips? If so, what was the nature of these experiences?

4.   What aspects (if any) of the wilderness trip program or of the participants in the program brought about or contributed to their spiritual experiences?

The subjects were participants in two wilderness adventure programs scheduled in the summer and fall of 1987. There were thirteen persons in each group who were eligible and who chose to participate in the study. The first group (Group A) consisted of persons with and without physical disabilities on an eight-day canoeing trip in northern Ontario, sponsored by Wilderness Inquiry, a non-profit organization which offers integrated wilderness trips. The second group (Group B) consisted of university students enrolled in a wilderness leadership class which involved a ten-day backpacking trip to the Beartooth Mountains in Wyoming and Montana. The first author/researcher was a participant/observer on both trips.

Group A consisted of thirteen persons (excluding the researcher). The group had three leaders, one intern, and nine participants, five of whom had disabilities (spina bifida, cerebral palsy, ataxia, and mental handicaps). Of the subjects included in the study, five were female and eight were male, ranging in age from 15 to 36 years of age (average age of 26 years). Regarding outdoor experience, only one person had never been on a wilderness trip of any sort. Nine people had moderate to high levels of experience in a wide variety of outdoor settings. Four people had limited experiences in camping, hiking, and canoeing.

Group B consisted of eighteen persons (excluding the researcher), four of whom were excluded from the study due to prior knowledge or involvement with it and one who was excluded due to not being available for the post-trip interview. Of the thirteen included subjects, eight were female and five were male. Their ages ranged from 20 to 36 years (average age of 26 years). Two participants had never had any previous wilderness experience. Five others had had limited experience back-packing, and the rest had moderate to high levels of experience in a wide variety of wilderness settings.

Prior to each trip, the researcher told the participants that they would be participating in a study looking at the spiritual dimension of wilderness experiences, although she did not disclose any of the interview questions. The researcher did not participate in any phase of the planning for these trips, nor did she prompt discussions about or activities relating to spirituality while on the trips. The researcher did not reveal her personal definition of spirituality to the subjects. The role of the researcher was to be a participant/observer, not a leader.

METHODS

The methodology used in this study was based on the qualitative paradigm of naturalistic inquiry[5] proposed by Lincoln and Guba (1985). There were four sources of data: pre-trip questionnaires, on-site observations (by the researcher), post-trip interviews, and analyses of participants' trip journals. The questionnaires included items regarding demographic data, previous wilderness experience, reasons for going on the trip, and anticipated benefits. The interviews, conducted as soon as possible following the trips (from three to forty-five days after each trip), included general questions (relating to how the trip affected participants physically, cognitively, and emotionally; what high and low points were; and whether or not participants' expectations of the trip were met), as well as the spiritually related questions. Both the pre-trip questionnaire and the interview were constructed by the authors, following guidelines established by Lincoln and Guba (1985) and Patton (1980). The interviews were recorded and transcribed for accuracy. On-site

---

[5]Naturalistic inquiry is a qualitative methodology based on the following tenets: Research is conducted in a natural setting, using humans as the primary data-gathering instruments; the researcher can use tacit knowledge in designing the study; participants are selected with a purpose in mind; and data analysis is inductive, as well as deductive. Theories, rather than being presupposed, emerge from the data, and the researcher checks those theories with participants at various stages in the study. The researcher presents the results in a case study, which provides a complete description of the situation, providing as many details as possible, so that readers can determine how similar or dissimilar their own situations are to those described. The results can be tentatively applied to other contexts, if the situations are similar enough to warrant application. Finally, there are standards, which are analogous to traditional measures of validity, reliability, and objectivity, that ensure the trustworthiness of the research (Lincoln & Guba, 1985).

observations, though of limited value in regard to spiritual experiences, were necessary for establishing context and rapport, as well as for forming complete descriptions of each trip.

Several steps were taken to establish the trustworthiness of the data (Lincoln & Guba, 1985). The researcher established credibility by forming a trusting relationship with the participants, through being familiar with the types of environments and wilderness activities included in the study, and through using multiple sources of data. In addition, another researcher, who was familiar with but not involved in the study, checked theories as they emerged to ensure that they followed from the data. The researcher sought (unsuccessfully) negative cases for analysis and had participants review both the data and the conclusions for further feedback. The researcher wrote a full case report and had it reviewed by an expert panel, including complete descriptions of both trips, in order to facilitate transferability (the degree to which the findings might be applicable to other situations).

RESULTS

Physical, Cognitive, and Emotional Experiences

Because spiritual experiences do not occur in a vacuum (i.e., they are most likely influenced by physical, cognitive, and emotional factors in our lives), the first research question dealt with how the trips affected participants in general. For both Group A and Group B, the respective wilderness trips were, overall, highly positive experiences. Participants in Group A found their trip to be fairly easy physically, while most participants in Group B felt that their trip was strenuous. These differences in perceived difficulty among participants were due to: 1) the presence or absence of physical disability; 2) the level of physical fitness; 3) the levels of difficulty in terrain, schedule, and physical activity; and/or 4) the addition of leadership or extra responsibilities. Both groups experienced cognitive learning in many different subject areas.

Participants in both groups experienced a wide array of feelings and emotions. On the positive side, participants reported feeling content, excited, happy, joyful, rejuvenated, peaceful, enchanted, moved, accepted, nurtured, more self-confident, complete, fulfilled, renewed in spirit, secure, relaxed, cleansed, close to others, and unstressed. On the negative side, participants felt frustrated, tense, burned out, nervous, over-extended, worried, sad, and fearful. Some comments regarding these feelings were:

It might be something that will take a month or so to process, but my immediate feeling [was] a simple sense of joy that I'd been part of something that I felt was very good, and I tapped into the lives of other people who I think are very good. I felt a smile in my heart, I guess would be a way to say it. Something wonderful had happened, all of the sudden. (Group A, interview)

Emotionally, it was a high of sorts, most of the time . . . . [But] at times I wish . . . I could have been there alone, or maybe with one or two other people . . . . There were times when . . . I didn't want to worry about what anyone else was doing . . . . But to [contradict] that, I was feeling very positive . . . . I have a hard time achieving that same amount of positive feeling when I'm in an urban environment. (Group B, interview)

Many of these general feelings were identical to those participants reported when identifying feelings and emotions associated with spirituality.

High points pertained to such categories as fellow participants (friendliness, diversity, closeness, laughter), the camaraderie of the group itself, physical achievements, the environment, and personal growth. Low points generally revolved around physical aspects of the trip (e.g., personal limitations due to disabilities, illness, sunburn, instability on the rocks, heavy packs, soreness, coldness) and interpersonal conflicts (impatience with and intolerance of other group members, tensions and difficulties in dealing with other group members). As noted below, there is a connection between those experiences reported as high and low points and those reported as spiritual experiences.

Participants' reasons for going on the trips included fun and enjoyment, getting away from the routines of everyday life, being in and learning about the wilderness, personal growth and awareness (physical, mental, emotional, and spiritual), learning about and working with people with disabilities, meeting new people, and experiencing the calming and rejuvenating effects of the wilderness. Their anticipated benefits from the trips, in addition to the reasons for participation listed above, included learning to cope with a new environment, learning to communicate with people who know little about you, gaining a greater awareness of self and the surrounding world, improving or learning new skills, slowing down and focusing energies, physical and mental conditioning, spiritual attunement and clarity, and sharing with others. Very few participants listed spiritual goals specifically. All participants stated that their expectations were met to some extent.

DEFINITIONS OF SPIRITUALITY

Personal definitions of spirituality were different for each individual, but many common themes emerged in both groups. These included the shared or common spirit between and among people; a power or authority greater than self; clarity of inner (or self) knowledge; inner feelings (especially of peace, oneness, and strength); awareness of and attunement to the world and one's place in it; the way in which one relates to fellow humans and to the environment (especially in relation to

---

Table 1: Definitions of Spirituality Reported By Groups A and B

Attributes or Characteristics of Spirituality:

- Awareness
- Human interconnectedness
- Attunement
- Inner feelings
- Connection or relation to a greater power/deity
- Inner or self-knowledge
- Faith or beliefs
- Inner strength
- Sense of wholeness, oneness, peace and/or tranquility
- Values
- Intangibility
- Shared or common spirit

Emotions and Feelings Associated with Spirituality:

• Accomplishment	• Exhilaration
• Optimism	• Awe
• Exuberance	• Peace
• Calmness	• Fear
• Quietness	• Centeredness
• Gentleness	• Reverence
• Clarity	• Happiness
• Security	• Contentment
• Hope	• Serenity
• Curiosity	• Humbleness
• Tranquility	• Empowerment
• Joy	• Trust
• Equilibrium	• Majesty
• Warmth	• Excitement
• Oneness	• Wonder

---

service); and intangibility. Table 1 lists the keywords that emerged from the definitions given by participants, broken down into both the attributes and the emotions or feelings they associated with spirituality or spiritual experiences.

Many participants' outlooks were shaped or influenced by traditional religious teachings, such as the acknowledgement of a deity, holding moral values, the importance of prayer, and the existence of faith. No one, however, confined his/her definition to a strictly religious view, and the majority of participants described broader or more general concepts of spirituality. Some typical comments were:

> It's a difficult thing to define, even after going through several wilderness experiences and having given that specific question ["What does the term 'spiritual' mean to you?"] some prior thought. I think there's a religious perspective to it, and I don't think that it necessarily means that one [subscribes to a particular religious belief], but I think you have to acknowledge the presence of a Power or of an Authority that's above and beyond anything we're capable of. I don't think you can experience the raw power of nature . . . without realizing that there really are powers much beyond what you can even articulate and understand . . . . (Group A, interview)

> I believe that there is a common spirit that is shared by everyone. I think spirituality is how each individual experiences that common spirit. And I don't think it's the same thing for everyone . . . . (Group A, interview)

I guess I've come to realize that it's all spiritual . . . . In a Christian sense, I likened [the trip] to the Eucharist in my journal . . . . We shared bread, we shared food, we shared laughter—which is the wine of the spirit . . . . [We] smelled one another's sweat, we heard one another belch, we entered into the lives of one another. And to me, that's all spirit; that's all shared experience . . . . It seems to me that there was a willingness to be comrades or to be with one another in that experience, and to me, that's spirit. We hugged, we kissed, we cried . . . . I think there's always this illusion that there's this spiritual plane that we seek to attain. But the more I study the Gospels, and the more I try to take on the life of Christ, I see that it's through the very act of living that that happens. It's not through some sort of mortification or extreme asceticism, or something like that. It's through the stuff of life: the dirt, the joy, the people . . . . (Group A, interview)

Spirituality is . . . getting down to the basic, essential needs. And looking for what's common . . . . I'll call it looking for the life force which is common to everything—plant, animal, rock, bird, etc . . . . A definition for me would be connecting, feeling literally and intellectually a connection with that life force. (Group B, interview)

It's almost an intangible quality that I sense in myself and in the world around me . . . . It's a sense of wholeness and being at one with everything that's around me, both with the people and the natural world. Wholeness, or maybe completeness. (Group B, interview)

Every participant stated that his or her definition did not differ in a wilderness context. Most went on to say, however, that their opportunities to experience their spirituality were greatly increased while in the wilderness and that being in the wilderness enhanced those experiences. One person said:

I think everyone has to find [spirituality] in a different way . . . . I have to be in the out-of-doors setting where things become real clear. The clarity is uncanny, because—maybe because of the pace? and maybe because the setting that we're in is really simple, yet complex . . . . There's a profound *power* out there—Mother Nature, or whatever people label it—that is totally unconquerable . . . . *That's* where my soul is . . . that's where I come alive . . . . I mean, if there's a God, that's where I feel closest to that God. That's where the peace comes from, that inner peace. (Group A, interview)

In general, the increased opportunities and enhancement of spiritual experiences in the wilderness were attributed to the absence of constraints and obligations that people usually had in their everyday lives. Since all participants lived in or near a metropolitan area, these pressures were described as being part of living in the city, and the wilderness represented a new and/or unusual living environment. Though several people said that their spirituality is based in the wilderness (as illustrated in several quotes included here), this was not the case for all participants. It might be surmised, therefore, that the operative factor for some participants was being in a *different* environment, free from normal constraints on time and energy, as opposed to being *necessarily* in a *wilderness* environment.

SPIRITUAL EXPERIENCES

Spiritual experiences were often thought of initially as cataclysmic, life-altering events of a traditional, religious nature by many participants. When they reflected on these definitions in juxtaposition to the definitions of spirituality they had just given, however, they realized that their concepts of spiritual experiences usually did not take into account their own definitions of spirituality. After this realization, all participants identified many different types of experiences they had had (on these trips and elsewhere) as being spiritual in nature.

Table 2 lists the spiritual experiences reported by both groups on their respective trips. The members of Group A described the unusual closeness that developed within the group, and so their reports of spiritual experiences were focused most often on the interconnections between people. Participants in Group B, exposed to the vast, stark, and unique beauty of an alpine environment, most often described spiritual experiences as involving an awareness of and appreciation for what they

---

Table 2: Spiritual Experiences Defined and Reported By Groups A and B

- Assisting other participants
- Conversations with other participants
- Facing personal fears and challenges
- Heightened levels of awareness
- Moments of intense feeling or emotion prompted by interactions with other participants
- Moments of intense feeling or emotion prompted by interactions with the natural environment
- Parting or saying good-byes
- Thinking in new ways about self, the world around oneself, and one's place in the world
- Times of solitude, personal reflection, and prayer
- Watching people work together

- Specific Activities:
  - Swimming
  - Portages
  - The final group talk
  - Being in the woods
  - Meals
  - Playing and listening to the guitar
  - Watching a full moonrise
  - Rock climbing
  - Summit ascents
  - Laughing and joking
  - Silent walk out on last day
  - An Earth Awareness exercise
  - A yoga lesson
  - A Native American ceremony

involved interactions with other people, just as persons in Group A described interactions with the environment. The majority of the responses, however, fell into the two respective categories listed above.)

A few of the comments were:

> Some of the days I was up before anybody else, and to be able just to go quietly about my business and get dressed and get the fire started, all those really important things . . . . Those are the very basic things you need to start your day. And [to] be able to look out over the river or the lake, and [to] be able to observe the eagles or the loons, or the osprey, or just the sunrise, those are all spiritual moments. (Group A, interview)

> [We] were walking out on the last day, and the whole walk was very spiritual for me. We didn't really talk at all. And we stopped quite a bit and just sat and listened and watched. And at that point, my senses were so in tune, after being out there [in the wilderness] for so long. In the back of my mind was the thought, "You're going back." And I just wanted to grab as much of it and stuff it in as I could. I just felt really happy, and . . . also the knowledge that I was going back wasn't bothering me, because I felt confident and content enough that I knew [that I could go back and deal with the things I needed to deal with back home] . . . . I remember looking around me, thinking, "God, the colors are so beautiful. Everything smells *so* good here." And it was just *special.* It was spiritual. I felt like I *belonged.* (Group B, interview)

> [For me, it was] just the people . . . and the fact that I have . . . some more friends . . . . We lose sight of that very sensible, crucial element of living, which is trusting other people and loving them, and tolerating their weaknesses, and maybe even getting disgusted with them, but still loving them. And I think that happened . . . . That was the spiritual awakening for me, you know, the friendship. (Group A, interview)

> One thing that comes to mind real quickly is joking and laughing, just really laughing hard . . . . Another time, was, I suppose, the high and low moments, when I was really struggling hard, and I . . . really felt some power from another person. All she did was walk with me and talk with me, and it was like I was able to absorb some of her power . . . . I find my Higher Power in other people, too. And spending time alone, all by myself, just allowing myself to feel whatever I felt . . . . (Group B, interview)

These participants' comments reflect several other people's feelings as well. Connection with other people—sharing a common spirit—was vital to many participants' experiences of spirituality. Often this connection included a component of service, either given or received, that helped strengthen the bond. Equally important were heightened awareness of or attunement to self and surroundings, and clarity of thought or feeling. The last quotation also illustrates that moments of great emotional impact (often reported by participants as spiritual moments or experiences) are not always positive; often negative and positive feelings are blended in a single experience.

A comparison of reported high and low points with reported spiritual experiences of both groups indicates that spiritual experiences are shaped or influenced primarily by the most memorable facets of the trip as a whole. The data also indicate that those experiences which are reported to be spiritual are also those which are reported to be the most emotionally intense. Furthermore, most of the emotions associated with these experiences are positive, and most of the experiences are accompanied by a heightened sense of awareness (of self, of others, of the environment, and/or of a greater power). These findings suggest that by giving participants opportunities to focus on and process the intense emotional experiences they encounter on trips, leaders may help participants to foster spiritual growth.

CONTRIBUTING FACTORS

There were many factors that were influential in participants' spiritual experiences in both groups. Table 3 gives a summary of both contributing and inhibiting factors mentioned by the participants in response to the questions: "What factors or components of the trip do you think brought about or contributed to this/these experiences?" and/or "What factors or components of the trip (or of yourself) do you think might have prevented you from having a spiritual experience?"

The two factors most frequently mentioned were other people on the trip—in terms of the sharing that occurred between group members and the variety of thoughts, opinions, and experiences that each person brought to the group—and being in a wilderness environment. Participants commented that the wilderness provides a place to find inner peace and tranquility, solitude, beauty, and spiritual rekindling; that it is a place in which one can learn and grow; and that the wilderness "prompted spontaneous [private] praise and worship, where other kinds of environments wouldn't."

The structure of the trips was both a contributing and an inhibiting factor for participants. "Time off" was seen as a crucial element in many persons' spiritual experiences; several people expressed the desire for more free time than was available to them. Other factors mentioned were personal awareness or a predisposition toward spiritual reflection, and the prompting of spiritual thought or discussion by other participants or the researcher (by virtue of conducting the study, not specific direction or prompting). As one participant said:

> Factors in myself are [that] I try to be accepting of my experience. Open to the
> experience, whether it's a challenge or whatever . . . . That's probably the biggest

---

Table 3: Factors Contributing To or Inhibiting Spiritual Experiences

Contributing Factors
- Prior awareness of one's own spirituality
- Camaraderie/The unusually close bonds between people
- Needing to confront and deal with personal questions
- Physical activity
- Predisposition toward spiritual reflection and/or experiences
- Previous spiritual experiences
- Prompting by other participants, leaders, or the researcher
- The natural environment/Being in a wilderness environment
- The people on the trip (sharing; the variety of thoughts, opinions, backgrounds, and experiences)
- Time off (from activities or from the group)
- Structure/Organization/Components of the Trips:
  - Changing paddling and tent partners
  - Opportunity to teach a prepared lesson to group
  - Food
  - Lack of responsibility for planning and leading trip (i.e., being a participant instead of a leader)
  - Physical challenges and demands
  - Relaxed atmosphere
  - Weather
  - Leadership styles

Inhibiting Factors
- Not enough time to feel, see, and/or process experiences
- Not having time/enough time off or alone
- Not looking for spiritual experiences
- Too large a group

---

single factor in myself. Another was my own awareness [of] where my spirituality is based. [It] is based . . . in the woods. Absolutely no doubt about it . . . . I don't get any closer . . . . That's where [the real world] is. Factors of the trip were that . . . it *was* the real world . . . . The trip wasn't a sightseeing tour of downtown Chicago. So the fact that it was wilderness. And then, the fact that the people on it had varied backgrounds and also were . . . quite accepting. I think that's good. I think those are important factors. (Group A, interview)

As previously noted, the major inhibiting factor was a lack of time alone or time off, either programmatically (i.e., not enough free time planned into the structure of the trip itself) or because of leadership responsibilities. Other factors mentioned were that participants were not seeking spiritual types of experiences and that the group was too large. One person said:

I think when it's been more spiritual, it's been because I've either been looking for a spiritual experience or looking to delve into something in myself, looking for soul development, and so I take the time for that. And I think it was just more a matter of time . . . . I didn't have the time to delve into my soul on this trip, because I was in a different role. (Group A, interview)

CONCLUSIONS AND PROGRAM RECOMMENDATIONS

These results indicate that the wilderness environment and experience was, for these groups in these situations, conducive to spiritual development. The spiritual experiences reported by participants in this study were emotionally intense in character. Furthermore, because most participants were readily able to recall and articulate these experiences approximately a month after their trips, the experiences seem to have had an impact on participants' lives to some degree. One participant, who is an avid outdoorsperson, said, "That particular experience, *that particular trip*, helps me every day." (Group A, interview)

The implications for experiential educators, programmers, and leaders are many. While one cannot automatically generalize to the population at large from these data (see footnote 5), this study indicates that wilderness adventure trips and programs have the potential to enrich the lives of participants, not only physically and mentally, but spiritually as well. Furthermore, once participants begin to contemplate and define their own concepts of spirituality, they may find that their opportunities for an enriched spiritual life are greater than they realize.

Based on the data reported in the study, the authors offer the following suggestions for planning and conducting trips (assuming the target populations and trip conditions are similar to those described here):

- Set aside group and personal time to think, talk, and write about spirituality and nurturing the human spirit. Specific tools that have been helpful to many people are journal writing, meditation, solos, and time off. Leaders can prompt thought about spirituality with inspirational readings at the end of the day or after significant moments in the trip. They can also encourage participants to bring along personal favorites, either to share with the group or to enjoy alone.

- Because the emotional intensity of wilderness experiences can be spiritually enriching, focus processing discussions around the spiritual nature of these experiences. Identifying and exploring these emotionally intense experiences may help participants to grasp their potential spiritual significance, if participants have had the opportunity to think about their own spirituality.

- Take people out of their everyday environments and normal constraints on time and energy. For someone living in a rural area, an urban adventure could be a powerful experience.

- Plan opportunities for people to be significantly affected on an emotional level. Include activities that provide physical challenge, enabling people to explore personal limits and to learn more about themselves.

- Because connections with others seemed to be a major factor in participants' definitions of spirituality and reports of spiritual experiences, encourage activities that help people explore and develop personal connections with each other, utilizing the variety of backgrounds and experiences that are present in any group.

- Similarly, because an awareness of the world around them was also a major component of participants' definitions and spiritual experiences, take advantage of the wilderness environment in which you will be traveling. Find out ahead of time what natural phenomena are prevalent (plants and animals, geology, full moonrise, meteor showers, times of sunrise and sunset, etc.). Take time to tell participants about the history of the area, creating connections between their experiences and the human and nonhuman past of an area.

This was an exploratory study on a topic which has received little emphasis. As the body of research on this topic grows, one can hope that we will be able to identify specific activities which foster or enhance spiritual development in the wilderness environment. Much more research will be needed to explore and define spirituality and spiritual experiences in the wilderness context. If experiential learning is a truly holistic approach to education, one should create opportunities for spiritual learning in programs.

A Final Thought

I guess what I would add is that I would hope, I would encourage everyone to open themselves up to how other people view the world, view the universe. And then, that they make for themselves a chance to go out into the wilderness—whether they define wilderness as a 40-acre plot of woods [or something else]—just so that they go out next to Mother Earth. It could be over the hill, behind a sub-division in Arizona. It doesn't matter where it is—Mother Earth is everywhere. I believe it helps to kind of peel back the pavement and rip down the boards . . . . But I would encourage everybody to go back and sit and touch and look at and be in earth, with earth, and open themselves up to just how that feels. And I think spirituality, although it may not connect up with words, will definitely take a new—and, hopefully, productive—meaning.

—a trip participant

Section II

Historical Foundations

7

A History of AEE

Dan Garvey

As the flight attendant announced our arrival in St. Louis, I awoke from a not-so-sound sleep, gathered my personal belongings from the overhead compartment and floor space in front of my seat, and shuffled off the plane into the airport. Another annual AEE conference! Could this possibly be number 16 for the association? My thoughts drifted back to previous gatherings of the association, and as I made my way to the baggage claim area, I privately reflected on these yearly get-togethers and the wonderful memories created during a brief four days every fall.

This conference will be different, not only in the way that all conferences take on their own character, but because my role within the association has changed. This year (1988), instead of arriving with one piece of carry-on luggage, I have arrived with three suitcases (actually, trunks would be a better word), because this year I come as the executive director of the association. In addition to several changes of clothes, these trunks contain most of the important records of AEE: minutes of previous board meetings, bylaws, ballots for the board election, and an assortment of other documents and office supplies.

Driving from the airport in St. Louis to the conference site at the Touch of Nature Environmental Center in Carbondale, Illinois, I attempted to piece together the history of AEE and found I couldn't even be sure of which years conferences were held in certain locations: Was the Portsmouth, New Hampshire, conference in 1978 or was it '79? Placing conferences with their dates was less difficult than attempting to put significant activities of the association within a historical context.

This paper is an attempt to write a brief history of AEE. I have not said "The History" because I expect others who have lived through the development of the association will continue to deepen our understanding of the activities of the past 16 years. In researching this paper I have attempted to read whatever I could find about the Association for Experiential Education (AEE). Of particular help has been the compilation of board minutes pulled together by my friend and former association officer, Betsy Dalgliesh. In addition to the "written word," I have also had formal and informal interviews with Joe Nold, Dick Kraft, Tony Richards, Keith King, Peggy Walker Stevens, and Jim Kielsmeier, each of whom has played a significant role in the birth and/or continuation of the association. There are many others, to be sure, who could/should have been contacted to gain insight and factual information. I hope this paper will serve as a beginning, and I encourage all who read it to offer their version of history for future updates.

AEE is a member-supported, international organization made up of approximately 1,300 individual and 120 institutional members. The association is committed to the practice and promotion of learning through experience, and to the collection and dissemination of information related to the broad topic of experiential education. One of the major foci of the association has been in the area of "adventure education." Since many of our members are involved in the use of experiential techniques in wilderness and adventure settings, the association has maintained a strong commitment to the development of safe practices for adventure programming. In 1980, the Adventure Alternatives Professional Group was formed within AEE. This group has been a powerful collective of practitioners interested in the application of experiential techniques with populations in corrections, mental health, and groups with special needs.

AEE publishes the *Journal of Experiential Education* three times per year, eight books specifically focused on the topic of experiential education and its application in a variety of settings (including the Directory of Adventure Alternatives, edited by Michael Gass, which identified 137 organizations and agencies "providing programs that link therapeutic strategies with experiential practices"), periodic newsletters, and the Jobs Clearinghouse, a listing of positions available throughout North America. In addition to publications, the association also convenes regional and national conferences to help practitioners upgrade their skills and provide a meeting time for like-minded people to come together to exchange ideas and renew friendships. Within the association in 1988 there are four professional interest groups: Adventure Alternatives, Programming for the Disabled, Schools and Colleges, and Women in Experiential Education. The AEE office is within the School of Education at the University of Colorado, Boulder.

THE FORMATION OF AN ASSOCIATION

The story might begin by placing the birth of AEE within the context of the "progressive" education movement, as has been described by Albert Adams and Sherrod Reynolds (1985). The purpose of my paper is to recognize the rich history of experiential education and to focus more directly upon AEE as a relatively unique adaptation of this educational philosophy. During the late 1970s, Outward Bound began to focus upon teacher training as one way to help influence the direction of the American education system. The apparent success of Outward Bound programs on previously disinterested students was well documented, and a small group of colleges and universities began to explore the idea of including these techniques within their formal teacher training programs.

In 1968, the Colorado Outward Bound School (COBS), under the direction of Joe Nold, began to affiliate with the University of Northern Colorado in Greeley in offering teachers practice. The goal of these "Teacher's Courses," as noted by Hawkes and Schulz (1969), was to produce a different type of teacher by addressing the criticism that ". . . methods classes, certification requirements, and eight-week, teacher-training courses, have failed to produce quality educators" (Hawkes & Schulze, 1969). Another program was located at Appalachian State University in Boone, North Carolina. In 1971, Keener Smathers, an assistant professor of secondary education, began to offer a summer teacher training program that included an Outward Bound course at the North Carolina school.

The success of this program and interest shown by other colleges and universities led Smathers to write to Henry Taft, president of Outward Bound, Inc., seeking his assistance to help organize a conference that would bring together members of the academic community with staff from the various Outward Bound schools to discuss the value of Outward Bound-type activities at the post-secondary level. Taft responded by sending John Rhodes, program coordinator at Outward Bound, Inc., to work with Smathers at Appalachian State, and the two of them planned a conference for February 1974 (Minor & Boldt, 1981). The First North American Conference on Outdoor Pursuits in Higher Education was convened February 10, 1974, at Appalachian State University. One hundred and thirty-six people preregistered for the conference, and over 200 attended. One of the attendees, Keith King, who was running his own program at Keene State College in New Hampshire, vividly remembers this first gathering: "I always took students with me to conferences, so I guess there were a dozen or so with me. When I heard about the conference, I just knew I had to go. There wasn't much support for what we were doing, most of us weren't sure if anyone else was trying to teach students this way." Dave Hopkinson, a student of Keith's recounted to me that he was "blown away by the experience of being with this exciting group of people at this first gathering."

Henry Taft delivered the keynote address, "The Value of Experience." He ended his talk with the following statement, "Finally, I would hope that some sort of national organization on outdoor experiential education at the college level may evolve from this trailblazing meeting. You are in unexplored territory, and about to be impelled into experience. Good luck" (Taft, 1974). A group of conferees, headed by Alan Hale, presented an outline for a possible national association as a follow-up to the conference. One of the recommendations included the formation of a national steering committee to oversee the development of a future conference and the possibility of a larger association. This first steering committee consisted of Bob Godfrey, University of Colorado; Don Kesselheim, University of Massachusetts; John Rhodes, Outward Bound, Inc.; Richard Rogers, Earlham College; and Keener Smathers, Appalachian State University.

The second conference was held 8 months later, in October, at Estes Park, Colorado. The organizer of this gathering was Bob Godfrey. The Estes Park conference was noteworthy because of the wide variety of educators who were in attendance. Unlike the previous conference in North Carolina, where Outward Bound staff had come together with college faculty, the Colorado conference was attended by "regular classroom teachers."

Reflecting upon this stage of what was to become AEE, Tony Richards suggested that this inclusion of educators from outside the outdoor pursuits area had opened the conferences to a diversity of participants, and had helped ensure that "you didn't have to be vaccinated with an Outward Bound course to be a member of this group."

Perhaps the most vivid memory of those in attendance at the Estes Park conference was the address delivered by William Unsoeld, which he entitled, "The Spiritual Value of the Wilderness." In this speech, Unsoeld provided a well-articulated rationale for "adventure activities." The effect upon participants was profound. Again quoting Keith King, "We came out of his speech 45 feet in the air, and we didn't come down until we hit New Hampshire."

The 1975 conference was convened by Alan Hale, at Mankato State University. The use of Outward Bound activities on university and college campuses was gaining popularity, and the need for a more formal organization was solidifying. Following the 1976 conference, hosted by Bob Pieh at Queens University in Kingston, Ontario, a group of interested participants met and finally pulled together this rather loose group of affiliated individuals and institutions into the Association for Experiential Education. Rick Medrick authored the Articles of Incorporation, which were filed in the state of Colorado on June 17, 1977. The stated purpose of this new association was to "promote experiential education, support experiential educators, and further develop experiential learning approaches through such services as conferences, publications, consulting, research, workshops, etc." (AEE 1977). The registered agent for the Association was Maria Snyder, who was working as a secretary with Joe Nold in his "Project Center" at the Colorado Outward Bound School in Denver.

This was the beginning of AEE. The need for college faculty using experiential methods to affiliate, and the financial and emotional support from Outward Bound combined to form a lasting bond that helped create this new organization. Though most of the early members of the association were "cut from the same cloth," AEE would soon move from its university focus to a much broader appeal to mainstream education and to people working with special populations of clients, primarily in the fields of corrections and mental health.

THE DEVELOPMENT OF AEE AND THE STRUGGLE FOR SURVIVAL

> A movement starts out with dedication and then, if it is to survive, faces success with noble resolution to deal with discomforts of size, with the need for professional recognition, with the issues of recruitment, training, the development of curriculum, the business of doing business and the insurance and management expertise this requires. (Shore, 1978)

Thus, Arnold Shore aptly described the development of AEE from 1977-84. The formation of the association was a concrete example of what a group of committed individuals interested in starting a movement within education could accomplish. Having created AEE, the next question facing the leaders was, "What should this association do?"

The administration of AEE was the responsibility of the newly organized "Coordinating Committee," which held its first official meeting on April 15-16, 1977, in Denver, Colorado. In attendance at the meeting were John Rhodes, Dan Campbell, Ron Gager, Rick Medrick, and Maria Snyder. The group discussed the need for increased member services and the production of the *Journal of Experiential Education*, which was scheduled to be published soon. In an attempt to more fully use the talents and energies of other interested members of the association, the Coordinating Committee created four standing committees: 1) membership and promotion; 2) networking, services, and publications; 3) conference; and 4) administration and finance. Much of the current organizational structure in AEE was established during the initial stages of these committees' efforts.

The founders could not rest on their laurels. The 1978 conference was held in St. Louis, Missouri. The choice of this site created substantial difficulties for many of the members, since Missouri had not been one of the states to ratify the Equal Rights Amendment. During the Annual General Meeting at the conference, a resolution, submitted by Linda Chin representing the Women's Issues Special Interest Group, was unanimously adopted by the membership. This resolution notified the Board of Directors that a boycott of the conference was taking place, and called for the following action:

1. That the location of subsequent conference sites be chosen in states that had ratified the E.R.A.

2. That the content of future conferences includes concerns particularly relevant to women more extensively than has been done in this year.

3. That efforts be made to eliminate sexist language in the presentations and publications of this association and its AEE conference (AEE, 1978).

This resolution called attention to the fact that AEE had an obligation to conduct its activities consistent with the values of its membership. Despite the contributions of several women such as Maryann Hedaa, Sherrod Reynolds, Gruffie Clough, and Maria Snyder in the early development and leadership of the association, AEE was primarily a male organization. Of the 130 people preregistered for the first conference in North Carolina, 17 were women. If AEE was to grow and fulfill the dreams of a broader representation of educators, it would have to address the problems presented in this resolution.

The next serious attempt to change the composition of the association occurred the very next year, at the Portsmouth, New Hampshire, conference. In the closing moments of the Annual General Meeting, Arthur Conquest was recognized from the floor and addressed the issue of minority representation within AEE. He urged the leadership of the association to seek ways in which those who have been participants in Outward Bound programs, often minority students from urban areas, could also be members of AEE. Conquest's comments resulted in a 27-point plan created by the Board of Directors to help increase the participation of minorities in AEE. Maryann Hedaa assumed responsibility for this endeavor.

One of the more significant problems to face AEE was looming on the horizon—financial solvency. As the association headed into the 1981 conference to be held in Toronto, there was a $6,288 deficit projected, with $7,531 remaining in the fund balance. The need for a financially successful conference was not apparent to the leadership.

When most of the expenses from the Toronto conference were calculated, the association was deeply in debt. President Rich Weider reported the following budget summary to the Board of Directors during their 1982 gathering: "In the 1981 budget it was planned to keep $8,000 in a fund balance in case of emergencies. Expenses were cut by $8,000, the Journal publication was deferred, bills weren't paid, and the Colorado Outward Bound School wasn't paid, so that with the $25,000 over budget of conference debt and $8,000 in administrative bills, the organization entered 1982 with a $33,000 debt" (AEE, 1982). In addition to the financial problems facing the association, Stephanie Takis, the executive officer resigned, stating her belief that AEE could no longer afford to pay someone in her position.

Faced with a substantial debt, the resignation of the executive officer, and the lack of funds to operate or rent an office space, the association was near collapse. Minutes of board meetings from this era reflect the tension and obstacles facing this group.

While no single person could claim to have saved AEE, the imaginative and dedicated activities of Jim Kielsmeier, Peggy Walker Stevens, and Dick Kraft certainly contributed to its rescue. Without the efforts of these individuals, and the other members of the Board of Directors, the association would certainly have floundered and collapsed. Kraft, a faculty member at the University of Colorado, offered space within the Education Department for AEE. The move of AEE from the Colorado Outward Bound School to the University of Colorado was, in some ways, an appropriate relocation. COBS and the University of Colorado had enjoyed a long history of cooperative activities, including the formation of a jointly run Master's in Education Program. In addition, many of the dominant forces within AEE had either been adjunct faculty in the Education Department (Bob Godfrey and Joe Nold, for instance), or they had studied with Kraft, John Haas, and Stan Ratliff, senior faculty members at CU (Jim Kielsmeier, Rocky Kimball, and Tony Richards).

The accounts of the board minutes from this period detail the dedication of a group of determined individuals who were resolved to keep the association alive. Peggy Walker Stevens arranged her vacation time so that she would be able to journey from New Hampshire to Boulder and work in the office. Kielsmeier and Kraft established the equivalent of martial law regarding the expenditure of money and the operation of the office. The other board members helped subsidize association expenses by covering phone charges and copying costs. The number of yearly board meetings was reduced, and when they met they slept on the floor of a host member's house to help save the costs of hotel rooms.

The efforts of these board members, coupled with a small but well-run conference at Humboldt State University in Arcada, California, convened by Mike Mobley, allowed the leadership and membership of the association to breathe a sigh of relief. At the Annual General Meeting in 1983, Dick Kraft reported "there were 554 people in attendance at this conference and the break-even point was 350." He said he had "come to the conference prepared to declare the organization bankrupt, but the success of the conference made that unnecessary" (AEE, "General Meeting," 1983). The financial scare of the early 1980s led to a conservative budget-planning process for the mid-'80s, so that the financial stability of the organization continued to grow. Despite the relatively healthy status of the budget, the last of the debts from the Toronto conference was only finally retired in 1987.

THE CERTIFICATION ISSUE

From the very first meeting in North Carolina, the question of how one determines the relative competence of outdoor instructors has been debated. This question has sometimes been whispered by the membership and at other times shouted from the floor of a general meeting. All discussions concerning the topic of certification were viewed by different factions within the association as biased. To help bring some order to this controversy, the board turned to the expert advice of Jed Williamson, Karl Johanson, and a small group of interested practitioners. This group, termed the Safety Committee, forged a near-consensus regarding the direction that should be taken by AEE in its efforts to help create and maintain safe wilderness leadership.

In 1984, the Safety Committee published *Common Peer Practices in Adventure Education*. This document was the culmination of endless hours of negotiation and hard work by the people involved. In addition, it brought the association together in a united effort to determine those techniques and practices that could be mutually agreed upon as contributing to the safety of adventure activities. This publication is perhaps the best compilation of standards in adventure programming available.

CURRENT TIMES AND FUTURE DIRECTIONS OF AEE

AEE entered a period of growth and maturity marked by a strong financial base and stable leadership. Questions concerning the board and the membership were ones of direction rather than existence. Discussion at Board meetings focused on concerns about how the association should be managed. The Association began to reach out to like-minded organizations in an attempt to broaden the base of support for mutually agreed-upon agendas for educational change. The 1983 conference at Lake Geneva, Wisconsin, was a joint project of AEE, The Council for the Advancement of Experiential Education (CAEL), and The National Society for Internship and Experiential Education (NSIEE). In 1985, AEE became a member of the Forum for Experiential Education, a group of 12 organizations that shared a common commitment to the goal of improving education through the application of a wide variety of experiential education techniques. These outreach efforts, coupled with a more vigorous recruitment program, resulted in a dramatic increase in the individual and institutional membership of the association.

At the January 1985 board meeting, Dick Kraft submitted his Executive Director's Report: "With this report, I believe that you will agree with me that the association is now again on solid grounds, so I hereby tender my resignation as executive director, effective on June 30, 1985, or at such time as a new executive director has been appointed" (AEE, Board of Directors, 1985). The board accepted his resignation and moved to hire Mitch Sakofs as the new executive director. Mitch had worked in the office as associate director with Dick for the past year and was a natural choice to fill the position. During the next years, Mitch computerized the records of the association, improved the publication of books and resource materials, and generally systematized the activities of the Boulder office. All of these activities were consistent with the major theme of this period: "the professionalization" of AEE. In 1987, Mitch resigned his position to take a job with Outward Bound, Inc., and was succeeded by Eileen Burke, who assumed the newly created position of association administrator.

The resignation of Mitch Sakofs resulted in a series of prolonged discussions regarding the long-term leadership of the association and the proper role for the board of directors. The result of these discussions was to begin the process of hiring a full-time, executive director. Throughout the history of AEE, there had been several discussions regarding the possible merits of a full-time executive director, but the association had never been in a financial position such that this could be recommended. Finances had improved to the extent that, in 1987, the association was in a position to hire a full-time director. Rita Yerkes, for the board, began a national search for an executive director in November 1987, and I was hired in August of 1988.

One would have good reason to be optimistic concerning the future of AEE. Our nation's educational system is suffering from a lack of resources, a lack of faith by students and parents, and a lack of clear direction for viable alternatives that can be implemented to help recapture the interest and intellect of our youth. The success demonstrated by member organizations of AEE has much to offer this ailing system.

In the past, those who comprised AEE were, in large measure, only marginally connected to the educational establishment. Outward Bound instructors and the highly creative classroom teacher have provided a model for many regarding the education that is possible, but they have not been in positions to effect broad-based, educational change. Today we are witnessing a new alliance. Large multinational corporations are sending their top executives on training programs that use experiential education approaches. Ernest Boyer (1987), former commissioner of education, writes in his recent book evaluating the college experience: "A good college affirms that service to others is a central part of education. The questions we pose are these: Are students encouraged to participate in voluntary service? Does the college offer the option of deferring admission to students who devote a year to service before coming to campus? Are the service projects drawn into the larger educational purposes, helping students see that they are not only autonomous individuals but also members of an intentional community? And does the faculty set an example and give leadership to service?" Service learning has long been an integral part of experiential education, and is one of the major tenets of the Outward Bound credo: "To serve, to strive, and not to yield."

The members of the association are not alone in their view that the educational system is in need of significant change. Conservatives and liberals are interested in listening to a voice that has, for many years, only been heard by a small group of progressive educators. AEE, and the educational philosophy it represents, will not be a panacea for the ills that have overtaken our educational system, but it may present sound alternatives for some of the problems.

The specific accomplishments of the association are less important than the fact that it exists and supports a different view of educational practice. AEE has evolved from the basic challenges of surviving, to solving problems of effective management, and finally to a position of leadership in educational innovation. I hope the next person to write the history of AEE will view it as a group that went far beyond an ability to support its members, to an organization deeply involved with supporting change within an educational system that sorely needs it.

8

Sketch of a Moving Spirit: Kurt Hahn

Thomas James

SOMEONE SAID ONCE THAT KURT HAHN WAS THE "MOVING SPIRIT" OF OUTWARD Bound when it began in Britain during World War II. Imported to the United States two decades later, Outward Bound, in turn, became a moving spirit of the experiential education movement. Now history has left the man behind—Hahn died nearly a decade ago—but his ideals are as ubiquitous in experiential education as is neoclassical architecture in Washington, DC. What was once innovation has become assumption, shaping and defining our vision. To ask about Hahn's ideals today is really to ask about ourselves as teachers and learners, whether in Outward Bound, in other experiential programs, or in the mainstream of American education. The answers we find should help us to understand, among other things, the meaning of our careers as educators. Work from the dream outward, Carl Jung once said. If we use history to probe the core of idealism that sustains much of experiential education as we practice it, we cannot help but encounter the man who founded Outward Bound in 1941.

"Moving Spirit" is a better designation than "Founder." What Kurt Hahn caused to happen was larger than the program he created to prevent men from dying in lifeboats when their ships were sunk by German U-boats in the North Atlantic. It was larger than the educational methods he applied to solve the problem at hand. It was, above all, a renewal of social vision.

Not a hero himself, Hahn infused others with a sense of heroic quest. He was an educator—the word comes from Latin roots meaning "to lead out." As a leader, he left enough unsaid that the people working with him were able to add their vision to the common pursuit. In each of the schools with which he was associated, not to mention the smaller programs he brought into being through the years, there was always, in the minds of those who were close to him, a sensation of having within their grasp a unifying aspiration with the power to strengthen individuals and transform social life. Kurt Hahn instilled a pervasive culture of aspiration that remains the essence of Outward Bound and a crucial part of experiential education to this day.

From where did this culture of aspiration come? What went into it that made it so compelling?

We might begin to address these questions by looking for the origins of Outward Bound in 1913 instead of 1941. In the summer of 1913, as an Oxford student vacationing with a friend in Scotland, recuperating from a lingering illness, a result of the sunstroke he had suffered a few years before, Kurt Hahn outlined his idea for a school based on principles set forth in Plato's *Republic*. This was without doubt an audacious, some would say foolish, act of the imagination. Hahn believed that the most extremely utopian conception or society ever formulated should be applied, purely and simply, to create a school in the modern world He was twenty-eight years old and had never run a school, nor even taught in one. The ideal school he imagined never came into being, but it exerted a profound influence on all his subsequent efforts as an educator and statesman. He launched Salem School, in Germany, in 1920; Gordonstoun School, in Scotland, in 1934; Outward Bound, in Wales, in 1941; and Atlantic College, in England, in 1962.

The main point is worth repeating. Though the youthful fantasy of a Platonic school never came into being, its influence crops up everywhere in the institutions he built and in the people he drew to his cause. In *English Progressive Schools*, Robert Skidelsky analyzes Hahn's debt to Plato as follows:

> Plato was a political reformer who sought to recall the Athenians to the old civic virtues eroded, as he saw it, by democratic enthusiasm and soft living. His aim was to educate a class of leaders in a "healthy pasture" remote from the corrupting environment, whose task it would be to regenerate society. Hahn must have been haunted by similar visions of decay as, inspired by these ideas, he drew up a plan in 1913 for a school modeled on Platonic principles. The war that broke out a year later and ended in the collapse of Germany was to give them a new urgency to convert what might have remained a purely academic speculation into an active campaign for social and political regeneration.

It takes little digging to find precisely the same intentions in the founding of Outward Bound in 1941. Men were dying an lifeboats; the English nation despaired of its strength and will to face the coming onslaught of the Nazis. Twenty-one years later, the founders of the Colorado Outward Bound School raised similar

"Always Bringing Out the Best in People"

by John S. Holden

Kurt Hahn was visiting our house in 1968 when Lyndon Johnson announced that he would not run for President again. At almost the same time, we heard of the tragedy of Martin Luther King. We watched the riots on television. Hahn was there when I took a phone call from one of our students who was doing volunteer work for the Southern Christian Leadership Conference in Washington. Here was "Whitey" in the Black stronghold. His description was far more graphic than what we were able to see on television. The conversation was cut off when the boy said he couldn't stand the tear gas any more.

In spite of this graphic warning, Hahn left our house the next day for Los Angeles. He went right to the Watts area to confer with a black man who had organized the youth there to carry out projects in their neighborhoods to make better living conditions for themselves and their families. He wasn't afraid of the Watts riots.

Except for the lifelong sunstroke affliction that kept him out of bright sunlight, Hahn had the greatest courage, both physical and mental. He wasn't afraid of jogging in the dark along the road during an April thaw when he visited us. He wasn't bothered by the fall he experienced on the way back to the house—just embarrassed and wanting a clothes brush to remove the mud from his suit. He always jogged in the dark, and that was neither the first nor the last fall he lived through .

He showed us another example of his courage one time when he was guiding us around Gordonstoun School in Scotland. We came to the watchtower manned by the boys every time there was a storm at sea. I think he was eighty-one years old at the time, and all his life he had been afflicted with unusual clumsiness. He called himself a physical illiterate. Nevertheless, he had to lead us up the steel ladder into the tower. I stayed close below him as he fumbled and almost slipped on his way up. The trip down was even more hair-raising.

At times I couldn't help thinking that this was the most unlikely man to have started the Outward Bound Movement. But, as I listened to his talk about Salem, about Gordonstoun, about Atlantic College, and about Outward Bound, I realized that he was always moving in the same direction, always bringing out the best in people, always stretching himself to the limit, and always demanding that same stretch in the people working with him.

The last time I saw him was in Cambridge, Massachusetts, after he had returned from Watts. He was full of optimism and hope, uplifted from his meeting with the black man who had calmed multitudes in the California ghettos by giving young people something that they could be proud of doing. Hahn was full of plans to bring together from all over the world the leaders of mountain rescue, Red Cross, water safety, firemen, and ski patrols. Prince Phillip was to foot the bill for this great conclave, which actually did take place in England the following year. Behind this was the theory: teach them to save lives and they'll never be willing to kill.

Kurt Hahn told us one of his favorite stories once as we were leaving the chapel at Gordonstoun. Prince Phillip, who had attended as a student, never returned to his old school until long after World War II when he was already very famous, married to Princess Elizabeth, soon to be Queen of England. Of course, there was great excitement. All the staff and his old teachers gathered around him as he toured the grounds. Suddenly, the Prince disappeared. There was speculation about where he had gone. To the chapel? To his old stand at the watchtower? When Prince Phillip returned, he smiled and said he had gone to see if the pigpen he had built in his student days was still there.

I'm glad we knew Kurt Hahn personally. He made it quite clear to us that the physical aspects of Outward Bound were secondary to the really important things. In his talk, he brought out the thinking part, the serving part, the spiritual part. As a warden of the Eskdale Outward Bound School put it, the aim was to arm students "against the enemies—fear, defeatism, apathy, selfishness. It was thus as much a moral as a practical training." Hahn was disgusted with any article or movie that didn't emphasize this more subtle and more important part of humankind.

concerns about the character of Americans. It had been reported that an alarming percentage of American prisoners of war in Korea had collaborated with the enemy. Americans were overweight, deluged by material goods and technology; the young were seen to be increasingly apathetic and often violently self-centered. In that year, 1962, Outward Bound took a hundred boys into the mountains and tried to teach them something about self-discovery. The purpose of the school could easily have been stated in the Platonic terms used by Hahn in 1921 to describe the purpose of Salem School: "to train citizens who would not shirk from leadership and who could, if called upon, make independent decisions, put right action before expediency and the common cause before personal ambition."

The Colorado Outward Bound School was not started to teach people how to live in the mountains. The idea was to use the mountains as a classroom to produce better people, to build character, to instill that intensity of individual and collective aspiration on which the entire society depends for its survival. Kurt Hahn summarized the school's idealism when he said that the goal was to ensure "the survival of an enterprising curiosity, an undefeatable spirit, tenacity in pursuit, readiness for sensible self-denial, and, above all, compassion." Another summary appeared in an article published in 1962 by the school's founding president, F. Charles Froelicher:

> Without self-discovery, a person may still have self-confidence, but it is a self-confidence built on ignorance and it melts in the face of heavy burdens. Self-discovery is the end product of a great challenge mastered, when the mind commands the body to do the seemingly impossible, when strength and courage are summoned to extraordinary limits for the sake of something outside the self—a principle, an onerous task, another human life.

Outward Bound places unusual emphasis on physical challenge, not as an end in itself, but as an instrument for training the will to strive for mastery. There is also the insistent use of action, instead of states of mind, to describe the reality of the individual. Education is tied unequivocally to experience, to what one does and not so much to one's attitudes and opinions. A thread running from Plato through Hahn and through Outward Bound is the responsibility of individuals to make their personal goals consonant with social necessity. Not only is the part subordinated to the whole, but the part cannot even understand its own identity, its relations, and its responsibility, until it has grasped the nature of the whole. This explains the connection between self-discovery and self-sacrifice in Froelicher's statement and it also shows where Hahn parted company with many others in the English Progressive School Movement who saw his stance as threatening to individual freedom. Having stood up to Hitler before being exiled from Nazi Germany in 1933, Hahn believed in individual freedom, but he believed that students should be impelled into experiences that would teach them the bonds of social life necessary to protect such freedom. He took from Plato the idea that a human being cannot achieve perfection without becoming part of a perfect society—that is, without creating social harmony to sustain the harmonious life of the individual. This is the overall structure of the argument in the *Republic* and it is also the most important lesson of an Outward Bound course, the lesson without which personal development is of questionable value. In a small group, the patrol, and in a "healthy pasture" away from the degenerate ways of the world, the individual student comes to grips with what must be done to create a just society, within which a human being might aspire to perfection. Here is the true, unadvertised peak climb of an Outward Bound course. An inner transformation precedes outward conquest. This is why Hahn placed compassion above all other values of Outward Bound, for it among all emotions is capable of reconciling individual strength with collective need.

The prospect of wholeness, the possibility, at least, of human life becoming an equilibrium sustained by harmony and balance, is what makes this form of education even thinkable. Skidelsky again offers a lucid analysis of the source of Hahn's thinking:

> The second idea which Hahn assimilated was Plato's notion that the principle of perfection was harmony and balance. The perfection of the body, he held, depends upon a harmony of its elements . . . . Virtue (the health of the soul) is the harmony or balance between the various faculties of the psyche: reason, the appetites, and spirit. Virtue in the state is the harmony between its functional elements: thinkers, soldiers, and artisans. The same principle can be extended indefinitely—to relations between men, relations between states, and so on.

This passage sheds some light on Hahn's interest in giving his students experiences that would complement their strengths and weaknesses. In his speeches, he said he wanted to turn introverts inside out and extroverts outside in. He wanted the poor to help the rich break their "enervating sense of privilege" and the rich to help the poor in building a true "aristocracy of talent." The schools he founded sent bookworms to the playing field and jocks to the reading room. He did not produce outstanding athletes, but his students exhibited consistently high levels of fitness, accomplishment, and social spirit. He said he valued mastery in the sphere of one's weakness over performance in the sphere of one's strength. To carry forward into Outward Bound today, the program is not meant to turn out virtuosos in any sense. Hahn would have liked what the Colorado staff call "ruthless compassion," the breaking of strong students by forcing them to keep a slow pace with the weaker members of the group. He would also have been happy with the not-quite-so ruthless encouragement of the weaker members to press beyond their limits.

If the miniature society that results is full of conflict, as is often the case in an Outward Bound patrol of widely differing abilities, we may find solace in the words of H. L. Brereton, Hahn's Director of Studies at Gordonstoun. In his book called *Gordonstoun*, Brereton accepts the life of aspiration, of struggling for a goal that always lies beyond the grasp of the society striving for it. He recommends that we follow Plato's use of a "fluid definition" of where we are in relation to the ideal form. Conflict is valuable, both for the group and for the individual, because "out of the inevitable conflict we can avoid complacent but narrow successes and reach after an elusive but much broader achievement." Brereton goes on: "It is the nature of a society trying to develop wholeness that it should be a sort of active debate, or even conflict. Plato demands that we accept complexity and the conflicts which result from it, not as avoidable evil, but as a necessary condition of health."

In a very real sense, Outward Bound and other experiential education programs are still trying to answer the questions posed by Socrates in the *Republic*: "What are we to do? . . . Where shall we discover a disposition that is at once gentle and great-spirited? What then, is our education?" Brereton speaks for all of us when he says, "We must seek to make the tough compassionate and the timid enterprising." He shows how this view, coming from Hahn, stands next to other educational priorities:

> Hahn, in his broadcast talk just after Gordonstoun was opened in 1934, said that there were three views of education, which he called the Ionian, the Spartan, and the Platonic. The first believes that the individual ought to be nurtured and humored regardless of the interests of the community. According to the second, the individual may and should be neglected for the benefit of the State. The third, the Platonic view, believes that any nation is a slovenly guardian of its own interests if it does not do all it can to make the individual citizen discover his own powers. And it further believes that the individual becomes a cripple from his or her own point of view if he or she is not qualified by education to serve the community.

The preceding paragraphs only scratch the surface of Plato's influence on Hahn. They do not begin to record his debt to other thinkers—Rousseau, Goethe, Max Weber, William James, to name a few of the major ones—whose ideas reach Outward Bound and experiential education in one form or another through Hahn. William James, for example, in *The Moral Equivalent of War*, asked if it is not possible in time of peace to build the kind of social spirit and productivity one takes for granted in time of war. Hahn saw Outward Bound as an answer to that question. Goethe wrote of an education that would need to occur in a place apart, a "Pedagogical Province," so that individuals could be strengthened and given skills to survive, individually and collectively, in the debilitating environment of human society as we know it. This has much in common with Plato's notion of a "healthy pasture," and it is the sine qua non of most adventure programs operating in the outdoors.

Like any idealist in education, Hahn was profoundly indebted to Rousseau, both for the idea that awakening an individual's collective concern is the key to healthy personal development, and for Rousseau's assumption that Nature is an educator in its own right, more akin to the true nature of a human being than is the society that humans have built for themselves. Hahn also drew heavily from the experience of the English school movement at the beginning of this century. But his genius was in applying ideas to emphasize the interdependence of the community as a whole, rather than a disproportionate excellence of some of its parts. A man of aphorisms more than of systematic theory, of aspiration more than of exact analysis, he lived out the aphorism of another great educator, Pestalozzi, who said, "To reach a worthy goal is better than to propound much wisdom."

If Hahn had been only an idealist, if he had not applied his ideals to the humdrum of educational programs—including Outward Bound—then we might be better off leaving him to his rest. As it is, however, his practical concerns are still concerns of Outward Bound and of experiential education.

First, for instance, Hahn asked his students to pledge themselves to a "training plan" that established personal goals and a code of responsibility. Outward Bound instructors make a similar appeal to their students today, though not in the detailed terms used by Hahn at Salem and Gordonstoun, and it is a crucial aspect of the Outward Bound experience. It is no exaggeration to say that the individual commitment of the student, the expressed desire to accomplish a worthy goal by means of the course, becomes, in effect, the moral basis of the community. It becomes the foundation both of compassion and of achievement, and it is, in addition, the ultimate source of value for the Outward Bound pin and certificate. These are not mere objects. At best, they come to represent the energy and determination that have been invested in them all along by students. They signify the pledge, the willingness to press beyond limits, the membership each student earns in a community of seekers. There are times when everyone wants to turn away from it all, just blast away from the cajoling of instructors and other students, but comes back because of the persistent lure of that self-imposed challenge, and the dishonor of withdrawing from it. The pledge imposes a necessary code of responsibility on people who have grown accustomed to a far different set of rules in our time. If the program taps previously undiscovered resources of courage and mutual support in the face of crisis among its students, even in what appear to be trivial situations like cooking a meal or getting up at an early hour, at least it will have opened the door to the revitalization of social life that Hahn had in mind. It will have started its students thinking about living up to an aspiration they have come to realize is possible.

A second concern that Hahn incorporated into all his educational programs had to do with compressing time. From Salem onward, he woke his students early, exercised them, controlled their activities. Even their time to relax and their time to be alone were strictly regulated. As one writer has pointed out cynically, every molder of character wants to control as much of the environment as possible. But on the positive side, this form of education, if it is handled sensitively to foster growth instead of merely to control, can be remarkably effective in leading students out of apathy and self-indulgence. The conflict that arises can be dealt with constructively so that it causes both the individual and the group to confront what must be done to meet collective goals without trampling on the rights of the individual. Any discussion of freedom that ignores this conflict has little basis in reality. Every Outward Bound instructor—indeed, every educator—has probably asked at one time or another: "Is it necessary to make such an incursion into the personal domain of students, their private world of choice and motivation and meaning, in order to give them a learning experience?" When they ask this, they are in effect arguing with

Kurt Hahn, and Hahn's answer would be: "Yes, but if it is done gently and with a caring spirit, it will not be such an incursion after all." The structuring of time is a critical factor in influencing behavior. To slow Outward Bound down, to shift its focus from action to sensibility and individual well-being apart from the needs of the group, would be to leave out an element ("*impelled* into experience") that Hahn saw as essential to the program.

Third, a centrally important element that Hahn brought to Outward Bound was adventure—with all the risk it entails. He believed that education should cultivate a passion for life and that this can be accomplished only through experience, a shared sense of moment in the journey toward an exciting goal. Mountaineering and sailing were integral parts of his program at Gordonstoun, and he made space in all his programs for student initiative—an expedition, a project, a sailing voyage. Hahn welcomed powerful emotions, such as awe, fear, exultant triumph. Part of his lifelong aspiration, part of the "whole" he sought through programs like Outward Bound, was that the experience accessible to any human being, at any level of ability, could be charged with joy and wonder in the doing. But the corollary is that he saw adventure in a social perspective, as an event of community life and not a private thrill. The adventure of the individual is always mediated to some extent by the values and needs of the group. This is why, almost forty years after the program was founded, Outward Bound retains an unusual world-view among the outdoor programs that have sprung up around it. Everyone touts adventure nowadays, but in Outward Bound the adventurer must still break down and learn to serve his companions The experience is individual; the pledge and the challenge are individual; the achievement necessarily belongs to all. Hahn saw his schools as a "countervailing force" against the declining values of the world at large. Perhaps among outdoor programs, Outward Bound is a countervailing force against narcissism and self-centered virtuosity.

Fourth, Hahn understood the educational value of working with small groups of students. He probably took this idea from military organization as it came into the youth movements of the late 19th century, especially the Scouting movement of Lord Baden-Powell in England. Oddly enough, military jargon persists in Outward Bound to this day in terms such as patrol, resupply, debriefing, and reconnaissance. Hahn saw small groups as a way to develop the natural leadership abilities he thought were present in most people, but were suppressed by the dependency, passivity, and bureaucratic impersonality of modern life. Such groups place heavy social pressures on individual initiative, yet at the same time they require it absolutely. Small groups require tremendous amounts of energy to reach the consensus necessary to meet objectives. In a wilderness environment, effective group dynamics are paramount to survival; they rank in importance with technical skills. Natural leaders emerge when the group must solve real problems instead of playing games with an unnatural reward system. A genuine community begins to appear on a small scale—at least the possibility is there. If it happens, each of the separate selves may glimpse an aspiration worth fighting for back home. At its worst, the small group is a troublesome obstacle to the fine experience any wilderness has to offer; but at its best, it opens a new dimension not accessible to solitary escapists, no matter how intense their devotion to the outdoors.

The fifth concern, which could be seen as encompassing all the rest, was Hahn's dedication to community service. It is possible to make a case that the Outward Bound concept was born when the headmaster of Gordonstoun looked around him during the 1930s and saw that the boys in Hopeman Village, near the school, were in terrible physical condition and that they fell into delinquent ways as soon as they reached puberty. Hahn believed the school should serve the community around it, so he allowed a few of his boys to go out on a project to teach the kids how to take care of themselves. The project grew, along with many other service projects he set up, ranging from craftsmanship to landscaping to rescue service. By the time he started developing a program to help sailors acquire the fortitude to survive in lifeboats at sea, Kurt Hahn already had an extensive outreach program from his school, including sailboats, mountaineering gear, tools, and other paraphernalia. As Hahn saw it, the link between individual and school depended for its meaning upon the link between school and society. The notion came into Outward Bound in the form of rescue service, and it has since been applied to diverse needs in communities and the natural environment.

These are a few of the ideas that Kurt Hahn brought to Outward Bound and to experiential education. Perhaps another writer would spend more time enumerating the man's limitations. I believe I have done enough by depicting Hahn's aspiration in a way that is true to the scale in which he envisioned it. Much more could be said about him that would be relevant to American education today. For example, his practice of hiring people who disagreed with him, and then challenging them to challenge him, is a tradition that ought to be perpetuated, even when the resulting conflict is painful. A more thorough inquiry into Hahn's life would undoubtedly turn up other treasures. But such an inquiry would eventually miss the point. The point is that he started Outward Bound with an immense aspiration that gave meaning to the program far beyond the needs being addressed at the time. The task facing Outward Bound and experiential education is to retrace some of that aspiration in the minds of all who come into contact with the programs. If this is done, other elements will fit readily within the whole. Instructional objectives, systems, models, policies, procedures, formats, evaluation schemes—all can play a part, alongside the irreplaceable devotion of staff, once we have come to terms with the essential nature of our business. All are a hollow shell without that recognition.

The staff of experiential education programs enter each course with a large store of technical skill and, in the outdoors, wilderness experience behind them. No student will ever see it all, but it helps to define their world throughout the course. In the same way, the social vision of staff can help to bring a world of dignity and compassion into being, if they are gentle and high-spirited enough. Each course, each student, each moment is an opportunity to use the mountains and other experiential "classrooms" to find the only mountain really worth climbing. This may sound wildly idealistic, but it is not out of keeping with the origins of Outward Bound or with the aims of experiential education. It is the tacit code that unifies and justifies the endeavors of all of us.

9

Change and Continuity in Experiential Education: A Case Study

Thomas James

Sooner or later, all educational programs confront the problem of adapting traditions to new circumstances. Traditions, even those only recently embraced, exercise a powerful influence on experiential learning, just as they do on conventional schooling. To define aims and standardize procedures is to set in motion the age-old dialectic of essence and existence, of core values and unforeseen contingencies. Much as we might wish to know in advance how to respond, only through experience do we learn what to hold constant or what to reshape in the educational process. As educators and as human beings, how can we discern when we have gone too far, either by manipulating the program so much that it is little more than a convenient response to external demands, or by becoming so inflexible amidst changing circumstances that we doom ourselves to earnest parochialism and a growing insignificance apparent to everyone by ourselves?

No program, no matter how innovative or how well established, can escape the uncertainties of programmatic change in light of this underlying dilemma. By studying one experiential program in some depth over the past few years, I have gained respect for all experiential educators as they respond to the environments in which they work while they deepen their understanding about what they are doing as teachers and learners. This article uses a case study of Outward Bound, specifically the North Carolina Outward Bound School (NCOBS), to develop an interpretation of change and continuity which may be helpful to people who work in non-profit educational organizations that confront similar tensions and opportunities.[1]

THE PRESSURES FOR CHANGE

To begin with, when NCOBS was founded in the 1960s, during the decade when the Outward Bound movement came to the United States,[2] the school quickly formed a core program around what has come to be called the standard course, a roughly three-week sequence of experiences emphasizing outdoor and fitness training, individual and group challenges, expeditions, a time for solitary reflection, and service.

The standard course was viewed as "public" in the sense that it was widely marketed for people within a designated category, such as adolescent boys, as opposed to a contract-type course established for a particular institution and designed for a special purpose. "Contract" courses, or more generally, special programs as they are now called at NCOBS, were relatively infrequent in the early years but have mushroomed in the 1980s. The dramatic growth of the curriculum beyond the standard course is a momentous issue that has raised the specter of conflict between educational traditions and new circumstances. Leaders at NCOBS have tried to fathom what is to be taken as essential and what is appropriately malleable in Outward Bound. For Outward Bound staff, no matter how long they remain with the organization, the evolution of this issue has implications for what they will be paid, the skills that will be expected of them, their trajectory of opportunities through and beyond Outward Bound, and the quality of professional culture they share with one another.

Before looking more closely at the changing balance of the curriculum at NCOBS, it is important to understand a key concept—institutional isomorphism—that helps to clarify the growth of special programs at NCOBS, particularly those contracted with external institutions larger than Outward Bound. At first frighteningly pedantic,

---

[1]My research on NCOBS is part of a larger project in which I an documenting the history of the school and writing a book on Outward Bound as a learning community in changing times. Other parts of the research that have been published so far include "Beyond Time and Place: An Essay in Honor of the Twentieth Anniversary of the North Carolina Outward Bound School," North Carolina Outward Bound School, Morganton, NC, April 1987; and "Old Allies in the Field: Outward Bound and Public Education," published as a series of articles in *The Effective School Report 6* (October 1988) and subsequent issues.

[2]See Joshua L. Miner and Joe Boldt, *Outward Bound USA* (New York: William Morrow, 1981); and Thomas James, *Education at the Edge: The Colorado Outward Bound School* (Denver: Outward Bound, 1980).

institutional isomorphism is a relatively simple idea: when two things are isomorphic, they are structurally similar. Drawn from biology, the word is used in the study of organizations to describe the similarity that typically emerges in the structure of major companies serving the same market. They may begin as highly individualistic and distinct from one another, but as they grow, they become more alike in response to the environment.[3]

The concept of institutional isomorphism can also be used to describe structural similarities between funding agencies and the organizations they support. For example, as school districts received more and more money from higher levels of government, or as defense contractors grew from small companies into major providers of weapons to the federal government, they developed more elaborate internal structures of information and control that corresponded to the structure and even the philosophy of the agencies that funded them. School districts also became more and more like one another, as organizations and as professional cultures, leaving behind much of their past distinctiveness and local flair. Defense contractors organized their incentives and logic of production to reflect the agencies they served, and top staff would then routinely circulate from one side to the other in their careers.

This concept cuts deeply into the difference between "public" and "contract" courses. The key to the contract course, as a historical trend in Outward Bound, is that it will be a more powerful agent of institutional isomorphism than has been the case with the standard course. Like school districts and defense contractors, though on a much smaller scale, NCOBS will have to develop more elaborate and internalized structures of knowledge, professional expertise, and specific programmatic elements to serve the complex organizations that replace individuals as its primary clients under the contract. Equally important, it will have to negotiate to some extent the aims and procedures of the special program to suit the organizational cultures on which it increasingly depends for its livelihood. In contrast, standard courses are designed and marketed by the school, and the key is to attract individuals to them.

The dilemma becomes more clear when it is overstated a bit for emphasis. To serve corporations, an experiential education program must learn to think like a corporation and know something about what goes on inside one. To serve adjudicated youth is to become enmeshed in strong incentives to adopt the therapeutic agenda and methodology of the referring institution. To serve public schools, it will be necessary to incorporate, at least to some extent, institutionalized literacy tasks and school-related behavioral objectives into the pedagogies of adventure and experience. To move into the health professions, counseling, or social work will require getting credentials and figuring out ways of responding to bureaucratic

---

[3]For an example of the literature on this subject, see Paul J. DiMaggio and Walter W. Powell, "The Iron Cage Revisited: Institutional Isomorphism and Collective Rationality in Organizational Fields," *American Journal of Sociology*, 48 (1983); pp. 147-60.

demands for accountability. It will mean creating the internal hierarchies and specialized staff needed to link up with the various kinds of organizations being served, both at the administrative level and among instructional staff.

By describing the change in this way, I do not want to imply that it is bad. It is, more likely, a necessary change that can be good if properly cultivated. However, one imperative certainly arises as Outward Bound or other organizations evolve toward greater complexity. The most discerning leadership imaginable is needed to articulate the identity of the program so that it will be real and honest for students, instructors, administrative staff, trustees, funding agencies, and the general public.

THE EXPANDING CURRICULUM

What are the differences between types of courses, and when did they arise in the North Carolina Outward Bound School? Recently, NCOBS developed curriculum guides for the various courses it offers. The order of presentation is as follows: standard, intensive, special programs, and other courses. The Outward Bound mission, course philosophy, and activity sequence are fully discussed in the first guide, which covers the standard course. Each subsequent guide explains only the variations from the standard course. For a number of reasons, this was the sensible way to proceed. The standard course—originally twenty-eight days—came first in the history of the school, followed by shorter or intensive courses, and then by other applications. Another reason is that many years ago, the national organization of Outward Bound defined the standard curriculum as a matter of policy. The national mission treats the public standard course for youth as the central feature of Outward Bound in the United States.

A third reason for starting with the standard course in describing the school's curriculum is that it reflects a prevailing assumption about the development of instructional staff. They begin by working with heterogeneous groups and with young people on the standard course. Subsequently, they move on to more special-ized instruction, first with homogeneous groups, generally including more adults on intensive courses, and then to more highly focused contract courses with learning objectives drawn from the different organizational environments of the students.

If the standard course is indeed the standard for Outward Bound, against which the development of everything else is understood, it is interesting to look at the statistics to see what is actually happening to the North Carolina Outward Bound School. From 184 students in 1967, when NCOBS began offering courses, standard course enrollments grew more than threefold to 587 by 1974, which was the first year that the school did not show an end-of-year deficit. But since 1974, standard course enrollments have remained virtually the same (see Table). In 1987, 614 students enrolled in these courses. These enrollments have been constrained by the summer capacity of the course areas in the peak months, by availability of staff, and by capital needs for program expansion.

Since the school opened, the standard course has not remained fixed. Its length, to take a superficial but hardly trivial example, has fluctuated from twenty-eight days down to twenty-one, before finally stabilizing at twenty-three, where it has remained since 1975, coinciding with the plateau in standard course enrollments. Other changes brought new course activities into the traditional sequence. Sometimes the staff added special events, such as a seminar at the end for educators on the standard course. Naturally, the activity sequence was adapted to different environments. But all in all, the standard course has been a constant in the school's curriculum; the more it has changed, the more it has remained the same. Instructors from fifteen years ago and those from last year could sit around today and swap tales without any need to define terms. Today, as much as ever before, course directors and instructors will say that they want to make sure their students "get a good Outward Bound course." They are referring to the peak experience for which the standard course is famous, Thus, one can still begin with the "standard" and work outward when describing the curriculum of the North Carolina Outward Bound School.

The evolution of the intensive courses is a different story. First of all, what is an intensive course? An easy definition would be that it is a shortened version of the standard course, aiming at a specific group such as adults, managers, women, parents with children, etc. Some adaptation is involved to address the needs of the group in question, but the course is public—that is, advertised and sold openly on the market to individual purchasers. While these courses differ in their sequence and mix of activities, or even in the instructional style, they are essentially compressed and adapted versions of the public standard course and do not demand a fundamental shift in educational aims.

Some refinement of our categories of courses is needed, since their meaning has changed over time. The distinction between "public" and "contract" courses does not seem to have been important in the early years of the school. Both were standard courses with only slight variations. For this reason, I take the liberty of grouping early "contract" courses under the intensive category up until 1981. In contrast, "contract" courses in the 1980s have developed new characteristics and seem to be a new type of endeavor.

The first intensive course, using this looser category that I have suggested for the early years, was a thirteen-day course for managers in 1968. It seems to have been an abbreviated version of the standard course, adapted to middle-aged men, although it was specifically for the employees of one corporation. In the following year, 110 students participated in those sorts of courses (see Table). The intensive course emerged on the roster in 1972 in the nine-day form which is the most common intensive course to this day.

Thus, in its first decade, NCOBS experimented with shortened and adapted versions of the standard course. These short "intensive" courses were either

Year	Standard	Intensive	Contract
Yearly enrollments for major categories of courses at NCOBS.[4]			
1967	184	—	—
1968	209	19	—
1969	304	110	—
1970	402	104	—
1971	323	266	—
1972	328	202	—
1973	425	115	—
1974	587	147	—
1975	592	149	—
1976	602	253	—
1977	539	345	—
1978	566	276	—
1979	596	350	—
1980	562	347	—
1981	534	316	74
1982	523	332	171
1983	562	344	289
1984	558	399	389
1985	567	395	642
1986	575	482	855
1987	614	492	940

contracted with organizations or presented as a public course, but there appears to have been little difference in terms of the course philosophy or content. The school also ran three-day and five-day seminars from 1969 onward, but the enrollments were minuscule in comparison with the standard course and other intensive courses. Overall, intensive course enrollments stood at 149 in the transition year of 1975.

One way of conceptualizing the growth of intensive courses is to look at their enrollments as a percentage of the standard course enrollments. In 1975, with 592 students enrolled in the standard course, the 149 students in the intensive courses were twenty-five percent in relation to the standard enrollment. Three years later, the intensive course enrollment was nearly fifty percent in relation to the standard course enrollment, and the proportion has continued to rise, up to about eighty-four percent in 1986 (see Table). This means that the short courses are approaching parity with the standard course in enrollments. While there is not a balance between the standard and intensive courses when figured in terms of student program days, it is important to remember that the short courses bring in more tuition per student program day (SPD). Their growth, therefore, has serious implications for the financial viability of the school. For the past ten years, intensive courses have generated about fifty percent more tuition per SPD than standard courses.

---

[4]This table does not include semester courses, alumni courses, and the programs of the Kurt Hahn Leadership Centre which amount to roughly 170 per year from 1985-87. These enrollments are at plateaus, amounting to less than 10% of the enrollments for each of these years. I would like to thank John C. Huie, school director, and his staff at the North Carolina Outward Bound School for providing me with free access to program files and school statistics, which formed the basis of my historical reconstruction of enrollment patterns.

Despite the magnitude of the trend, the growth of intensive courses can be viewed as an outgrowth of the standard course in most respects. Intensive courses represent curricular adaptation based upon a known model. Once staff have been trained to instruct the standard course and have acquired some experience in the field, they can move easily from one course to another. They require little more than some predisposition for working with the group in question, perhaps some in-service preparation, and a pre-course briefing.

A New Departure

The "contract" courses and other special programs of the 1980s represent a new departure because these courses often require knowledge, skills, and preparation not available through working on the standard course. The growth of these contract courses has been spectacular. In 1981, the 74 students enrolled in these courses represented a mere fourteen percent in relation to the 534 students enrolled in the standard course (see Table). Over the next three years, the proportion rose approximately twenty percent per year to almost seventy percent of the enrollments in the standard course. Then in one year, from 1984 to 1985, the number of students enrolled in contract courses rose from 389 to 642, for the first time exceeding enrollments in the standard course, which have remained virtually constant. From now on, it is necessary to reverse the calculation, figuring standard course enrollments as a proportion of contract enrollments: eighty-eight percent in 1985, sixty-seven percent in 1986, and so on. Based upon long-range planning figures from NCOBS, the enrollments in contract courses will achieve parity with those of standard and intensive courses combined by 1991.

It is true, once again, that enrollments are not the same as student program days (SPD). One enrollment in a three-day contract course represents a statistic quite different from one enrollment in a 23-day standard course. Nevertheless, the comparison of enrollment figures is more meaningful than it might appear on the surface. First, the contract courses produce substantially more revenue per SPD than the standard course. The difference is even more disproportionate than with the intensive courses, but it varies more widely by individual contract and by the type of contract. Second, contract courses are organizationally complex for NCOBS. Although it is difficult to calculate, I suspect that it takes more effort to mount a contract course than to put another standard course on the calendar. Third, the labor input is more costly for the contract course, and it is generally more difficult to staff than the longer standard courses, since the instructors with adequate preparation are more scarce. The human capital—knowledge, skills, experience—required for contracts is greater, or at least more specifically focused, requiring familiarity with methods and environments beyond those of Outward Bound. Sometimes the school must enter into cooperative relationships with instructional staff drawn from the organization sending the students.

The rising enrollment figures show that contract courses are becoming increasingly important. What they do not show is the programmatic pressure inherent in the contractual relationship. A contract is a mutual agreement in which the parties specify something that will be accomplished and under what conditions. Offering goods in an open or "public" market—as is the case with the standard course—is also a contractual situation, but we can make a useful distinction here. When you buy something that is advertised and sold on the open market, you take it as it comes. The product is fully developed—with your needs in mind, but it has already been designed, produced, and finished. The automobile you buy is essentially non-negotiable as a product, except for a few superficial options. The same is true for educational programs, despite occasional rhetoric about negotiable learning and mutual goal-setting. When you enroll in a private school or a college, you are buying a product that has been developed by others. You have a contract only in the sense that you are buying entry to the institution just as it is. You will bring your own needs to the transaction, you then derive your own experience, but you have not planned, decided, organized, or produced the program; nor have you negotiated how these things are to be done in advance of your purchase.

A contract course is different from open-market or public courses in one fundamental respect. When you purchase it, you can to some extent negotiate the process that will give you the outcomes you desire. This does not necessarily mean that you will negotiate, but you can. The contract course represents more than an adaptation of the standard course, for it alters the set of relationships that sustains the planning and production of the course.

This change has many implications for the North Carolina Outward Bound School, not the least of which is the opportunity to reach more people with the transforming values of Outward Bound. Some of the implications for staff, such as the potential for longer Outward Bound careers and greater professional and personal growth, are welcome. Others, such as the complexity of instructional relationships, the different pace of varied course formats, and the unpredictability of future demands, are viewed at times with trepidation. Some instructors have qualms about sacrificing the rigor and intensity of Outward Bound. What if courses are negotiated into smaller segments involving challenges less disruptive of the normal routines of daily life, or if journeys become luxurious by the traditional standards of Outward Bound? Occasionally such qualms give rise to an unabashed nostalgia for the good old days when Truth and Beauty came in the form of a tough, no-frills, no-nonsense, standard course that "knocks their socks off."

On the other side, it is widely recognized that the growth of contract and intensive courses has exerted a tremendously beneficial influence on the North Carolina Outward Bound School. Besides making it possible to reach numerous clienteles outside the predominantly young, white, middle-class population that has traditionally filled the standard course, the new programs have strengthened the school as an educational organization. The special programs have demonstrated that more can be done to provide pre-course information and orientation, not only for contract courses, but for all types of Outward Bound instruction. The specific group needs that come along with contractual relationships have caused planners and instructors at NCOBS to consider new ways of increasing the transfer of learning from Outward Bound back to participants' normal settings. Greater flexibility in programming may serve, on balance, as a countervailing force against the dangers of stagnation in the standard program.

In Search of the Enduring Core

The heart of the matter is not to be found in the divisions that exist in the Outward Bound program. The key to understanding the direction of change is the fact that the standard and contract courses share a single reality. They seek and serve common aims through different means. At best, they both probe for the deepest and most enduring values that animate Outward Bound—but not without setting achievable expectations that will lead to tangible outcomes for the population in question.

Here the experience of NCOBS should be highly relevant to experiential educators working in other settings. By design, the contract courses force planners to innovate while also working to express the essence of Outward Bound. Ideally, the same should be true for the standard and intensive courses. All these courses can and must reflect the dynamic creativity of Outward Bound as an educational movement because they require ceaseless pioneering along with a search for sustaining continuity. By the very fact that it is continually transforming its program structure, Outward Bound is reaching for its most deeply felt aspirations as an educational organization while dealing realistically with what works to make the learning experience fit the needs of the students.

One cannot help but be impressed by the magnitude of change under way in the program at NCOBS. The question naturally arises: How is the school strengthening itself internally, both to deal with the many new constituencies, and perhaps more importantly, to maintain its integrity under the pressure of institutional isomorphism as it serves those constituencies with its courses?

Some of the needed strength comes in the form of documenting how the newer and older strands of Outward Bound are developing in relation to one another. Curriculum guides, staff training, and a residential leadership program are healthy steps in that direction. Another source of coherence is the course directors and other senior field staff who bridge the field and office cultures of the school. Their informed vision is crucial for keeping the staff culture in tune with shifting strategies of the school for developing contract opportunities.

Beyond this, the shared vision embodied in the school's top management and board of directors is essential to the survival of Outward Bound's values through changing times. They will be making the decisions that will require the school to internalize the priorities, professional cultures, and methodologies of contracting agencies. To the extent that they can resolve among themselves the structural and professional tensions that arise from the impact of contracting on the school, they will project to others a firm sense of integrity that is the future of Outward Bound. And to the extent that they can discern the moral order that continues to define and defend what is quintessentially Outward Bound, they will have accomplished something truly valuable for Outward Bound schools everywhere. But there is no higher law for assigning priorities to standard and contract courses in the development of the curriculum. Outward Bound was both idealistic and pragmatic in its origins. This dualism continues to apply to both the public and the contract sides of its activity, and I would be surprised if it ever disappeared. A similar dualism can be found at the heart of all educational programs connected in any way with experiential learning.

The tension between idealism and pragmatism draws attention to the fundamental question of identity. What is Outward Bound? The striking differences in what shapes Outward Bound as an educational organization in different societies are good cause for skepticism about any simple answer to that question. In Holland, Outward Bound is funded by the agency that tries to rehabilitate the chronically unemployed in a full-employment society. The credentials of instructors are similar to those of social workers. Some developing nations, by contrast, embraced Outward Bound as part of their rise to independence. Programs are in essence fully contracted to the government, infusing Outward Bound with statist ideology and military culture, along with the traditional values. Such a vision would be anathema in the United States, where Outward Bound schools are more like semi-sovereign independent entities, each with its own distinctive ethos.

To explore this issue of identity, to find out what educational organizations are really teaching in various societies, or even in various kinds of courses within one school, we must look beyond the mission statements and activity sequences to the nature of the social contract, the underlying relationships of power and authority among those who agree to stage a course. This is especially true for contract opportunities: What is the implicit social contract? Who is doing what to whom? Why? Is this "hidden curriculum" consonant with the values of Outward Bound and with the shared culture of staff and trustees? Here, the issue of institutional isomorphism can become tricky, since the values of organizations that fund contract courses might in some respects or in certain instances stand at variance with those at the heart of Outward Bound.

THE IMPLICATIONS OF CHANGE

The increasing shift to contract courses for Outward Bound in the United States after years of developing mostly public standard courses will push a number of important issues to the forefront. I am stating several of these boldly because they strike me as worthy of further consideration by other educators who might encounter similar issues within their own organizations.

First, it is not uncommon these days to find the perception in NCOBS course reports that students on contract courses arrive with different objectives than those of the sending company or organization. This disparity will not go away as contracts expand in the school. Should Outward Bound consider its values as autonomous of the institutions with which it makes contracts? Or should it, on the contrary, adapt to different contractual arrangements and relationships, carrying out the educational objectives that it negotiates for each? A third alternative: Should it do neither, but instead serve only the developmental needs of the individual as these are recognized and negotiated on the course through the activity structure of Outward Bound?

Second, because of its underlying values and sponsorship, the public standard course in the United States began as an implicit social contract with affluent, upwardly mobile, white parents who wanted to motivate their children to succeed. The scholarship students who joined the children of these parents on courses were, in a very real sense, Outward Bound's first contract clients, especially when they were referred by urban social agencies and community-based organizations. But they never enjoyed the kind of responsiveness and interest that Outward Bound now shows toward contracting organizations under more lucrative conditions. They form a lost chapter in the history of Outward Bound which is waiting to be recovered. What sort of institutional isomorphism would Outward Bound need to develop in order to connect with communities sending minority and low-income students?

Third, in any form of education, what can be offered to the student is dependent on the vitality of the teacher. Outward Bound took hold in the United States in part because it recruited and hired college-educated men and women in their twenties who were looking for adventure outside of mainstream institutions, but who embodied positive aspects and potentials of those institutions. One way to plan the growth of contracts would be to continue to base practices on the excellence of the people who come to Outward Bound. If many instructors will work until they are thirty, becoming adept in adventure programming and safety systems, how many will pursue new opportunities in Outward Bound until they are forty? And of those who will continue (or will come anew with the proper skills), what would they most like to do? The planning of contract courses should be influenced by the ethos of staff and their chosen paths of personal and professional development, just as the standard course has been influenced by staff culture through the years.

Fourth, there is an implicit social contract underlying different methodologies that are adapted to work with certain groups of students. Coming from a university where all this is out in the open, I am surprised that there is not more dissension when Outward Bound becomes mingled, for example, with behavior modification interventions in the programs developed for delinquent and "at-risk" young people, or with school retention programs that do not address the sources of student attrition in schools and communities.

Fifth, when Outward Bound develops new contracts, it must create a more elaborate structure of knowledge and skills within the school. It must become more complex and internally differentiated as an organization. One side effect is that if program developers shift ground too abruptly in the external environment to capitalize upon new contracts, or if funds are suddenly withdrawn from a major contract already under way, then the jolt could create chaos on the inside. Each time a new linkage is forged, a new internal structure must coalesce to make it work. It is often the case in smaller nonprofit organizations that the overload on administrative staff comes from not having settled upon a clear trajectory of development for contracts, one that will organize the needed documentation, staff training, and outside liaison into predictable patterns. The strategic decision about how to form such a trajectory usually cannot be made by those who are actively developing the contracts. By experience and temperament, they tend to be inclined to maximize application and extension of the product line to reach new clienteles with what they know to be a good thing. More often, the decisions on direction are made by the funding sources, who stabilize a desirable market by offering long-term subsidies for predictable outcomes, or by the board of directors and executive director, who set priorities.

Sixth, the principle of *congruence* is valuable for thinking about contractual relationships. NCOBS could build up a few, sustained, long-term alliances with institutions that share at a deep level an awareness of and commitment to the humane goals which animate Outward Bound. Another useful principle, the opposite of congruence, would be *purposeful dissonance*. When there are differences in fundamental values between Outward Bound and the institutions with which it enters into contracts, rather than serving as a "hired gun," Outward Bound could develop pro-active strategies to change and influence mainstream institutions. By working to prevent dropouts, for example, Outward Bound is not only trying to get dropouts back into school; it is trying to change schools and schooling so that there will be experiences that can hold young people there by choice.

Finally, instructors discover the potential of various educational practices through the different courses offered by the program in which they work. An exciting dialogue is taking place within the North Carolina Outward Bound School about the differences, challenging everyone who cares about education to reflect on what it means to achieve the aims of experiential learning. There are no simple answers, but a new chapter in educational history is being written by those who bring the best they can give and discover what it means to be both a teacher and a learner.

10

Babies and Bath Water: Two Experiential Heresies

Theodore F. Wichmann

THIS PAPER CENTERS ON THE PHILOSOPHIES OF JOHN DEWEY AND EDWARD HALL by exploring two heresies that presently limit, and may ultimately threaten, the modern Experiential Education Movement. Practically, this movement is defined by an annual conference which began in 1973, the Association for Experiential Education, incorporated in 1977, and the *Journal for Experiential Education*, first printed in 1977. Philosophically, the movement still self-admittedly lacks a "crisp, broadly accepted definition." In the first issue of *Journal*, Murray Durst identified certain assumptions about the members of AEE. He saw them as working within and from without various educational institutions, at all levels and across many disciplines, with a unifying interest in "the nature and process of experience for educational purposes." Furthermore, he viewed the members' perception of their role "to be at the leading edge for educational reform" (1977).

One purpose of this paper is to provide a brief historical perspective that may reveal the subtle, suicidal tendencies of the Experiential Education Movement. Although this may seem unduly pessimistic, I can't help but see the parallels between this modern movement and the now dead Progressive (or Experimental) Education Movement: both movements accepting Dewey as mentor; both being highly holistic and multidisciplinary; both seeking learning through experience; both operating largely outside traditional institutions; and neither one well researched. In fact, one of the few scholarly works on Progressive Education served as an epitaph with the following obituary: "The death of the Progressive Education Association in 1955 and the passing of its journal, *Progressive Education*, two years later marked the end of an era in American pedagogy. Yet one would scarcely have known it from the pitifully small group of mourners at both funerals" (Cremin, 1964). I somehow cannot avoid the image of this as handwriting on the wall. In order to survive, experiential education must help both the individual learner and the culture, of which it is a part, to grow and evolve.

The credibility of the school is its tradition. The credibility of innovative experiential learning must be its demonstrated effectiveness in promoting the survival and growth of the individual. As with the American Progressivism Movement, many modern programs and practitioners have often interpreted experiential education as "learning by doing." In our enthusiasm for developing alternatives to traditional schooling, we have overlooked the fact that experience can be noneducative or even miseducative. In our rush to innovate, many of us have thrown out the babies of experiential education philosophy with the bath water of traditional pedagogy. The philosophy and theories born in the work of Rousseau, Pestalozzi, James, Dewey, and Piaget should be nurtured rather than discarded or ignored. These educators refused to resort to the popular experiential euphemism that if you have to ask the question, you won't understand the answer. Rather, they each dared to ask the question that Dewey phrased: "What is the place and meaning of subject matter and of organization within experience?" (Dewey, 1938, p. 20)

As learning promotes the survival and growth of the individual, educational reform must contribute to the evolution of the culture. As with Progressive Education, many modern programs and practitioners have often interpreted educational reform as improvisational reforming by doing. We are all too acutely aware that traditional education's primary function has been to transmit and maintain culture, and, in so doing, has been "the principal instrument for setting limits on the enterprise of mind" (Bruner, 1962). However, in developing alternatives to traditional education, we have sometimes merely scrambled the internalized cultural program that is mind. We have thrown out the babies of cultural insight with the bath water of educational bureaucracy, with all its violations of cultural norms that limit the development of self. We must dare to ask, What is the place and meaning of experiential education within the culture?

FORTY YEARS OF EITHER-ORS

Forty years ago John Dewey (1938) began *Experience and Education* by observing that educators had been formulating their instructional theories in terms of "Either-Ors." More importantly, he deplored the fact that the Progressive Education Movement, which had recruited Dewey as symbolic father, had not progressed past a philosophy of rejection. Progressivism represented a radical reaction against three primary learning assumptions of traditional education: 1) subject matter and proper conduct from the past are imposed upon students, 2) books are the representatives of this past, and 3) teachers transmit this subject matter and enforce rules of conduct. Thus, the basic learning tenets of progressive education were: 1) to ignore organized subject matter, 2) to emphasize the present and the future to the exclusion of the past, and 3) to view any form of direction by adults as an invasion of individual freedom. Dewey saw that these negatively based principles were vague and inadequate guides for conducting and managing education.

Progressivism also represented a radical reaction against the following cultural assumptions, which Edward Hall (1977) saw as implicit in traditional education: 1) the dominant WASP culture is imposed upon cross-cultural or ethnic groups that are segregated through homogeneous groupings, 2) time schedules and spatial ordering are sacred and rule everything, 3) bureaucracies are real and organization is placed above everything else, and 4) winning and losing are not necessarily dependent upon the context of the subject matter or the real world. Thus, the basic cultural tenets of progressive education were: 1) ethnic minority groups were generally not included or were integrated through heterogeneous grouping with no concern for cross-cultural differences, 2) time schedules and spatial ordering were ignored, 3) organization was placed below everything else and bureaucracies were considered unreal, and 4) winning and losing were deemphasized, but not necessarily made dependent upon context. Traditional schools were not developing enterprising minds, but were producing good citizens who could maintain a culture that is extremely linear, monochronic, and low context. Unfortunately, it is a culture that is not able to adapt to the future shock of rapid technological change. The Progressivists, of course, realized this, but in their haste to react, failed to actualize Dewey's dream of an education that "is the fundamental method of social progress and reform" (1929). In fact, at the end of the Progressive era, American education found itself in a quandary, surrounded by pseudo-reforms.

Levin (1975) recently attempted to resolve this quandary by legally defining the goals of education by identifying a set of broad societal expectations. He described the following four major mandates for education: 1) to certify the achievement of technical competence, 2) to develop physical, emotional, and intellectual skills and abilities, 3) to generate social integration among individuals and across cultural groups, and 4) to nurture a sense of social responsibility for the consequences of personal and group actions. In spite of Hall's insight and Levin's redefined social mandates for education, we are faced with very similar "Either-Ors," forty years after *Experience and Education*. The opponents have updated their banners to: Competency-Based Education versus Experiential Education.

The Competency-Based Education Movement (CBE) described by Spady (1977) as a bandwagon in search of a definition, appears to be here to stay—at least until it is renamed and resold as another hot, McCarthyistic political issue. In spite of vague popular definitions, this movement looks suspiciously like Dewey's "traditional education" of 1938 with its emphasis on subject matter, books, teacher dominance, and a rigid, dinosaurian, cultural structure. Likewise, the Experiential Education Movement resembles the Progressive Education Movement in that its present impetus comes from a negative reaction to traditional education and those forces that support CBE. It is interesting to note that both of these movements are highly unidimensional in relation to Levin's societal expectations. CBE is concerned with the certification of students' achievement of technical skills, while the Experiential Education Movement is limited to the development of physical, emotional, and intellectual skills and abilities. Neither has done more than pay verbal homage to social integration and social responsibility.

There is little hope for reformation of education or society through the CBE Movement. It is highly static, self-perpetuating, and reactionary. In its popular "back to basics" or "3 Rs" form, it in fact represents the traditional, American education thought of the past 100 years. On the other hand, the Experiential Education Movement presents the same promise for educational and social reform as did the Progressive Education Movement. Its advocates are innovative and dynamic and appear to be more concerned with learning and reform than with institutional self-perpetuation. However, this potential is limited by its continuing, self-conscious overreaction to traditional education. This self-consciousness has restricted multidimensional, holistic approaches and produced an obvious reluctance among experiential educators to risk philosophical and theoretical exploration. Most have been content to criticize traditional education and to limit affirmative positions to vague generalities and mystical metaphors. This has created a dangerous philosophical vacuum between the "Either" and the "Or."

THE LEARNING BY DOING HERESY

The paradox of the Experiential Education Movement is that its strengths are sometimes also its weaknesses. An educator's personal discovery of the charismatic power of an educative experience can make an unquestioning convert of him or her. A small group of secondary teachers, for example, shared an intense Outward Bound course in which they collectively overcame various exciting challenges and very real physical and psychological stress. They all felt emotionally reborn at the end of the course. They felt they had changed and had increased their self-awareness and self-confidence. They knew it worked. However, in trying to adapt the model to their own traditional school, the educators were unable to explain to their administrators why such an experience was educational. The experience was never examined from an historical or theoretical perspective, for that would have seemed to decrease the mystery and the importance of the educators' own experience. If one of these teachers explores the possibilities of taking Mohammed to the proverbial mountain, he or she will find that most experiential programs exist as alternatives well outside the educational mainstream. Money, security, and training opportunities are scarce. This has caused practitioners and programs to constantly struggle for survival. This struggle has stimulated innovation and excellence in some cases, while also creating high staff turnover and a paucity of lifelong careers in experiential education. The educator who does carve out a career niche, within or without traditional education, is likely to become addicted to the process of discovery. He or she may then ignore past knowledge and experience and opt for the self-indulgent joy of reinventing educational wheels. This, of course, limits the advancement of the state of the art to one generation. Each discovery addict begins and ends where his/her predecessor began and ended. Cold turkey treatment involves the revelation that many of the addict's anecdotal, axiomatic "discoveries" are 75 years old and have been found to be theoretically and empirically unsound. All of these paradoxes have, of course, limited the growth and influence of experiential education and have contributed to the development of the "learning-by-doing" heresy and its three syndromes: 1) the blind faith syndrome, 2) the cookbook syndrome, and 3) the process-centered syndrome.

The limited literature of the modern Experiential Education Movement is saturated with examples of the blind faith syndrome. Nold (1977), in "On Defining Experiential Education: John Dewey Revisited," wrote that:

> Some feel about experiential education the way Hemingway felt about making love: Don't talk about it, you'll only ruin the experience. We know it's good because it feels good, and as G. E. Moore, the philosopher said: good is good, and that's the end of the matter. It can only be defined in terms of itself, it has intrinsic worth so there is no other standard to judge it by, it requires no further justification. The values are "self-evident." Let the mountains speak for themselves!

Arnold Shore (1977) attempted to define the Experiential Education Movement in terms of its past and its present. He stated that " . . . we conceived of something undefined that was larger, but closely related, that is, experiential education. Not unlike the bead game in Hesse's *Magister Ludi,* this central concept can remain undefined with its purpose yet safe to get us beyond ourselves to something which must be grander." Both of these quotes describe a typical attitude within the Experiential Education Movement. There is no reason to ask questions or verbalize answers. You must know intuitively that all experience is good because it is good. There does exist some support for intuitive knowledge, from Socrates through the present. Of course, the belief in an Inner Truth makes proving any point possible. Whether all experience is good or not from an educational perspective is the focus here and will be further discussed later.

The cookbook syndrome is not as obvious in the literature, but is prevalent among instructors and teachers. Often they must buy a bag of tricks rather than learn the complex magic. They want lists of experiential education activities that work. How does one know if an activity works? It works if the students can do it without losing too much interest. It works if it fills the time slot. It works if it has a reputation for working. Line staff who demonstrate the cookbook syndrome often have little choice. They have received little or no training in experiential education and need "tricks" if they want to survive their apprenticeship. Of course, this is not very different from colleges of education where teachers are trained primarily through memorizing curriculum and compiling related lists of activities called lesson plans. The difference becomes only the nature of the tricks. The traditional educator learns tricks for imposing multiplication tables or grammatical rules on unwilling children, while the experiential educator finds out how long a wilderness solo should be, or what kind of questions and people should be used for interviews by students in his or her cultural journalism class.

Walsh and Golins (1976), Gager (1977), and Greenberg (1978) have all developed process-centered experiential learning theories. These three papers are examples of the process-centered syndrome. Each of these papers describes in detail how the experiential learning process flows, but all avoid any detailed discussion of *what* is to be learned. In terms of Bruner's (1966) framework for a theory of instruction, they have generally included the predisposition to learn and a very general sequence of learning. None of these theories, however, develop an optimal structure of the knowledge to be learned or specify the form and pacing of reinforcement. In our reaction to traditional information transference, we have made process the end rather than the means. There has been little discussion of behavior and knowledge resulting from the experiential learning process. Even more importantly, we have discussed this process as if it were common to all learning and all learners. Should the learning process be identical for enactive, iconic, and symbolic learning; or for personality development, language, and mathematics? Should it be the same for persons at different levels of biological cognitive development? The same for formal operators as for concrete operators? For learning disabled as well as the gifted? We seem to have become parsimonious in our theorizing by ignoring what has been discovered recently about learning and development and by even avoiding Dewey's questions related to the meaning and organization of subject matter within experience.

The fallacy that is basic to the "learning-by-doing" heresy and that unites each of the three syndromes discussed above, is that experience and education can be directly equated to each other. Dewey stated that, "The belief that all genuine education comes about through experience does not mean that all experiences are genuinely or equally educative" (1938, p. 25). Experience can also be "noneducative" or even "miseducative." A noneducative experience is one that does not promote the growth of further experience. A miseducative experience is one that arrests or distorts the growth of further experience. Furthermore, there is a two-dimensional, qualitative difference between educative experiences. There is the short-term quality of the immediate agreeableness or reward, and there is the long-term quality in terms of its influence upon later experiences. In its broadest definition, experience includes all stimuli and all response, everything that happens to us and every thought or action we make. We must whittle this down to size. We must carefully decide what to leave in our educational plan, and more importantly, what to omit.

Furthermore, we must better understand the nature of experiencing, including the subtle, but all important, differences.

Thus, it seems obvious that blind faith, activity cookbooks, and even process-centered theories are not only inadequate, but can be miseducative. All three syndromes can limit the growth of further experience for educators and students by avoiding the issue of miseducative experience and by failing to provide complete criteria for determining the relative quality of a situation-specific and learner-specific educative experience. What is needed now is the development of specific theories of experiential learning and instruction, based upon a general philosophy of experiential education. As Dewey wrote:

> Unless experience is so conceived that the result is a plan for deciding upon subject matter, upon methods of instruction and discipline, and upon material, equipment and social organization . . . it is wholly in the air. It is reduced to a form of words which may be emotionally stirring, but for which any other set of words might equally well be substituted unless they indicate operations to be initiated and executed. (1938, p. 28)

THE REFORMING BY DOING HERESY

Why educational reform? Because as learning promotes the survival and growth of the individual, educational reform must contribute to the evolution of the culture. Why cultural evolution? Because the increasingly rapid advance of technology is shocking our culture to its very foundations. Increasing crime, suicide, divorce, child abuse, resource depletion, pollution, and nuclear proliferation are symptoms of this shock and of our culture's inability to adapt and control technology. As educators, we must not shirk our responsibility to do what we can through our own educational medium to help our culture adapt and evolve. This is, of course, the long-term goal of any education in any culture. Why should the fledgling Experiential Education Movement concern itself with reform? First of all, in terms of its own survival, it must serve a culturally adaptive function. Perhaps more important is the fact that few other educational organizations or institutions are doing it. George Counts's words to the Progressive Education Association's national meeting in 1932 are strangely descriptive of the present situation:

> That the existing school is leading the way to a better social order is a thesis which few informed persons would care to defend. Except as it is forced to fight for its own life during times of depression, its course is too serene and untroubled. Only in the rarest of instances does it wage war on behalf of principle or ideal. Almost everywhere it is in the grip of conservative forces and is serving the cause of perpetuating ideas and institutions suited to an age that is gone. But there is one

movement above the educational horizon which would seem to show promise of genuine and creative leadership. (1932, pp. 2-3)

In 1979, this movement is the Experiential Education Movement.

However, an examination of the programs and philosophies of Experiential Education reveals certain inherent cultural obstructions to effective reform The first and most obvious problem is the one of cultural homogeneity. Nearly all experiential educators within the movement are white Anglo-Saxon Protestants and Agnostics (WASPAs). There seem to be several reasons for this. One is that most educators from ethnic or minority groups may presently be concerned more with basic needs, such as security, than with such idealistic needs as social reform. Secondly, they may be more concerned with providing educational opportunities for their youthful constituents who are often more limited to traditional schooling than are WASPA children. Thirdly, the Experiential Education Movement has demonstrated little or no sensitivity or affirmative action toward involving minority students or educators in their programs or professional activities.

Another problem is that of hidden cultural meanings within both traditional and experiential education. Since this problem is so complex, the discussion here is meant to be only illustrative, not comprehensive. Any educational transaction can be placed along a cultural continuum, from low context to high context. High-context transactions depend upon the immediate environment as well as information the receiver has. Low-context transactions depend almost totally upon the content of a particular lesson, in order to make up for what is missing in the context. Traditional education is, of course, very low context, while experiential education is typically high context. The traditional educator is most concerned with the curriculum (content), while the experiential educator is more interested in the environment (context). More importantly, high-context communication, in contrast to low context, is efficient and satisfying as long as the communicators are both tuned into the particular contexts involved. If one is not tuned in, the communication is incomplete. Thus, the experiential educator has great difficulty communicating to the traditional educator or bureaucrat what it is they do or want to do. The typical reaction is frustration on both sides.

Another important aspect of the problem of hidden cultural meaning has to do with how time and space are used as organizing frames for activities. Most Americans use what Hall calls "monochronic time" or "M-time" as opposed to "polychronic time" or "P-time." M-time emphasizes time schedules and spatial segmentation. P-time is characterized by several things happening at once with little regard for spatial segmentation. P-time emphasizes the completion of transactions rather than adherence to preset schedules. Traditional education is, of course, very monochronic, while experiential education is ideally polychronic. This makes integration of experiential learning into the school very difficult. It is one thing to end a history lecture at the ringing of the bell and take up where you left off the next day. It is quite another thing to be involved in a powerful learning experience only to have it cut off before completion at the end of 55 minutes. Similarly, most traditional schooling is designed to take place in very small, well-defined spaces—classrooms, laboratories, gyms, etc. Realistic experiences do not always lend themselves to such simplistic spatial segmentation.

Besides these cultural obstructions to easy integration of experience into traditional schooling, there is the more subtle problem of the experiential educator's own acculturation. He or she is a product of the dominant culture and probably operates most comfortably in low-context, monochronic situations with little or no conscious awareness of this fact. Thus, as Hall states, "Given our linear, step-by-step, compartmentalized way of thinking, fostered by the schools and public media, it is impossible for our leaders to consider events comprehensively or to weigh priorities according to a system of common good, all of which can be placed like an unwanted waif on culture's doorstep" (1977, p. 12). These problems of cultural homogeneity and hidden meaning have also limited the growth and influence of experiential education by contributing to the "reforming-by-doing heresy" and its three syndromes: 1) the lollypop syndrome, 2) the missionary syndrome, and 3) the culture-free syndrome.

In order to explain the lollypop syndrome, I have to tell you a simple story from which the lollypop metaphor was derived. This story was told me on several different occasions by various experiential educators. It goes something like this. Unlike most children, there are some who have never experienced a lollypop. If you give these children a lollypop once or several times, they know what lollypops taste like and may even grow fond of them. Then these children go back to their lollypopless world. They will be all the worse for this experience since they may now want lollypops and not have them. The storyteller then goes on to explain that the same is true in relation to providing experiential education for students from ethnic and minority backgrounds. Thus, the experiential educator can return to doing his own thing with his own kind. There is no need for understanding complex, cross-cultural differences or for adapting programming to meet minority students' needs.

The experiential educator who does not buy the lollypop metaphor may demonstrate the missionary syndrome. This syndrome is based on the fallacy that mind is not synonymous with culture, but rather is created in the image and likeness of God. Minds which appear to be different from our own must, therefore, be inferior or distorted. This belief frees us to practice what Hall describes as "an unconscious form of cultural imperialism which we impose on others" (1977, p. 206). This syndrome makes educational and cultural reform nearly impossible. We become like the missionaries who left their mother country to avoid religious persecution, only in turn to impose their own beliefs on others in a new land. Because we have left the cultural imperialism of traditional schooling, we feel all the more confident that God is on our side. Although we may have developed innovations in our approach, it is doubtful that we have changed all those practices that are synonymous with culture. We become stagnant with our own self-righteous belief that we are reforming education and society through doing "good works."

The culture-free syndrome is the most subtle and sophisticated of the three syndromes. This syndrome centers around the fallacy that education and culture are two separate entities. We may be aware that mind and culture are related. However, we believe that education that deals with information, thinking, and simple forms of behavior can be kept distinct from such things as morals and culture. This makes things much simpler. We can now reform education, and to some extent society, without having to understand the complexities of culture and mind. It becomes just a matter of inserting appropriate experiences or experiential processes into the classroom. The culture-free syndrome was demonstrated recently by an experiential educator who stated, "Because I dream of the day when my nine-year-old son Danny will not have to sit through an entire unit on plants, as he did last month without a single plant in the classroom. He needs us" (Leiweke, 1975, p. 5). One assumption here seems to be that all Danny was supposed to learn was information about plants. Our linear logic tells us that this is a safe assumption. However, from a more comprehensive point of view, we might perceive that Danny was learning more than just botany. He was also learning how to function in and maintain a low-context culture. Another assumption here seems to be that plants in the classroom would have been a significant improvement. How would such changes affect the classroom study of nuclear physics, evolution, or elephants? The point is that such changes as plants in the classroom could easily sublimate real educational reform.

The fallacy that is basic to "reforming-by-doing" heresy and that unites each of the three syndromes discussed above, is that experiential education and educational reform can be directly equated to each other. Hall stated that, "Those features of education that are synonymous with culture are very likely to change when the educators start innovating, when they try opened and closed classrooms, permissive and nonpermissive discipline, fast and slow tracks, reforming curriculum, and the like. This point is crucial, and its importance is frequently overlooked" (1977, p. 206). Thus, it seems obvious that cultural segregation, cultural imperialism, and the fallacy of culture-free education will not effect reform and bring us closer to fulfilling Levin's mandates for social integration and social responsibility. We must begin to see the interrelatedness of education and culture, and begin to understand such cultural features as action chains, situational frames, and extensions, and how one uses them. We must reappraise our philosophy and practice in realizing that "denying culture can be as destructive as denying evil. Man must come to terms with both" (Hall, 1977, p. 7). Otherwise, the Experiential Education Movement will not contribute to the evolution of the culture, and being useless, will be selected for cultural extinction.

CONCLUSION

In discussing Progressivism in American education, Cremin (1964) pointed out that "the transformation of the schools" has always been incomplete at best, and often produced inconsistent or contradictory organizational elements. Effective and politically acceptable education programs can be developed only if the historical alternatives are understood within a theoretical framework and subjected to systematic research. In order for the modern Experiential Education Movement to be more successful than Progressivism in surviving the onslaught of reactionary critics, to develop effective educational programs, and to influence traditional education, it must be more than merely reactive. In other words, it must: 1) reexamine its present operations and theories in light of the learning-by-doing and reforming-by-doing fallacies, 2) develop a more sound theoretical framework based upon an understanding of historical and cultural alternatives and philosophies, and 3) provide for the ongoing empirical investigation of subject matter, methodologies, processes, and outcomes. In other words, we must work toward reliable criteria for distinguishing between the babies and the bath water.

Section III

Psychological Foundations

11

Experiential Learning and Information Assimilation: Toward an Appropriate Mix

James S. Coleman

I MUST SAY THAT I ADDRESS YOU THIS MORNING WITH A GREAT DEAL OF DIFFIdence. For in any consideration of experiential learning, it is those who *do* it, and not those who theorize or talk about it, to whom one's admiration must flow. Those of us who attempt to analyze, to dissect, to generalize about experiential learning are as parasites, gaining our life blood from the vitality of those who do it. Perhaps the one justification for the kind of analysis I'm attempting here is the same as that which occurs in the discussions that typically follow specific experiences themselves: such analysis can sometimes aid understanding and give greater value to the experience. My aim here will be, then, to attempt to stimulate some insights about the functions of experiential learning in education, and how it can best accomplish these functions. For if experiential learning is to have a strong and secure place in the learning environments of the future, we need a better understanding of just what functions it fulfills.

Having begun with the diffidence, I will nevertheless go on to say that the formation of an Association for Experiential Education in A.D. 1977 is curious indeed. For at first it appears to be a throwback, an anachronism. One might expect the formation of an association for computer-augmented education in 1977, but hardly an association for experiential education. For experiential education has always been with us. The innovation is elsewhere. The innovation is in education through assimilating information, education through being taught via a symbolic medium, learning by being given the distilled experience of others, direct memory-to-memory transfer of information. Those innovations are extraordinary, for they have made it possible for persons in one generation to assimilate a vast store of accumulated knowledge, and for persons in one part of the world to know a great deal about what is going on in other distant parts.

It is, however, the very abundance of these innovations in learning through symbolic media that makes necessary now, as never before, a focus on experiential learning. For the very wealth of information with which we are bombarded, the very richness of the accumulated knowledge that is thrust at each neophyte to the society, increases an imbalance which has become extreme, and can have serious consequences for the making of a person. This is the imbalance between information and experience. So long as the techniques by which information is gained *without* experience were scanty and primitive, much of a person's information came through experience, and such an imbalance could not come about. The experience, and information gained through experience, constituted a strong contextual base for assimilating the information obtained by methods that bypassed experience. The latter was made meaningful by the former. For a child who has seen a grandparent grow old and die, the words "old age" and "death" have a rich fabric of meaning unknown to the child without such experience. And when the child grows up, and reads news stories about nursing homes and participates in political decisions about the elderly, the fabric of meaning provided by those experiences provides a context for action that is otherwise missing.

Suddenly, we have a poverty of experience in life. And children, who most need this nourishment, are most deprived of it. The household, which was once a productive unit, overrun with people, activity, strife, demands, love, and work, where the child could gain experience without undue danger, has now become antiseptic, a boardinghouse where family members come to sleep, and sometimes to eat, a place where their paths cross as they go back and forth to their specialized activities.

The child's specialized activity is the school which acts as a protective shield against the mine, the factory, the farm field, the streets, where the child was once exploited by adults and where he learned in the school of hard knocks.

We have intentionally cut off the child's nourishment by experience, for experience always contains difficulties and dangers that parents, looking back on their experiences, want to protect their children from. This deprivation of experience is accomplished largely by the school, aided by the increasingly sterile home which houses the child between school days.

It is at least partly in this context that one can see the various aspects of the youth movement that burst forth in the mid-sixties: that is, as a demand for experience—first in the pilgrimage from the cities of the North to the sit-ins and demonstrations and marches in small towns of the South, and then in the demonstrations and violence on college campuses. The subsequent accounts of these experiences by those who took part in them describe far less the goals of the actions and the larger aims of the movement than they do the texture of the experience itself, the feeling of oneness with one's fellows, the sense of collective euphoria, the emotions upon witnessing a demonstrator being beaten, how it felt to spend a night in jail, the excitement of confronting authorities to whom one once paid deference.

Can we say then that something is wrong with the school, that it is too rigid in its focus on basic academic skills of reading, mathematics, and the like? Certainly not without some serious question. David Copperfield went to a school far more rigid than those of today. But this narrow focus upon learning through symbolic media that took place in his classroom was preceded by and accompanied by an overwhelming torrent of experience—on the streets of London, in his friendship with Mrs. Peggity and with Mr. McCawber, his experiences with Uriah Heep, his struggle to get from London to Dover, and the odd assortment of households in which he found himself. For children of his time and experience, the narrow concentration of the school provided supplementary information that enriched, and could be assimilated by, the base of existing experience. The school of today is in the same role for some children, but for most children, two changes have occurred: there is a multitude of *other* media outside the school, from books to newspapers to television, to supply information which bypasses experience; and there is, for many of these children, only a weak experiential base on which to build.

To say, then, that the school is too rigid, that the school is blind to experiential learning, that the school must change, simply misses the point. For the point is that what goes on inside the school and what goes on outside, play important complementary roles. We cannot say what the school should be and do in abstract, without knowing what goes on in the life of the child outside the school. For the school has always existed to provide a set of *auxiliary* skills and *supplementary* knowledge, to augment the basic skills and knowledge the child gains through experience.

The task, then, if we are to be serious about designing appropriate environments for children and youth, is to carry out a detailed examination of just what functions experiential education is intended to perform. What do we want experience for?

To carry out such a detailed examination certainly goes beyond what I can do this morning. I can, however, suggest some points that are preliminary to such an examination.

It should be apparent to anyone who reads the program of this conference, or to anyone who talks to two or more people involved in experiential learning activities, that different people are looking for different things. There is not a *single* goal, but different goals. I'll try to identify a few of these.

I will begin with a function of experience that is most close to the traditional and central aims of the school, and most fully implements these aims. I will consider the two "basic" skills around which most achievement testing and most achievement concerns are focused: reading and mathematics skills. The property of these two skills is that they both involve manipulation of symbols, symbols used to stand for other things. The symbols of language are designed to stand for the whole range of human activity, while the numbers and operations of arithmetic are designed to stand for certain types of operations with quantities.

There are two ways of learning a language, as anyone who has tried to learn a second language in school knows. One is the way all children learn a first language: the "natural" way, by being in the linguistic environment, by trying and failing and finally succeeding in making oneself understood and understanding others. It is a painful, time-consuming, and emotion-producing experience, but an effective one. The second way is the typical method of school-learning of a second language: learning the rules of grammar, learning the meanings of words, not in terms of experience, but in terms of the words of the first language one knows. This process is less painful, less emotion-producing, and less effective. Why? Because the first method grounds each word, each phrase, each declarative statement, each question, in a rich bed of experience. One remembers a word, a phrase, because of the very emotions it provoked when it was not understood by another, or when it was understood and evoked a response from the other. One cannot forget it, because its usage is an intrinsic part of the fabric of experience that institutes one's life.

Or at a more mundane level, there is the common expression about new words in one's first language: "Use a word three times and it's yours." The statement is not, "Have a word defined three times . . . ," nor even "Hear a word three times . . . ," but "*Use* a word three times . . . ." Usage is action, and action generates response and becomes a part of one's experience, a part of one's personal history.

Language is a reflection of experience, of the daily activities one carries out. Murray Durst reminded me last night that Eskimos have one or, at most, a few words for plants, corresponding to the English "tundra." But they have many words for snow, for their activities revolve around snow. Or as Otto Klineberg, the social psychologist, once pointed out, Arabs have many words for our one word, "camel."

Learning to read is of course different from learning a language. But there are ways of learning to read that are experiential learning, and there are ways that are not. Word games, crossword puzzles, games involving letters, stems, and parts of words—all these embed the written language in one's own experience in a way that some traditional methods of teaching reading do not. As an aside, I believe that the major difference between "advantaged" children and "disadvantaged" children in learning to read is the extensive experience in playing with words and with language that the "advantaged" child has from an early age, long before school begins, and the "disadvantaged" child does not. One of the reasons for the success of Sesame Street, I believe, is that it recognizes this: *it plays* with letters and words, and the child who watches it has, not a true experience, but a vicarious one, with those letters and words.

With numbers and the operations of arithmetic, it is the same. One of the things I have done, of which I am most proud, is to devise a game for playing with numbers, a game in the order of chess, but with numbers as pieces, and one which a six-year-old can play. I've played it a lot myself, and I've watched children play it, and as a result of playing it myself, I have a different view toward odd and even numbers than I ever had before. I think of a three in a special way, and a four in a different way. Or there is an arithmetic game devised by Layman Allen, which has been used in some schools, and with which some research has been done by psychologists at Johns Hopkins. They find an extraordinary effectiveness of the game, and of team play with the game, in raising scores on basic ability tests which involve numerical operations. The rich experience of acting in a setting that involves responses of others, that evolves emotions, that generates mutual aid and support, appears again, as in the other instances, to create a structure of meaning and association that provides a base for further learning.

This then, is one goal, one function, of experiential learning: the creation of a solid experience base, in one's own life, for the very symbolic media that are subsequently used to transmit information bypassing experience. It needs hardly be said that only if these experiential foundations are strong—whether they are built in the home or by an extensive use of school time in play with language, games with printed words, or in still another way—only then can language and reading serve as the vehicle by which information that bypasses experience can be assimilated.

But this has very little to do with Outward Bound, very little to do with alternative schools as we know them, very little to do with urban explorations, not much more to do with Lance Lee's Apprenticeshop, although perhaps something more to do with Eliot Wigginton's cultural journalism, and certainly more to do with Mary Kohler's children tutoring children.

I have begun with this one function that is most close to traditional goals of schools to show the fundamental importance of experiential learning even there. But obviously many kinds of experiential learning are intended for different goals, designed to do different things to a young person. What are these?

Consider first a program like Outward Bound. (Here, as I discuss these programs about which others have so much more experience and understanding than I, my diffidence increases, because I will surely be in error. But perhaps these errors will themselves stimulate the necessary corrections by those who can do so.)

It seems clear that one of the central functions of an experience like Outward Bound has to do with a person's relation to *himself or herself*. A person after Outward Bound is a different person—perhaps more confident, perhaps with more humility, and sometimes with both. An activity like Outward Bound has to do with the *intense* experiences from which many young persons are now protected in the sterile environments we have created for them. It is intense experiences, critical events, that give us of ourselves, that put us closer to ourselves, make us less fearful of our faults, more able to address them in a straightforward way, without fear or favor. This the school was never designed to do, and in a society that provided a rich set of intense experiences, like David Copperfield's early life in London did for him, the school was properly unconcerned with such things. But it has come to be time to recognize that for many young persons, there is a vacuum outside the school, devoid of such intense experiences that give one self-knowledge. And it has come to be time

or else they are intense experiences that hamper knowledge.

to design learning environments, whether in school or in another setting, that contain those experiences that move one along the path to self-knowledge.

This discovery of oneself is, of course, not all that happens in an Outward Bound program, or in other intense experiences engaged in with other persons. But I will content myself here with this one function, that I believe is of central importance, and turn to other kinds of experiential learning.

One kind of experiential activity that is widely engaged in, and takes on a number of different forms, is community studies—whether as urban exploration, as cultural journalism in a rural environment, or in another form. A few of these experiential activities produce a product, such as the Foxfire books, that is of clear value to others beyond the participants, although many do not. The importance for the participants themselves of such an externally valued product is great, for it provides an external validation of the value of one's activities. But I want to address another function, shared by all these community studies. This is the function of providing a direct experience with persons, events, settings, neighborhoods, life histories that would be totally outside the realm of experience of these young persons. Again, the need for such experience lies in the "sanitizing" of a young person's environment which has resulted in part from the conscious attempts by parents to protect their children from bad experiences, and in part from the general movement of society toward institutionalization of the young in schools. In the age of the small, heterogeneous community, where children from all social classes rubbed elbows and walked down the same streets, such experience was part of life itself. For some young persons of today, whose parents move a lot, or those whose parents suffer sudden reverses that throw them into a different environment, or those who on their own seek out such experiences, the vacuum is partially filled. (The demand by protected youth for such experience is not a weak one, and leads at times, as I have suggested, to movements like the civil rights marches in the South in the '60s.) When I was in college, I felt such a need, and went to Chicago one summer to live and work in skid row, West Madison Street. That experience was an important one for me—but not one my parents or school would have designed or even approved of. And such individual search for experience is far more prevalent among the protected young of today than it was among the less protected young when I was growing up. This very increase in search by youth themselves, this very demand, indicates the vacuum, and the need for some way of filling it, or at least some way of facilitating the young person filling it, short of self-destructive activity. It is worth pointing out, in this connection, that not only has the search for diverse experience by the young increased in recent years; also, self-destructive actions such as suicide have sharply increased as well, as Edward Wynne has cogently pointed out in his book, *Growing Up Suburban*.

It is not clear just how this vacuum of experience beyond one's orbit can be filled; it is clear, however, that the experience of community studies of various sorts, such as those practiced by some of the persons at this conference, constitute a stride in this direction.

In outlining these three functions of the various activities that are called experiential learning, I have not attempted to be comprehensive. I have tried to show that some forms of experiential learning are essential to acquisition of the basic skills that schools attempt to teach, that other forms provide the kind of intense experience that begins to bring self-knowledge, and that still others give a young person some direct experience with other lives and settings far beyond his own. I have not discussed the function, shared by many forms of experiential learning, of broadening and deepening the kinds of relations one has with others—both those his own age and others of different ages. And there are other functions as well that I have ignored.

But the reason I have attempted to separate these functions, to identify them as distinct kinds of things that a young person learns, is this: I believe that if we are to provide not merely schools for the young, but environments which aid them toward a satisfying adulthood, it is important to identify the separate components. For then we can work toward providing the mix of various kinds of experiential learning and classroom learning that will address these components. I view this analytic activity toward which I have made a small attempt this morning, as parasitic upon the creative experiential activities which are represented by persons in this room. But as with some parasitic relations, the analytic activity may itself aid the central activity on which it depends, by helping to establish a firmer place in the young person's environment for these activities.

12

Programming the Transfer of Learning in Adventure Education

Michael A. Gass

WHEN EVALUATING THE EFFECTIVENESS OF ANY LEARNING EXPERIENCE, EDUCAtors have often focused on how learning will serve the student in the future. This concern has become particularly true in the field of adventure education. Whether it has been a young adolescent developing more appropriate social behaviors, a freshman student obtaining a more beneficial educational experience at a university, or another program where adventure is used as a valid educational medium, the credibility of programs using a challenging environment has been based upon the positive effects they have on their students' or clients' futures.

This effect that a particular experience has on future learning experiences is called the transfer of learning or the transfer of training. In our attempts to simplify the essential, most adventure educators call this phenomenon "transfer." Transfer is valuable to many programs in the sense that their success, continuation, and/or livelihood is based on the effect their program has on the future of their students or clients. For example, when describing the value of adventure programming as a milieu used to prevent delinquency, the U.S. Department of Justice states that despite having some plausible theoretical or correlational basis, wilderness programs without follow-up (transfer) into clients' home communities "should be rejected on the basis of their repeated failure to demonstrate effectiveness in reducing delinquency after having been tried and evaluated."

While transfer is critical to the field of adventure education, probably no other concept is so often misunderstood. Much of the confusion plaguing the transfer of learning has resulted from two main factors. First is the concern that the initial learning usually takes place in an environment (e.g., mountains) quite different from the environment where the student's future learning will occur. Second is the lack of knowledge concerning the variety of methods available to promote transfer. Neither of these problems is limited to adventure education, but there are certain theories, models, and techniques that pertain directly to the field and can assist in eliminating much of the confusion surrounding the topic and enable individuals to strengthen the transfer of their program's goals.

THEORIES CONCERNING TRANSFER

Concerning the application to adventure education, three central learning theories pertaining to transfer exist that explain how the linking of elements from one learning environment to another occurs (see Figure 1). Bruner describes the first two, specific and non-specific transfer, in attempting to show how current learning serves the learner in the future.

> There are two ways in which learning serves the future. One is through its specific applicability to tasks that are highly similar to those we originally learned to perform. Psychologists refer to this specific phenomenon as specific transfer of training; perhaps it should be called the extension of habits or associations. Its utility appears to be limited in the main to what we speak of as skills. A second way in which earlier learning renders later performance more efficient is through what is conveniently called non-specific transfer, or, more accurately, the transfer of principles and attitudes. In essence, it consists of learning, initially, not a skill but a general idea which can then be used as a basis of recognizing subsequent problems as special cases of the idea originally mastered. (1960, p. 17)

The following example from a student's notebook serves to illustrate the use of specific transfer in adventure education:

> Today during the class we learned how to rappel. Initially I was quite frightened, but I ended up catching on to the proper technique and enjoying it quite a bit! One thing that helped me in learning how to rappel was the belaying we did yesterday. With belaying, our left hand is the "feel" hand while the right hand is the "brake" hand. With rappelling, it is the same; our left hand is the "feel" hand and our right hand is used to "brake" our rappel and control our descent.

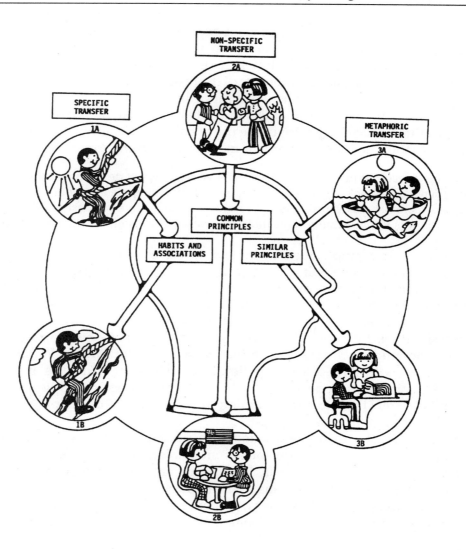

Figure 1. Three Theories of Transfer in Adventure Education. The above diagram illustrates how learning in adventure education is linked to future learning experiences. In the first theory, specific transfer, the learner takes the habits and associations acquired during a previous experience (Diagram 1A - the hand skills of belaying) and applies them to a new experience to assist him in developing a new skill (Diagram 1B - the hand skills of rappelling). In the second theory, non-specific transfer, the learner generalizes the common underlying principles received from a previous experience (Diagram 2A - developing trust from an initiative game) and employs them in a new learning situation (Diagram 2B - developing trust with peers at school). The third theory, metaphoric transfer, shows the learner transferring the similar underlying principles from canoeing (Diagram 3A) to working with other individuals in a business corporation (Diagram 3B).

In this example, the student's previous experiences of specific hand skills learned while belaying positively affected her ability to learn the necessary and correct hand skills of rappelling. Figure 1 illustrates these events occurring—the initial stage of learning how to belay, the development of the proper and safe habits while belaying, and finally, the use of these skills while rappelling.

The next example from another student's notebook highlights what Bruner describes as non-specific transfer, or the use of common underlying principles in one learning situation to assist the student in a future learning experience:

> . . . (as a result of the wilderness course) I've seen myself developing more trust in my friends at school. The no-discount policy[1] helps me quite a bit, but I think what helped the most was learning how I receive as well as give support to others. I felt that this was the most important thing I learned (while on the wilderness course).

In this second example, the student had the common underlying principles that she learned about developing trust (i.e., receiving and giving support from/to others) from the wilderness course and generalized those principles and attitudes to a new learning situation (i.e., school). This ability to generalize by the learner is crucial for non-specific transfer to occur. Figure 1 shows the connection of two learning situations by common underlying principles or non-specific transfer. In this example, the student, through an initiative such as the Willow Wand Exercise[2] supplemented with a no-discount policy, learns valuable principles and attitudes about developing trust in peer relationships. She takes these principles, generalizes them, and transfers them to a new learning situation, such as developing meaningful relationships at school based on trust.

The third transfer theory associated with adventure learning also requires the student to generalize certain principles from one learning situation to another. But the principles being transferred in this theory are not common or the same in structure, but are similar, analogous, or metaphorical.

The following passage illustrates a student making the connection between the similar underlying principles of canoeing and his group working together:

---

[1]The no-discount policy is a technique from Gestalt psychology used by some adventure programs. It asks that all participants (voluntarily) enter into a "contract" with the other group members, agreeing not to discount their feelings as well as the feelings of the other members in the group. Members of the group are asked to confront any discounting behavior and this will often lead to a group discussion.

[2]The Willow Wand Exercise is an initiative used to introduce the concept of trust to a group in an adventure experience. It often serves as a lead-up activity to a Trust Circle or Trust Fall.

There has been a certain jerkiness in the group. It's like the progress of a canoe. When the people on each side paddle in unison, with each person pulling his weight, the canoe goes forward smoothly. If certain people slack, or if there is a lack of co-ordination, progress becomes jerky. The canoe veers (from) side to side. Time and energy are wasted. (Godfrey, 1980, p. 229)

In this particular situation, the student is not using the principles of efficient canoeing for future aquatic learning experiences. He is instead transferring the concepts or principles of canoeing as metaphors for another learning experience that is similar, yet not the same.

This third type of transfer, metaphoric transfer, is also illustrated in Figure 1. Here the student takes the similar underlying principles mentioned in the example above, generalizes them, and applies them to a future learning experience with similar elements. The future learning experience represented in Figure 1 for metaphoric transfer is a group situation where the necessity of everyone working together efficiently is vital (in this case, working for a business corporation).

Probably the individual who has done the most investigation into the use of metaphoric transfer with adventure learning is Stephen Bacon. In the following passage, he further explains how using experiences that are metaphoric provides a vehicle for the transfer of learning:

The key factor in determining whether experiences are metaphoric is the degree of isomorphism between the metaphoric situation and the real-life situation. Isomorphic means having the same structure. When all the major elements in one experience are represented by corresponding elements in another experience, and when the overall structures of the two experiences are highly similar, then the two experiences are metaphors for each other. This does not imply that the corresponding elements are literally identical; rather, they must be symbolically identical. (Bacon, 1983, p. 4)

A Program Model for Transfer

When reviewing the three transfer-of-learning theories discussed previously, it can be seen that the key to increasing transfer often lies either in the selection or design of appropriate learning activities or in the teaching methodology. One of the major faults of adventure education has been the lack of planning for the transfer in these areas. Transfer must be planned, much in the same manner as an educational objective, or a properly planned learning skill.

Figure 2 portrays the learning process of an adventure program interested in procuring positive transfer for a student.

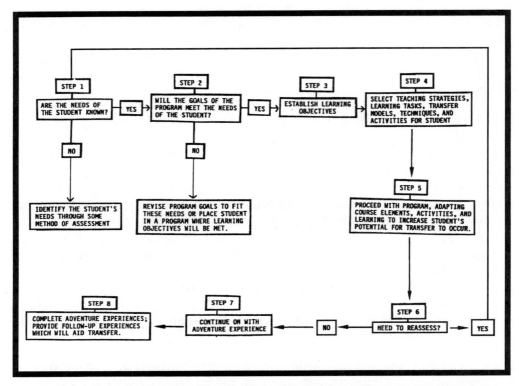

Figure 2. Learning Process Model with an Emphasis on the Transfer of Learning

As seen in the model, once the needs of the student and the goals of the program are properly identified and matched, the learning skills, activities, teaching strategies, and transfer models and techniques are planned. A strong emphasis is placed here on providing the connection between the present and future learning environments to increase the amount of transfer which will occur. Note that throughout the program, if the needs of the student change, the model directs the instructor to assess these changes and adapt new learning activities and transfer elements to the student's new behavior. At the completion of the adventure experience, follow-up activities are also used to enhance positive transfer.

FACTORS/TECHNIQUES THAT ENHANCE THE TRANSFER OF LEARNING THROUGH ADVENTURE ACTIVITIES

Given the information in Figure 2 for programming transfer, what are some of the factors or techniques adventure educators can use to assist them in increasing the transfer of their students' learning? (Shown by Step 4 in Figure 2.) Many researchers have presented exhaustive lists of elements which can lead to positive transfer, but some of these are unalterable (e.g., genetic factors concerning intelligence), while others have little application to the "non-traditional" atmosphere where most adventure learning takes place.

As stated in the program model, it is necessary for the adventure educator to select not only the proper transfer of learning theories, but also the techniques and activities involved with the increase of transfer applicable to their program. Ten techniques adaptable to the transfer of learning occurring with adventure activities are presented here as examples. However, many other techniques exist and should be selected for their ability to transfer the goals of the specific program and what theory of transfer one is using. (A bibliography is included with this article and sources that address this topic to a greater degree are noted by ***.)

1.   *Design conditions for transfer before the course/program/learning activities actually begin.* Several steps can be done prior to a learning experience that can aid in the transfer of learning from an adventure activity. Examples of these steps include:

  a)   Identify, develop, or establish a commitment to change in the student.

  b)   Have a student set goals for the experience.

  c)   Write and set tight learning objectives for the student in the program.

  d)   Place the plans and goals made by the student in writing to create a stronger commitment for transferring the learning.

2.   *Create elements in the student's learning environment similar to those elements likely to be found in future learning environments.* Learning environments with strong applicability to future experiences have greater potential for a more positive transfer of learning. The following example of a disaffected youth in a wilderness program shows how elements of the program were created to assist him in transferring a behavior, in this case, a greater self-concept, into a subsequent learning environment.

> Throughout the course, Kurt was presented with a variety of challenging tasks. He overcame strong personal fears and doubts and succeeded at many of the tasks that required a great deal of initiative. The staff noticed that after he had developed a stronger belief in himself, he was especially zealous on tasks that required a great deal of trust and responsibility (e.g., belaying). Throughout the course, the staff continued to place Kurt in progressively more difficult situations that demanded a strong, realistic belief in himself as well as other members in the group. Many of the discussions at night were about the relationships between the elements they faced

as individuals and as a group in the wilderness and those they would find when they returned to their communities.

Other learning behaviors are often presented in a similar manner to increase their relevance and application to future learning environments for students. Certain programs have found that by approaching problem-solving and decision-making skills in a general manner, their students succeed in creating elements valuable for future use (Gass, 1985, p. 5).

3.   *Provide students with the opportunities to practice the transfer of learning while still in the program.* There was probably no better time for Kurt to practice the skill to be transferred (i.e., an increased self-concept) than during the course. The variety of contexts in which to practice transfer, the number of times Kurt could practice transferring the skill, and the strong support group that developed during this outdoor adventure program all helped Kurt to focus on the generalizing and conceptualizing skills he needed to strengthen the bond that his transfer needed for different learning situations.

4.   *Have the consequences of learning be natural—not artificial.* One can think of the consequences of learning as either being natural or artificial. "Natural consequences are those that follow or would follow a given act *unless* some human or human system intervenes. Artificial consequences follow or would follow a given act, if, and only if, some human or human system *anticipates* or responds to the initial act and causes the artificial consequence or modifies a natural consequence" (Darnell, 1983, p. 4).

Superficially viewing the field of outdoor education, one would think that all learning that takes place in the outdoors would have natural consequences. Unfortunately, far too often this is not the case. Whether it has been from an "overly" caring instructor or an overpowering one, too often the student becomes dependent on, is shielded by, or anticipates the instructor as a reinforcer of learning. Once the course is over and the reinforcer (i.e., the instructor) is removed from the student, learning behavior is severely hampered or terminated. In this way, with artificial consequences, the result of learning transfer is extremely limited.

However, if outdoor programs could make their students' learning more experiential, natural consequences would be more likely to occur. This would result in the stronger formation of learning behaviors likely to be available in future learning situations, hence, the increase in the amount of transfer. Some experiential learning techniques that could foster the development of natural consequences include relying upon the student's intrinsic rather than some external source of motivation; placing more responsibility for learning on the student (see 8); and not shielding the learner from the consequences of their learning, whether they be positive or negative.

5.   *Provide the means for students to internalize their own learning.* The ability for a student to internalize his/her own learning creates the concepts and generalizations central to the transfer process. Adventure educators have differed to a great extent on how this is best accomplished. Many believe that by getting their students to verbalize, or place their own learning into words, the internalization of the concepts to be transferred is increased through self-awareness and reflective thinking (Kalisch, 1979, p. 62). Others feel that conscious efforts such as verbalizing are secondary to other methods of internalization, such as the subconscious development of metaphors for transfer (Bacon, 1983, p. 2).

All methods which ask students to internalize learning behaviors from adventure programs strongly support the use of *reflection* to aid internalization. It seems that any process an instructor can use that enables the student to identify personal learning would lead to a greater applicability of learning for future situations.

An example of a process often used by adventure education programs that increases transfer through reflection is the "solo" experience. Certain programs feel that such an experience reinforces the learning that occurs in the adventure program and helps students/clients to identify how they are going to use the experience in the future (Gass, 1985, p. 6).

6.   *Include past successful alumni in the adventure program.* Sometimes the incorporation of successful alumni in courses or programs assists in the transfer of learning for students/clients. The following example demonstrates how one program uses this technique:

> By listening to how these alumni used the skills they had learned from the program in their lives, students began to envision how they might use elements of the program in future situations. While not always advisable or possible for some programs, many individuals felt this "vicarious" method of planning future transfer strategies aided in the transfer of learning for students. (Gass, 1985, p. 5)

7.   *Include significant others in the learning process.* The inclusion of other individuals closely associated with the student's/client's learning process has often been found to heighten the transfer of learning (Gass, 1985, p. 2). Some of the persons used to fill this vital role have been peers, parents, counselors, social workers, and/or teachers. The following example illustrates how one program includes significant others in the learning process to provide positive transfer for a student:

> Before Cristina participated on the adventure portion of the family therapy program, several objectives were established for her family, counselor and school teacher—as well as herself. Cristina and her family met with the staff, other participants and their families prior to the adventure experience in order to familiarize both the students and the parents of the reasons for their participation on the course. Another reason for this meeting was to inform them of possible changes in the student that could occur. The program continued to stay in close contact with Cristina's family in order for them to adjust to and support possible changes in Cristina's personality and behavior.
>
> Cristina also created several "goal contracts" in a pre-trip meeting with the assistance of a staff member in the areas of personal, family, school and peer development. The contracts were discussed on the course and monitored monthly, with proper adaptations, for the next six months. Cristina's teacher also participated on several portions of the wilderness course, enabling him to support, reinforce and try and use the observable changes during the adventure program with Cristina in the classroom.

8.   *When possible, place more responsibility for learning in the program with the students/clients.* Many programs, especially those invested in teaching adventure education experientially, believe that placing more responsibility with the students, in the program not only increases their motivation to learn but also their incentive to apply their learning in future experiences. Examples of this range from some programs involving students in the planning of food menus to other programs that have students organize and conduct an entire adventure experience on their own. Certain programs have implemented strong service components that have a definite focus on future experiences outside of the adventure experience (MacArthur, 1982, pp. 37-38) and enhance the self-responsibility within the student which could lead to a greater transfer of learning.

No matter what techniques programs use to involve their students/clients in the planning and operations of an adventure learning experience, their involvement should depend on their ability to accept responsibility for learning and their willingness and desire to do so. A person who willingly accepts responsibility for learning will transfer information much more readily than an individual who approaches such a task with a sense of indifference or resentment.

9. *Develop focused processing techniques that facilitate the transfer of learning.* In many adventure education programs, processing/debriefing/facilitating is often used to enrich a student's learning experience. The length and intensity of these debriefings can differ from a quick and informal sharing of the day's occurrences to a lengthy and formalized discussion of a particular incident with a specific set of rules and guidelines. Despite this vast difference in the application of techniques, there are certain general characteristics that, if included in the processing of an experience, will assist in the transfer of learning. Some of these characteristics are:

    a) Present processing sessions based on the student's/client's ability to contribute personally meaningful responses.

    b) Focus on linking the experiences from the present and future learning environments together during the processing session.

    c) When possible, debrief throughout the learning experience and not just at the end of it, allowing the students to continually focus on the future applicability of present learning.

10. *Provide follow-up experiences which aid in the application of transfer.* Once a student begins transferring learning, the presence of follow-up activities (e.g., continued communications, feedback on learning decisions, processes, and choices) serves to heighten transfer abilities. Again, one reason for this might be the positive effects of reflection between learning situations. Reflection gives the student the opportunity to see and evaluate the results of past learning behaviors, garner learner motivation, and plan future learning strategies and directions.

CONCLUSION

As educators who use the outdoors and challenging situations to help students to learn more efficiently, we all aspire to teach our students something useable—and therein lies the value of our program. But, unless we assist our students in providing their own linkages, bridges, and connections to their learning, the utility of much of the education we care and work so hard to bring about is put away in the equipment room along with the ropes and backpacks. As we strive to become better educators and proponents of the value of adventure education, let us look upon transfer as a device to excite students by showing them the future value of their current learning experiences. This motivation, provided by the opportunity to use their learning again, can furnish one of the strongest incentives for our students' continued learning and the field's success.

13

Internalizing Learning: Beyond Experiential Education

Larry Prochazka

LEARNING WITHOUT DOING MAY NOT BE LEARNING AT ALL. YET, EXPERIENTIALLY designed learning activities do not ensure learning occurs either. What is learning? How does learning take place? How does an individual learn to internalize information, integrate it into his or her personal life, and assimilate it to determine what fits and what does not? These interesting issues pose a challenge to those in education and learning-related fields.

WHAT IS LEARNING?

Surprisingly few teachers have a clear working notion of learning. Most know what teaching is. It is generally the delivery of information, the one-way process of telling learners about information. In this traditional view of teaching, learning is measured by test scores and written assignments. But does this system really measure learning or simply assess an individual's test-taking and memorization ability?

Educators favoring experiential methods of teaching would have a broader view of learning than teachers ascribing to more traditional views of education. To them, learning somehow involves "doing." Learning activities are centered around getting students involved in experiencing situations illustrating relevant information. By absorption in the activity, students are learning the material. But, is there something beyond experiencing a process? Is a deeper level of learning possible?

AN EXPERIENTIAL DILEMMA

The question of going beyond experiential learning was raised for me several years ago. I was teaching a class in communication skills. This was one of my first major tests at designing and applying the experiential process. I believed learners would really learn communication skills if they "did" communication skills. Off to the library I charged! After I reviewed a variety of textbooks and journals, I collected numerous experiential exercises which support the basic "content" I had identified as essential to enhancing communication. The class learned about active listening and then performed active-listening exercises. They learned about barriers to effective communications and then experienced situations where these barriers were present. After three weeks of this exciting adventure, the class took a "thinking"-oriented test. Questions were designed around real-life situations. Learners were to analyze the situation, identify one communication skill recently learned, apply it to the situation to enhance the described communication pattern, and imply how the outcome could be modified by using the skill they selected. They did marvelously well on the test. However, over the next few days, learners showed little or no change in their communication pattern! What happened? If experiential activities enhance learning, why were communication patterns left unchanged once the obstacle (the test) was hurdled. What does it take to go beyond the experiential exercise; for an individual to draw the information inside themselves and somehow integrate it into his or her life? This was my next challenge, to go beyond experiential learning to the process of internalizing learning.

INTERNALIZING LEARNING

A large part of education centers on information and facts. Information may enter the brain and be recorded for a short period of time before evaporating into the universe. For example, how much do you remember from your high school civics class? Probably very little. Data is stored by memorization until its usefulness is terminated. Then, poof! It's gone. This is what I will call the first level of "learning." At this level, memorization is the primary process involved and the focus is on content.

The next level involves a little more than memorization but is still primarily intellectual or cognitive activity. At this level, the learner may have an attitude of interest, an attitude of "I think I know what this means." They are primarily working with data and may or may not be involved in experiential activities. There is perhaps a feeling of familiarity with information, but the ability to apply it is lacking. Mastery of "content" is again the focus of the learning process.

The third learning level is experiential. Here the data has been organized in such a way to allow learners the opportunity to experience it. In the communication example, learners listened to and discussed information concerning communication skills. Then they participated in activities structured to accommodate experience and use the skill. The experiential level is deeper and more personal than the first two levels of learning. It involves not only a focus on "content" but on the "process" of learning as well. However, it may not connect with the individual in such a way that they take new skills away from the experience. A glowing example of this is the statement, "Do as I say, not as I do." It genuinely indicates there is information stored somewhere in the gray matter that has not been registered in the organism, the person. Consequently, intellectual awareness of facts is not an indicator that learning occurred "internally."

Now we arrive at the level of "internalized" learning. At this level of learning, learners ask themselves such questions as, "What can I create with this new information? How can I make it a part of my life and use it? What can I choose to do differently now?" It is at this level that the individual learner becomes intimately involved in the "process" of bringing the data into reality. Content is still involved, but the process of bringing the content into a personal reality is of greater significance.

"Internalization" can be thought of as an inside-out process. The learner takes the information inside themselves to a deep, personal, feeling level, a level deeper than that of cognitive recall. Here the learner has responsibility for creating something with the new information, a responsibility to take the information and integrate it into their life, and act upon it. The learner acts on it by looking outside themselves into the real world around him or her, and identifying a goal for applying this new learning. The learner might ask, "How do I get there from here? What is it going to take? How can I use this information to get there?" It is in this process of "getting there" that learning becomes internalized and a part of the individual. As an example, if I had encouraged learners involved in the communication session to keep a diary, and the purpose of the diary would have been to "live" one communication skill and record the experience, learning would have taken place at a deeper level. Had the learners taken the information on active listening, designed a plan to live it and use it for one day, and recorded their feelings about the experience, learning would have occurred at a deeper level. They would have been personally responsible for literally trying on new information and seeing how it fit into their life. Learning at this level has significant impact on the individual! They are touched and involved at a deep personal level.

So what happens inside? Information is no longer sterile. Learners are invited to become intimately involved with growing, changing, and learning. They become their own teachers and guides. They are, in essence, learning how to learn. The "process" used during internalization can be transferred to any aspect of their life, any class, any new information they wish to learn.

THE ROLE OF THE TEACHER

I remember reading once that learners learn more from "who" you are as a teacher or person than from "what" you say. Therefore, the first responsibility of the teacher is to role-model what he wants learners to learn. Strict "black or white" thinking will not model creativity, open-mindedness, or curiosity. "Right answer thinking" models conformity. "I have all the answers" thinking models "you are only a student" behavior. Whatever the subject, the teacher must be aware of his behavior and what it is saying. To believe in internalized learning is to demonstrate it. Some Native Americans had a concept called the "give away." During certain rites of passage and celebration, a family would give away everything they owned. The only reason to own anything was to give it away. You cannot give away anything you do not have! The same is true for the teacher. A teacher can only share what they have developed as a person.

A role important for teachers to play is "asker" instead of "teller," of questioner instead of possessor of all the answers. People learn more from talking than listening, yet perhaps 80% or more of the time spent by learners is spent listening. The mind disengages while the hand furiously takes notes. This is a nice exercise to improve motor skills but not for developing higher order "thinking." An example of this was shared with me by a man who was trying to help children understand why it is wrong to tell a lie. The child was told it was wrong to lie and did not understand. He could not connect the action of lying with the command not to lie. But when the child was asked if he told Johnny the truth, he replied, "No!" When asked how he felt inside, he felt nervous and uncomfortable. He felt like he was unfair and dishonest with Johnny. Now he understands why it is improper to lie. The feelings of anxiety and dishonesty were the real teacher, the teacher became a questioner directing the child to discover his own answers. Teachers must be proficient at asking questions that guide learners to new awareness rather than meeting them head-on and "telling" them all they need to know.

Positive manipulation can be a powerful tool. The martial arts teach learners how to use the momentum of an opponent for their defense. Go with the flow and use the momentum, never go against it head-on. Teachers can use the same principle to create more stimulating learning environments. For example, there is a strong survival mode among learners. They will do nearly anything that is required of them for points or credit. This momentum can be used to involve students in stimulating learning activities. I have begun requiring cognitive maps at the beginning of class when new topics are to be presented. Learners have to read the material to complete the map. The map is designed to be done on one page and includes the major concept covered in the reading, sub-topics related to the major concept, and supportive information for each sub-topic. The mapping process integrates the hemispheres of the brain and facilitates greater understanding. Never before have

I had an entire class read what they were asked to read. Now, not only have they read what they were asked to read, but they are prepared to discuss key concepts from the material. Rather than resort to lecturing on the topic, we can now share in discussion. I bring my questions, learners bring theirs, and off we go into a world of curiosity, discovery, discussion, and personal involvement. Higher levels of thinking and communicating are involved as well as intimate, internal views of the learners. Significant internal levels of learning are achieved when emphasis on memorization of information is reduced and greater emphasis is placed on understanding and discussing. Learners are encouraged to use the information, to try it on and "live" it! Furthermore, interpersonal skills are being developed, which is seldom a priority in traditional classrooms.

CONCLUSION

There are as many different definitions of learning as there are teachers. Most have not explicitly defined it, so they subconsciously stab at accomplishing it. It may be looked at in terms of the level of learning a teacher hopes learners can reach. Memorization is a rather shallow and short-term intellectual skill. Deeper levels of learning are possible which encourage the personal commitment to grow and improve as a person. It is only by experiencing this growth that teachers can share it with others. Perhaps a guiding question would be of use to teachers interested in the internalization process: "What do you want learners to know or be able to know when they finish your class?" Do you want them to be masters of information and the memorization process, or do you want them to grow as people?

14

Piaget—A Psychological Rationale for Experiential Education

Mitchell Sakofs

BROADLY DEFINED, EXPERIENTIAL EDUCATION IS A PHILOSOPHICAL ORIENTATION toward teaching and learning that values and encourages linkages between concrete educative activities and abstract lessons to maximize learning. Through these experiences, it is hoped and believed that learners attain a qualitatively superior level of knowing than can be achieved through abstract lessons alone: this goal is accomplished by confronting the learner with elements of reality which augment their understanding of the materials under investigation, because reality demands that the learners more fully engage themselves in the learning process (i.e., experience the learning process) in ways that abstract teaching tools, such as books, cannot accomplish. It important to note that experiential education refers to a philosophical orientation and method of presentation rather than a content area. In fact, experiential programming can be applied to all academic fields.

Although much has been written on the philosophical aspects of experiential education, when front-line educators seek to implement experiential programs within their schools, they often find that the administration is resistant to promoting such projects. This resistance is often rooted in the failure of the experiential education movement to overcome its association with the now-tainted progressive education movement led by John Dewey, and legitimize itself with currently accepted psychological learning theories.

To aid teachers to generate more support for the development and implementation of experiential programs within their school-based curricula, the following brief discussion of some recent research in the field of psychology is offered.

STAGE THEORY

How children learn is a direct function of how they think and grow intellectually. To an understanding of these processes, the Swiss psychologist Jean Piaget devoted much of his life and developed a theory of learning with which all involved in education should be familiar. Through his more than 30 years of research related to learning, Piaget identified various stages of cognitive development in children. The stages of development which Piaget identified were:

1.   Sensory motor (ages 0-2)

2.   Preoperational (ages 2-7)

3.   Concrete operational (ages 7-11) and

4.   Formal operational (ages 11-14).

Although the age parameters have been identified for each stage, Piaget acknowledged that they may vary from culture to culture and/or as a function of experience.

Although children operating within Piaget's sensory motor, preoperational, and concrete operational stages are dramatically different, a fundamental thread which ties them together is that in each of these stages, the child is dependent upon concrete interactions with the world in order to promote intellectual growth and true learning. Thus, it is not until the last stage, the stage of formal operations, that children are capable of cognitively manipulating abstract concepts in an effective manner.

Since, according to Piaget, most people attain the level of formal operations between the ages of 11 and 14 years, it seemed reasonable for schools to develop lessons which required such capabilities, for conducting lessons on an abstract plane is more efficient in terms of time, money, and energy, than structuring experiential lessons. Evidence to the acceptance of this position can be found most everywhere in our nation's schools. For example, at a very early stage in a child's schooling, the vast majority of lessons are taught through abstract means, i.e., various media such as books, movies, filmstrips, and the like. Since these tools of education are essentially one dimensional, and thus devoid of stimulation beyond the abstract manipulations of the mind, they require the student to possess the cognitive capabilities to effectively process this information; that is, they must have the cognitive constructs which Piaget defined as Formal Operations.

Unfortunately, however, although the lion's share of information presented in our nation's schools is done so at the abstract level, recent research has shown that the vast majority of students attending these schools operate below this level of functioning. More specifically, work by Epstein and Maynard indicate that nearly

85% of all middle school and 69% of all high school students in the United States are functioning within Piaget's stage of concrete operations. Thus, the research indicates that our educational system is emphasizing methods of knowledge acquisition which require the students to use cognitive skills which they do not possess. Furthermore, the research also suggests that the byproduct of such demands on the students is that they "turn off" to school and learning, and become frustrated and dissatisfied with education.

EXPERIENTIAL EDUCATION

In contrast with traditional school programs, which emphasize learning formats requiring formal operations, i.e., the use of books and other media to facilitate learning, experiential programs, by their very nature, focus on concrete experiences to facilitate learning. As a result of this focus on the concrete, experiential programs are more in tune with the cognitive capabilities of the majority of students in attendance in our nation's schools on up through high school.

These facts are critical for all educators to understand if they are to teach effectively, minimize the frustrations experienced by their students, and promote true learning. In addition, such information provides teachers with a psychological foundation upon which to base a proposal to develop and implement experiential programs into their curricula.

15

The Spiritual Core of Experiential Education

F. Earle Fox

WE TAKE FOR GRANTED THINGS THAT ARE GOING WELL. IT IS WHEN GEARS grind and axles squeak that we focus our attention upon them. Experiential education is no exception. One might say that the very experience of education has become problematic, so that special courses, even whole curricula, are being devised to focus on what in ages past must have been taken quite for granted. Indeed, I would say that even more profoundly, the very ability to have experience at all and to make rational sense of it is becoming increasingly marginal for many people.

To have experiences is a given part of life. But to be able to make coherent sense of these experiences, to experience a coherence between oneself, the world, and the source of life does not seem to be a reliable part of the modern package. For several decades, our art forms have been signaling danger. Dramas such as *Endgame* or *Waiting for Godot* by Samuel Beckett, or on the music scene, the appearance of punk rock (or rock at all), are clear signs of a culture in deep trouble. We are at once the most individualized and independent and freewheeling culture in history, and at the same time, it seems, the least comfortable with our individuality.

And so, as might be expected, we are appointing committees and writing books and inventing curricula to deal with this strange malady. It is not merely that educational *systems* are out of whack or not doing their job with the 4 Rs (add "religion"), though that is certainly true. It is rather that for an increasing number of young people coming through our educational systems, experience of *any* sort is not educational. One might say that it never was. Youth has always been recalcitrant. But the fact is that the educational systems of the past were on the whole able to discipline and train and shape experiences of their students so that a common culture and common values were possible and shared to a degree we find impossible. It would be facile to assert that that was simply because of the autocratic and authoritarian nature of old educational processes, which were able to stamp out mechanically produced specimens made to fit the preconditions ordained by the inherited culture. Clearly, any culture has a certain amount of oppression and conformism. But looking back in particular at our own Western history, the ages of greatest artistic achievement have come out of a substratum of basic values and a world view shared more or less freely and openly by the populace. A great deal of conformity has been genuine and powerful and immensely productive.

But something has happened to us in the 20th century that will require more than another committee, another curriculum, another Ph.D. thesis to set aright. For despite our intense pride on being modern, the most educated and most informed people at any time in human history, we have a strange panicky sense that it is all coming apart at the seams.

And so we focus on what seems to be the area of deficiency, namely experience. We put together "experiential education," as though education could have ever been anything else. The irony is that we do indeed seem to have invented a nonexperiential sort of education, not by design so much as due to the fact that our whole culture has drifted strongly in a schizoid direction. We have retreated over a period of several centuries from feelings and relationships into individualization and abstract thinking. We are living to an extraordinary degree in our heads rather than our emotions. When experience gets too chaotic, we try to control it by force or manipulation, or we retreat from dealing with it into thinking about it. Rock music, self-discovery courses and workshops, gurus and meditation, and experiential education programs are all various ways of trying to deal with that fact through a "new kind" of experience.

I would like to offer some suggestions about the nature of experiential education and its relation to the spiritual life. My connections with experiential education in the institutional sense of the word are not yet extensive, having only recently become a chaplain at an institution that engages in experiential education. But listening to talk about programs, aims, failures, and successes, and engaging in some of it myself, I am very impressed with the correlation between what is happening at (in my case) Becket Academy and what I gradually and somewhat painfully came to experience my job to be during ten years of parish ministry.

I am also impressed with the fact that, without exception, all of the successful reform movements in the Church have been non-academic (not anti-academic) but rather experiential in nature—from the early desert fathers, through the Benedictines, the Franciscans, the Jesuits, the Quakers, Methodists, right down to the present day "charismatic renewal." All this was not to the exclusion of serious academic work. But it was the experience that came first which provided the fodder for the rational mind to work upon. The Judeo-Christian tradition is profoundly experiential, not to the exclusion of reason, but as the precondition of it. That is, the material upon which reason exerts itself is precisely those experiences of ours which need ordering and coherence.

Let us add one further element to this picture. Faith, for the Judeo-Christian community, is not "belief in something no matter how stupid." It is not blind belief. It is not dogmatism or belief despite all the evidence to the contrary. Nowhere in the Bible from Genesis to Revelation is faith presented in such a manner.

On the contrary, nothing in the Biblical story makes sense unless faith is taken to mean "a teachable spirit." Not a gullible spirit, but a spirit that is *open* to experience and to reasoning about that experience. Faith means openness to reality.

THE PROBLEM AT THE CENTER

So how can experiential education make a difference to the massive needs of our time? Sometimes answers are staring us in the face, laying about the landscape, as it were, though we are blocked by our prejudices from seeing them.

The Judeo-Christian tradition is not available to most moderns. It is too close to us and we are in rebellion against it. And yet it is infinitely far away, out of reach, because it seems so contrary to the modern secular mind-set concerning the nature of the world. (Viewers of Carl Sagan's brilliant TV series, "Cosmos," would have experienced this in a powerful way.) But even more important, the Judeo-Christian tradition is simply not known. It is a forgotten wisdom. We moderns, despite our pretense to knowledge, are abysmally ignorant of the spiritual and cultural foundation stones long ago laid, and upon which still rests the great weight of contemporary Western culture insofar as it still holds together at all. We do not know our own roots.

It can be said that the Western spiritual tradition rooted in the Bible has wrestled with two elemental themes—one the problem, the other the solution.

The problem is the child side of ourselves, our contingent, dependent, and somewhat broken nature. We experience our dependency as an unwelcome aspect. We yearn for self-sufficient adulthood, the immortality of the gods. Our vulnerability to the slings and arrows of outrageous fortune is more than we can tolerate, and so we tend to build a closed, defensive circle about ourselves.

One might imagine oneself as three concentric rings, the outer ring representing the body, the middle ring the soul, and the center the spirit.

The soul is composed of our psychological aspects of mind, will, and emotions or feelings. But the soul, not being self-sufficient, cannot be its own center. The spiritual center is inhabited by whatever we choose to put at the center of our lives, that which we depend on for our integrity, identity, and sense of well-being. The spiritual center is the throne room. Whatever occupies that throne will shape and form how we think, choose, and feel, our three psychological aspects.

Our problem lies in finding something to put at the center that is itself secure and strong enough to rely on, and at the same time friendly to and supportive of our well-being. There are not many such possible friendly, supportive, and secure centers in the world. And so we tend to experience our center as insecure, as in need of protection from outside threat, and also as itself ambiguous toward our well-being. The very thing we rely on is not all that trustworthy. We experience the center of our life not as something we can freely share in relationship. There is a part of me that I keep hidden even in my most intimate relations.

The most common way we try to deal with our dependency and vulnerability is to deny it. If we cannot be at the center of ourselves, and if we cannot put something there that is "on our side" in the game of life, we try to create the illusion of invincibility and invulnerability and self-sufficiency by putting something there that we can at least control or manipulate. International power struggles are nothing more than this process writ large. The child within continues to dream of the mythical adulthood, super-hero self-sufficiency, failing which we resort to defensive walling strategies. If you can't beat them, hide from them.

The troubled youth who are the clientele for so much experiential education are no exception. A large part of their maladaptation to life can be explained as faulty dealing with the experiences of being not self-sufficient.

Dealing with our hurts and fears and insecurities through defensive mechanism, power plays, and manipulation works for a while, or we would not be tempted into these ploys. But most of our defenses have the disadvantage of increasingly cutting us off from reality. That part of us that is being defended, the hurting, frightened child within, by that very defense is frequently cut off from the learning experience that could possibly heal and strengthen and mature. Our castles become our prisons, and finally our tombs. The resentment I harbor against being accused prevents me from discovering and working creatively with the truth of the matter, whatever it may be.

THE RISK OF FAITH

The second elemental theme after the problem, naturally, is the solution, namely faith. Now suppose that faith, as taught and lived in the Bible, is not the nonsense that so many Christians and non-Christians alike have tended to treat it as. If that is the case, then this kind of faith becomes the sine qua non of experiential education. Openness to experience and to reasoning about it is clearly a prerequisite to any truly educational process. Faith, then, is not the closed attitude that bars one from true knowledge (scientific or otherwise); it is the precondition of living in reality and of having any serious knowledge at all.

The problem is that reality is not always experienced as a friendly place in which to remain open and vulnerable to learning experience. The school of hard knocks can be just that. And so we can develop habitual responses to life that, in fact, preclude the fullness of the learning experience. We defend ourselves against any vital and sensitive contact with the very reality we supposedly want to know and understand. We keep reality at a distance, we build walls, we paint and therefore distort our public image so as (we believe) to preserve our acceptability and our viability in a hostile and alien land. A defensive move is always a move of un-faith.

The life of faith, then, is the choice to risk the hurt and rejection and disappointment, at whatever cost, to experience and know the truth, whatever it may be, and to put that at the center. We are saved and made whole, as Jesus indicated, by our faith. That works, of course, only if, in fact, ultimate reality turns out to be gracious and friendly despite the hard knocks. If it is not, to expose oneself in such a manner is to be annihilated. That is the risk of faith. That is the leap. But the leap is into the light, not the dark. It is the leap out of my defenses into intimate touch with the truth, the relationship, the person I want to know.

Faith, then, also necessarily means learning with the whole of me. I become, as it were, my own antenna by which I receive messages from reality "out there." If a part of me is cut off by defensive walls, that part of me will at best perceive and relate only in a distorted and partial way.

The Judeo-Christian view wants to say that God, the ultimate reality, has invested Himself in this process as well. The very meaning of Biblical revelation presupposes that investment. The impact of the Christian view of the incarnation of the Son of God is that God makes Himself supremely available and vulnerable—able to be touched, experienced in the deepest kind of mutual sharing, which is holy communion. God does not "defend" Himself—which is the only possible basis upon which we can shed our defenses. To paraphrase D. Frank Lake, an English psychiatrist: The only foundation possible for mental health is the gracious nature of God, . . . for that alone transforms our brokenness from that which at all costs must be avoided to that which at all costs must be accepted.

Thus, not only because God is my creator, but because God is not hiding behind walls of defense, He alone is able to be the center which can speak to and touch and heal and mature the whole of me.

EXPERIENTIAL EDUCATION AND RENEWAL

What then of experiential education? A great deal, though not all, of experiential education is remedial or therapeutic in intent. Many wilderness or "outward bound"-type programs are intended to benefit people who have learning or behavioral or emotional difficulties. They are programs which subject students to a great deal of stress along with the experience of personal loyalty which will see them through to success. One is unavoidably confronted with one's dependencies—hopefully in a way that one can begin to accept oneself and to share that real self in the student-teacher and peer relationships.

What I am saying would certainly apply to such programs, but I believe it would also apply to *any* type of education that aims beyond the surface into the depths of learning and maturation.

If experiential education is to fulfill the goal it has taken for itself—a profound reordering of the educational process which can assist the healing and maturing of the whole person—then it must provide the context within which one can experience the *need* and *desirability* and *possibility* of facing, rather than avoiding, the brokenness within. That is, experiential education must provide the context within which one can reexperience one's dependency and come to terms with it as a good thing, rather than a thing to be denied and defended against. I must experience the ability and the right to be myself and to share that self without denying, hiding, or making excuses for my dependency and lack of self-sufficiency. Until I can find some place (ultimately some person) in which to invest my dependency, my spiritual center, which I can experience as safe and nourishing and supportive, it will never be possible for me to let the defenses down which prevent the growth and maturing I hopefully seek.

Needless to say, this is never a one-shot process. It is a way of life, a pilgrimage. But as experiential education provides the context of unfailing acceptance with uncompromising discipline—what might be called the mothering and fathering sides of life—the hurting child within begins to experience the encouragement to return to full relationship with life. And that means learning and growth. The child begins to experience the freedom to choose the open road of faith rather than the closed circle of defensiveness. That is the context of Tough Love: I will never let you down, I will never let you off. It provides the space where I can fall apart and still be accepted. I can experience success *with* my dependency. And that is exactly what has to happen at the very deepest level of our existence.

That kind of loyalty, combined with toughness that characterizes so many experiential education programs, is I believe, one of the foundation stones of success. Both the religious and educational institutions of our culture, church and school, have by and large abandoned any such concept of education. The signs that we may be recovering some of that Tough Love are encouraging.

I would suggest that we find the archetypal model for that kind of love right in the mainstream of the Judeo-Christian spiritual tradition in the person of Yahweh who called Abraham, Moses, and the prophets into a living experience of His presence, and even more concretely in Jesus' relation with His disciples. Tough Love leads us through the holocaust of facing our brokenness, death to self, and into the fullness of personal resurrection on the other side.

Our experiential education programs must introduce students not only to the abstract and theoretical reality of their spiritual center and dependency, but to its concrete reality, real people, real feelings, real decisions. That is the function of Tough Love—absolute love and acceptance married to absolute truth and discipline. Wilderness programs have the virtue of having discipline and hardship built in, along with isolation from so many extraneous distractions. But the same crucible of maturation and healing can be created in any community where the leadership is committed to that kind of openness and sharing and self-discipline, and where the leadership will share together a common center of that quality.

That is part of the meaning of being made in the image of God. We become like what we worship. We have not a choice about that. That choice lies in whether sitting on the throne will be something which itself is dependent and defensive and impersonal and, therefore, inadequate, or whether it will be the person who is, in fact, the source of my being, gracious, personal, and totally secure, who Himself lives by faith and therefore can afford to allow me to live by faith.

16

Teaching for Adult Effectiveness

Douglas Heath

I INVOLVE MY STUDENTS IN EXPERIENTIAL LEARNING IN EVERY COURSE THAT I teach: fieldwork in nursery schools, alternative schools, old age homes; cooperative modes of teaching and learning; action research on significant social issues; experiential involvement in the classroom with theoretical concepts; student participation in the teaching process itself. What have been the effects? Upon students? Apprehension about what will happen next; avoidance of my courses by the overly intellectualized as well as the academically weak student; arousal of emotional ambivalences in a few toward me; increased "aliveness," motivation, and curiosity in many but not all students; great spurts by some in fulfilling academic potentials not previously sensed; a feeling of emotional intellectual exhaustion by the end of the course; an understanding of the power of learning by praxis.

Upon colleagues? Distrust and wariness of what Heath is up to now; dismissal by some of such experiences as frivolous, time-consuming, and not "basic"; desire by others to block such courses out of the curriculum, or at least consciousness, but inability to do so completely because enhanced student interest and growth, even mastery of basic content, are known; mystification: the feeling that "Heath can do it, he can get away with it; I can't."

Upon me? More emotional hassles with students as they struggle with formerly suppressed ambivalences toward teachers; greater demands of me for energy, time, and, most of all, sensitivity; increased awareness of the maturing effects in students when they assume responsibility for their own growth; fleeting desires to return to the infinitely easier, authoritative, didactic role in which it is clear that a teacher is a teacher and a student a student; strengthening my belief that if what we learn is to endure, it must affect the character of a student—his passions, values, concept of himself, personal relationships as well as his mind; recognition that such experientially based courses will not survive in the long run if they are not also academically demanding.

I have learned other important lessons. The academician needs the insights of the experiential educator about how to create more powerful, transforming, educational settings. The experiential educator needs the academician's knowledge of intellectual skill development as well as his rigorous demands that can assist a person to use his problem-solving talents in a diverse range of settings, including the academic. Perhaps the two most important lessons that I have learned are that both need to be much clearer about their priority goals and that both need a persuasive, coherent, theoretical understanding of what healthy growth means and what the educational conditions are that promote such growth.

Regardless of our different perspectives, all of us face an extraordinary challenge: how to prepare today's young people to be effective adults for the uncertain, perilous world of the 21st century. It is the rare faculty that has self-consciously sought to identify the qualities that will be required to live in those unpredictable years. Proctor Academy, one of our country's leaders in experiential education, identified the three most important qualities to be compassion, self-confidence, and adaptability. It is an even rarer faculty that deliberately seeks to educate for such qualities and then has the courage to assess whether it is successful or not. I think of the faculty of Alverno College that has dared to do just that. Common to such efforts and to the thinking of those at the forefront of education in many parts of the country, is the growing conviction that a priority goal should be to empower a youth to become a more adaptable, self-educating, autonomous learner. Unfortunately, such a goal remains more a slogan than a specific program for action. Although some academicians and experiential educators claim they achieve such a goal, I remain skeptical that most of us are as successful as we may believe.

How can we go beyond slogans and rhetoric to discover what are the actual qualities that make an adaptable adult? Presumably, such a person is one who has learned to fulfill various adult roles reasonably well. I suggest that we examine in depth just what such adults are like in our society. What qualities predict their effectiveness? Can we begin to draw out of such studies and our own collective experience as academicians and experiential educators insights about the principles that further such adaptability that can be implemented in our work with young people?

EFFECTIVE ADULTS: WHAT ARE THEY LIKE?

I have just completed a study of men in their early thirties who typically fulfill our American stereotypes of successful, effective persons. They are highly educated and productive contributors to society. They are physicians, lawyers, scholars, engineers, business managers, poets, accountants, writers. Most are married; they have at least two children. They are financially comfortable. More importantly, they are living very full lives; they rate themselves to be between moderately and very happy persons. I have more than a hundred different measures of what they were like as adolescents and more than 400 measures of their competence as adults. Extensive material about the men has also been secured from their wives, closest friends, and colleagues.

What have I learned about effective adults, persons who have learned how to cope with the demands of diverse adult roles? First, as an indicator of their adaptability and ability to continue to grow, the men had continued to become more mature and psychologically healthy since their graduation from college. Growth does not have to stop once one has reached 17 or 21 or even 30. Second, the men who were well adapted vocationally were also much better husbands and more competent fathers. This singularly important finding tells us that there is a set of qualities that apparently mediates effective adaptation in a wide variety of different adult roles. If we knew what such qualities were, we might be able to nurture their development more directly in school. Third, the men's happiness was not related to their academic grades when in school, their income when adults, or to most other measures of material achievement in our society. Instead, the happier person was the one who had continued to grow and become more mature since he had graduated from college. It was the person who had not changed much, whose attitudes and values had not been challenged, whose relationships remained in the same old ruts, who was less happy. Also, the happier person was more mature, particularly interpersonally. Fourth, measures of the men's adolescent scholastic aptitude and college achievement just did not predict much later in life. What the aptitude tests did predict, however, was unsettling. The men who had higher quantitative aptitude scores when in high school, for example, were, 15 years later, less well integrated persons, had less accurate views of themselves, were rated by their colleagues to be more distant and aloof in their relationships, were less mature. As other studies of gifted young people have shown, high intellectual aptitude and achievement in and of themselves do not guarantee subsequent happiness or effectiveness. More likely than not, too accentuated cultivation of just such potential strengths during adolescence to the exclusion of other kinds of growth may imbalance the personality in the long run and rob a youth of the socio-emotional growth that contributes, apparently, to adult effectiveness. When I studied the qualities that contributed to the men's vocational effectiveness, I found an impressively large variety of traits that most of our academic measures just do not assess: ability to anticipate, imaginativeness, empathy, tolerance, interpersonal sensitivity, persistence, ability to schedule and plan, and so on.

But the most important finding from the study was the clear demonstration that it was the psychological maturity of a youth and, later on, of an adult, that was the most powerful predictor of his subsequent effectiveness. Of the hundreds of qualities that I measured, it was his psychological maturity that contributed most to his vocational adaptation, happiness, marital sexual compatibility, and his competence as a father. My findings confirm the results of other studies of highly competent, creative, and productive persons. A highly effective adult must be an adaptable person, capable of creating some optimal satisfying relation between the demands of his own needs *and* the demands of the various roles that he plays. The more mature the person, the more likely he will have the qualities necessary to continue maturing and adapting. Maturity is its own condition, in other words, for continued healthy growth.

THE ADAPTABLE, SELF-EDUCATING PERSON

I have mentioned that the emerging consensus among educators is that we must more self-consciously educate a youth to be a more adaptable, self-educating person. Four qualities are essential to be such a person: each is enhanced by a person's maturity. We know that a self-educating person has a self-concept that he is growing and can continue to learn and grow. Since what we think we can do can affect our motivation to risk trying, our ideas about ourselves can become self-fulfilling prophecies. A solo experience in the Hurricane Island Outward Bound program can reassure a youth that he can survive on his own and powerfully alter his estimate of his competence to achieve in other ways as well. A student who believes that he cannot learn algebra frequently will not try to learn. Self-confidence in one's capacity to learn and adapt, therefore, becomes an indispensable quality that enables a youth to risk extending himself. Much evidence now indicates that the more, in contrast to the less, mature person has greater confidence in himself.

A second attribute of a self-educating person is that he has a desire to learn, a curiosity about his world that spurs him to explore and to learn. Yet we teach in our traditional schools, even our best ones, in ways that tend to snuff out that curiosity. A study of one of New England's best public schools has shown that only 43% of the fourth-graders and 13% of the 12th-graders evidenced any genuine intellectual curiosity or eagerness to learn in the classroom. The relation between healthy growth and curiosity becomes very clear even by third grade. Studies show that it is the healthy, mature third-grader who's the more curious student.

A third attribute of a self-educating, healthy, growing person is openness to learning from his peers and teachers. A defensive youth, whether manifested in hypersensitivity to criticism or in passive negativism, is not educable. Again, we know that the more self-disclosing, interpersonally open person is a more mature, well-integrated person.

The final attribute of a self-educating person is that he has learned that knowledge and those skills that can assist him to educate himself. He has learned how to get control, so to speak, of the processes of his own growth. For example, a self-educating person knows how to establish realistic goals, organize his available resources to achieve such goals, and evaluate whether he has achieved his expectations. Yet we seldom teach for such skills in our traditional classrooms; and I am not certain that we teach for such goals as systematically as we could in our experientially based programs. Too frequently, we reverse the logic of the educational process. We select a course or program to offer primarily in terms of its content or appeal and ignore the more functional adaptive skills a youth needs. The traditionalist plans to "cover" the content of the course, even if it means racing through to the final chapter, progressively leaving more and more students behind, ignoring the effects of such pacing on their self-concepts, and intensifying student passivity as lectures dominate more of the classroom. The experiential educator becomes enamored by a novel experience, a simulation, or some other "turn on" experience which, sometimes, becomes *the* goal in and of itself. Mastery of self-educating skills is too often only a fortuitous consequence of either approach. Why? Primarily because we have not clearly identified the priority skills we want our students to learn and *then* planned, organized, and educated in ways that deliberately furthered such skill development. I have identified for each course that I teach the principal skills it lends itself to teaching most effectively. Then I focus very systematically on the process of teaching to create the learning conditions in and outside of the classroom to further such skill development. For example, a self-educating skill that students will need in the years ahead is induction, one that experiential education ideally is capable of nurturing. One of the potentially more powerful ways to learn such a skill is to become immersed in the complexities of a real-life problem, like trying to understand and work with nursery school children. Simply working with such children several hours a week does not necessarily lead to improved inductive skill. I have learned that much more active, teacher-reflective involvement is required, however, if the skill is to be "fixed." I deliberately confront students by having them discuss together questions like, "What did you learn? What generalizations or principles were evident in the behavior of the children? What is the relation of what you have been observing to the material you have been reading?" But I find that this constant prodding in many diverse ways is not very productive. My hunch is that a more effective way to teach induction is to be with the student while working with the children and illustrating the process by modeling it at the actual time such inductions are appropriate.

What prevents the contributions of the traditional and the experiential teacher from synergistically assisting the other is the lack of a common philosophy of education, or, as I have already suggested, the lack of a shared conception of healthy growth and of the outcomes of the educational process. If both can accept that a primary goal of education should be to enhance a youth's adaptability and capacity to educate himself, then I think we can create a more rational theoretical underpinning for our joint efforts. The demonstration that psychological maturity not only contributes to a student's ability to educate himself but is also the best predictor of how effectively a person adapts to a variety of adult roles provides the opening to the creation of such a common developmental understanding of our goals.

THE PROCESS OF HEALTHY GROWTH

What do we know about the process of maturing, and what are we learning about the educational principles that we can implement to further the maturational process? Any growing person, regardless of his or her sex, ethnic, social class, or cultural background, grows as an organismic system, not just in the head. All persons grow in certain common ways as I have described elsewhere. If we stretch that growing person out of shape by emphasizing too exclusive development in only one sector of his personality, like the academic, we eventually create stresses in his personality that may interfere with continued growth in the overemphasized sector. I think this is one reason why many very talented persons have turned away from formal academic work to immerse themselves in experiential learning. But too exclusive involvement primarily in the affective modes of learning may also satiate a person, particularly those who sense that they also need the rigorous demands of a disciplined intellectual education if they are to fulfill their nascent talents. We are systems that need to integrate both the affective and the cognitive if we are to release the full adaptive potential of each. We hobble a gifted youth if his talent is not yoked to passion; we drown the passionate youth if his emotionality is not disciplined by intellectual skills.

So how does a person grow healthily? He matures in five interdependent ways: he becomes more able to *symbolize* his experience, more capable of taking a *multiplicity of perspectives*, more *integrated*, *stable*, and *autonomous* in his concept of himself, his motives and values, interpersonal relationships, and intellectual skills. I describe each dimension and then illustrate one of several educational principles we are now discovering that contribute to healthy development on that dimension.

Toward Increased Symbolization

When confronted with a difficulty, one of the most powerful, potentially adaptive responses that we can make is to represent the elements of the problem symbolically. We notice its details, different meanings, and seek to articulate the essence of the problem that is troubling us. Such awareness enhances our power to retrospectively learn from our past experience to similar problems, imagine the possible outcomes, and anticipate their consequences. Our increasing ability to label and articulate more carefully leads to increased reflectiveness, self-insight, and understanding of our motives and those of others.

How can we more systematically prod healthy growth on this dimension? At this point, I must distinguish between an educational principle and a technique. I am dismayed by teachers who ask me how I teach, believing that my specific teaching methods will necessarily help them. We do not empower others by offering them our techniques; we empower them by helping them internalize principles of broad generality that provide guidelines to them for creating their own techniques. For example, one educational principle of which all of us are aware but few self-consciously implement in furthering healthy growth is to *contrast, confront, and challenge*. This principle is close to the heart of the success of many experiential programs. While good teachers use such a principle to provoke thought about course content, few of us use it to disrupt a student's typically passive and dependent mode of learning to help him learn how to become more aware about his own idiosyncratic way of growing. One *technique* that I use the first day in a class of 35 students is to immediately break the class into small groups of five each. I present each student with a list of goals, one of which is to begin to learn the skills of cooperatively helping each other learn. I then list a detailed series of steps by which they can begin to learn such a skill. After 45 minutes, the class is brought back together for the first time as a class. I challenge them to tell me why I began the course that way. Some are usually perceptive enough to know that I am disrupting their typically passive mode of learning as well as their assumption that I am there to "teach," if not "entertain" them. They know that I am forcing them to confront the fact that most are not very autonomous learners. Such disruption of years of passive learning creates frustration, in most, anger in some, and great anxiety in all. But they are involved, many for the first time, in the first step leading to reflection about their own learning processes. Now such a technique may not be useful or appropriate for other teachers or students; the underlying educational principle, however, remains valid. If you wish to provoke a person to become more aware, learn how to reflect, think freshly, then disrupt his usual patterns by forcing him into situations that create contrasts, confrontations, and challenges.

Toward Increased Allocentricism

The second interdependent dimension that describes the adaptive process or maturing is technically known as allocentricism, the growth away from self-centeredness and narcissism to self-objectification, and the capacity emphatically to take other divergent points of view toward issues and toward one's self. Such a growth underlies the capacity, when confronted by a difficulty, to analyze the problem from different viewpoints, to think more logically, to communicate more clearly. It enables a person to predict more accurately what others think of him; he becomes a more tolerant accepting person as he more deeply understands how others feel about the issue that may be the source of the difficulty.

Of the several educational principles I am learning that further such growth, there is one that again, many experiential educators intuitively know: namely, *provide opportunities for students to assume alternative roles*. One of the powerful contributions to healthy growth that drama, for example, offers a youth is that it sanctions playing a role, dramatizing a range of feelings or interactions, that he otherwise might not be able to allow himself to experience. As one learns on the stage how to be affectionate or cry, even be dependent or assertive, one learns that such feelings are not necessarily evil, that one can control their expression, and that there are ways they can be integrated into one's experience. Within an academic classroom, I use the technique of encouraging students to assume the role of teacher, first in dyads, then in small groups, and then in the larger class itself. Scarcely a novel technique—one that may fail with some students, with some faculty. But the underlying principle is one we could more deliberately use in more imaginative ways to further allocentric maturing.

Toward Increased Integration

A maturing person gets himself together, his thinking becomes more differentiated and relational; he is more natural and spontaneous in that he can be himself in his relations with others; his values and actions become more consistent; and he becomes more able to work cooperatively in mutually respectful ways with others. When adapting to a difficulty, a mature person not only is more aware of its various aspects and seeks out alternative solutions, but also tries to formulate some line of solution that brings together, synthesizes, integrates the various elements of the problem.

Much of the maturing power of experiential education is due to its integrative potential. Unfortunately, in most traditional classrooms a student passively sits and inefficiently absorbs information that is not integrated with his experience. As wise educators have always known, a critical educational principle that furthers healthy growth is to *provide reflection upon experiential types of learning.* Experience forces action; when we must act, our intellects, concepts of ourselves, values, feelings, and interpersonal skills are involved. What we learn becomes integrated with many different action systems and so becomes stabilized more readily. But as the early Greeks knew well, experiencing is not enough; there must be self-conscious reflection about it if it is to have integrative, maturing effects. For example, for years I taught students about psychoanalytic theory by talking about repression, resistance, and free association. But even those who recited back the correct definitions of such terms never seemed to really understand what such concepts referred to. So now as an optional experience, pairs of students, each alternatively assuming the role of patient and the other that of a psychoanalyst, actually free associate for twenty minutes and, in the process, discover that at times their minds become blank, that nothing comes to mind, and that such blocking is what Freud meant by repression. They then reflect about what they discovered that interfered with their associating. Finally, the larger group comes together to reflect similarly about the variety of ways that "resistance" to associating had occurred. A student now knows by way of his body, not just by way of his head, what the abstract concept of repression means.

Toward Increased Stability

A maturing person becomes more stable, though not rigid. Recall that too-extended development on one dimension, relative to growth on the others, can distort a person's integrity and result in maladaptation. A person's intellectual skills become more stable, though still resilient; when confronted with personally meaningful or anxiety-arousing challenges, a more mature person is able to maintain his judgment, his analytic efficiency, his ability to recall the relevant facts of a problem. And if his judgment does become colored by his biases or he temporarily blocks on an exam, he can recover more quickly than the immature person can. As Erikson has told us, a mature person also has a more stable sense of who he is; his values are more stable and he has the capacity to create more enduring relationships with others.

Of the educational principles necessary for mature stabilization to occur, the requirement for *constant externalization of what we think we know and its correction by action* is very familiar to experiential educators. By virtue of their emphasis on action, experiential educators are several steps ahead of traditional educators in creating more powerful conditions for stabilizing what is learned. The value of constant practice in action is scarcely a revolutionary insight; it has been known since parents first began raising their children. But most of us do not *self-consciously* capitalize on the value of the principle. For example, few high schools and colleges require students to write frequently; if they do, they seldom ask students to re-write and then re-write again until they have made perfect what they have written. They are externalizing their students' thoughts and language skills but not correcting them by remedial action! No wonder students do not know how to write. One technique that I use to "fix" what the students learn is to use students as guides, resource persons, and teachers whenever possible. For when they explain, demonstrate, assist, they externalize what they think they know. They soon discover in the process how well they communicate to and teach others. Too often, even in experiential programs, the teacher or leader fails to "let go" his teaching or leadership at the appropriate time, when students verge on the edge of being able to accept the responsibility of becoming teachers or leaders themselves.

Toward Increased Autonomy

A maturing person becomes a more independent person: he can take what he has learned in one situation and apply it to increasingly different problems. He can stand up for what he believes and resist the lures of peer pressure or the imperious demands of his own impulses. He gradually comes into command of his own talents and energies.

Experiential educators have told us much about the educational principles that further mature autonomy that could be applied to the traditional classroom. Again, the principles are obvious, but again, most of us fail to implement them systematically in the way that we teach in the classroom. Few of us deeply understand, for example, the psychology of learning that is involved in consistently encouraging *a youth to assume responsibility for his own growth early in life*. Experiential programs that test a youth's capacity to assume responsibility for himself and for others can profoundly alter a youth's concept of himself. An Outward Bound program taught my son that he could alter his own life if he but chose to do so. He has a self-confidence now that has freed him from the fear that he cannot make it on his own wherever he goes. But I know few academic programs that similarly challenge their students to become autonomous, self-educating persons and that progressively wean them of the need for directed guidance and structure within the classroom. I try to teach so that students assume more and more responsibility for their own education as they progress through each course. I share with them as much of the educational process as they are willing responsibly to assume. And as I have already mentioned, I alert them the first time they come to class that I expect that they will become in time more self-educating, autonomous persons.

Maturing and Experiential Education

We experiential educators, sometimes because of anti-academic attitudes, sometimes because of our failure to bring a disciplined reflectiveness to what we are doing, sometimes due to a reluctance to analyze and examine what the enduring effects of our programs are upon the participants, sometimes because of our lack of understanding about the adaptive potentials of our own programs, have not communicated as persuasively as we could what we have been learning about how to create more effective learning conditions in the traditional classroom. Given future budgets, the retrogressive implications of the "back to basics" movement, the increasingly conservative educational temper in the country, the experiential education movement as a movement risks suicide if it does not articulate more convincingly what it is learning about how to help a youth become more mature and so, more adaptable. The model of maturing I have proposed may provide the theoretical map by which to identify the potential strengths of experiential education; it may also provide the bridge to synthesize the strengths of both the traditional and the experiential approach to education. It maps the core qualities that facilitate effectiveness in a wide range of adult roles. Society expects schools to prepare youngsters to be more effective adults. Experiential education offers numerous educational principles which, if consistently implemented within the classroom and school experience, could greatly enhance the power of education to contribute to a youth's future adaptability.

A future task for all of us is to identify those educational principles that contribute to growth in the symbolization, allocentricism, integration, stability, and autonomy of a youth's self-concept, values, interpersonal relationships, and intellectual skills. Contrasting, confronting, and challenging, providing opportunities for assuming different roles, encouraging *reflection* upon experiential learning, requiring constant externalization and correction by action, and consistently encouraging the assumption of responsibility for one's own growth are only the more obvious principles that experiential educators know well. I believe that there are numerous others, known to educators for centuries, but ones that need to be reaffirmed and given new meaning through the vehicle of experiential education to the wider educational community. If we accept that challenge, our contribution to the broader educational scene will justify society's continued support of our innovative searching efforts to create more humane and transforming learning experiences for our students.

Section IV

Social Foundations

White Awareness and Our Responsibility to End Racism

Karen Fox

Note: This article discusses white awareness and the responsibility to end racism in the context of a series of short articles in the *Horizon*, the newsletter of the Association for Experiential Education (AEE). Although it explicitly responds to previous *Horizon* articles, it goes beyond them to bring a conceptual and critical analysis to these issues from a white perspective. In order to facilitate the reading of this article, the series of articles in the *Horizon* by Arthur Wellington Conquest III, Roberto Velez, and Dan Pervorse and Jim Garrett are reprinted immediately following this article. The Conquest and Velez articles originally appeared in the January 1991 *Horizon*, and the Pervorse and Garrett response to them appeared in the May 1991 *Horizon*.

I WAS PLEASED TO SEE THE DISCUSSION CONCERNING RACISM AND PREJUDICE IN the field of experiential education. As a white woman from the United States teaching in Canada, I was also saddened and angered by the comments of Messrs. Pervorse and Garrett because of the lack of attention to the meaning of words, critical thinking standards, and previous work on the meaning, origin, and effect of racism. I believe it is essential that we choose and use words wisely and think critically about emotionally charged issues. I believe it is our professional obligation to express thoughtful and well-reasoned opinions as we develop programs in a multicultural world. I wish to deal only with a few of the issues raised in their argument.

THE DIFFERENCE BETWEEN RACISM AND PREJUDICE

Messrs. Pervorse and Garret use the words prejudice and racism interchangeably throughout their letter. This was unfortunate because the words have very different meanings. The definition given by Messrs. Pervorse and Garrett (see paragraph two of their article below) is only one aspect of prejudice. "Prejudice" comes from a Latin stem meaning to pre-judge or have a preconceived opinion or feeling which may be favorable or unfavorable. Racism, on the other hand, is the "belief that human races have distinctive characteristics that determine their respective cultures, usually involving the idea that one's own race is superior and has the right to rule others."[1] It is important to note that racism involves the belief in the superiority of one's own race and the involvement of systems of power to promote that belief. Building from results of the Kerner Report, Whitney Young (1970) states:

> Most Americans get awfully uptight about the charge of racism, since most people are not conscious of what racism really is. Racism is not the desire to wake up every morning and lynch a black man from a tall tree. It is not engaging in vulgar epithets. These kinds of people are just fools. It is the day-to-day indignities, the subtle humiliations, that are so devastating. Racism is the assumption of superiority of one group over another, with all the gross arrogance that goes along with it. Racism is a part of us. The Kerner Commission has said that if you have been an observer you have been a racist; if you have stood idly, you are racist. (p. 730)

If one attends carefully to the words and their definition, a distinct difference between requesting representation of an under-represented group (i.e., people of color) and racism (i.e., belief in the superiority of a particular race) emerges. The demands by Messrs. Velez and Conquest were for representation of an under-represented group and awareness of underlying racist and oppressive behavior patterns of the Association for Experiential Education (AEE), which is dominated by white people. Those demands are not the same as expressing a belief in superiority of one race over the other.

---

[1] I base my definitions and use of words on the Random House Dictionary of the English Language. I have tried to be faithful to the list of definitions for each word since such a strategy supports a more honest and complete discussion of the concepts. Simple definitions are adequate when there is an agreement about an item (e.g., chair, bicycle), but a more comprehensive discussion is needed when we are exploring the meanings of abstract concepts. To that end, it is extremely helpful to use research results and philosophical discussions about racism and prejudice that include context, meaning of words and syntax, and current associations with the concept.

ATTENDING TO THE STANDARDS OF CRITICAL THINKING

Even if one were to agree with the definition of prejudice provided by Messrs. Pervorse and Garrett, they do not support their claim that Messrs. Velez and Conquest "cross the line into racism." Messrs. Velez and Conquest made generalizations (a logical process) from their own personal experiences with AEE professionals. Making generalizations from experience is not an irrational process. It is instructive to closely examine the structure of the writings of Messrs. Velez and Conquest.

Mr. Velez states that he, himself, had several experiences (notice it was more than one experience) with outdoor educators who were "bigoted and know-it-all." Notice that Mr. Velez does not generalize the label to *all* outdoor educators; he merely says that he was *reluctant* to attend the conference, given these previous experiences. In addition, Mr. Velez does not indicate that he thinks people of color are superior and does not invoke a power structure or system to oppress white people—two of the conditions necessary for racism. Finally, Mr. Velez tests his original generalizations and conclusions by attending the conference.

Mr. Conquest presented an analysis of power structures within AEE and associated organizations. Although one may disagree with his analogy of the plantation, it is a proper use of constructing an argument using analogies. Mr. Conquest supports the analogy by drawing connections between the power relationships on a plantation and the power relationships between personnel roles and functions, i.e., assistants often serve their bosses with little or no access to power or policy development. In addition, Mr. Conquest merely requests that people of color have control over programs designed for them and about them. He never once indicates that he thinks people of color should have power over white people or that they are superior to white people. He simply states that people of color should have a strong voice and control in programs designed for people of color. As in the case of Mr. Velez, there is no sign of racism (the belief that one race is superior and should have power over another race) in the words of Mr. Conquest. A dialogue using critical thinking skills would address the topic at hand and present evidence to counter the analogy or disprove the supporting evidence.

Furthermore, their generalizations seem warranted (and necessary for their own survival in a world where white people hold the power) given the generations of oppression and violence toward people of color and the barrage of daily reminders of that history. When referring to individuals, we assume the individual has white skin unless so noted. Therefore, we identify black athletes or scholars but not white athletes or scholars. It is implied that the norm or standard is white skin and this leaves people of color excluded. In addition, one only has to watch the nightly news to hear examples of white police officers beating people of color, the low number of people of color represented in positions of power, the high number of people of color in jail, and the higher percentage of infant mortality for children of color, to see the continuation of the racism and prejudice within the institutions of power (Kaufman, 1989; Robson, 1990; Klauda & St. Anthony, 1990; Klauda, 1990; von Sternber, 1990; Weiner, 1990).

Racism and White Privilege

What is missing in the response by Messrs. Pervorse and Garrett is an understanding of racism as a problem for whites (Katz, 1978).[2] It is people with white skin who have access to power structures and do not have to think about the color of their skin. It is part of what Peggy McIntosh (1991) defines as "white privilege." We tend to think of racism as disadvantages for people of color without seeing the corollary aspects which put people with white skin at an advantage. White privilege is an "invisible knapsack" of invisible but important special provisions that can be used when needed. What are these provisions? Ms. McIntosh gives us some examples:

1. I can, if I wish, arrange to be in the company of people of my race most of the time.

2. I can go shopping alone most of the time, pretty well assured that I will not be followed or harassed.

3. I can turn on the television or open to the front page of the paper and see people of my race widely represented.

4. When I am told about our national heritage or about "civilization," I am shown that people of my color made it what it is.

5. I can be sure that my children will be given curricular materials that testify to the existence and excellence of their race.

6. Whether I use checks, credit cards, or cash, I can count on my skin color not to work against the appearance of financial reliability.

7. I can arrange to protect my children most of the time from people who might not like them.

---

[2]See J. H. Katz (1978), *White Awareness: Handbook for Anti-Racism Training*. Katz carefully builds a case for the need of white people's awareness of their own attitudes and behavior that unintentionally and unconsciously still perpetuates racism. In addition, she notes the negative costs for white people when they unknowingly operate from these racist attitudes. Also see E. Lee (1985), *Letters to Marcia: A Teacher's Guide to Anti-Racist Education*. Lee presents the many facets of subtle racism in the school, and lesson plans for addressing the various issues.

8.   I can swear, or dress in second-hand clothes, or not answer letters, without having people attribute these choices to the bad morals, the poverty, or the illiteracy of my race.

9.   If a traffic cop pulls me over or if the IRS audits my tax return, I can be sure I haven't been singled out because of my race.

10.   I can speak in public to a powerful male group without putting my race on trial.

11.   I am never asked to speak for all the people of my racial group.

12.   I can remain oblivious of the language and customs of persons of color who constitute the world's majority without feeling in my culture any penalty for such oblivion.

13.   I can go home from most meetings of organizations I belong to feeling somewhat tied in, rather than isolated, out-of-place, outnumbered, unheard, held at a distance, or feared. (p. 5)

White privilege is an elusive subject and the tendency is to avoid facing it because it questions the myth of meritocracy. If these things are true, the United States is not such a free country, one's life is not what one makes it; many doors open for certain people through no virtue of their own.

Even the word "privilege" seems misleading. Privilege is normally considered a favored state, whether earned or conferred. Yet some of the above conditions work to systematically over-empower certain groups. Such privilege simply *confers dominance* because of one's race. There is a difference between earned strength and unearned power conferred systematically. Power from unearned privilege can look like strength when it is in fact permission to escape or to dominate. But not all the aspects of white privilege are damaging. Some, like the expectation that neighbors will be decent to you, or that your race will not be counted against you in court, should be the norm in a just society. Others, like the privilege to ignore less powerful people, distort the humanity of the holders as well as the ignored groups (McIntosh, 1991).

Messrs. Pervorse and Garrett's statement that we (white people) "have done everything we can," is a statement originating in white privilege. It assumes that white lives are morally neutral, normative, average, and ideal; that we white folks can work to allow "them" to be more like "us." The statement implies a power over others, not a power working with others to oppose all forms of oppression. The statement assumes that it is responsible (and good) to act for others and that we can be sure of our own moral intent and wisdom. Such assumptions prevent us from seeing the destructive consequences of our well-intentioned projects. Although many of our projects are meant to "help people of color," these projects can and do inflict more damage and oppression.[3] This is directly related to a lack of interaction with and transfer of power to people of color. The statement leaves people of color in the role of "victim," not as actors determining their own roles. The statement leaves in place a power structure dominated by white people deciding the fate of people of color. Messrs. Velez and Conquest do not want more charity or programs designed by white people. Messrs. Velez and Conquest are claiming what is rightfully theirs—the power to define their own programs to support the freedom and self-dignity of people of color (Gibson, 1989). Such a commitment from AEE means material changes in structure, number of people of color in positions of power, and content of the programs.

The examples of role models chosen by Messrs. Pervorse and Garrett is also insightful. A study of children who are African-American indicates that African-American children are so inundated with white role models and symbolism that they point to children with dark skin and say they are dirty, ugly, and bad, or even wish they were white. It is the overwhelming whiteness of role models that does not assist a young child of color to imagine that she or he could obtain a particular level of achievement. It is white people who lack a broad perspective of role models across racial and cultural arenas, not people of color. For instance, how many scientists, scholars, politicians, social activists, or authors of color in American history can one name? In addition, I fail to see the significant relevance of athletic role models to experiential education. There has been a long history of racism in sports. Initially, many of the major sports were closed to people of color. The latest series on racism in a Minneapolis newspaper indicated that athletes of color still encounter racism and many teams do not even promote their games within communities of people of color (Weiner, 1990). The example would have been much more relevant had the examples come from experiential education, education in general, outdoor education, or a similar area.

THE ROLE OF CRITIQUE BY PEOPLE OF COLOR

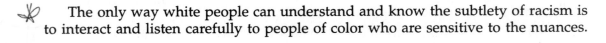

The only way white people can understand and know the subtlety of racism is to interact and listen carefully to people of color who are sensitive to the nuances.

---

[3]For an excellent discussion about the costs of racism for the people who have access to the power structures over people of color, see Susan D. Welch (1990), *A Feminist Ethic of Risk*. Welch convincingly argues that many projects developed by white people to help people of color fall short because of a lack of interactive dialogue that acknowledges the damage of oppression, sees the need for ongoing work toward freedom and justice for all people, and conceives of people of color as both victims and courageous fighters of oppression.

People of color have an "epistemological privilege" (Narayan, 1988)[4] by virtue of living in two racial worlds and having to survive in a world dominated by white people. People of color must not only maintain their own cultures and dignity but also learn how to relate to white people who are in power and control much of the lives of people of color. We, white people, do not live in a world where we have to be conscious of the color of our skin and hence, must learn this knowledge from listening to people of color. If we, white people, truly want to resist racism and prejudice, we must learn how we perpetuate it in our systems and practices through ignorance and lack of awareness and attention.

The anger expressed by Messrs. Velez and Conquest reflects generations of oppression, racism, and prejudice that their families, friends, and even they themselves have undergone. The only way to address such subtleties is people of color taking the risk and expressing their righteous anger toward such situations. Although it is not pleasant, those of us who are white must be accountable for that history as well as our own perpetuation of the system because we are the ones who have access to the privilege and power system. Messrs. Velez and Conquest are setting healthy examples in this field by voicing their justified anger at the situation and taking the risk of exposing their own feelings.[5]

We are a long way from being diverse together, and the statements of Messrs. Velez and Conquest indicate we must listen more to people of color. It is people of color who help us see how our actions, even well-intentioned actions, perpetuate racism and prejudice. It is they who will point the way to resolving some of the issues. It is they who have fought racism and prejudice for years. It is we white people who need to listen and hear their anger that there already has been too much damage.

This critique is not to replace the responsibility of white people to speak out against racism, as men need to speak out against sexism. It is not the responsibility of people of color to educate white people about their racist behavior. It is the *responsibility of white people* to acknowledge their access to privilege and power based on skin color, remain accountable for the history of oppression of people of color by white people, and change their attitudes and behaviors as well as work toward justice for all. I agree with Messrs. Garrett and Pervorse that people of color and white people cannot hold others at arm's length. But I fail to see how expressing

---

[4]For an extensive explanation of epistemic privilege, standpoint epistemology, and methodological humility, see Uma Narayan (1988), *Working across difference: Some considerations on emotions and political practice*, and P. H. Collins (1991), *Learning from the outsider within: The sociological significance of black feminist thought*.

[5]Susan Welch (1990) discusses the privilege of white, middle-class people that allows them to retreat from discussions about racism when righteous anger is expressed concerning the history and effects of racism on people of color.

anger and defining the subtleties of racism and prejudice as seen by people of color is pushing people away. Susan Welch (1990) states:

> It is painful to learn we have caused others harm, either as individuals or as members of a dominant social group. Change occurs when the response to this knowledge is not guilt but repentance, a deep commitment to make amends and to change patterns of behavior. Such changes are not losses but gains, opportunities to live out our love and respect for others. (p. 174)

We cannot stand side by side if one race is not allowed to express its anger.

If AEE is truly opposed to oppression, prejudice, and racism, we must enter into a dialogue with people of color and hear their critique of the plans and actions designed by white people. As a mature and ethical organization, we would invite such critiques and explore their meanings. We must unflinchingly recognize not simply the evil consequences of our thoughtless or greedy actions but also the negative consequences of our attempts to pursue good. We must, in effect, create a matrix of resistance to all forms of injustice. We could start by listening more to the details and suggestions of brave people like Messrs. Velez and Conquest.

DIVERSITY: ACCEPTING/RESPECTING COLOR

Arthur Wellington Conquest III

It has been more than twenty-five years since the historic Civil Rights Bill was signed by President Lyndon B. Johnson and the doors of "the dream" were supposed to magically open for people of color (POC) in America. In the name of misleading terms like "integration" and "the melting pot," and at a time when large numbers of POC were being recruited as course participants, POC were lured into the outdoor field with powerless positions such as assistant instructors, urban specialists, and, in rare cases, instructors. In reality, however, the basic foundations of slavery and the plantations it supported remained fixed: Whites, as masters, gave the orders and controlled everything, while POC, as the house servants, accepted their subservient status and did as they were told. This system, unfortunately, continues full-steam-ahead today.

As long as POC have to idolize individuals who don't represent or speak for them, then those individuals only serve as wardens of (outdoor) institutions that have POC locked up in economic, political, and mental prisons in America. [About 500,000 POC are literally locked up in prisons.] Malcolm X once said, "If you stick a knife in my back, if you put it in nine inches and pull it out six inches, you haven't done me any favor. If you pull it all the way out, you (still) haven't done me any favor."

While AEE, along with the rest of America, prepares for the drastic changes that will occur with the Workforce 2000, emotionally seductive words like "diversity," "pluralism," and "cultural differences" are being used more frequently. Are these terms code words for "integration" and "affirmative action?" What do these terms mean and are POC going to allow whites, especially white males, to continue to set themselves up as the custodians of their communities? Are these signals specifically designed to distract attention from the conflict, tension, and pressure intrinsic in eliminating prejudice, discrimination, racism?

If white individuals and/or organizations associated with AEE are going to seriously address issues encompassing diversity, then they must begin to embrace the notion that cultural/racial differences as they relate to POC, especially skin color, are on a par with their own. Historically, most things associated with POC in this country are assumed to have less value than those of white people. Jazz vs. classical (European) music, is but one example. Even today, all but the most racially healthy whites at some point in their lives have an assumption that POC are somehow tainted and/or inferior. [I see and experience the superior/inferior posture daily—at the 1990 AEE conference in St. Paul, too—and when I refuse to submit, many whites become extremely indignant.]

Diversity must not mean that POC have to reject their cultures and adopt the values of white society to participate as equals within mainstream outdoor institutions. POC should be allowed to accept and like being who they are. Taking this a step further, white outdoor educators must be willing to accept POC's desire to control their own institutions and educate children of color accordingly so they do not feel compelled to define themselves in relation to a society which has not yet come to terms with accepting and respecting color. Diversity is accepting and respecting a colored heart with a colored face, a nation within a nation.

THE ST. PAUL CONFERENCE WAS "HIP!"

Roberto Velez

Reluctantly, I attended the 1990 AEE Annual Conference in St. Paul, Minnesota. I was reluctant because my experiences with elitist, "know-it-all," bigoted, outdoor educators made me apprehensive about the possibility of spending any time with large numbers of them at a conference. But this conference was different for a variety of reasons. First, there were more people of color present than I had expected and many of them ran workshops that addressed their cultures and their oppressive experiences in America. Second, I took part in a "special workshop" made up of about forty people of color. Together we developed a set of goals for social change and empowerment within the experiential education field. Third, I was inspired and rejuvenated with a sense of hope by brothers like Arthur Conquest and McClellan Hall who have been "in the fight" for justice and equality in the outdoor education movement for a number of years. Finally, I met a number of sincere white people, such as Rick Hall, who demonstrated throughout the conference that they, too, were willing to stand up and speak out against racism.

I'm glad I attended the conference and I look forward to the 1991 conference in North Carolina, where I hope to see, talk to, and work with my brothers and sisters again.

RACISM AND PREJUDICE IN THE FIELD

Dan Pervorse and Jim Garrett

The January 1991 issue of *The AEE Horizon* proved to be quite enlightening and, at the same time, perplexing. It was enlightening to read the many thoughts and viewpoints of the various members, yet at the same time, some of those views caused some anxiety. Two articles in particular, one written by Roberto Velez and the other by Arthur Wellington Conquest III, dealt with the topics of prejudice and racism, particularly as they relate to the experiential education field.

As with both of these gentlemen, we too are concerned about and despise racism and prejudice in any form. This of course includes the form that took shape at the hands of both Mr. Velez and Mr. Conquest. For the purpose of clarification, Webster's Dictionary defines prejudice as "an irrational attitude of hostility directed against an individual, a group, a race, or their supposed characteristics; preconceived judgment or opinion; an opinion or leaning adverse to anything without just grounds or before sufficient knowledge." Additionally, racism is "racial prejudice or discrimination."

Mr. Velez crossed the line into racism from the outset of his letter in the *Horizon*. He stated that he was reluctant to attend the 1990 AEE Annual Conference because of the large numbers of "elitist, 'know-it-all,' bigoted, outdoor educators" who would be there. We are glad that his experience at the conference was much to the contrary of what he expected. However, by making such a statement about any of us, based solely upon his own experiences with others in this field, he fits the above definition of a racist. He is the very epitome of what he is speaking out against. It angers us to be lumped into such a category by him when he has no knowledge of our persons or character. His very words violate the stance that people of color (POC) claim to take against such attitudes.

The letter composed by Mr. Conquest does make a meaningful attempt at addressing these issues in this field. However, this letter also seems to be structured around a foundation of racial prejudice. Mr. Conquest's presupposition that all programs that are directed by whites ("Whites, as masters," giving orders and controlling everything, while POC act "as the house servants") are continuing to perpetuate the slavery and plantation system is basically a gross overexaggeration of reality. We have done what we can in our respective agencies to bring in POC at leadership positions in order to effect necessary changes and to address the pertinent issues of our communities. We are tired of being blamed for the history of discrimination of the past. We don't doubt that POC do, in fact, still face prejudice, but we are not perpetuating it and are tired of POC who point their fingers at us and blame us simply because of our skin color.

Mr. Conquest states that "white outdoor educators must be willing to accept POC's desire to control their own institutions and educate children of color" so that they can deal with their own cultural values. In this same light, POC need to allow us "white outdoor educators" to do the same, without putting us down for doing so. In an effort to delineate and understand their own cultural heritages over the years, some POC have denied the existence and/or importance of a white cultural heritage. Do not deny us the same rights that you so desire for yourselves by labeling our own efforts to grow as being racist. It would be wrong for anyone to deny anyone else of their right to learn and grow and to be involved in their heritage.

There is also another perspective that must not be overlooked. One of the purposes of many experiential education programs is to provide the participants with positive role models. Based on the statement quoted above, is Mr. Conquest suggesting that the only proper role models for children of color are POC (and conversely white role models for white children)? If this were true, then why are Michael Jordan and Larry Bird such powerful role models for many children in this country irrespective of color?

If we are serious about breaking the cycle of racism and prejudice in this field, should we not be setting healthy examples in our own programs? The healthy example that must be promoted is for programs to have a racially and/or culturally diverse program staff. If we perpetuate the idea that the only proper role models for children are those of their own race, we will be guilty of promoting segregation and racism.

Additionally, according to Mr. Conquest, "diversity is accepting and respecting a colored heart with a colored face, a nation within a nation." This definition is too narrow in that it seems to say that diversity is a function of color. Diversity is accepting/respecting differences in others regardless of color (and for that matter sex, age, the way people dress, geographical location, program affiliation, etc.).

One of the main reasons for the existence of AEE is to bring together people from all walks of life who are interested in perpetuating the philosophy and goals of experiential education. In other words, it is to unite people of like minds yet of different life experiences. Those differences are what we would call diversity. Each of us brings something special and truly unique to this organization, regardless of whether our differences flow out of an educational, professional, racial, sexual, or any other, perspective. This is the essence of true diversity.

We agree with Mr. Conquest that terms such as "melting pot" do not describe the true essence of diversity. The melting pot presents a picture of a cauldron where all are boiled together into one large indistinguishable and dysfunctional glob. Much to the contrary, we each need to maintain our uniqueness and our own heritage. But it will only hurt all of us if we continue to segregate and throw bigoted barbs at those who don't fit our particular special interests. POC should not hold others who are different than they, in particular the white male, at arm's length because they don't understand POC issues. How will we gain an understanding of your issues or you of ours if we continue to push each other away? Instead, we need to stand side by side and learn from one another about our differences in order that we all might grow. The beauty of true diversity in AEE is that we are diverse together.

18

Healthy Expressions of Diversity Lead to Positive Group Experiences

Denise Mitten

THE EXPRESSION OF DIVERSITY IS ONE OF THE MOST IMPORTANT FEATURES OF A healthy group. It is a key to safety, good decisions, participant enjoyment, and trip or expedition success. Recognition of diversity, recognition of people's fears about diversity, and a commitment to encourage participants to express their perspectives and wants is part of the challenging job of a group leader. The typical result in groups where acknowledging and using diversity constructively is a norm, is the ability to set goals and accomplish tasks. Group members will feel validated as individuals and contribute to group discussions and decision making in a positive, constructive manner.

THE VALUE OF DIVERSITY

Diversity means variety, distinctness or separateness of being. People can be different or alike in many ways; these include trip or life expectations, cultural background, learning styles, communication styles, political persuasions, interests, race, economic status, spirituality, age, gender, skills, physical condition, sexual preference, educational background, diet preferences, stress tolerance, and goal orientation. Any and all of these aspects can bring people together, have no effect, or keep them apart. As leaders and educators, it is important to realize that we bring all the ways we are different from each other in our cities and towns with us on an outdoor trip. We have a wonderful opportunity to structure an environment where the expression of diversity is welcomed. Some people for the first time in their lives can feel part of a group and can feel that as individuals, each one of them matters to the leader and to the other individuals in the group. People can feel that they can be honest about their trip expectations, talk about important concerns, and feel heard and validated.

In a society which teaches us to minimize differences, it is often difficult to establish a group norm of sharing and celebrating them. Diversity itself is value-free. There is no good or bad diversity. On the other hand, how people perceive others as individuals, including their opinions and behaviors, is often value-laden. Each person brings her or his own history of exposure to differences, including both fears and appreciation of differences, to an outdoor trip.

Historically many people have been afraid of diversity. Those who have different aspirations may be seen as threats to achieving one's own goals. Some people think that only one kind of person will be liked. Some will not initiate a conversation with someone who is obviously different from them. Many people have learned to minimize the ways in which they differ from others, to look and act like they fit the "mold." It is easy for a norm to be set that everyone has to want the same thing or at least everyone has to say they want the same thing. A common phenomenon in the early 1900s for immigrants to the United States was to completely give up speaking their native tongues and participating in their cultural traditions in order to become as American as possible, so as to be able to achieve success and feel safer. It was not uncommon for people who spoke differently to be ostracized, beaten up, and overlooked for jobs. Many immigrant families refused to teach their children their native language.

A group that does not accept diversity can feel unsafe to its members. They may not say they are tired and need to stop for a rest or that they want to walk slowly and are content to stop short of the summit. Others may not feel it is appropriate to say, "I want to push hard and go all out to reach the summit." People can be worried about violating a norm, stepping on someone's toes, or losing the respect of the trip leader.

Diversity helps build strength in a group just as it does in natural environments. There are a number of ecological principles that apply both to our natural environment and to the human population. Ecological communities with high diversity are healthy, have a greater chance of surviving and continuing to evolve, and are better able to adapt or cope with disasters such as weather, pests, and other catastrophes. Human populations are similar. Positive, diverse groups are more stable, can endure hardships, and can cope with disasters better than groups that are not diverse or groups where the expression of diversity is not encouraged.

Diversity in personalities can be an asset in a group. One person may think of the details, one person may think about the whole picture, another person may recognize the importance of feelings. We cannot expect each person to embody all the personality qualities that are needed for a successful expedition; however, people who are allowed to express their personalities can come together and create an effective team.

For example, by developing a board of directors that includes a lawyer, bank president, fund raiser, doctor, homemaker, farmer, and business manager, we acknowledge that these people have different skills, are diverse in their interests and competencies, and come together to perform a service or govern a business or organization. It is in the best interest of the organization for the group to express and use this diversity. The goals of the organization can be better accomplished because of the variety of expertise. The healthy expression of this diversity takes place when the chairperson encourages each of the individuals to use his or her talents and expertise to problem-solve for the organization. Conversely, there is not a healthy expression of diversity if the chairperson indicates that the board members are to follow directions and not question decisions. The board members may become apathetic and resign, rebel against the chairperson, or subtly sabotage the organization's goals.

I see diversity among individuals as a useful and a highly desirable aspect of groups. As a leader, I use the group's expression of diversity to attain goals not otherwise possible.

ELICITING THE EXPRESSION OF DIVERSITY

Within the Woodswomen program model,[1] there are helpful tools for working with diversity. Our model has been successful when working with groups on day, weekend, or week-long trips, as well as major expeditions. It has been successful with women's groups, women and children's groups, mixed-gender groups, and men's groups. This approach to the healthy expression of diversity is widely applicable to group settings beyond the specific, outdoor-trip context which is discussed below.

A necessary ingredient in this process is having leaders who are comfortable with themselves and the ways they are different from the perceived norms of society. Accepting one's own self is crucial in helping people embrace their own differences and themselves. It is also useful for leaders to know about a number of different lifestyles and perspectives. Leaders are more accessible if a person can chat with them about their interests and hobbies, no matter what they may be.

Some educators are worried about diversity-run-wild. Does embracing diversity mean that there are no rules and the trip is chaotic? What happens if everyone does different things? How will the trip be safe, how will the leader stay in charge, how will programming goals be accomplished?

---

[1]Woodswomen, Inc., is an adventure program for women of all ages that offers wilderness trips. It is working to build a strong international network of outdoors women.

It is important to distinguish between the healthy expression of diversity and the suppression of diversity. Often in the guise of keeping control of a group or maintaining order, a leader will accidentally suppress diverse perspectives. For example, if a leader knows that one person may want to hike faster than the pace of the group, the leader may choose to ignore that observation and hope that the fast hiker will conform to the pace and be content enough so that there will be no conflict. Often, however, the leader's fear of talking about and working with diverse expectations will lead to the very conflict the leader was trying to avoid. If diversity is stifled in a group, members may become discontent, rebellious, and defiant, and, for example, decide to paddle fast forward in a rapid even though it would be safer to backpaddle. This can lead to unsafe situations.

Many leaders confuse inappropriate rebellion against authority, which comes from people being suppressed, with the expression of diversity. This makes the leaders reluctant to allow the healthy expression of diversity. If a leader is fearful or confused about what the healthy expression of diversity is, then it will be hard for that leader to create the space for its expression.

An example of a situation where the leader missed an opportunity to create the space for participants to express diverse expectations occurred on a leadership

Photo courtesy of Wilderness Inquiry II.

course. We were talking about the backpacking trip we were planning for the last five days of our course. One woman did a great job of explaining the alternatives for our hike location. Then she opened up the discussion for questions. Another woman asked about hiking farther than the proposed route. Someone else said she would like that, too. The woman heading the discussion did a common thing: She asked who else wanted to go farther. No one raised a hand. The woman leading the discussion concluded that since "the group" did not want to hike farther, the matter was closed. This situation left the women who spoke up feeling alone. A more appropriate response would be "Pat, Cathy, and perhaps others may want to hike farther. We can certainly explore the option of part of the group hiking farther. What other questions are there about the routes?" After questions about the routes are fielded, go back to the question of what each individual wants to do. I think it is important to keep an open mind and to be sure that as a leader, one guides the group to openly consider both the group's and the individual's options. The final decision will be better accepted by all group members if they believe that the leader explored with them the alternatives that they wanted.

There are ways that groups covertly and overtly discourage or suppress diversity. In a men's group, a participant related a trip experience. Jeff was asked by players on his baseball team to go to the Boundary Water Canoe Wilderness for a week. He thought that would be a great idea. He showed up at the appointed time and off they went. He related that he woke up the first morning scared to death as he was hearing shotgun blasts near his head. He got up to find five dead gulls lying in the water. He was horrified to realize that his comrades had done the shooting and, in fact, were planning to drink and shoot for much of the trip. He said he did not dare to speak up for fear of his life or at least ridicule. Jeff was scared to say he was different or that he did not want to shoot the birds. He said that he was able to confide in his brother-in-law who was also on the trip, so he did not feel totally alone. The other men in my group confirmed that this situation is not unusual. Many had been on trips where they did not agree with the behavior of the most vocal or popular men, but felt helpless to speak up.

An optimistic programming model incorporates the idea that it is possible and desirable for group members to be different, have different goals, backgrounds, and strengths, and still enjoy a wilderness trip together, and, in fact, better accomplish group goals than if there were no diversity. This approach emphasizes respect for the individual and the belief that if the individual has a chance to say what she wants in a comfortable, supportive environment, and feels she is heard, then that person will be a willing, active, and constructive group member. Having a group norm of realizing and acknowledging differences is important because a person who feels uncomfortable or embarrassed about sharing what she considers an important part of herself, may tend to withdraw and isolate herself, especially if she perceives that she will be labeled as "different" from the other group members. That person will not be eager to participate in risky situations. Groups with a negative attitude about diversity reinforce people's fear that they will not be accepted if they reveal certain things about themselves. Suppressing themselves can add to low self-esteem and self-denial, making it hard for individuals to trust enough to establish healthy relationships. Of course, wanting to share an aspect of oneself, but having a fear of being ostracized, is different from a situation in which a person may not choose to share of himself while establishing casual relationships. If people feel secure enough to say what they want or talk about how they are feeling—tired, sick, happy, driven—then, as leaders, we are setting the stage for a successful trip.

Leaders sensitive to the importance of individual expression work hard to reinforce the positive aspects of diversity. They are available to talk and be with the participants in both quiet and direct ways. Leaders use inclusive language and do not make assumptions about who is in the group or what people will want to do, nor do they assume that everyone is the same and thinks in the same way. Spending time with each participant and being obviously supportive to all helps make it safe for participants to approach each other. Humor and frankness are also helpful. Leaders meet people where they are, encourage participants to be responsible for their actions, and are not confrontive. They encourage people to say what they want, express their opinions, and feel comfortable about who they are. Leaders encourage a feeling of being included in the group process, which I consider different from "belonging" to a group. It is important that a person retain the feeling of individuality and choice in participating in the group process and group activities. In order to participate fully and to build self-esteem, participants need to consider themselves as individuals who can freely come and go from a group.

There are certain specific steps a leader needs to take in order to elicit the healthy expression of diversity. The stage is set for the group to be receptive to diversity at the initial trip gathering. As the leader meets the group, it is important to make verbal contact with each person. During initial introductions, group members learn about each other and start to learn about and have reactions to the diversity in the group. For example, some women come on a women's trip assuming that since we are all here, we are similar and present for the same reasons. During introductions to one trip, I saw one woman's face drop as she heard another say, "I am so glad to be here with others like me who have left our husbands and children at home. We can have a girls' week out in the woods." The woman whose face dropped felt that this description did not include her and was uncomfortable thinking that she was possibly the only group member who did not have a husband and children. In fact, the group was a typical diverse mix of women in a variety of personal relationship situations. It was up to the leader to be sure the conversation reflected the group's diversity instead of waiting to see if it happened. People are not used to being direct about differences. The leader can model directness and the participants can learn from this modeling.

At this first meeting, time and emphasis is given equally to each individual's expectations. The leader also creates the space to allow people who do not have expectations to share at the first meeting, to freely voice them any time during the trip, stressing that differences in timing is a normal way that people vary. Within twenty-four hours, the leader repeats the question regarding expectations to the group to allow for a potential timing difference. During the trip, leaders periodically check in with individuals regarding their expectations.

At the end of the initial meeting, many people may think, "How are we going to make this work? We are all so different." The leader expresses overtly what many people may be thinking by stating in an up-beat, positive tone, "that to have different expectations with a diverse group of people is a perfectly normal and healthy occurrence for a group." Continuing in a matter-of-fact tone, the leader says that some individual's expectations will probably change as the trip progresses and invites people to keep him posted on their thoughts. The leader emphasizes that one of the goals of the trip is to have fun, which is certainly possible with the great diversity in the group.

Leaders greatly influence trip norms. The leader reinforces the notion that it is valued to say what you think by making a personal connection with each person in a way that gives them permission to be comfortable being who they are on the trip. Leaders can support a positive attitude toward diversity by avoiding disparaging remarks, jokes, and discussions about different groups (i.e., women talking about all men's groups, backpackers talking about canoeing groups, ethnic and racial minorities, etc.).

The example that follows illustrates how to work with diverse expectations rather than suppressing them. A group was scheduled to climb Pisang Peak in the Himalayas. After walking six days to the base of the peak, we were turned back from our attempt by a storm that dropped twelve feet of snow in four days. Because of time constraints, we had to decide whether to attempt the summit again and return to Kathmandu the way we walked in, or abandon the summit and continue our circuit around the Annapurna massif. I asked group members for their preferences. Two women wanted to do the circuit and four wanted to attempt the summit again. At first the women began to make cases for their preferences. However, since it is a strong value for us to encourage participants to meet their individual goals, and in this case it was safe and practical, I suggested we divide into two groups. Groups often resist separating because in our society, we often learn to separate when we are not getting along, not because we have different goals. It is important for leaders to redefine separation to mean that we all get to do what we want and still support and like each other. This is a healthy relationship model for people to learn and to transfer to their personal relationships. If healthy diversity had not been encouraged in this group, it is unlikely group members would have been willing to state their preferences and to part amicably for a portion of the trip. If we had stayed together, it would have been unsafe to attempt a summit with climbers who were ambivalent. In this case, the group divided for a period and rejoined later in the trip.

The leader must be aware of the individuals' goals and expectations before an ambitious endeavor. For example, on a ski mountaineering trip in Colorado, we were to attempt a peak ascent on Day Five. One question I have learned to ask group members is, "What are your goals for the day?" For example, "Do you want to get as far as you can but not necessarily to the top? Do you want to have fun, take pictures, and not focus on the ascent? Do you want to focus on getting to the top?" It is important that each group member be honest with herself and the group about her goals. The group and individuals have a greater chance of personal success if everyone says what they really want for the day. I ask people these questions in several different ways. A peak ascent is too important and the safety considerations are too great to not do all I can as a leader to get participants to speak up about their desires. In this case, all group members said their goal was to have a fun day and get as far as they could, but not necessarily to the top. In fact, seven out of eight of us went to the top. The eighth woman, 56 years old and on touring skis for the first time four days ago, stayed forty-five minutes below the summit, resting. The crux is for participants to feel secure enough to be candid about their goals.

If a leader does not deliberately elicit or support the expression of diversity, a variety of scenarios can occur. Here are two illustrations:

A woman related a story where she was on an outdoor educators' course. On Day Two of the trip, the more vocal group members began making fun of "process." It quickly became the norm to not talk about personal concerns. The more vocal members were smoking marijuana. This concerned the participant, but she felt unsupported by the instructors who were laughing at the jokes. She did not want to risk being ostracized by the group by pushing against the norm to bring up what she perceived as a safety issue.

Two other people reported they went on a guided wilderness trip together expressly to share the experience with each other. On Day Two, the group held a kangaroo court, saying that these two people could not be affectionate on the trip, not because of safety, program philosophy, or inappropriateness, but because it bothered some of the group members. They were fifteen miles up-river from the nearest town, unable to leave the trip, and feeling unsupported by the leader and other participants. The leader, of course, thought she was doing what was in the best interest of the group since during the kangaroo court, it seemed as if the majority of the members said they wanted these two to change.

Individual differences in groups can bring about catastrophes, whatever the setting. The challenge is to encourage the expression of diversity rather than suppress it. By respecting individual differences, we allow and encourage participants to take responsibility for their own health, safety, and well-being. This in turn creates a safe and fun atmosphere in which major goals can be accomplished.

19

"Borrowing" Activities from Another Culture: A Native American's Perspective

Gordon W. A. Oles

THE ENTIRE SPECTRUM OF THE WILDERNESS/ADVENTURE EDUCATION EXPERIENCE is a most dynamic phenomenon. Many of the programs and experiences which adventure education practitioners facilitate are exciting, innovative, affective, and effective. Moreover, the profession has not developed to the point where the calcifying effects of organizational rigor mortis threaten to overtake it. There is still room for new ideas. In fact, if a wagging finger were to be pointed, it would have to be directed toward the tendency to jump on a bandwagon whenever an idea, concept, or practice captures one's fancy. It seems that one of the more pervasive bandwagons has been the trend of latching on to the rituals and practices of various Native American tribes and other aboriginal groups.

My concern stems from my experience in working with a number of agencies that conducted wilderness rehabilitation programs for troubled youth. One aspect of the various agencies' programs included sweat lodge ceremonies, giving of names, vision quests, fasts, etc., yet no cultural context was appropriate for the things which they were doing. Additionally, I believe that these agencies and individuals had no right to take these religious activities and put them to use in that setting.

I have had deeply spiritual experiences that I do not share with others, yet they are of profound meaning to me, for the context in which they occurred was appropriate to my cultural heritage. There are other events which I share with others of my culture, for we have these experiences in common; however, those who are outsiders must always be excluded.

By attempting to adopt Indian ceremonies into their adventure leadership programs, these well-intentioned, but misguided leaders have desecrated things that should have remained sacred and holy. From my perspective as a Native American (who also happens to be an outdoor leader), these contrived, pseudo-Indian activities were tantamount to a non-believer taking the Emblems of Communion and passing them out along the trail as a snack.

What if I were to come into St. Patrick's Cathedral, clad only in moccasins and a breechclout, and attempt to take the place of the priest? Or suppose that I went into a synagogue on Yom Kippur and sang *Kol Nidre* instead of the cantor? Can you see the incongruity? Even if I say the correct words and do the correct things, I certainly do not have the right to do so, and I would most likely offend the religious sensibilities of those within their respective congregations. It works both ways.

Many non-Indian people within Western society seem to think of Indians as a separate species from them, with a cosmology based upon fear and superstition. Worse, they may view us as curiosities, or as stage props instead of people. In the short story *Sun and Shadow*, Ray Bradbury pointedly demonstrates the cultural insensitivity that far too frequently occurs when Westerners deal with indigenous peoples.

> We must understand each other . . . . I will not have my alley used because of its pretty shadows, or my sky used because of its sun, or my house used because there is an interesting crack . . . . We are poor people. Our doors peel paint, our walls are chipped and cracked, our gutters fume in the street, the alleys are all cobbles . . . . Did you think I knew you were coming and put my boy in his dirtiest clothes? We are *not* a studio! We are people and must be given attention as people. Have I made it clear? (Bradbury, 1953)

Our religious beliefs may seem strange. I will agree they are different from the Western world's cosmology; however, that difference does not make them less valid as a means of expressing reverence for the divine. From a Western viewpoint, land is a commodity to be bought and sold, or to be plundered and conquered. To the Native American, the earth is our mother. Western thought arrogates to humankind the sole right of reason and being. One Native American perspective takes the viewpoint that all animals are sentient beings. Moreover, the very rocks themselves are alive. Western thought conveniently divides the sacred from the profane; yet in the cosmology of a Native American, one may see the Hand of the Creator in all things; therefore, all is sacred.

How often over the centuries has our religious expression been ridiculed by the West? Yet, at the same time, if *their* religious institutions fail them, many non-Indians think that by adopting some Indian rituals or ceremonies (or a "reasonable facsimile"), they will find their way back to truth and light. *It just isn't going to happen!*

I seriously doubt that Western society is without spiritual meaning, and I cannot subscribe to the notion that the West is morally bankrupt (as yet). All enduring societies must have been built upon a spiritual and moral foundation, or else they would not have endured. In all of these societies that have risen and fallen, there was a spiritual drive that sustained them in their growth. Western society is no exception, though it seems in many cases that this spiritual dimension has been either denied or demythologized.

Western society has had its full complement of culture heroes, but what has it done with them (or to them)? If the heroes have displayed any human failings, they have been unceremoniously removed from their pedestal. Any element of the supernatural was dealt with in just as cavalier a manner. *Consequently, there remains a spiritual void when the culture heroes are dismantled, and we vainly search for their replacement.* It has been popularly stated in Western thought that "God is dead (also the culture heroes)." It must be remembered, however, that it is we who have killed them in our de-eschatological hubris. In Native American mythology, however, the hero remains inviolate; *it is we who must live up to the myth.* Therein lies a critical cultural difference between a Native American perspective and the Western cosmological viewpoint.

AUTHENTIC CULTURAL CONTEXTS

In order for a religious institution to work, it must be founded within the appropriate cultural context. Its adherents then practice their beliefs within that cultural milieu, and do so appropriately with their society's full sanction. For example, the religious ceremonies that are integral to any given tribe will be central frameworks of that tribe's cultural identity. Trying to juxtapose certain ceremonies into Western society would be disturbingly jarring. By the same token, those tribes also recognize the absurdity of trying to do the reverse. Hence, virtually all outsiders and outside distractions are excluded from most activities within the tribal religion, and rightly so. The hero motifs, cosmological perspectives, etc., remain forever intact—a standard that the tribal members strive to attain in their lives.

"Putting new wine into old bottles" is a timeless adage now, even as when it was first uttered. Adventure educators should critically examine the activities that are adopted. Activities must be *authentic* in order to be effective. In this definition of terms, authentic activities must be congruent to one's cultural framework. Therein lies the dilemma. Though people may recognize the value of certain activities (and Native American ceremonies have been perennial favorites), they cannot effectively make use of them if these activities and ceremonies come from a culturally dissimilar framework. To do so would make them appear unnatural and contrived. No amount of "cultural appreciation" or "cultural sensitivity" can make them fit within the Western cosmology, because the necessary perspective is lacking. Nor can these elements which have been appropriated (stolen) be of lasting efficacy, for the simple fact that they have been practiced without the proper sanctions. There is neither the cultural precedent, the cultural framework, *nor the authority* to conduct any sort of tribal activity—even if couched with Anglo terminology—even if conducted with the purest motives—even if those conducting these activities are doing them in a manner that is "sensitive" to the feelings of the Native Americans' tribal ceremonies that have been appropriated. In all honesty, I would have to say, "Find your own ceremonies; don't take ours."

Finding Western Cultural Contexts

Within the framework of non-Indian culture, there is a rich legacy that has been bequeathed if people will only look. Western society is not devoid of examples that could be emulated, if only one could look beyond one's cultural myopia. For example, if an individual only went so far as to read the delightful stories that Laura Ingalls Wilder (1976) wrote about her growing up, a very effective program could be developed using the subsistence skills that were once common to America's settlers. Wilder was not alone; there were others who left behind a record of early American life and institutions. Virtually every library has some sort of account of a pioneering family that could be effectively used with further research. A most simplistic example perhaps, but it could be easily incorporated into a program. Wigginton (1974) has done much to preserve America's heritage with the Foxfire efforts. Surely there is much that could be critically examined and incorporated from that source—and numerous others.

The nice thing about this approach is that it is *authentic* in the previously defined sense. Moreover, I doubt that many people's sensibilities would be offended, as might occur with some of the pseudo-quasi-religious-mystic undertones of some "Indian style" activities. Certainly, they would not take on the trappings of the "cigar-store" Indian and the inherent tawdriness that comes from such an unnatural union.

> . . . pseudo-Indianism is a passing fad. It cannot last. A sacred pipe torn from the body of a living heritage soon dies and becomes meaningless. (Hawk, 1990)

This is not to say that sweat baths, solo experiences, quests, walkabouts, and so on are inappropriate for use in programs. Just don't couch them in language or metaphorical contexts that cause them to appear to be something that they could never be. Once something has been shown to be a forgery (despite all the careful attention to authentic details), its baseness becomes glaringly apparent.

The Value of Rites and Ceremonies

It seems that there is a need for formal rites or ceremonies to validate human experiences within a society. In Western societies, there are christenings, bar mitzvahs, weddings, graduations, funerals, retirements, etc., all done with much ceremony. They are formalized ways in which each person's place in a Western society is validated. In Native American societies, there are rites and ceremonies as well. Upon closer examination it might well be said that activities of the types under discussion are essential for the complete development of a human being. One example must suffice.

Among many Native American tribes, the training of the young boys to become men was long and thorough. For instance, one of the great Crow chiefs, Plenty-Coups, had this to say:

> In all seasons of the year most men were in the rivers before sunrise. Boys had plenty of teachers here. Sometimes they were hard on us, too. They would often send us into the water to swim among cakes of floating ice, and the ice taught us to take care of our bodies. Cold toughens a man . . . . In we plunged amid the floating ice. The more difficulties we faced, the better for us, since they forced us to use our heads as well as our muscles. Nothing was overlooked that might lead us to self-reliance or give us courage in the face of sudden danger. (Linderman, 1967)

As I come to the end of this discourse, I feel it necessary to explain a few things. As a Native American, I felt that I could share some perspectives, but please keep in mind that I have only spoken for myself; I do not speak for my tribe. I certainly do not speak for all Native Americans. Nonetheless, I felt that it was important that I should share some of my feelings with you, so that there may be greater understanding between us.

I have no quarrel with those who see the value of developing men and women among our youth by making use of certain activities such as a solo experience, a fast or vision quest, bathing in a sweat lodge, or whatever other activity has been included within an adventure program.

Native Americans are not the only societies in which these activities occur or have occurred; consequently, we don't have a monopoly on them. What I will always object to is couching these activities in the realm of "Indian lore." I am not a museum specimen; my beliefs are not for sale. I am a human being. Treat me as such.

I realize that many people may strive to do these things because of a desire to emulate certain ideals, but please remember, the Noble Savage has existed only in literature, and perpetuating that myth only perpetuates stereotypic ideas. Romance is very seldom reality.

If you feel that the clients whom you serve may benefit from a sweat bath, fine, *but* don't say it's a Dakota sweat lodge ceremony. If you feel you want to change your name, fine. Just don't tell me that it's an Indian name. (If it really were your true name, I would hope that you wouldn't tell me.) If you want to fast, go ahead; that's your business. And, if you are in search of a vision from your Creator, please seek earnestly. All I ask is that you keep those things sacred to you. There are numerous models within the Western cultural context that can be deemed to be worthy of emulation—why be ashamed of them because they originated in Western civilization?

20

Snips and Snails and Puppy Dog Tails . . . The Use of Gender-Free Language in Experiential Education

Deb Jordan

"WHAT ARE LITTLE BOYS MADE OF? SNIPS AND SNAILS AND PUPPY DOG TAILS . . . ." "What are little girls made of? Sugar and spice and every thing nice . . . ." These childhood singsongs portray subtle attitudes and expectations of the roles for women and men in today's world. Research has shown that these gender role stereotypes have changed little over the years: women are still viewed as soft and yielding while men are seen as strong and assertive (Werner & LaRussa, 1985).

Through television shows and commercials, magazine advertisements, and radio voice-overs, the media continually depicts women and men in traditional social roles: women are wives, mothers, and helpers; men are money earners, supporting women and children. Gender influences also are depicted in our nonverbal, verbal, and written communications. Women tend to take up less physical space with their bodies and gestures, men talk and interrupt conversations more, and written language is filled with generic [sic] male pronouns. This article will help you rediscover the implications for use of gender-identified language and behaviors in experiential education.

CHANGE IS SLOW

While there certainly has been a move toward gender-neutral language in general, and in the field of experiential education in particular (admonitions from journals such as this for use of inclusive language), there also has been resistance (Shivers' exclusive use of the male pronoun in a recreation leadership text published as recently as 1986; Shivers, 1986). Newspapers, news magazines (*Time*, January

1978) and news shows continue to use "he" and "man" as generic, gender-neutral terms, even though research has shown that these terms are not perceived as being gender neutral. Miller and Swift (1988) have demonstrated that "he" and "man" conjure up images of male persons to the exclusion of female persons. Persistent use of these gender-specific terms will continue to reinforce the notion that being male is better (Connell, 1987).

In experiential education, we are all guilty of some gender bias. Most of us were socialized in a society that is heavily male oriented. Although we may have been exposed to non-traditional family models, the media, schools, and religious institutions inundate us with pro-male messages. As long as the overriding message is that boys are better than girls, we are, in a sense, trapped. Intellectualizing, while a necessary beginning to breaking free of these inhibiting attitudes, does not totally eradicate the lessons of youth.

The theory of expectation states and gender-role theories tell us that high power, high potency, and high status are attributed to those things we value. In our society, the male sex is more highly valued; therefore, those characteristics and materials associated with the male gender are more highly valued. The female gender is accorded low value, low legitimacy, and low status; therefore, those items and characteristics associated with females are attributed little or no respect (Berger & Zelditch, 1985; Eagly, 1987). We can make similar comments about differences in ages, races, and any other categories we establish.

While conscious efforts are being made to reduce gender bias and lessen these misattributions of status, change is slow. As a group, experiential educators and outdoor professionals appear to make a sincere effort to minimize gender bias in the field. They appear to be open to new ideas, support participation by both sexes, and encourage skilled individuals to develop personal skills to their full potential. There is, however, one very prevalent example of gender bias that pervades the field of experiential education: the use of gender-identified language and terminology.

THE BIAS IN LANGUAGE

In examining the impact of sexism in language, we need to look at the three functions of language bias. Sexism may ignore one gender, define the genders, and/or depreciate a gender (Pearson, 1985). Ignoring one gender is accomplished through the use of so-called "generic" terms. This includes the use of the masculine pronoun in describing both sexes (i.e., man for both female and male persons) and in the of such terms as chairman, man-hours, mankind, and two-man tent. This function serves to make the female gender invisible, and in reality is not inclusive.

Sexist word usage also may define a sex in relation to something else. An example of this would be the lumping together of "women and children" in the same phrase. This type of definition effectively reduces women to the level of children: having few rights, having little world experience and maturity, and needing care.

Another example of defining a sex in relation to something else, thereby reducing its value and power, is when people refer to adult females as girls (or ladies) and males as men. I often spend time in my classes discussing "words that go together." Those words include girls and boys, women and men, ladies and gentlemen.

While listeners have little difficulty in seeing the problem with using "girls and men" in a phrase together, they can't seem to see a problem with using the term "ladies and men." The problem, of course, is in the connotation of the words. Females well know the differences; remember when you were a child and your mother scolded you to sit or walk "like a lady"? Not once have I ever heard of anyone being scolded to walk "like a woman." I dare say a child never would have known what that meant. There is power in the word "woman," and I believe that's why most participants balk so strongly at the word. To facilitate every participant to reach their full potential, we should allow them equal access to the power of words.

A gender may also be defined in terms of relationships in ordering of words. Thorne and Henley (1975) suggest that consistently utilized word order is similar to ranking by importance and status. The accepted ordering of "men and women" in a phrase, rather than "women and men," indicates power and dominance of the former over the latter. Similar ordering of the terms "hard skills" and "soft skills" rather than "soft skills" and "hard skills" also illustrates a type of ranking, whereby hard skills are given more importance and status than soft skills.

Depreciation of a gender occurs when adjectives discredit one gender. "Dumb jock" as a referent to male athletes identifies them as wholly physical beings with little or no mental capabilities. Similarly, as a term, "women's work" is often used disparagingly. Adjectives to describe work that women do include such words as nice and pretty, while the same work attributed to men is described as masterful and brilliant (Sargent, 1984). Another example of the negative use of adjectives is found in the connotations of adjectives used to describe similar women and men. While assertiveness and a sharp mind are desired management and leadership skills, those traits manifested by females often result in characterizations of bitchy, aggressive, aloof, and cold. Those same behaviors exhibited by a male, however, are considered assertive, indicative of having a keen mind, and demonstrating competence (Sargent, 1984).

HARD SKILLS/SOFT SKILLS:
THE POWER OF GENDER BIAS

In addition to the implication of ordering, the generally accepted terms, hard skills and soft skills, also can depreciate the female gender and its contribution to the field of experiential education due to the phallocentric nature of the words. Hard skills and soft skills generally have been recognized as two types of skills in the practice of outdoor leadership. Hard skills are those that encompass such things as logistics, planning, and technical skill development; soft skills are those that involve human relations, communication, and social skills (Swiderski, 1987). For a long time, hard skills were the more highly valued of the two (Swiderski, 1987). Technical skills were those competencies people bragged about (and some still do), and at which people trained long and hard to become the best. Interpersonal skills, on the other hand, just sort of "happened" as the experience evolved. There was little or no formal training in interpersonal skills since it was assumed that everyone could successfully work with people. After all, people practice social skills in everyday living.

Recently, however, it has been recognized that both interpersonal and technical skills play an equally important role in experiential education. In training sessions, journal articles, and conference programs, more and more attention is being given to such skills as processing, debriefing, conflict management, and group dynamics. Currently, the development of people skills is being stressed as heavily as activity skills in many experiential programs. If, as a profession, experiential education truly believes that interpersonal skills are as valuable as technical skills, this is the time to alter our language to agree with those beliefs.

There have been assertions that terminology is a matter of personal semantic preference and that the use of hard and soft or technical and interpersonal as skill descriptors is not a matter worthy of examination. After all, these terms have the same meanings and everybody understands the lingo, right? A word is a word is a word, so to speak. The importance of semantics in the understanding and full acceptance of one aspect of experiential education, however, has been long overlooked. Word choice can alter meanings, result in misunderstandings, and provide only partial information (Pearson, 1985).

Gender-identified language often obscures the contributions and existence of the disregarded gender; it presents imprecise and half-true information. If we always talk in terms of one grouping of people (i.e., male people), we effectively negate the contributions of the other grouping (i.e., female people). Pearson (1985) states that language shapes the way we perceive reality: therefore, if we continue to promote one sex over the other in the course of everyday language, we will continue to define reality in terms of that one gender. This would perpetuate a pro-male bias in an already biased society and essentially maintain female oppression.

The choice of hard and soft as accepted synonyms for technical and interpersonal tends to slight the female gender, define the importance and status of maleness and femaleness in experiential education, and tends to depreciate the contributions of female leaders and participants . These terms are laden with subtle messages about valuing, status, and acceptance of women and men in this field. Much more accurate descriptors of these skill areas, which are also gender-free descriptors, are interpersonal and technical skills.

The concern with gender-identified language (i.e., hard and soft as descriptors, use of "man" as in two-man tent, etc.) is with the images and expectations conjured up by that particular word usage. As mentioned earlier, research has indicated that when exposed to "he" and "man," respondents imagined male persons, not female and male persons. Examining the impact of hard and soft as skill descriptors illustrates the gender-identifying qualities of the terms. Webster's New World Dictionary (1978) defines hard as "having firm muscles; vigorous and robust," while soft is defined as "giving way easily under pressure." Comparatively, masculine and feminine as terms indicating characteristics attributed to males and females are also related to the connotations for hard and soft. Masculine is defined as "having qualities regarded as characteristic of men and boys, as strength, vigor, etc." (snips and snails and puppy dog tails . . .). Feminine is defined as "having qualities regarded as characteristic of women and girls, as gentleness, delicacy, etc." (sugar and spice and everything nice . . .). Males are perceived as being hard in musculature and emotionally and mentally tough, while females are perceived as physically soft and emotionally and mentally delicate.

A distinct relationship between the meanings of male, masculine, and hard exists; hard may be characterized as being masculine and, therefore, attributed to men or boys. Since the male sex is more highly valued and attributed more status than the female sex, it is easy to see why, in the past, hard skills have been more highly valued—they are masculine and, according to social norms, masculine is the way to be.

Definitions of feminine and soft reveal a similar connection. The term feminine elicits an image of gentleness and delicacy—one may certainly argue that it also portrays softness and giving way under pressure. Most would agree that society does not view softness with much respect. One who is considered soft often is denigrated by being referred to as a wimp, pansy, or softhearted. In the out-of-doors and in many business situations, being soft or giving way under pressure is a highly undesirable trait. A leader who is able to make sound decisions without being unnecessarily swayed by popular thought is preferred over the leader whose decisions can be influenced by the most vocal group members.

By their very definitions, the use of the terms hard skills and soft skills makes a statement about underlying beliefs of femaleness and maleness in outdoor skill development. Although we verbalize the importance of interpersonal skills in experiential education, we will continue to deny the essence of that in our choice of terminology if we persist in using gender-identified language. The order of wording in written and spoken language also is a subtle manifestation of sexism. Why and how has it come about that we should always speak of hard (or technical) skills before soft (or interpersonal) skills?

It has been suggested that hard and soft as descriptors are evidence of a phallocentric history (Wilkinson, 1986). Experiential education has this history in that traditionally it has been a male domain where males are the doers. Perhaps we should change the linguistic approach to a more vaginocentric stance by utilizing dry and wet as adjectives. While it might take some getting used to, wet and dry make just as much sense in describing interpersonal and technical skills as do soft and hard. In fact, dry actually may be more accurate than hard. *Webster's New World Dictionary* (1978) defines dry as "having no personal bias or emotional concern." Technical skills are those very skills that (generally speaking) can be reduced to objective, tangible tasks and knowledge. The phrase "cut and dried" is an apt representation of skills that are supposed to be logical and relatively emotion-free. As an antonym, wet could be utilized adequately to characterize interpersonal skills.

WORDS TO ACTIONS

Why all this fuss about semantics? Because as noted by Spender (1980, as cited by Miller & Swift, 1988):

> For women to become visible, it is necessary that they become linguistically visible . . . . New symbols will need to be created and old symbols will need to be recycled and invested with new images if the male hold of language is to be broken.

In addition to linguistics, behaviors are prime areas for discovery of subtle sexism. Leaders and teachers in experiential education need to examine behaviors, not only between themselves and participants, but also between and among participants. Leaders should be aware of how they address participants—who is referred to by name most often, boys or girls? Calling male participants by their names more frequently than females (which, by the way, is quite common) has the impact of legitimatizing males, while negating females.

Praising males for their competence (Good decision! Nicely done!) while praising females for their appearance and domestic abilities (Great dinner! Pretty outfit!) is another insidious example of sexism. Related to this is the way we handle someone who is having difficulty with a given task—let's say using a compass. Study the way you (as the leader) handle the difficulties experienced by female and male participants. Telling a female participant to "not worry, girls are never very good at compass work anyhow," or, even more subtly, giving up on, even helping her, can imply to that female that she doesn't have the inherent abilities to succeed. Yet challenging a boy with the same problem, "Come on, try again, you can do it," and letting him struggle through the course, acts as a cue that expectations are different for him (he will succeed) because his inherent abilities are different.

Tolerating a wider latitude of behaviors from male participants than female participants is another way sexism from leaders/teachers rears its ugly head. Easily seen in structured classrooms, rowdy and loud behavior from boys is tolerated much more readily than rowdy or loud behavior from girls. This includes talking out of turn, cutting in lines, physical positioning, and working with other students. Until we get a handle on how attitudes are being manifested through language and behaviors in experiential settings, this subtle sexism will continue.

Leaders also need to monitor intergroup behaviors and word usage to facilitate a gender-neutral environment. It is very common for participants in mixed-sex groups to fall into those roles which are most comfortable, yet those roles have been accepted based on heavy, but subtle, social pressure. Leaders need to keep an eye on participants who short themselves by buying into a restrictive belief system and on participants who short others by limiting their experiences. The ever-helpful male who always lifts heavy objects, the female who always calls for help before fully assessing her own capabilities, the participant who puts down another because they dared to step outside the bounds of socially accepted roles, these are individuals who, while perhaps under the guise of cooperation and courtesy, restrict another's experience.

Steps Toward Equality

Now is the time for all of us in experiential education to share in the effort to make women visible, to further reduce sexism in the field, and use terminology and behaviors that accurately reflect the nature of described skills. We can do this by referring to the specific bodies of knowledge with appropriate adjectives (i.e., interpersonal and technical). In written and spoken language, we should continue to encourage and utilize gender-free and gender-neutral terms such as two-*person* tent and chair*person*. Fully value both sexes by using and encouraging the use of "words that go together." It is also appropriate to encourage the reordering of terms. When discussing the sexes, discuss women and men rather than men and women; when discussing skills, discuss interpersonal and technical skills rather than the reverse.

When examining behaviors with participants, investigate how you use names of participants, what types of behaviors you tolerate from whom, and how you react to difficulties experienced by females and males. Investigate how participants relate to one another, try to isolate and deal with those behaviors encouraged by sexist thinking and attitudes. Listen to the group talk. How do individuals refer to one another? What are the underlying expectations as seen through behaviors and word usage? As a profession, we can continue to respect all persons and their individual abilities by permitting and openly supporting cross-gender skill and social development.

21

Learning to Cross the Street: A Male Perspective on Feminist Theory

Gary Rasberry

THE INHERITANCE

I AM IN THE PROCESS OF MOVING INTO A NEW HOUSE LOCATED ON A QUIET STREET. It is actually a very old house—one which has been abandoned and empty for some time. It has been in the family for centuries, passed on from father to son through the ages. From the outside, and from a distance, the house looks impressive. It is handsome, with grand facades that have been carefully crafted. The house itself has had very little work done on it over the years and although things have begun to break down with greater frequency, it still has a comfortable feel to it.

So here I stand, faced with a house in decay—my inheritance—already full of excess baggage passed down to me through the family lines. Of course, I already have my own baggage with me. I would like to move in right away and make myself comfortable—at home. But there is something fundamentally wrong.

The slow and insidious wear and tear resulting from countless years of neglect now requires much work and attention—repairs, reorganizing, rebuilding, cleaning—the list is long. But where do I start? It is apparent that the house has some serious structural problems. Taking a close look at the structure and foundation seems like a logical place to start but I don't always pay attention to logic, even when it is staring me directly in the face. Why not just start with the easier items? Straighten up a few things, sweep the floor, clean the windows, and fix the broken floor boards. As logical as it may be, working on the structure of the house seems a daunting task. Besides, I'm not sure I can afford it. It could be costly. I can always get to the structure later.

MALE POWER AND PRIVILEGE

The structure that I speak of metaphorically is male power and privilege. The house that requires my urgent attention today is the same house that seemed adequate yesterday, but it suddenly looks different as a result of my experiences as a male studying feminist theory for the first time. My attempts at developing a working relationship with feminist theory have led to a recognition of the work I must do in my own life—on my own house—in order to live more comfortably with myself and with other men and women. I signed up for a feminist theory course as part of my graduate studies, thinking I would take a quick tour through the literature with a feminist perspective as my guide. What resulted instead was a personal journey—an exploration of my life experiences as I encountered new ways of examining them. Male power and privilege represents the lens with which I have begun to view my life and build new understanding. I offer the following account of my exploration, not as truth to be entertained by others, but as an invitation for others to explore or to reflect on their own personal experiences.

As a male, I am a full-fledged member of the patriarchy—an automatic representative of the socially constructed, male-dominated hierarchy. Membership affords many luxuries, some subtle, some not so subtle. It allows me access to power, wealth, and privilege in ways that I am only beginning to recognize. Why, then, is it so difficult for me to understand how this masculine privilege works?

Hegemony is a practice by which the interests of the dominant group become "normalized" (Gramsci, 1971). In this practice, the dominant class projects and imposes its own reality so successfully that it seems to be the natural order. The dominant view is seen as common sense by the subordinate group. A short form for hegemony is "that which goes without saying." We tend not to question the things we do in our daily lives.

Studying feminist theory exposed all of this to me. As a man, I learned that I cannot know what the experiences of women are. My job is not to understand women's experiences of being oppressed, but rather, the ways in which men act as oppressors. I had to examine the practices in my own life that granted me status and privilege as a male. I recognized this as a step toward reworking the structure in my ancestral house, but the task still seemed prohibitive. Why was it so difficult to look at the practices in my own life? The instructor of the feminist theory course I was taking responded in this way: "Perhaps it is because these everyday practices are so naturalized that they are made to seem so normal" (Lewis, personal communication, 1990).

In terms of inheriting the house, I recognized that in my own exploration of male power and privilege, I needed to deal with some of the easier, more manageable tasks first, as they made sense for me, before I could get at the structure.

I have learned a great deal. I have learned that I have a great deal to learn. I have experienced a whole series of feelings, thoughts, and reactions, which include confusion, guilt, resentment, defensiveness, anger, bitterness, and a distinct lack of comfort. I have also learned that many, if not most, of these reactions are not necessarily helpful in gaining better understandings. The course instructor commented,

> You're right—feeling sorry and feeling bad are not very helpful and I encourage people not to indulge themselves. What is helpful is trying to understand what's going on and more to the point, why. This may be quite disquieting and discomforting. Hopefully it will also make us think, question, face ourselves, transform.

I recognized the wisdom in these words, I intellectually acknowledged them as correct, but they were not my own. I was just beginning my own struggle to make sense of them from my own experience.

Many new impressions were formed through my reading and discussions of feminist literature, all of which addressed the myriad of forms in which women are oppressed in a male-dominated patriarchy. I was greatly affected by what I was reading and hearing. Some of it was familiar, much of it was not. I received this new information partly disbelieving, partly denying, and partly embarrassed. This initial exposure, however, was from a theoretical perspective. I was learning a great deal, but I had not established my own personal filing system with which to organize my understanding. My frustration resulted not just from the violations to women that I was discovering, but from my own inability to do something with this new information in my life. How to engage? How to make it my own? I knew that my house needed work, but I didn't know where to start.

CROSSING THE STREET: THE JOURNEY BEGINS

A significant change in my thinking occurred one day in a class discussion centred around a scenario involving a man walking behind a lone woman on the street. The discussion of this scenario revolved around the issue of whether or not a man should cross the street in order to alleviate the fears a woman might be experiencing as a result of being followed. Initially, I was angry at the thought of having to cross the street in order to alleviate the fear a woman might have of being attacked or raped by me. I felt that I was admitting some kind of guilt—as though I might be mistaken for someone who would rape. I also felt that in crossing the street, I was acknowledging that all men, including myself, are bad. In fact, I resented being grouped with all men. After some discussion, however, I came to the realization that I have a choice in the matter. This is my male privilege. I will not rape, but I could. A woman does not have this choice. I do not have to live with the fear that the possibility of rape generates, although I occasionally experience a general fear for my safety (being mugged, for example). A woman, however, may experience a deeper fear every day of her existence. My understanding of this allows me the opportunity to cross the street and show a silent form of solidarity. It's a concrete way of beginning to change my thinking and my behaviour.

It also becomes a way to dissolve some of the male pride, and the power, that fuels the above notions of admitting that I might be a bad guy or a rapist. In essence, it becomes a willingness to experience a sense of isolation because I am trying to understand the fear that a woman experiences by understanding my role as a member of the oppressor group.

ONE STEP FORWARD, TWO STEPS BACK

I now recognize the evolution of my understanding as steps along the metaphoric journey which involves crossing the street. The first step was to acknowledge that a major change or shift in my acting and in my thinking was needed. The second step was to recognize male power and privilege as the problem that needed to be addressed. The third step was to examine my own practices and privileges as a male. The fourth step was to put my new understandings into action for change. The fifth step was to share my understandings with others. I did not progress through these steps in a smooth, linear progression. I stumbled regularly, and one step forward was often followed by two steps back. An example of this back-and-forth movement and uncertainty was my realization that I could not understand the fear a woman experiences. What I could do was understand the fear that I do not experience. I could then translate this into an understanding of what it means for a man to experience the world without this kind of fear.

It is still a complex thing to try to describe. I had heard the statement that uncovering domination and oppression is uncomfortable for a male but it is painful for a woman. It took a long while to understand that I needed to recognize that pain, although I could never own it. In recognizing it, however, I could begin to look closer at my own discomfort and the isolation that accompanied it. I became extremely conscious of the eye-contact that I made with women as I walked down the street. I hesitated to smile or even give the suggestion of looking at their bodies. I wondered if I was, in fact, missing simple opportunities to be friendly, or possibly even to make acquaintances. I tried to hide my own sexuality.

This recognition is subtle but profound. It has helped me develop a concrete practice from the theory that I have been studying. I can take this practice and, in turn, develop new theories of my own, which in turn influence my practice. In doing so, each example of women's subordination became an example of male dominance or privilege. Readings and discussions, as well as life experiences, took on new meaning as I began to experience this shift in perspective.

It helped me see that crossing the street did not necessarily mean moving farther away from women in order to show solidarity or to stand beside them. It meant "reorganizing the terms by which we come together" (Lewis, personal communication, July 1990). This reorganizing does not take place by simply moving the furniture around in the old house. My own experience demonstrated that cleaning up and moving the furniture was a necessary step in preparing for the major work still required. The major work involves deconstructing before constructing. That is, the old structures must first be taken apart, allowing one to examine and understand how the old structures work, as well as to make room for the new ones.

All of this deconstructing of my experiences and constructing of new theory is part of the process leading to an eventual change or transformation in both thought and action—a paradigm shift. Learning to cross the street provided me with a vehicle for examining the nature of this paradigm shift. This shift in perspective itself causes a change in thinking and in actions, so that the same incident (crossing the street) looks different before and after the shift.

The metaphor of crossing the street helped me to identify these five stages or steps that I have experienced in my first exposure to feminist theory. These include recognizing a need for change, identifying male power and privilege as the structure behind the need for change, determining what this means for my life, implementing change, and eventually, sharing those changes with others. These stages have helped me to deal with the many questions that have arisen and, in turn, to hang them on to an identifiable framework. Consequently, they have been much easier to keep organized as I sort and unpack them. For example, if I am crossing the street, "Where am I coming from?" And in turn, "Where am I going to?" "Why am I crossing the street?" These are questions that I had not really considered asking before this time. Having a sense of them better enabled me to determine how I would get there.

I needed to start with where I was coming from. I am a male—a product of the patriarchy; in fact, a representative of the patriarchy. As a student in a feminist theory class, I brought all of my baggage with me, an accumulation of a lifetime of male upbringing and socialization. I would have liked to think that I could check it at the door, but it all belonged to me. I arrived determined not to represent all males, although I was, in fact, the only one present. I was nervous and apprehensive. I hoped that I could somehow be objective. I have since learned that this in itself is a male characteristic. I see now, through the lens offered by the feminist perspective, that the subjective, or personal, feelings are the issue.

The blatant and tragic violation of women was not in question. It was more of a trapped feeling for me as a male. "Yes, I acknowledge this subordination of women by men, but I'm a man." My first response was to take the information and internally sort it. "I know that happens, but I would never do that kind of thing. I must be different. After all, I'm taking this course, I'm at least showing interest."

In fact, at this point, I very much questioned taking the course. Where was I supposed to stand? It seemed there was no safe place. I did not really want to be a male, with my accompanying patriarchal membership, and it appeared that the women did not want me on their side either. At this point, I was merely entertaining the notion of crossing the street. I had not thought about why I was even choosing to cross—it seemed like a good idea at the time. I liken it to stepping off the curb and finding the road filled with a tangle of traffic, both men and women, moving in different directions. I started to second-guess my decision. It might be safer just to stay on this side. Besides, what lies on the other side? I was looking for a pat on the back from women for even beginning to think this way. My feelings were hurt. I had fallen into what our professor called the "wounded [male] ego pattern."

All of this, however, made me ask myself, "Why did I take the course?" I wanted to learn about feminist theory, of course—to become informed. I was interested in studying it intellectually. I was curious. Initially, I came as a spectator, almost as a novelty. Perhaps I was taking it to further myself and my own understandings in some way. Perhaps I wanted to feel good about myself. Perhaps it was also because I cared.

At first, I was not prepared to think about actually changing. This is what a colleague and friend (Mac Freeman, personal communication, 1989) calls experiencing "river-bank meaning" versus "river-meaning" in life. That is, I stood on the banks, watching the river flow by, attempting to understand something that was moving and changing, while I remained stationary.

I did not initially sign up for the course in order to truly understand the feminist perspective, let alone embody it. This marks the stage in which I wanted to change, but didn't know how to go about it. I thought the thing to do was to avoid my maleness and the associated domination that it represented, and instead sympathize or even empathize with women and their oppression. I felt this way for some time. I was still looking in as a spectator.

In an effort to understand how I was feeling, I went back to an article on men's reactions to feminism by Ned Lyttelton (1987), which I had read at the beginning of the course. It helped me develop an understanding of how men were beginning to organize themselves in response to the feminist position. Lyttelton describes men's reactions to feminist theory as ranging from open hostility, to those who pay lip-service, to those who make some attempt to deal with male privilege as a reality in their lives (Lyttelton, 1987). Reading and re-reading this article convinced me that if I was going to change, I must examine my own practices and privileges as a male. The following statement by Lyttelton (1987) remains as one of the most important influences on my thinking:

Unless an analysis of masculinity deals specifically with male power and privilege as its basis and starting point, it is likely to be more or less subtly anti-feminist. It will ignore or implicitly deny the basic tenet of all varieties of feminism, namely, that between women and men there is an imbalance that gives power to men and disempowers women. (p. 472)

He goes on to provide an analysis of some of the men's groups which he categorizes as either "anti-sexist" or "men's liberation." He is particularly scathing of men's liberation groups which he says have formed in an effort to bring men together in support of each other. Specifically, these men come together to re-discover and nurture the many characteristics traditionally thought of as female. These include intuitiveness, cooperativeness, and intimacy, to name a few (Lyttelton, 1987). Lyttelton criticizes this aspect, claiming that their "rhetoric is couched in seemingly pro-feminist terms" (p. 474). He points out that:

. . . men's alienation from ourselves is in reality the price that we pay for male supremacy. In fact being oppressors dehumanizes, but does not oppress us. Men's Liberation seeks to find ways to keep the power and avoid paying the price. In other words, let's ignore the power differences and learn women's stuff, so as to get all the goodies, all the power (1987, p. 474).

Anti-sexist groups are quite different, although Lyttelton is quick to point out the inherent difficulties associated with them. He explains that sexism is the practice of male privilege or the "acting-out of male power" (Lyttelton, 1987, p. 474). Thus, anti-sexism must begin with the recognition of that power and begin to divest the privileges that go along with it (Lyttelton, 1987).

He states that intention is essential. Without it, it becomes easy to recognize male power, enjoy it, fight it, and keep it (Lyttelton, 1987). Lyttelton sums up the process:

The intention unfortunately doesn't guarantee any action or movement, but you certainly can't move anywhere without it. At first the intention wavers, with lots of resistance, a little movement—a pattern any feminist who has pushed a man on sexism knows only too well. But ideally the practise develops the analysis, and the analysis makes sense of the practise. After repeating our mistakes over and over we learn to recognise them by ourselves and start to change our actions. Where we have always expected and taken access to women's lives and bodies, we become less obtrusive, take up less space. Where we have been used to dominating, taking over, appropriating, we listen. Where we have never had to notice that what we assume to be universal, what we take for granted, is just one reality, we become aware of more realities than our own and feel really guilty for a while. But guilt is a paralysing state that prevents action, and it quickly turns to resentment. So we start again, but from a new place. Instead of withholding access we give women fuller access to our groups, our thinking, our emotions, our lives. We risk making mistakes and being criticised (and we are and will be), but we try not to be defensive or to retreat into a safe place. (1987, p. 475)

There is much for me to learn in these words. In a sense, they offer suggestions for re-building the structure of my house. They also offer advice for those interested in learning how to cross the street. When I first read this article, the words were in the right place, but I had not yet reached my crossing-the-street understanding. It was knowledge, not knowing. Since then, I have started to understand what is on the other side of the street. I have started to think about where I am going. Lyttelton (1987) reminded me I am a product of the patriarchy taking the opportunity to examine my privilege of power, and discover and practice ways to divest it through a new understanding and awareness of a feminist perspective.

DIVESTING POWER

What are those practices and processes that give me advantage? How do I begin to think about divesting power and privilege? How can I best put the house that I inherited in order, before living in it myself or before passing it on to the next male occupant? As Lyttelton pointed out, power cannot be divested without acknowledging it first. Change must then occur through action. Extending the metaphor of crossing the street, it means that men must be committed to changing their street language and their behaviour. This means looking for everyday opportunities to disrupt the norm. Once this process is begun, it brings about other possibilities that might not have been predicted. As Lyttelton (1987) suggests, we must begin by being less obtrusive, taking up less space, listening instead of talking, and by taking over less. It means taking a very close look at our own homes, our relationships, our parenting, and our notion of work. My work as a teacher has been greatly influenced by this view as I have begun placing more emphasis on learning from my students, listening more, being less "teacher-like."

A colleague of mine, a woman who has spent many years teaching and living feminist theory, stresses the importance of making a commitment to divest the power of the everyday practices of our lives. She stated: "There must be a commitment to divestment, and the integrity of that commitment will determine how well it works" (B. MacDonald, personal communication, 1990). She also discussed the need for authenticity in this process. How others interpret our divestment practices is critical. They must be genuine and real, and perceived as such by others.

There is always the possibility that other men, and possibly other women, will view me as weak—not a man. I must keep in mind, however, that I am beginning the process of changing what people consider normal—and what it means to be a man. A change in my behaviour has the potential to precipitate a whole series of changes in others. This can be threatening—for me and for those with whom I teach, and learn, and work, and play. The true work is in developing a practice, crafting a lifestyle. This certainly must involve sharing my new perspective with others.

HELPING OTHERS LEARN TO CROSS THE STREET

This brings me to the issue of sharing my new understandings and helping others learn how to cross the street. I make the distinction between helping someone learn how to cross the street, and helping someone across the street.

As a man, I must begin to develop ways to demonstrate to other men the process through which I am working. Men, of course, have a choice as to whether they will acknowledge and embrace this new paradigm or will simply adhere to the status quo of a male-dominated society. One would have to ask, "Why would men want to change?" There appears to be little incentive to do so. For the most part, men have their cake and the ability to eat it where and when they choose. In fact, a large part of men's initial work is in recognizing a choice even exists. There is much to explore through issues surrounding the benefits that might exist for men who choose to divest their power and privilege. Another world of possibilities exists through partnership, between men and men, and men and women.

The task that confronts us together, as men and women, is to deconstruct the patriarchy and replace it with a better system. As a male, I now face the prospects of challenging the dominant norms by dialoguing and working with both men and women. I feel that my impact can be extremely significant in both cases. I have seen and experienced the negative and often adverse reactions men have as women describe how it feels to be oppressed. There tends to be resistance, no matter how clear the facts are. There are, in my mind, then, many potential benefits to men initiating social change. It certainly would appear less threatening to fragile male pride, to be educated and helped along by another understanding male. Similarly, it is an interesting phenomenon to consider males sharing their personal insights, stories, and understandings of feminist theory with females who have not been exposed to it.

As in any teaching situation, the context within which this sharing takes place is all-important. The emphasis must be on a sharing of stories and personal experiences, as opposed to an indoctrination with facts. The timing must be right, and attention must be paid to both the apparent willingness of the recipients to learn, and their openness to change. During the past year, I have been involved in teaching and learning situations where narrative methods have been used to examine curriculum, where curriculum is defined as a set of life experiences (Connelly & Clandinin, 1988). The life experiences of both learner and teacher are honoured, as they mutually carve out their own ways of knowing.

Just as in thinking about repairing the old house, a certain amount of risk must be taken. It may not always be possible or practical to wait for all circumstances to be right. The situation will dictate what must be done. There is much to gain, less to lose.

RE-EXAMINING THE INHERITANCE

Most people would be excited at the thought of inheriting a beautiful old house. It's not until you take a much closer look, that you begin to uncover the hidden costs. It is still possible to ignore them or pretend that they are not there once you discover them. A coat of paint here—some wallpaper there—rearrange the furniture to hide the flaws. All of these actions can postpone the major work and help one avoid getting at the real problems. It is my belief that men have much to gain by risking the initial discomfort of uncovering the hidden costs. It is worth the work required to look beyond the wallpaper and the furniture in order to examine the structure of our houses and our lives.

Once we begin to do so, things can never be the same. Once begun, the structural work required is not as daunting as it seems initially. It just appeared that way as I thought about renovating the house in one great sweep. Building a structure or foundation is not something done in order to get it out of the way, as though it were an inconvenience preventing one from getting on with other work. The structure influences everything else that follows and determines how the rest of the work will be done. Male power and privilege create the structure that underlies my life. They are a part of everything I do. The way I go about working on my house is what is critical. It is the most important thing that I can do—the only way that I can begin to create change—slowly and deliberately.

I must start where I live. In fact, the street on which I learn to cross is the quiet street in my own familiar neighbourhood. This shift in perspective that I am experiencing means that my house, my street, the neighbours, may never look the same again. My neighbourhood is no longer quite so familiar.

22

Sharing Lesbian, Gay, and Bisexual Life Experiences Face to Face

Mary McClintock

I FIRST EXPERIENCED A PANEL PRESENTATION ON LESBIAN AND GAY ISSUES WHEN I was a college student in the mid-seventies. Members of the campus Lesbian Alliance spoke to dorm groups as part of an effort to improve the climate for lesbians at the women's college I attended. It was both scary and exciting to sit in the dorm living room with other women from my dorm and discuss our concerns, as lesbians, heterosexuals, and women who did not want to define their sexual orientation. By the end of the evening, I felt proud to be a lesbian and part of the organization that sponsored the discussion, and relieved that it was possible to talk about myself with other women in the dorm. The dialogue that occurred helped set a context for discussing everyone's concerns, whatever their sexual orientation. Fifteen years later, my experience of hearing a speakers' panel when I was in college was echoed by a student in one of the classes I teach. He said, "Listening to the panel made me feel proud to be a gay man. It was the first time I realized that I could feel good about myself and stand up to the harassment I'm facing in the dorm."

Currently, I am a member of Face to Face, a gay, lesbian, and bisexual speakers' bureau based in Amherst, Massachusetts. We speak to a wide range of groups, including classes in elementary schools through colleges, social service organizations, and religious organizations. We have spoken at several Association for Experiential Education (AEE) Northeast Regional Conferences. Similar speakers' bureaus exist in Boston, San Francisco, and at many colleges. Speakers volunteer for a number of reasons. I am a member of a speakers' bureau because talking to people about being a lesbian feels like one small thing I can do to make the world a better place for lesbians. I do not want other lesbians to face the discrimination and pain that I have experienced.

This article explores the importance, rationale, process, and effective use of lesbian, gay, and bisexual speakers' panels as an educational tool. Why should experiential educators be familiar with and use these panels? Lesbian, gay, and bisexual people are everywhere, including learning and working as students and staff members of experiential education programs. Homophobia (the fear and hatred of lesbians, gays, and bisexuals) is also everywhere. Like other forms of oppression, homophobia works on many levels, including interpersonal and institutional levels. As students and staff of experiential education programs, we are subjected to jokes and comments about lesbians and gays, harassment, and institutional policies that discriminate against us. All of this serves to hinder our ability to learn as students or work effectively as staff members.

My own experience bears this out. As a staff member of an organization that provided therapeutic wilderness programs for adolescents, I experienced harassment from students with whom I worked and the potential of losing my job if anyone found out I was a lesbian. Prior to my starting work in the program, a gay man on the staff told other staff that he was gay. Right after he disclosed his sexual orientation, the Board of Directors of the organization met and removed "sexual orientation" from the non-discrimination clause in the personnel policy. They decided that they wanted to reserve the right to discriminate against lesbians and gays in hiring. When I learned of this policy, the message to me was clear: being open about being a lesbian could cost me my job. In that job and others where I could not be open about being a lesbian, I found that I was less able to be effective in my work. Hiding something as basic as the identity of my life partner took a tremendous emotional and mental toll. Being emotionally shut down meant that I was less available to my students and my co-workers. I had similar experiences as a student in experiential education programs.

As experiential educators, we spend a great deal of time and energy working to make sure that our students can get the full benefit of our educational programs and that staff can perform their jobs. However, if we do not work to eradicate homophobia and other forms of oppression in our programs, we are essentially saying that it is acceptable for some of our students and co-workers to not receive all that we have to offer and, potentially, to be hurt by our program. I believe that it is essential for all experiential education programs to work on improving their ability to be a setting where lesbians, gays, and bisexuals can be fully affirmed as students and staff members. These beliefs have been echoed by AEE members who have been panelists and participants at lesbian, gay, and bisexual speakers' panels at AEE Regional Conferences.

Speakers' panels are one of the most powerful methods available for educating people about lesbian, gay, and bisexual issues. What exactly is a lesbian, gay, and bisexual speakers' panel? Although the format varies depending on the context of the panel, the basic format consists of an introduction to the panel; each panelist speaking briefly about his/her life as a lesbian, gay, or bisexual person; and a time for questions, answers, and dialogue. On the surface, this design sounds quite simple, and frankly, not very experiential or profound. However, I can say honestly that profound experiential education does occur at every panel.

After many years of being a panelist and using panels in the courses I teach on social justice issues, I have begun to examine the question: What makes this form of social justice education so successful? I have come up with a number of possible reasons. First, homophobia is both similar to and different from other social justice issues. An understanding of homophobia's uniqueness with respect to other forms of oppression sheds some light on the power of lesbian, gay, and bisexual speakers' panels. A second key factor in the success of these panels is that they are designed and facilitated in a manner that attends to the emotional safety of both the panelists and the participants. Finally, speakers' panels are grounded in basic principles of adult and experiential learning theory. These principles include an understanding of the importance of personal experience to adult learners and the use of processing discussions to complete the experiential learning cycle. These are all key issues in the success of this form of social justice education.

HOMOPHOBIA IN RELATION TO OTHER FORMS OF OPPRESSION

One of the main ways that homophobia works is through silence and lack of information. From a very young age, many of us are taught not to talk about "that kind of people." For many, the only context in which they hear about lesbians, gays, and bisexuals is whispered jokes and stereotypes or shouted taunts. For most people, there is virtually no accurate information available about lesbians, gays, and bisexuals. Two comments by college students who experienced panel presentations in their classes attest to the lack of accurate information available. A woman in her sixties commented, "Thank you for coming to talk to our class. I never met a lesbian before. I need to think more about this. You are not what I expected a lesbian to be like." A twenty-year-old man said, "I used to think fags were all really sick . . . , but being in this class and hearing the panel made me realize that maybe the stuff people say about gays is like the stuff people say about Jews like me . . . maybe it's all lies."

Panels about lesbian, gay, and bisexual issues have similarities to and differences from other forums where members of oppressed social groups speak about their lives. Some other oppressed groups, such as women, Jews, and people of color, have been more visible than lesbians, gays, and bisexuals. Lesbians, gays, and bisexuals are often invisible because many of us do not reveal our identities. Because men of color and all women are more visible, they are more likely to be put in an educator role: to be asked questions about the "women's point of view" or the "African-

American's point of view," etc. Many members of oppressed social groups, especially women and people of color, are tired of being educators and do not want to be in this role. Lesbians, gays, and bisexuals are less likely to have been put in this educator role because of our relative invisibility and because heterosexual people have not been clamoring for education about our lives. While forums of speakers on other social justice issues can be powerful, lesbian, gay, and bisexual speakers' panels are particularly powerful because of these contextual differences.

My experience as a woman and as a lesbian illustrates these differences. I do not feel compelled to speak on panels about my experience of being a woman. There are many opportunities to talk to other people in daily conversations about the issues that concern me. A growing number of written and media materials address women's issues. Many times other people have assumed that I would be an educator or speak about women's issues because they know I am a woman. On some occasions, the educator role has been all but forced on me. In contrast, as a lesbian, I choose to speak on panels for a number of reasons. Speaking up is a self-empowering act in a world that continually tells me I should hide and be ashamed of who I am. I speak about my experience of being a lesbian in a homophobic world because it is one way that I can break the silence about our lives. Unless I make a point of saying that I am a lesbian and bringing up lesbian issues, I do not have conversations with people about lesbian issues. Prior to my having taken on a more visible role as a lesbian educator, other people did not assume that I would fulfill this role. Recognizing the difference in my experience as a woman and as a lesbian has helped me understand that educational strategies should not be uniformly used to address all social justice issues.

CREATING A SAFE ENVIRONMENT FOR LEARNING

Lesbian, gay, and bisexual speakers' panels are only successful to the degree that they are capable of creating an atmosphere of emotional safety for panelists and participants. This safety is a crucial condition for everyone to feel able to speak honestly about their experiences and beliefs. A number of design elements and facilitation strategies are used to create a safe atmosphere. One element that contributes to a safe atmosphere is the use of panel members who are not members of the group or students in the class. This serves the dual purpose of not putting pressure on members of the group/class to be "out" (i.e., open/public) as lesbians, gays, or bisexuals, and of allowing students/group members to choose to share their experiences if they wish, but not to force them to take on an "educator" role. It is also crucial that speakers, whether they are outside speakers or speakers from within the group, are speaking voluntarily, that they are not pressured into speaking.

All lesbian, gay, and bisexual speakers' panels should have as part of their format the setting of guidelines for how the panel and participants interact with each other. Commonly used guidelines include the following:

- everyone agrees to maintain confidentiality about what is said during the session;

- everyone acknowledges that because there is a general lack of information about the lives of lesbians, gays, and bisexuals, there is no such thing as a "stupid" question; panelists may choose not to answer a particular question, but participants should ask;

- panelists speak from their own experiences and do not represent all lesbians, gays, and bisexuals, acknowledging that there is a great diversity in lesbians, gays, and bisexuals;

- participants are requested to speak from their own experience, using "I" statements rather than we, they, you, etc. For example, saying "I, as a student in this school, have experienced . . . " rather than "the students in this school believe . . ." .

Guidelines are presented as part of the introduction to the panel. The guideline of confidentiality is especially important for many speakers and participants. Some speakers only share their first names and ask that the names of panelists not be revealed because they fear that if their sexual orientations were widely known, they could lose their jobs or their children. Discussing these real concerns often helps participants understand the kind of discrimination we face.

Having a method for participants to ask questions anonymously greatly enhances the sense of emotional safety, and often, allows for a broader range of questions. One way to do this is to pass out index cards at the beginning of the session and have participants write questions on the cards after panelists finish their initial speaking. All participants are asked to either write a question, or write "I do not have a question" on their cards. The cards can then be collected and responded to by the panelists. It is important that everyone write something or it will be clear who is writing, and the process will not be anonymous. Methods such as guidelines and anonymous questions create a setting that allows panelists and participants to feel safe enough to share their own experiences and hear the experiences of others.

ADULT LEARNING THEORY

Adult learning theory helps to explain the success of lesbian, gay, and bisexual speakers' panels. This form of social justice education is particularly appropriate for adult learners. A characteristic common to most adult learners is that they bring a great deal of personal experience to a learning situation. It is common for adult learners to relate their own experiences in a learning setting and to frame new learning in the context of how these experiences can be applied to future situations. Malcolm Knowles, in his book *The Modern Practice of Adult Education* (1980), points out that "adults define themselves largely by their experience" (p. 50). Recognizing this centrality of personal experience, Knowles (p. 50) concludes that adults "are themselves a rich resource for learning" and "have a richer foundation of experience to which to relate new experiences" (and new learnings tend to take on meaning as we are able to relate them to our past experience). Adult learners in particular can benefit from lesbian, gay, and bisexual speakers' panels because they emphasize the sharing of life experiences and facilitate applying the understanding gained to future situations.

SPEAKERS' PANELS AND EXPERIENTIAL LEARNING THEORY

In many ways, speakers' panels on lesbian, gay, and bisexual issues are not unlike many other forms of experiential education. The core of experiential education is the experiential learning cycle: having an experience, reflecting on the experience, analyzing the experience, and then using that analysis to generalize learnings to future situations. Lesbian, gay, and bisexual speakers' panels provide this type of learning experience for the panelists and for the participants. Although the "experience" varies for panelists and participants, for both it can be an experience that defies social norms. One way in which panels differ from activity-centered experiential education and from panels related to other topics is that they draw primarily upon the life experiences of the panelists and, often, the participants. Sharing life experiences is a valid tool in experiential education related to social justice issues. To paraphrase the feminist saying, "the personal is educational." The individual life experiences of members of oppressed social groups are the reality of social injustice. If reality is not one fixed measurable phenomenon external to people, but is something socially constructed by people, then the telling of life experiences and learning from each others' experience is a way to move from a unjust present reality to a just future reality.

For panelists, the act of articulating life experiences, speaking out loud about one's life, and breaking the silence surrounding lesbian, gay, and bisexual issues is an experience that defies our pervasive invisibility. For participants, meeting lesbians, gays, and bisexuals, hearing them speak about their real life experiences, and entering into dialogue with panelists allows participants to replace whispered stereotypes with complex human reality. For both panelists and participants, spending time together talking about a subject that is normally taboo is in itself a profound emotional and intellectual experience.

As contexts for panels vary, so do the means in which the experiential learning cycle is completed. In some settings, course instructors or the panelists lead the group through a more formal processing discussion of the experience. As an instructor of a college course on social justice issues, I have facilitated discussions directly following panels. In these discussions, I ask students to reflect on messages they received in the past about lesbians, gays, and bisexuals and relate those messages to what they have just heard from the panel. I also ask them to consider how the experiences related by the panelists fit into the larger context of social justice issues. We discuss how this experience will affect their future interactions with lesbians, gays, and bisexuals.

Not all settings lend themselves to prolonged, formal processing discussions. In settings where the participants are all part of an organization or group, some processing can be built into the question-and-answer period. For example, as a panelist in a presentation to a social service agency, I have asked participants how they previously addressed gay, lesbian, and bisexual issues and individuals in their agency, and how they will change based on what they have heard from panelists. In open forum presentations to groups of unrelated individuals, little formal processing occurs. Panelists weave into their presentations the notion of examining past beliefs and using the experience of hearing the panel to inform their understanding of lesbians, gays, and bisexuals. In this way, panelists model learning from experience rather than directly facilitating such learning.

In addition to the processing discussions facilitated by or demonstrated by panelists or instructors, a great deal of informal processing occurs in discussions among participants and panelists after the presentation. The format and safe atmosphere created by the panelists provides the groundwork for individual participants to continue learning from the experience in the future through conversations with colleagues, friends, and family.

All of the above components are key to the success of lesbian, gay, and bisexual speakers' panels. However, above and beyond these components, there is one factor I would emphasize. Crucial to the success of panels is the personal element. Spending an hour or two eye to eye with someone who is a real, live, complex human being goes a long way toward breaking down the myths and stereotypes of lesbians, gays, and bisexuals as sick, unhappy, or perverted people. I often ask participants to think about me, the other panelists, the laughs we have shared, and the serious things we have discussed the next time someone says something hurtful about lesbians, gays, and bisexuals. For heterosexual people, speakers' panels put a human face to an "issue" that for many has been clouded in secrecy. For lesbians, gays, and bisexuals in the audience, panels provide more positive images of how we can live our lives. For everyone, they foster learning and understanding because they are truly "face to face."

23

In Our Own Words: Service Learning in Native Communities

McClellan Hall

One of the things that has interested me over the years in terms of Native education is that what you call Service Learning, is how Native people transmitted knowledge and culture in their own communities. (Roger Buffalohead, remarks during the First Annual National Conference on Service Learning, 1991)

THIS QUOTE IS ONE OF MANY THAT HAVE COME TO OUR ATTENTION IN RECENT years and captures the spirit of the National Indian Youth Leadership Project (NIYLP) in its efforts to initiate and promote active, thoughtful, authentic service in Native communities. Over the past twelve years, we have discovered numerous examples of how service learning has been practiced in Native cultures and have identified several terms that describe the process in Native languages.

As a Cherokee, I am most familiar with the concept of *gadugi*, a traditional practice based on interdependency and recoprocity among clans and families. A call for *gadugi* results in people coming together, much in the same way as the early pioneers in the American West came together to raise a barn or help a family in need. The *gadugi* tradition has been the blueprint for the service component of the NIYLP.

Back in 1980, when the ideas for the NIYLP model were germinating in Cherokee country, one of the best examples of contemporary *gadugi* was the project corrodinated by Wilma Mankiller in the small Cherokee community of Bell, Oklahoma. In those days, Wilma was Director of Community Development, while I was Director of Stilwell Academy, the Cherokee Nation alternative high school. Wilma, myself, and other Cherokee Nation staff may not have been aware of the roots or the approaches of the "Service Movement," as it is now called, but we had our own models. While this project contained all of the elements recently described by Eliot Wigginton (1986) in the project-planning process used by his Foxfire classes, it was organically Cherokee.

A thorough assessment in the Cherokee language was the starting point for the Bell project. Consistent with the traditional approach, the assessment looked closely at, and placed great value in, the strengths and skills already present in the community as the foundation upon which this project was to be built. Through a consensus-building process, it became clear that people in Bell really wanted running water in their homes and were willing to work to make it a reality. In spite of many warnings that the project would not succeed, the residents of Bell did their share and more. The community came back together around the *gadugi* concept. Rather than asking the government to do the project *for the people*, this project was done *by the people*.

The experience of the NIYLP with Native communities across the United States and Canada has identified several other terms in Native languages that describe the service ethic. In the Keres language, spoken by the people of Acoma, Laguna, and Zia pueblos, the term *si-yuu-dze* translates to "everybody's work" and refers to communal service, where people get together to clean the irrigation ditches in the spring, plant corn, clean the plazas for ceremonies, etc. In the Zuni language, the term *yanse'Lihanna* has a similar meaning.

These concepts can be traced to the original teachings, passed on through oral tradition for thousands of years, in Native as well as in other cultures throughout the world. In the Cherokee tradition, it is taught that the Creator made the different races of people and sent them to different parts of the world with specific instructions and responsibilities. The Native people of the North American continent were entrusted to be caretakers of this place. The songs and prayers used in Cherokee ceremonies, for example, acknowledge the other races of people by name and emphasize our relationship to each other. With the five hundredth anniversary of our reunion on this continent, it is clear that most of those who came from Europe didn't recognize the Native people here as relatives. Many of the early missionaries did not realize that our ancestors were providing a valuable spiritual service. Prayers for the benefit of the entire creation would seem to be a common ground that people of all cultures could support.

The importance of service in the reclamation of the continent cannot be overstated. It represents a place to start, a way to empower people, especially young people, to regain control of our communities, on our own terms—in our own words.

We are all learning more about the power and nature of dependent relationships from the extensive body of knowledge on co-dependency in our society. It is clear that dependent relationships exist, not only in classrooms where students are not encouraged to think for themselves, but rather to wait for the teacher to provide the "answer," but they also exist on a community level. As the result of generations of paternalistic government policy, many contemporary Native people have somehow lost their focus on the true significance of what is reserved in our treaties. As proud, independent people, it is difficult to imagine that our ancestors intended treaty language to be a prescription for a lifestyle of dependency.

The NIYLP uses an approach that focuses on "habilitation" of both young people and communities. This term is simply defined as a process of becoming capable, not through self-centered individualism, but through interdependency. To accomplish this, we promote three levels of service: traditional/community-generated service, program-generated service, and student-generated service.

Traditional/Community-Generated Service

These would be the *gadugi*-type projects that were described earlier. In addition, we include activities where the community or individuals come together to recognize, through ceremony and celebration, the rites of passage that young people traditionally go through in the process of reaching adulthood successfully. Recently, the NIYLP has been involved in reviving these recognition events where they are no longer practiced. In the Navajo tradition, for example, the puberty ceremony for females is still commonplace. Unfortunately, the ceremony for boys has nearly been forgotten. In the spring of 1992, we brought several 12- to 14-year-old boys together near Sweetwater, Arizona, for the initial phase of the ritual. A medicine man who remembers the procedure took the boys through a sweat lodge and began the instruction in the roles and responsibilities of manhood. We want to provide what our young people need to help them take their places as productive members of their communities.

Program-Generated Service

Through examining a spectrum of issues all the way from the local to the global levels (i.e., environmental concerns), and building consensus on priorities, we have initiated the following activities:

- Establishing a state- and tribally-sanctioned search and rescue program made up of high school aged youth from Zuni Pueblo.

- Developing an integrated unit at Twin Buttes High School (Zuni) which focuses on issues involved with the recent Zuni land claims settlement. Students are studying erosion and its impact on their reservation, and are creating a "before and after" slide show based on ideas for improvement projects that students will plan, conduct, and evaluate.

- Working on restoration of a 250-year-old church at Picuris Pueblo. The community is rebuilding the church with all volunteer labor. We provided a crew of sixty youth and adults and made one thousand adobe bricks by hand. We still hold the record for most adobes made in one day.

- Painting the tribal office buildings, including the governor's office at Jemez Pueblo.

- Working with the National Park Service, cleaning and preserving Anasazi ruins, and providing trail maintenance and erosion control.

- Adopting several miles of highway on the Acoma Pueblo for which Acoma students are cleaning and caring.

- Developing the "Buddy Works" program at Acoma Pueblo, where seventh- and eighth-graders adopt kindergarten buddies and provide reading and tutoring service. The older students prepare lesson plans and make materials.

STUDENT-GENERATED SERVICE

Several examples of student-generated projects are:

- Students participated in a field-based Navajo history unit in Canyon DeChelley on the Navajo reservation where they learned about the destruction of Navajo homes and food supplies at the hands of Kit Carson and the United States Army in the 1860s. One student was so moved by the presentation that he suggested that we could begin to do our part by planting new peach trees all over the canyon. Although this project was originally somewhat symbolic, we did plant the peach trees and have continued to do so since 1989.

- Zuni high school students decided they wanted to spend quality time with senior citizens. They are now painting murals on the walls of the new seniors' center, and they are involved in intergenerational cultural exchanges, where both groups take turns doing the teaching and learning.

- Junior high students in Taos, New Mexico, were recently recognized by their tribe for helping with a Pow Wow and raising money for local runners.

SERVICE AS AN ENTRY POINT

In the early 1980s, as director of the Stilwell Academy, I often visited Crosslin Smith, a religious leader of the Keetoowah Cherokees, a traditional group that still practices the traditional religion. In one conversation, as I was sharing my frustrations and concerns, Crosslin talked about how, long ago, Cherokee spiritual leaders fasted and went to a sacred place, performing the necessary rituals to see into the future. "We already know these things will happen," he warned, "we have seen it coming," referring to the difficult times young people are facing. Although he never prescribed what could or should be done, I took this as a challenge to see what difference I could make.

Judging by the newspaper headlines, drop-out rates, and reports about gang activity in Native communities, we're now living in the times that the Cherokee elders saw when they looked into the future many generations ago. The negative opportunities for our youth often seem to outnumber the positive, and young people are trading away their culture for something far less valuable.

As Native people, I've always felt that we have a responsibility to give something back. As parents, teachers, coaches, and mentors, we have an exciting opportunity to provide the most valuable service of all, that of simply providing a positive example. Changes need to be made in Native communities; there are some extremely destructive cycles that need to be interrupted by positive, caring individuals. Service can provide an entry point to bring those young people who have been alienated back into the circle. There are exciting new programs waiting to be developed, based on a template that has been available to us all along. We can start anywhere. Let's begin by taking a look at our communities, not to identify problems, but to find the strengths on which we can build. Let's look for those things that need to be done and for those who can do them. Let's not overlook those whose greatest need is to do something that will be recognized and appreciated by others. We can start this process from a traditional values base that has been with us for as long as anyone can remember. Service can represent an act of faith—both in our communities and in our young people.

As Bernie Bearskin said in Studs Terkel's book *Division Street America*:

I think perhaps that my early training in the home impressed me with the philosophy of our forebears. It was taught to us that if one could be of service to the people, this is one of the greatest honors there is.

Section V

Theory and Practice

24

What is Experiential Education?

Steve Chapman, Pam McPhee, and Bill Proudman

INTRODUCTION

HOW MANY TIMES HAVE I BEEN ASKED THE "WHAT IS EXPERIENTIAL EDUCA-tion?" question by a person unfamiliar with the field, only to find myself looking at my feet in a paralyzed state before finally coming up with some sort of circuitous answer which inevitably starts with the comment that experiential education is not easy to define in a few words. Yes, there are whole books written on the topic, but the questioner is not typically looking for a book, just a straightforward answer. As editor of the *Journal*, I would often like to say, "Here, just take a look at this brief article." But when has there been an article in the *Journal* which deals with this? I have to go all the way back to a 1981 essay by Laura Joplin, entitled "On Defining Experiential Education" (Vol. 4, No. 1, pp. 17-20). I find it hard to believe that nothing has changed in over a decade—are experiential educators avoiding basic definitional questions? I wonder; I have not seen a direct attempt to address this topic come across my editor's desk in five years.

Who should be writing this sort of essay? My answer is "each and every experiential educator." But that is not practical for the *Journal*. So where does one start? Surely not with those who use lots of long and hard-to-follow academic words; they would likely confuse my naive questioner. If things have changed, maybe one should search beyond familiar authors who have written at length? Yet it seems it should be people with a good deal of experience in the field, and people who are reflective of what they are doing and why—at least this seems a sensible start if one is asking that the subtleties of the definitional question be dealt with in a short space. Moreover, it seems highly unlikely, given the history, that just one answer could or would ever satisfy everyone.

This sort of reasoning led Karen Warren, the publications representative on the AEE board, and me to approach a number of people with the request to tackle this question—experienced and reflective practitioners who have not written on the topic previously. We were not asking for ultimate answers, but just a willingness to take on the challenge of re-opening the question with their personal thoughts and feelings. The following three essays comprise the initial response. There are many other perspectives, but hopefully these efforts will provide some valuable ideas and re-open the debate. The field cannot afford to avoid this issue if it is to evolve and develop in relation to the rapid social and educational changes that confront us all.

WHAT IS THE QUESTION?

Steve Chapman

People sometimes ask me for a definition of "experiential education." One would think that, as the director of a department of that name and a practitioner for about fifteen years, I should be able to answer those questions easily. The truth is, I can't. It isn't really that I don't know. I'm just not always sure what people are asking. Rather than try to define experiential education, I will just reflect on my own experience. My background is in school programs, but perhaps my experience in that arena can also shed light elsewhere. Several commonly asked questions help frame my thoughts.

"Oh, experiential education! That's ropes courses, right?" Experiential education cannot be understood simply as a particular set of activities. Yes, outdoor adventures, new games, and ropes courses all are linked to "experiential education" in the minds of many people. Yet as valuable as backpacking, rock climbing, canoe trips, and ropes courses are, they comprise only a small part of the potential arena. Cross-cultural homestays, community service projects, urban adventure programs, work-study programs, internships, cooperative education approaches in the classroom—all these (along with much more) provide great opportunities for students to become directly and enthusiastically engaged in real learning.

"What is it your students learn out there?" Sometimes people want a definition of experiential education to be presented in terms of content, just as science, history, and math usually are. Actually, experiential approaches are better understood in terms of style, and any topic can be explored using such techniques. Whatever is being studied, the point is to place students into a different, more direct relationship with the material. Students are actively engaged—exploring things for themselves—rather than being told answers to questions. Although practitioners

often cite their particular favorite outcomes (i.e., development of self-confidence), experiential approaches are not restricted to a specific set of goals or domains.

"Students need to be active rather than passive. Is that what you mean?" That depends on what you mean by active. Typical field trips seldom represent what I am talking about. When students are asked to absorb seemingly irrelevant information while walking through a zoo, their senses may become just as dulled as if they were completing classroom worksheets. Active mode refers to how the students' minds are used, not their legs. I can as easily run a bogus program in the woods as I can in the classroom, carefully explaining the workings of the world to everyone around me.

The adventure aspect of activities is not necessarily the focus. One issue for me is precisely the degree to which many people currently do equate experiential education with various high-adrenalin, high-challenge, highly physical ventures. Perhaps the role of adventure programs—Outward Bound and the like—in the most recent surge of the experiential education movement accounts for this confusion. Group initiative problems, wilderness programs, rock climbing, and ropes courses are especially fun and motivating. But if used thoughtlessly, they become mere diversions—fun, but educationally pointless.

"I've heard experiential education deals with material that is more 'real.' Is that the key?" Well, it comes closer than defining it by content or by the mere presence of adrenalin. But what does "real" mean in this context? Surely simulations are not out of bounds just because they are fake. It is the question under consideration that must be real; students must perceive it to be relevant, and the activity must provide a worthy vehicle for approaching the issue.

The truth of a metaphor is not measured literally, after all. Getting a group over a specially constructed "challenge wall" is a common and effective initiative problem, but how many of us must actually help someone over a fifteen-foot plywood wall on our way to work each morning? Similarly, a mock trial can be a great example of an experiential approach, though the question may be about a fictional circumstance (i.e., "Is Jack, in the novel *Lord of the Flies*, guilty of murder?").

"If experiential education is supposed to be student-centered, what is the role of the teacher?" The description that works best for me is "providing minimum necessary structure." In other words, the teacher's role is to give just enough assistance for students to be successful, but no more. If the teacher carries out the role properly, students will accomplish more than they ever could on their own. Yet if the approach is truly student-centered, they may not be aware the teacher had a role at all.

Another critical role for the teacher is to help students make connections. I think most of us would agree that students must eventually understand the point of an experience for it to be educative, and that point seldom emerges fully developed on its own. Some argue that the teacher's primary role is to guide an effective "debriefing" discussion (Kjol & Weber, 1990). Getting full value from even the best metaphors requires closure, and that takes a good guide.

Others suggest that the leader's principal function is to create the experience in the first place. With some combination of insight, skill, and input from the group, the best facilitators can create experiences so analogous to real-life situations that the key points are bound to emerge from within the group's discussion (Gass, 1991). But whether through actively leading a good closing discussion, or by crafting a group's activities so carefully in the first place that the group will naturally process them well, the role of the leader in helping students make connections is essential.

Finally, a fundamental role of the teacher is to be intentional—to have an objective and then to teach toward it. Ropes courses, new games, and tent-camping are just tools, like lectures and textbooks; they do not themselves represent the goal. I like to compare the teaching process to setting a trap. The ultimate goal is to create a situation from which "springs" some revelation—some meaningful insight—for the students. A thoughtful, intentional approach allows the teacher to recognize and develop many seemingly unrelated elements of a course or experience.

For me, the art of teaching has much to do with the ability to develop many disparate pieces of experience—to bring them into place while resisting the temptation to make the points for students. Only when many elements are put together can the trap be sprung. Then all the pieces suddenly fall into place and students have important insights—they suddenly "get it." The teacher must understand the point of activities in these terms in order to set a good trap, and must intentionally teach toward that climactic moment.

"Are there particular arenas in which experiential techniques are especially effective?" Though my own schooling suggested otherwise, my adult life has shown that there are many right ways to do most things. Solutions to problems are right if they work. Of course, they are better if they are more efficient or more elegant or otherwise more satisfactory, but there are multiple ways to be right. I believe this principle should lie at the heart of experiential education.

In terms of achieving particular outcomes, I think experiential techniques are especially effective when trying to address community issues. For example, mainstream schooling offers plenty of practice in competition, and until recently, the more cooperative approaches have been largely ignored. If I want to encourage an understanding of the power of cooperation, I must have my students do more than discuss it. They must experience it—feel it. For many of my students, the experience of what real community feels like has been more important than their experience of adventure or personal accomplishment.

An example comes to mind. A ninth-grade boy was struggling with muscular dystrophy, yet wanted very much to join his peers on the five-day backpacking trip that serves as our upper school's orientation program. He did so, but walked with such an unusual gait that the leader asked him quite often if she could check his feet for blisters. The extra attention embarrassed him, but a peer suggested that every time this student took off his shoes and socks to check, they all should do the same. It was an important moment. I imagine that for this student, his personal accomplishment reigns supreme. But for another in the group, that spontaneous act of understanding and compassion represented the most significant event of the trip.

"So . . . . What is experiential education?" It is an approach which has students actively engaged in exploring questions they find relevant and meaningful, and has them trusting that feeling, as well as thinking, can lead to knowledge. Teachers are cast as coaches and are largely removed from their roles as interpreters of reality, purveyors of truth, mediators between students and the world. They are asked to believe that students can draw valid and meaningful conclusions from their own experiences. Learning in this way ultimately proves more meaningful than just relying on other people's conclusions about others' lives.

ASKING THE QUESTION

Pam McPhee

Of all things that might be true about experiential education the one thing that is unassailably true is that you can't find out by defining it.

John Huie

Having started with this disclaimer, let me follow with descriptive events, experiences that eventually led me on a personal quest—"What is experiential education and what is the use of defining it anyway?"

I have often wondered, How could I spend an average of five hours a day for 180 days in front of the same teacher and not remember who he or she was? So maybe elementary school was a while ago. How about the fact that the average college course and minimum studying time consist of 126 hours and I can not even list the courses I had in college. Contrast this with the fact that I can remember many of the different influences that the Greeks and Romans had on modern day architecture—thanks to a trip with Janny Campbell to New York City to photograph the buildings (two trips to be exact because we forgot to put film in the camera the first time). Or that in fourth grade, I understood what propaganda was by bringing in empty cereal boxes from the breakfast table. Now don't get me wrong, I do not want to equate memory with learning. However, I do want to stress the impact of "direct first-hand learning opportunities" (Dewey, 1938).

If you have not read *Experience and Education* by John Dewey (1938), do it. It won't give you many answers but it sure will start you thinking about what constitutes an "educational" experience. And that is the point. If we do not ask ourselves the question, "What is experiential education?", we are in peril of being "technicians implementing techniques rather than educators who teach through the understanding of their trade" (Peters, 1970). The definition is not the answer; rather, it is the asking of the question that encourages learning. It is important to see knowledge not only in a consumptive manner, i.e., "If I learn this, how will it help me get the things I want," but also in terms of the intrinsic appreciation of knowing:

> And we know that of all the issues in education, the issue of relevance is the phoniest. If life were as predictable and small as the talkers of politics would have it, then the relevance would be a consideration. But life is large and surprising and mysterious, and we don't know what we need to know . . . . A student should know that he [sic] needs to learn everything he can, and he should suppose he needs to know more than he can learn. (Wendall Berry)

The risk of defining experiential education is that once done, the definition is available for those to regurgitate it at will—a written sentence copied and lost between the yellowing pages of one's notebook. The value is the asking of the question, the ever-elusive attempt to understand, not solely to be better learners and educators, but for the excellence that is intrinsic to it.

Experiential Education as Emotionally Engaged Learning

Bill Proudman

I believe that experiential education, as promoted by the Association for Experiential Education (AEE), is at an exciting crossroads. We must choose between refining our craft as a unique teaching and learning *process* that is applicable in many learning environments, and defining experiential education as simply a set of activities (usually active and taking place outdoors). My purpose in this essay is to argue for the process-oriented path. It is time to shift our educational paradigm to be more inclusive of multiple cultures and perspectives. One place to start is in examining what experiential education is not.

Experiential education is not simply "learning by doing." Living could be described as learning by doing. Often, this is not education, but simply a routinized, prescribed pattern of social conditioning that teaches us to stay in pre-determined boxes for fear of being labeled as outside of the norm.

I have grown tired of listening to professionals describe their "experiential stuff" in terms of what their students are doing, which usually means doing something outdoors with an emphasis on physical, adventurous activity. Experiential education is not simply a matter of replacing flag football in the physical education curriculum with a ropes course. The introduction of a tool such as a ropes course does not guarantee that the learning will be experiential. I have seen good educators make flag football more "experiential" than a ropes course.

Good experiential learning combines direct experience that is meaningful to the student with guided reflection and analysis. It is a challenging, active, student-centered process that impels students toward opportunities for taking initiative, responsibility, and decision making. An experiential approach allows numerous opportunities for the student to connect the head with the body, heart, spirit, and soul. Whatever the activity, it is the learning and teaching *process* that defines whether a learning experience is experiential. Further, an experiential learning process can be conducted almost anywhere and with any type of activity or learning medium.

Experiential education engages the learner emotionally. Students are so immersed in the learning that they are often uninterested in separating themselves from the learning experience. It is real and they are a part of it. Rather than describing experiential learning as "hands-on" learning (an insensitive and offensive term connoting that one must have hands to learn experientially), maybe we should think of experiential education as emotionally engaged learning.

Experiential Education as a Set of Relationships

The experiential process can best be described as a series of critical relationships: the learner to self, the learner to teacher, and the learner to the learning environment. All three relationships are important and are present to varying degrees during the learning experience. These relationships are two-way and highly dynamic.

Learner to Self: This relationship involves the learner making sense out of the experience. The learner controls this outcome and is ultimately responsible for the learning and growth that takes place. The learner processes new experiences, information, and values within a personal and holistic framework. The opportunity for guided and structured reflection is a valuable element of the experiential learning process. Examples of this learner-to-self relationship in action include activities such as structured journaling and small-group processing that specifically ask the student to engage in self-reflection and introspection.

Learner to Teacher: This relationship is a crucial one, both because of the learner-teacher interaction and because the teacher is responsible for designing and creating the parameters within which the learners will interact with their learning environment. The teacher's role is to define the boundaries to ensure a safe learning environment (physically, emotionally, intellectually) within which a student can become totally immersed. The teacher's role is to provide opportunities for the student to make sense of their experiences and to fit them into their ever-changing views of self and the world. It is an atmosphere where mistakes are expected as part of the learning process.

As Keith King (a former AEE Practitioner of the Year) has often said, "The teacher is responsible to, rather than for, their students." The teacher's primary role is that of problem poser, mediator, and coach.

For example, I once designed and led a student-planned, eighth-grade class trip where the students worked with one another throughout the course of the school year to decide where the five-day trip would go and what it would involve. I first articulated a series of planning guidelines, consisting of elements such as mandatory activity components (e.g., need to incorporate service, physical adventure); budget guidelines; and a planning schedule outlining steps and issues to be decided. Over the school year, small subcommittees worked on and reported back to the class about the trip. The class worked within this framework of guidelines and were accountable for the various deadlines prescribed within the planning outline. The planning process itself became as meaningful and significant a learning experience as the trip. Once the trip guidelines were articulated to the students, I simply acted as a mediator and coach.

Learner to Learning Environment: The learning environment is a broad concept that includes the content material being covered, the people and their relationships directly and indirectly involved with the learner, and the surrounding physical environment. Each context looks very different, depending on who the learner is. This relationship involves multiple layers, all interacting in differing ways and intensities with the learner. It is obvious that different learners have different learning experiences. Take, for instance, the varying reactions students have to the same learning environment.

During a recent urban exploration, a group of Euro-American adult students, who were doing a neighborhood investigation in a predominantly African-American section of the city, were invited into a church where they experienced a cultural celebration that was different from their own. The students reacted differently to the environment, partly as a result of their own social conditioning and their perceived stereotypes previously developed about that culture. It led to interesting follow-up discussions amongst the students that allowed their differing perceptions to re-question their cultural stereotypes and attitudes, as well as resulting in powerful discussions on American racism.

Too often teachers are so focused on the activity (and their own learning experiences as a student in that activity) that they blindly assume their students will have similar experiences. Besides being myopic, it also is a culturally biased perspective that negates other cultural and personal interpretations. As experiential educators involved with process, we need to be ever aware of how our own cultural conditioning colors our interpretations of others' learning experiences.

Experiential Education as Methodology

Simple participation in a prescribed set of learning experiences does not make something experiential. The experiential methodology is not linear, cyclical, or even patterned. It is a series of working principles, all of which are equally important and must be present to varying degrees at some time during experiential learning. These principles are required no matter what activity the student is engaged in or where the learning takes place.

1. *Mixture of Content and Process*: Often, experiential educators are considered to be too process-oriented at the expense of content and/or theory. We need a conscious mixing of content and process. Theory is the critical glue that holds powerful learning experiences together. Edward Demming, the management guru who transformed Japanese corporations, once said that experience was meaningless without theory.

2. *Absence of Excessive Teacher Judgment*: If the teacher truly believes in the experiential process, the teacher will create the safe working boundaries for students and then get out of the way. Responsibility cannot be nurtured in the learner if the teacher creates or expects the learner to learn for the teacher's (or someone else's) sake. While this does not mean that students get whatever they want, I am advocating that within the teacher-defined boundaries, students should have full run of the premises.

   Each person is a product of his or her cultural environment. Each person is conditioned over time to react in certain ways to given situations. It is critical that teachers recognize the effects of their conditioning in order to allow students to have their own experiences minus teacher judgment.

   As an example, I have experienced teachers excitedly telling students exactly where to place their hands and feet while on a climbing wall, under the guise of helping the student succeed and "get to the top." But this approach raises several critical questions: Whose experience is it? Whose definition of success is being used? What is the goal of the activity for the student? How invested is the teacher in guaranteeing a certain student outcome? Too often, teachers allow their unconscious conditioning to interfere with opportunities for student self-discovery.

3. *Engaged in Purposeful Endeavors*: There needs to be meaning for the student in the learning. It needs to be personally relevant. The teacher works in the

program design phase to identify opportunities for students to find meaningful interpretations of their experiences. This can be a daunting task for the educator as this means highly personalized instruction. However, the necessary paradigm shift here is to recognize the learner as a self-teacher, or to view a group of learners as providing mentoring and coaching for each other.

A workshop on valuing cultural diversity provides an example of engaging in purposeful endeavors. In this instance, the students are given early opportunities to engage in one-to-one talking/listening dyads as a means to articulate their own personal goals after the workshop parameters are identified (the facilitators' assumptions about the workshop content, the group operating agreements, and the workshop goals). The dyad process gives students an opportunity to assess what they wish to get from the experience in their own terms without critical feedback from the teacher or another student. Dyads give students the opportunity to be listened to, rather than to be questioned or evaluated by others.

4.   *Encouraging the Big Picture Perspective*: Experiential methodology provides opportunities for the students to see and feel their relationships with the broader world. It opens doors to limitless relationships and develops in the students an appreciation, understanding, and involvement with ideas, other people, and environments that can be both similar and different from the students' own experiences. Students need opportunities to better understand and interact with complex systems and environments in order to understand firsthand the interconnectedness of all things and their place in the web.

For example, I recently worked with a group of educators and wanted to have them experience firsthand the ways in which persons who are members of underrepresented segments of American society have to conform silently to the norms of the groups who have received preferential treatment from being on the up side of the power chart. Two volunteers were blindfolded for the duration of a problem-solving activity. The well-intentioned group generally ignored the two and simply "packaged" them for the purposes of completing the problem at hand. The two blindfolded members were not involved with planning, weren't asked to volunteer their ideas and opinions, and, in the words of one of the sightless group members, were made to feel "stupid and worthless."

Following the experience, group members shared their feelings and perceptions. Light bulbs came on for many. The processing resulted in a powerful discussion about the obvious and subtle forms of institutional and internalized oppression around issues of gender, physical ability, sexual orientation, age, ethnicity, and class. It was a transformational moment for many in the group and acted as an invitation for the group to explore many of the personal ramifications of oppression.

5. *Teaching with Multiple Learning Styles*: David Kolb's experiential learning model is a good touchstone here (Kolb, 1976). Experiential learning is not simply the active, doing part. Rather, Kolb's model describes a learning cycle that emphasizes that for a person to learn experientially, a teaching routine must include a cycle of all four learning styles: concrete experience, reflective observation, abstract conceptualization, and active experimentation.

It makes sense that if experiential education professes to address the whole person, then it should teach in a routine that touches all four learning styles. Again, the implication is that experiential learning is not simply a process of adventurous physical activity with some discussion thrown in at the end.

6. *The Role of Reflection*: Piling one experience on top of a previous experience is really no different than the worst childhood nightmares of rote learning in school. The need to mix experience with associated content and guided reflection is critical. The dissonance created in this mixing allows the learner opportunities to bring the theory to life and gain valuable insights about one's self and one's interactions with the world at large.

7. *Creating Emotional Investment*: This element provides one of the major differences that I see between other forms of significant learning and what experiential educators often facilitate. I believe that any experiential learning model which does not recognize the importance of emotional investment diminishes its potential effectiveness for the learner in the long run. The process needs to engage the learner to a point where what is being learned and experienced strikes a critical, central chord within the learner. Learners' motivations to continue are no longer based on what they have to do because someone or something else tells them they must. Rather, they are fully immersed and engaged in *their* learning experience.

The teacher's challenge is to create a physically and emotionally safe environment (in the eyes of the students) so as to encourage emotional investment. There must not be teacher judgment or a dismissal of the learner's feelings. It means creating an environment where people are fully valued and appreciated.

In working with groups, I make a regular practice to verbally remind students that they are in control of deciding how or even if they wish to be involved with the learning experiences. Giving students true power to make meaningful, self-determined choices within a teaching/learning context is extremely important to validating each student as a competent, capable member of a group, and developing a climate of mutual trust, respect, and regard for each person.

Often, as a facilitator, I have to introduce and model this concept in a number of ways because individuals' conditioning and experiences have negated their own inner voices. The net effect is that the atmosphere of trust and acceptance allows students the space to determine their own level of emotional investment.

8. *The Re-Examination of Values*: When students feel valued and fully appreciated, there is a greater likelihood that they will re-examine and explore their own values. The creation of a safe environment for students is initiated by the teacher through clearly defined educational parameters—group working agreements, activity learning goals, a big-picture design plan, etc. Creating opportunities for personal transformational growth is a hallmark of meaningful experiential education.

9. *The Presence of Meaningful Relationships*: Learning is not an abstract process. It is fully embraced when it is experienced as a series of relationships—learner to self, learner to teacher, and learner to learning environment. Learning that takes place without reference to relationships is not experiential as it does not allow learners an opportunity to see how they fit into the bigger picture.

10. *Learning Outside of One's Perceived Comfort Zone*: A learner often needs to be challenged in order to be stretched by a new experience. While experiential learning need not start from a place of discomfort, learning is enhanced when students are given the opportunity to operate outside of their own perceived comfort zones. By comfort zone, I am referring not only to the physical environment but also to the social environment (i.e., being accountable for one's actions and owning the consequences).

In Summary

Experiential education is transformational. A well-conceived and well-led experiential learning endeavor does not just happen to the student. Meaningful education is not something that can be easily packaged. While society tempts many educators to market a cookbook approach, I believe that experiential educators, like all good educators, are artists using a palette of tools and abilities that are ever expanding and changing. As artists, it is dangerous to ever become complacent about how we define and perform our work.

Experiential educators need to continue to grapple with the questions of just what is experiential education and, similarly, what is good teaching. Let's continue to push the edges of our emerging profession. Let's also recognize that if we truly subscribe to the idea of lifelong learning, then our understanding and definition of experiential education will also change and expand.

I am reminded of the simple phrase, "The best way to learn something is to teach it." Here's to all of our students who have given us, as teachers, the gift of continued learning. May our journeys continue to be enriched.

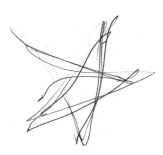

25

The Student-Directed Classroom: A Model for Teaching Experiential Education Theory

Karen Warren

HOW CAN WE TEACH A THEORY OF WHAT WE PRACTICE? HOW CAN WE COME down off the ropes course, return from interviewing Aunt Arie, or put away our New Games props, and sit down in the classroom to learn experiential education philosophy? How can discussions about Dewey's ideas, lesson plans, Summerhill, moral development, ethics of teaching, motivation, and a host of other questions grounded in the basic foundations of experiential education come alive in a classroom setting? How can we give future teachers a sound theoretical framework to use in teaching experientially? The answer, of course, is experientially.

THE MODEL

The student-directed classroom is the method I have used to introduce the theory of experiential education to college students, many of whom want to use experiential learning in their future teaching careers. This model has been in existence for five years at Hampshire College. It takes place within four walls, sandwiched in a two-hour time-block twice a week in a busy college schedule.

The experience in this model is the students' active creation of the class itself. Students determine the syllabus, prioritize topic areas, regulate class members' commitment, facilitate actual class sessions, undertake individual or group-inspired projects, and engage in ongoing evaluation. Because it is different from traditional educational theory courses which attempt to convey a body of knowledge that the teacher or the institution deems important, the student-defined curriculum promotes a shift from giving an education to, in the words of Adrienne Rich, "claiming an education."

In the student-directed classroom, the question often posed by the back-to-basics naysayers is "Will students choose to learn what they are 'supposed' to learn in such a class?" I find it fascinating that during the five years of the Philosophy of Experiential Education course, an appreciable body of key concepts and questions has always been addressed.

Consistently, students want to learn what experiential education is all about and search through its historical and philosophical roots to arrive at a definition. They look at current developments in the theory by studying more recent program models: expedition education, cultural journalism, and various therapeutic, adventure, and alternative programs. Students are generally interested in the social issues which inundate educational theory. Issues such as oppression, multicultural perspectives, ethical and moral dilemmas, diversity, and social change all have become important subject matter. Teaching methodology and applications of experiential education are also primary topics. Finally, most students are curious about their own place within the experiential education movement and philosophy—how their own education and learning style can benefit from such an approach. In essence, they are striving to achieve a sense of themselves in an often vast and impersonal educational process.

So while the doubters question the magnitude and appropriateness of the content, the students have successfully devised a class experience rich in both content and process. An added benefit is that students are able to address the continuing questions that often override the content. Questions such as, "What is learning?" and "What are the goals of education?" which pervade and color all classes, can be explored in this format.

POWER IN THE MODEL

The goal in the student-directed model is to empower rather than to hold power over. Therefore, the elimination of authority, the chief power dynamic in a teacher-directed situation, is a primary technique. This does not mean teachers withdraw from power by denouncing their authority. If a teacher abdicates power without transferring it to students, confusion results, the class lacks leadership and direction, and a miseducative void is created. Instead, the teacher needs to use the respect and position they enjoy at the onset of the class to promote student empowerment.

To foster this shift in the locus of power, the teacher introduces students to the tools of empowerment in the beginning class stages. (These tools are shown in the diagrams and explained later in the article.) Concurrently, the students accrue power as their initial promise of academic freedom becomes realized. The teacher relinquishes authoritarian influence and becomes an integral member of the evolving group.

After the students have attained self-determination, intervention by the teacher acting as a leader rather than a group member occurs only in situations when the group lacks the skills to deal with obstacles they encounter. For example, a student-led class meeting on the philosophical basis of experiential education was hopelessly jumbled one semester. I perceived the need for further focusing and for discussion leadership skills and offered these to the class for future use.

There are situations where the students want to give power back to the teacher. The teacher then must decide whether they are giving power back legitimately. Do they need help with process tools, direction setting, or just a morale boost? Or do they in fact have the problem-solving capabilities but have declined responsibility by relying on the traditional power structure? The following sections on teacher role, student role, and evaluation will make it more clear how this power transformation is achieved.

TEACHER'S ROLE

The teacher's role in the student-directed classroom is challenging in its subtlety. I sometimes feel as if I'm tiptoeing the line between intervention and stepping back. As most experiential educators can affirm, it's an intuitive guess at times whether to: 1) actively facilitate the process either to maximize learning or to keep it from becoming miseducative, or 2) let the students' struggle with the experience serve as the didactic lesson. I have identified several components of the teacher's role in this model that may make this easier.

Informed Consent

Students need to know what they are getting into so they can make responsible choices. They make initial decisions based on a sketch the teacher provides of the student-directed classroom. A precise course description and detailed introduction to both the potentials and perplexities of the class are methods to provide this information.

Establishing a Concrete Vision

I remember my first exposure to an open classroom in junior high. The teacher pushed back the desks, promised us we were about to embark on an exciting educational journey, and told us we could do anything we wanted. As thrilled as I was by the prospects, I was totally lost as to how or where to proceed. My classmates must have had similar trials because after a couple of weeks, this grand experiment fizzled, the desks were returned to rows, and we got down to the business of being taught English.

The lesson I took from that early exposure to a student-directed classroom was that students who are a product of a traditionally teacher-directed system need some assistance in making that exhilarating but unfamiliar jump to self-determination. The teacher's role, then, is to provide some initial structure and focusing.

In this model, the initial structure is the framework on which students can build their self-direction. The teacher conveys a concrete vision of the class by suggesting the course goals and what the students might expect from such an endeavor. The task of creating the curriculum then becomes the concrete focus. The teacher also facilitates the first several weeks of class to give direction and to set a model for future facilitation. Creative, well organized class sessions set a standard for students to follow when they undertake their own facilitations.

Ground Rule Setting

In the introductory stages, the teacher sets the basic operating principles by both statement and example. These ground rules are the safety net which allows students to take risks to involve themselves in the frightening but compelling class maelstrom. Some ground rules stressed are: use of "I statements" to express feelings, active listening, commitment, use of inclusive language, constructive feedback, and intolerance of oppression.

Process Tools

Since interdependence reigns in this collective effort, students need the appropriate group skills to accomplish their goal of self-determination. The teacher is responsible for imparting the following process tools:

1) Skills in thinking as a group. In order to come up with what they want to learn, students are introduced to brainstorming and prioritizing strategies, and quickly find these to be of use in synthesizing their syllabus.

2) Decision-making skills. Consensus decision making is explained and tested out. Practicing with smaller decisions at first, the group builds proficiency in the empowerment stage and is able to orchestrate very complex decisions in the self-determination stage.

3) Leadership roles. Since a group needs leadership rather than set leaders to function effectively, the teacher points out available leadership roles. Impelled by the situation, students actively take on the various roles of timekeeper, feelings articulator, group collective conscience, minority opinion advocate, question framer, summarizer, focuser, and gate keeper.

Teacher's Role in the Student-Directed Classroom

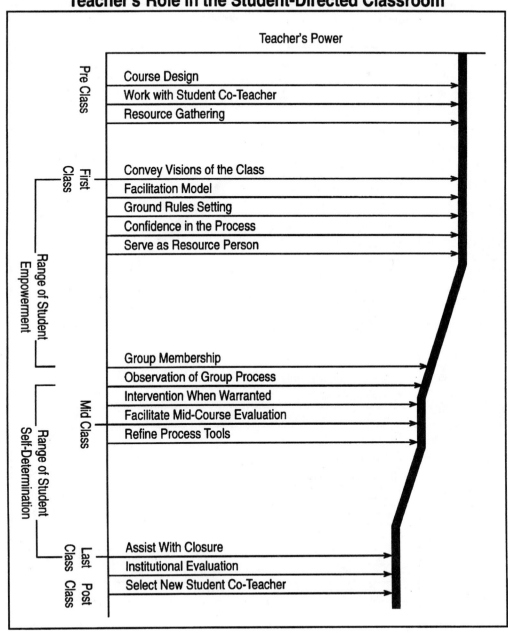

Student's Role in the Student-Directed Classroom

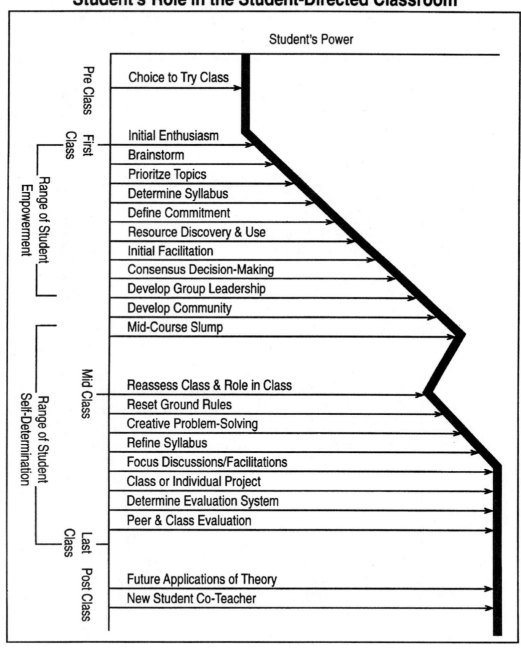

4) Problem-solving skills. Through a series of simple initiative problems, the group is equipped with the tools as well as the belief that they can creatively solve problems together.

5) Feedback and debriefing skills. Because debriefing is critical to experiential education, the teacher's job is to ensure it happens. Insisting on quality feedback time early in the course sets an expectation for continuation during the latter sessions.

Resource Person

After the students have brainstormed what they want to learn, the teacher becomes the resource for readings, speakers, films, and programs. By having a ready repertoire of provocative resources, the teacher can influence the quality of the course content.

This sequence of events often occurs. During the first few classes, students finalize an ordered list of topics for each class session. I then attach readings and other resource ideas to each subject. These ideas are presented to the group for acceptance and rearranging. Usually the give-and-take of resource selection helps refine the topics even further. Finally, the student facilitators have the option of adding to or changing the resources for their sessions.

Confidence in the Process

The importance of the teacher as cheerleader can not be underestimated in this model. As students are learning that self-regulation can work, they often need someone to point out that the struggles are an important part of growth toward success. In this regard, the teacher can reframe the conflict in a positive light, have faith in the students, and exude a contagious delight with the process.

Closure Assistance

Termination can be a difficult time. The teacher assists in this stage by helping the students understand what they have accomplished. It's time to marvel at results. As they articulate their growth, students can better internalize what self-determination has taught them about experiential education theory. They can also postulate future applications of the theories learned. Asking for written and verbal self-evaluations and encouraging a closure celebration are ways the teacher can support the transition.

STUDENT ROLE

The student role in this model is best elucidated by example.

Facilitation

The refinement of teaching skills resulting from the opportunity to facilitate are of great benefit to future experiential educators. Student-led class sessions are often a forum for innovation that illuminates experiential education theory far better than lectures or discussions.

For example, one year the class co-facilitators recreated the atmosphere of a traditional teacher-directed classroom with all its subtle nuances of authority. They dressed up in their best teacher clothes and put on an aura of professional aloofness to set the stage. We arrived at the classroom to find our usual circular seminar seating arranged in proper rows with assigned seats for all. Class started with a quiz on that day's reading, "A Process Guide to Teaching." Having focused on the ideas of teaching effectively outlined in the article, we had neglected to memorize the character names in each vignette which were the basis of our quiz questions. Even before we exchanged papers to be graded, we knew we were failures. Our only avenue was rebellion from the authority so perfectly play-acted before us. Spitballs flew and chaos reigned while our teachers finished their lengthy lecture on John Dewey. The lessons of student powerlessness in an authority-centered class were firmly entrenched by the enacted experience.

Develop an Effective Group

There is a noticeable increase in group efficiency as time passes in the course. As students risk more of themselves over time, discussions gain depth, facilitations find a focus, and the content becomes more compelling.

Project

Class or individual projects support an in-depth look at a particular aspect of experiential education theory. Individual projects have included experiential education applications to such topics as: cognitive learning, education in China, environmental ethics, women in the wilderness, the creative arts, and wit as a sign of gifted intelligence.

Some years the class decides to do a collective project. On one such occasion, an educational consortium was set up to create a school. After an over-arching philosophy was determined, students worked in teams to establish different experiential education programs for the school. One team visited a junior high classroom to gather background resources. Another labored on lesson plans which would address the needs of disenfranchised kids. The project culminated with each team producing a comprehensive brochure of their program in the school.

Reassessments

The group finds itself reworking many class components as they learn from their experiences with self-regulation. They refine the syllabus—"If we want to see how experiential education theory works in practice, let's *go* to an alterative school." They focus discussion—non-productive tangents are more quickly identified and avoided. They reset ground rules. For example, the group typically has set time aside to redefine their commitment to the course. Collectively they determined what, specifically, being prepared for the class meant, agreed they wanted to start and end class on time, and verbally announced to their peers what their level of commitment was. Their expectations of each other were much more exacting than anything I would ever attempt to have a class follow.

Student Co-Teacher

Every year I enlist a student from a previous class to co-teach the course. Having participated in the struggles of self-direction firsthand the preceding year, the student co-teacher brings an invaluable voice of experience to the new group. Their perspective and credibility as a peer to the new class is yet another way to redistribute power.

EVALUATION

Since evaluation in the traditional school situation is the primary way for the teacher to maintain power over the students, restructuring it in this training model emphasizes that students and teachers share equally in the learning process. It eschews the idea of evaluation as motivation in favor of its use in enhancing learning through immediate feedback.

In the student-directed class, evaluation takes three major forms. Facilitation feedback, where students in charge are critiqued on how they ran the particular class, encompasses the debriefing stage of the popular experiential education models. It allows class members immediate access to ideas on how to structure future teaching attempts.

The second evaluation tool is the mid-course assessment. Invariably there is a mid-semester slump when other commitments, conflicts within the class, and lethargy arise. The mid-course evaluation is the device to get things back on track. Directed by the teacher, it's an opportunity to gauge satisfaction and frustrations with the class. We figure out what things we're doing well and what needs fixing. Because we do the repair work at mid-semester instead of waiting until the end, students feel as if they have power to change their immediate educational experience.

The final major form to measure progress is peer evaluation. Class members record observations of other individuals' growth in the class and write evaluations to be used as part of the institutional evaluation.

While I realize that institutional constraints of traditional evaluation sometimes serve as barriers, with some effort student involvement in the evaluation procedure can be creatively incorporated. At Hampshire College, accepted evaluation practice is for the instructor to write a short course synopsis, followed by an evaluation of the student's work in the course. One-year students in the experiential education class decided they wanted to write the course synopsis collectively so it would truly reflect what the class had meant to them. They decided to represent the class diagrammatically—a dramatic departure from the institutionally accepted practice. Speculating on what this would look like in their permanent record and if it would be accepted by the powers that be at the college, there ensued an intense discussion about the goals and purposes of assessment in education and how we can faithfully document experiences as education. This dialogue was far more complex and intriguing than if I had come in that day and said the topic was evaluation of experiential education.

CONCLUSION

To integrate experiential education into the mainstream of American education, it is essential to validate its theoretical base. We must move beyond simply giving teachers-to-be the tricks of the experiential education trade. Additionally, we must challenge these students to discover a comprehensive understanding of the theories behind the techniques. This article has suggested one model to experientially convey the underlying theory to future teachers.

A word of caution is necessary. There is no pat formula for success in the student-directed classroom. As stated in the course catalogue description, "this unique educational collaboration requires that students be willing to struggle through the perplexities and frustrations of the responsibility of creating a refined educational endeavor." Instructors who wish to utilize this model must decide that the students' experience in the process of claiming their education is more important than a perfectly crafted, smooth flowing, predictable class. But after all, isn't taking risks and exploring options precisely what experiential education is all about?

Note

I would like to acknowledge and thank all the students over the years who are the true co-creators of this model.

26

The Design of Intellectual Experience

Donald L. Finkel and Stephen Monk

WHY TEACH?

BENEATH THE CONSCIOUS GOALS AND MOTIVATIONS THAT DRIVE A TEACHER'S daily activities lies a basic human impulse: the desire to share intellectual experiences. Most teachers have felt for themselves the striking pleasure that results from the work of intelligence, whether experienced as insight, beauty, connectedness, or resolution. Ideally, they would like to lead their students to such pleasures; yet the accomplishment of this ideal is rare.

Few teachers adopt the explicit goal of sharing experience, and those who do must be struck by the difficulty of actively pursuing such an aim. This is not the sort of pedagogic goal about which one's colleagues talk. Moreover, what kind of methods could be formulated for achieving such a personal and insubstantial goal? Too easily, the dimension of experience is ignored altogether, leaving teachers with only the products of their disciplines to present. Yet it is the processes that lead to these products which yield the intellectual excitement they wish to share. For students to experience such excitement, the formal systems of knowledge must be undone, so that students can feel what it is like to put those systems together for themselves. Thus, *teachers must learn how to convert academic subject matter into activities for students*. Because it is just these intellectual activities that lead to understanding, the students' gains and the teachers' gratification stem from the same process.

This article will describe a framework for converting formal knowledge into structured activities for students. We shall examine an example and draw from it six principles for designing such activities. This discussion should make concrete the goal of sharing intellectual experience and indicate its benefits to both students and teachers. We must begin, however, by confronting the dilemma which faces any teacher who takes this goal seriously.

THE DILEMMA OF SHARING

Suppose you return home from a trip to Nepal. You are brimming with the excitement of the experience and wish to share it with your friends. Your first inclination is to describe to them in detail all you can about the people, the landscape, and the customs, illustrating your adventures with as many slides as possible. Your first impulse is the *Impulse to Tell*. After several hours of slides and talk, you cannot avoid a conclusion: Since your friends have never experienced anything like Nepalese culture, they cannot possibly get from your description what you feel you are putting into it, or anything like what you got from the trip.

Perhaps it is impossible to tell about important experiences, to give them directly to others. Maybe you should wait until your friends' lives naturally take them to Nepal. Then, when they return, you will finally be able to share the experience. The Impulse to Tell has given way to the *Impulse to Let It Happen*. Following this impulse is not satisfying either, since you may have to wait forever, and you want to share your trip now. Compromises are possible, and you may urge your friends to travel. Yet even if amenable, they will probably experience Nepal quite differently. More likely, however, your urgings will awaken a long buried desire in them for travel up the Nile, and then you will be faced with the inevitable evening of Egyptian slides and monologues.

These two opposing impulses, The Impulse to Tell and the Impulse to Let It Happen, are inherent in the attempt to share experiences, and each has the unfortunate tendency to drive you to an extreme. If you sense you are telling unsuccessfully, you are likely to tell more and more, and to tell it in greater and greater detail. If you withdraw to let something happen, careful to avoid imposing your own experience on others, and nothing happens, then you will withdraw even further to leave a wider arena free for the others' experience. The dilemma of sharing is this: What do you do when you have discovered that neither telling nor refraining from telling is a successful mode of sharing?

Teachers also find themselves caught in this dilemma. In the classroom, the Impulse to Tell leads to lecturing or expository methods of presenting subject matter. The Impulse to Let It Happen is found in various, nondirective teaching modes that have arisen in reaction to exposition. We do not oppose these forms in themselves but rather the results that flow from them. Teachers who seek change by following one of these impulses find themselves either expounding in ever more exquisite detail or refining even further the role of non-leader. Since telling does not provide a genuine experience and letting things happen does not produce the particular experience you had in mind, neither of these impulses leads to the genuine satisfaction that comes from sharing an intellectual experience.

This claim immediately raises two questions. What are *intellectual* experiences and what does it mean to *share* them? Does going to a Beethoven concert with your friend constitute sharing an intellectual experience? What about watching a football game together? Returning to the previous example concerning the trip to Nepal, you cannot be sure that even bringing your friends with you to Nepal would have satisfied your desire to share the experience. To address these questions, we must distinguish between the external events or objects (the musicians, the musical sounds, the football game, the people of Nepal) from what we make of them (our perceptions, ideas, interpretations). These mental constructs are what we *use* to interact with the external events: without them we can have no experience. Thus, events in themselves are neither intellectual nor nonintellectual. These terms refer only to the nature of our interactions with events. Interactions may be characterized as more intellectual to the degree that they may engage and promote the development of more elaborate and comprehensive systems of ideas. Listening to Beethoven can be nonintellectual depending upon *how* one is listening, while watching a football game might be a most intellectual activity if it were part of a comparative analysis of games.

Sharing Intellectual Experiences

The solution to the dilemma lies in the intriguing possibility that a teacher can design an experience which has intellectual consequences for students, the very consequences the teacher wished to share in the first place. Our central thesis is that such pedagogic activity is possible and that teachers can best share intellectual experiences by designing them.

Now, what does it mean to *share* an intellectual experience? Suppose you are listening to a record of a Beethoven quartet with which you are not familiar, and you suddenly become aware of a structural similarity among all of Beethoven's late quartets. Full of excitement, you invite a friend over to hear your new record. You have had an intellectual experience and wish to share it. As you listen to the record together, are you sharing an intellectual experience? It is most unlikely that your friend will make the same discovery you made by just listening to the record. When the record ends, look at your friend expectantly to see if "it happened," and then you recall that for a teacher to merely expose students to archetypal examples is precisely to yield to the Impulse to Let It Happen. It is tempting to think that something fruitful must result from such exposure. After all, how could one read Shakespeare and not be improved by the experience? However, teachers who simply trust in such invisible and delayed effects forgo a sense of direct contribution to their students' understanding. Implicit in the idea of sharing is that we teachers have something valuable to give, not Beethoven or Shakespeare, but ways of thinking about them, ways of understanding and ultimately of interacting with music and words. We would like to give our students the systems of ideas, the perspectives, the concepts that make possible these interactions with music and words. Yet, to adopt such an approach sounds as though we are back to Telling. If only we could collar our students, reach into their heads with a mental hand, and alter their patterns of thought! Once again, we face the dilemma of sharing.

To resolve this dilemma, we must focus on two crucial propositions about these patterns of thought we would like to alter. First, there is no way to interact intellectually with anything in the environment except through such mental patterns. Every student brings some form of conceptual system to new material: the student initially understands the material in the best way he or she can, interpreting it according to his or her present patterns of thought. This proposition is encouraging because it means the teacher is not attempting to get students to elaborate complex theories from nothing. It can also be discouraging, because it means that the teacher must work with students' systems no matter how primitive, fuzzy, or ill-conceived those systems may seem when compared to the system the teacher would like the students to develop. The second proposition is that the structure of the system of ideas which engages with an external event will never match perfectly with the structure of the event. One's own mental system will inevitably influence the way one "sees" the event. At the same time, interaction with the event can influence the system of ideas.

It is possible to influence someone else's patterns of thought by means less direct than a mental hand. *The teacher can design an environment, and activities for students within that environment, which will engage their current conceptual systems in such a way that these systems will be induced to develop.* These activities must aim to create a kind of mismatch between internal structure and external event that leads the student to refine, differentiate, and restructure the conceptual system. This approach to teaching is neither Telling nor Letting It Happen. In designing such experiences for students, the teacher must draw upon personal intellectual experiences, but the students will have their own experiences in working through the activities. No one can directly engineer an experience or guarantee the outcome for another person. However, designing focused activities within a concrete environment makes the chances of converging experiences likely, and such a convergence is as close as we can come to sharing.

We thus propose designing intellectual experiences for students as a means for sharing the pleasures of the mind with them. To design, in this sense, is to structure a specific environment for student interaction in order to promote the restructuring of the students' systems of ideas. We take the goal of conceptual restructuring to be of paramount importance because it is the students' systems of ideas that stay with them and shape their vision of the world. Moreover, it is the act of restructuring such systems which provides the pleasures of intellectual work we assume teachers wish to share with their students.

AN EXAMPLE

The most prominent feature of teacher-designed intellectual experiences, or "workshops" as we call them, is that students work on their own in groups ranging in size from two to seven. The teacher roves from group to group, observing, guiding, questioning, and "teaching," in response to the needs of specific groups or individuals. The students' work is directed by a set of written instructions and questions which we call a "worksheet." Thus, the teacher is present in the students' environment only through the written worksheet and occasional interactions.

The following worksheet is for a college-level workshop in developmental psychology, sociology, or the philosophy of education. The intellectual experience it attempts to share is the understanding that the way one thinks about child development is inextricably linked to one's conception of society. The authors hoped to induce their students to make this connection and to crystallize it by formulating alternative versions of the possible relations between society and the developing child.

There are four parts to the worksheet. As you read them, try to picture a classroom full of students engaged in these activities. Further, try to determine how each part of the worksheet requires a different style of work from the students. Finally, ask yourself these questions: Is the worksheet likely to engage the students' current patterns of thought about development and society? Is it likely to result in a restructuring of the students' ideas on this topic?

ELOISE AND THE PHILOSOPHERS

There are four parts to this workshop. Part I is to be performed in pairs. Parts II and III are to be done in groups of six, formed by combining three of the previous partnerships from Part I. Part IV will be completed with the class together as a whole.

Part I

Eloise is an 11-year-old girl who has decided to keep a diary during her sixth-grade year, which she has just begun. You will find attached the first entry in her new diary, written during the lunch hour of the first day of school. After reading the entry [which appears below, after Part IV], agree on and write down the answers to the following five questions.

1. List the five different activities in which Eloise participated during her morning.

2. For each activity, describe what you think were the teacher's underlying goals (or strategies) in having the children participate in such an activity.

3. Now consider that the school and its teachers are primarily agents of society, and that one of society's tasks is to employ the school to affect children's emotional and intellectual development in such a way that they are prepared to enter society and be useful members. Then each of Eloise's activities can be viewed as meeting society's goals well or badly, but on *two* levels: on the level of *content* (fractions, writing skill, ecology, etc.) and on the level of *form* (the way the activity is organized). Ignoring the content of Eloise's morning, describe how society is affecting her through the form of each of the activities. Why is each activity structured the way it is?

4. Note the basic similarities and differences among the five activities, based upon your responses to Question 3. Overall, do the forms of the different activities tend to be consistent with each other, or inconsistent?

5. What are some different ways to view the possible relationship between the developing child and society? List at least three different relationships.

Part II

Form groups of six by combining three partnerships. Each group should choose a scribe to keep a written record of its results. The group will be given a set of 14 index cards, each with a quotation on it. [See below for example.] These quotes are from philosophers and educators, old and new.

1. Each quote implies a certain relationship between the developing child and society. Sort the quotes into a small number of categories (between 3 and 5) that reflect the differing relationships. Try to agree on the groupings.

2. Formulate and agree upon descriptive labels for each of your categories.

You will probably have to go back and forth between questions 1 and 2, sorting some cards, deciding upon a tentative label, and re-sorting some of the original cards. If you cannot reach agreement, record minority opinions.

Part III

Remain in the same group of six.

1.   Together with your original partner from Part 1, share your answers to Part 1, Question 5, with the group. Compare these answers to the categories your group devised in Part II. Did categorizing the quotes alter your original views significantly? If so, in what ways? Compare the effects of Part II on your views with its impact on other partnerships in your group, and have the scribe record general trends.

2.   Using your current set of categories from Part II, your group should place each of the following systems into the appropriate category:

(a)   Summerhill (as seen in the film last week),

(b)   the school you are now attending,

(c)   the way your parents treated you (in general),

(d)   the way you intend to treat your children,

(e)   today's workshop.

Part IV

The class will reassemble as a whole. We will hear the results of each group's work from the scribes, and then discuss the entire exercise

ELOISE'S DIARY

Dear Diary: It was great to get back to school and see my friends again, especially Susan. Before the bell rang, I told her all about our summer trip to Mexico, and about Manuel, and our trip to the beach together. This year I got Mrs. Morgan. She's okay, but I wanted Mr. Brown. Susan's so lucky she got him! After attendance, the first thing we had to do was write a paper about what we did over summer vacation. Why do teachers always give that dumb assignment? Well, I wrote about Mexico City, and the market place, about all the things you can buy there. Some people read their papers out loud, but I didn't. Then we had math. Mrs. Morgan explained about multiplying and dividing fractions. We had all that stuff last year, but no one seems to remember it. Even Mrs. Morgan made a mistake at one point! Of course, everybody loved that. We learned a little poem, so we know when to flip the fraction upside down, and when not to. (I forgot the poem already! I never was good in math!!) Then we saw a movie about a lake in Africa—like the ones on TV. Mrs. Morgan said for science we are going to learn a new thing called *ecology*. The first thing we had to do was list all the animals we saw using the lake and tell how they used it Then Mrs. Morgan asked us what would happen to all the plants and animals if the hippos got killed and could never bathe in the lake. Richard said there would be a lot of dead hippos around and the whole class laughed. Richard's so dumb! But Mrs. Morgan wouldn't tell us the answer, even after we tried. Then we had gym. I love gym, but Mr. Brown's class creamed us in volleyball. If only I could get those creeps in our class to set up the ball, I'm sure we could win. When we got back, there was a policeman waiting in our room. Everyone was excited for a minute, but it turned out to be a lecture on drugs. He showed us all these pills and needles and stuff and said it was all bad. Borrring! Now it's lunch time. Oh, here comes Susan—see you tonight, Diary.

Sample Quotes

We include the following three quotations to give the reader of this article a flavor of the quotations used. We have chosen three rather extreme cases, but the full group of 14 index cards presents a formidable task of differentiation and categorization.

"Give your scholar no verbal lessons: he should be taught by experience alone; never punish him, for he does not know what it is to do wrong; . . . May I venture at this point to state the greatest, the most important, the most useful rule of education? It is: Do not save time, but lose it."

"Having thus very early set up your Authority, and by the gentler Applications of it, shamed him out of what leads towards any immoral Habit . . . (for I would by no means have chiding used, much less Blows, till Obstinacy and Incorrigibleness make it absolutely necessary) . . . ."

"What is the least that we can say about an organism's development? Everybody admits that two things must be said: First, it develops by getting habits formed; and second, it develops by getting new adaptations which involve the breaking up or modification of habits."

To appreciate the experiential flavor of the workshop, you should now switch gears and actually *do* the problems which make up Part I. Readers usually tend to resist becoming more active in this way, but you will sense the power of this approach only if you overcome this resistance.

PRINCIPLES OF DESIGN

The most striking quality of this worksheet on first reading is its variety. The students work in pairs, groups, and as a whole class. They read the imaginary diary of a sixth-grader and later classify quotes from philosophers. In addition to reading and sorting cards, they must express themselves to classmates, argue for their views, and reflect upon their own experiences. In order to reveal the orderly design within this apparent kaleidoscope of educational activities, we must break down the overriding goal of workshops into a set of interlocking principles. Recall that the teacher's goal is to convert an intellectual product into a sequence of activities for students. The six principles that follow will suggest how such a conversion may be facilitated and will illustrate why the authors of the previous worksheet designed it as they did.

A worksheet must always set forth an environment, and activities for students in that environment, which engage their current conceptual systems in such a way that these systems will be induced to develop. We will first examine the nature of that *environment*, then describe the structure of the *activities*, and finally discuss the resulting role of the *teacher*. Our six principles emerge from the discussion of these three elements of workshops. They are italicized in the text and summarized in a list at the end of this section.

Environment

The student's environment in a workshop has two chief components: an external shared event and the other students in the group. The external event can take many forms; in the above example it was Eloise's diary and then the quotes on index cards. Whatever the form, *the event must be specific, concrete, and present*. These features are required to engage effectively the students' conceptual systems. Any material (texts, data, graphs, journals) with which the students are going to work must be ready at hand in manageable quantities. The material must be sufficiently challenging to engage the students at diverse levels of sophistication, but not so complicated as to overwhelm them.

The group of students working together on a worksheet provides a second aspect of the environment. Students can help one another in a number of ways: They can provide mutual support and a sense of common purpose; their exchanges can promote the externalization and articulation of ideas; finally, the diversity of points of view provides a continuing source of puzzlement and constructive friction. This last feature of group work propels the card-sorting task in *Eloise*, while externalization and clarification of ideas lies behind the use partnerships in Part I, the analysis of the diary. The teacher designing a workshop must think through these issues in advance in order *to exploit consciously the collective potential of the group.* Such devices as requiring agreement, fostering debate, inviting exchange of work, and assigning specialized roles use the group productively. With whatever techniques you use, your instructions must implicitly communicate your trust in your students' capacity as a group and your genuine expectation that together they have the resources to complete the task.

However, simply to place your students on their own in groups to explore a stimulating event is insufficient. Beyond the group and the event, a third aspect of the environment is required. *Specific questions and instructions must be written in advance and given to each student.* These questions and instructions constitute the worksheet itself. Sometimes the activities required will not be clear unless they are written. Even when the instructions could be communicated orally or on the board, it is important to distribute them to each student. With the worksheet at hand, the students can interact directly with the event and each other without the need for the teacher's constant personal mediation. These written questions and instructions embody the teacher's wisdom on the subject, yet in this form, they permit the students to take the initiative.

Activities

A great deal of activity can be generated by placing students in an environment that contains concrete events, other students, and specific written questions about these events. However, student activity in itself is not our goal. We wish to induce intellectual change in order to allow the sharing of intellectual experience. To effect intellectual change, activity must have a particular structure. This structure may be summarized by saying that *every worksheet requires the students to solve a problem.*

The best way to alter someone else's thought is to provide a problem which cannot be solved with his or her present conceptions. This requires a three-phase process. First, the student must be made to see the problem as a genuine problem that is disturbing and requires resolution. Such a problem must be formulated from the student's own view of the phenomenon. Thus, the first phase requires *activities which elicit the student's current mental structures.* People always have common-sense concepts, intuitions, or general rules of thumb for exploring anything new. These are what must be elicited by the first phase of the worksheet, because it is only from these mental constructs that intellectual change can proceed. The problem itself only comes into consciousness as a result of *questions that force upon the student the inadequacy of his or her present conceptions*. This is the worksheet's second phase. It must throw the student into a state of intellectual disequilibrium. Conflict between the students' differing conceptions or between obdurate phenomena and unsophisticated theories must make the student feel the problem in all of its perplexing force, and lead him or her to want to solve it.

It is not enough to perplex students and leave them hanging. Relevant information, guides, questions, and examples must be provided so that the students have a reasonable chance of making new distinctions and tying ideas together in a different way. *Activities which lead to intellectual restructuring* mark the third phase, which should result in the creation of a new mental equilibrium. The teacher must strike a balance between withholding too much information, on the one hand, and giving out a prepackaged solution, on the other. Repeated experience in workshops watching students restructure their ideas will guide most teachers to this balance.

In *Eloise*, the single problem which organizes the activities is this. How can we describe the system of mutual implications between views of child rearing and conceptions of social organization? As a question, this is very abstract and is unlikely to lead to a productive discussion. With this problem serving as a focus, the teacher must ask: What activities or tasks would be most likely to lead students to understand these implications? In this case, the authors decided to use a categorizing task. By articulating different ways in which a view of child development contains a conception of society (or vice versa), students will be forced to make distinctions and ask questions that are new to them. The workshop now has a central activity, one that will constitute the second phase (disequilibrium) of the three-phase structure. Sorting quotes almost inevitably reveals the inadequacy of students' intuitive views about children and society, and may well produce intellectual conflict as the students argue over which cards belong in which piles and why. Indeed, the card sorting is the center of this workshop and will perplex students and challenge their current thinking.

However, to present the student with fourteen wordy quotes with no preparation might well throw them too far off balance. First, they need to have their own ideas about children and society elicited in a more familiar and concrete context. The questions about Eloise's diary fulfill this function. By the end of Part I, the students' own ideas would have been articulated, clarified, and written, so they can face the test of the card sorting.

If the workshop were to end after Part II, the students would have only their own shaky products, the set of categories, which might well seem ad hoc and of little significance. The students now need to use the categories, applying them to phenomena to see if they shed new light. In addition, they need to bring their ideas into the public arena of the class to present them to their peers and teacher. Parts III and IV of *Eloise* address these needs: they supply the resolution and closure to the experience. Certainly a total restructuring of ideas will not occur as a result of *Eloise*, but a first step will be made in the process. After the groups have compared their categories in Part IV, they will try to resolve their differences through synthesis in the ensuing discussion. Their original ideas (e.g., about free children and harsh societies) will have been shaken, and they will be on their way toward a more refined and complex system of ideas.

In all this, it is important to remember that, intellectual or otherwise, *a genuine experience has a style and texture* as well as an organization. Matters of rhythm and timing must not be neglected. Moreover, it is essential that the worksheet not speak to the students in a voice that is didactic or pedantic; it should speak in the author's natural voice. The finished worksheet should bear the teacher's personal stamp, reflecting a sense of play and purpose. *Eloise* requires students to shift activities repeatedly. It does not try to exhaust the meaning contained in any one source: it progresses, allowing for student work in new modes and in new combinations. The authors attempt to write in the style of a sixth-grade girl and provide physical props, the cards with quotes, so that some of the action can be physical. The important point to remember when you are composing a worksheet is that students will actually be doing the things you ask of them, and you must try to envision what it would be like to experience the activities you are designing.

Teacher

In writing a worksheet, you have provided a blueprint for an experience. By working backwards from the products of your discipline to activities for students, you have drawn on some of your most creative and pedagogic impulses. Yet your presence at the workshop itself will still be necessary, both to facilitate the students' interaction with the worksheet and to give you the necessary information upon which to base future worksheets. However, your role will be quite different from that of the conventional teacher. Most teachers are held captive by the need to continually direct and organize the activities of the class. The students' attention is almost always focused on the teacher. He or she is bound in place by the students' conviction that the teacher is the vital link between themselves and the subject matter. This traditional role puts the teacher at the hub of the wheel, the common source of support and cohesion. In contrast, the teacher's role in the workshop may be summarized by the phrase: *The teacher is there, but out of the middle.*

In a workshop, it is the worksheet, and not you, which provides the "carrying energy" for the students' work. They are in direct contact with the material and one another, so that you remain outside of their immediate experience. This is just what you need in order to be free to move around and respond to groups of students in a flexible fashion, tailoring your contribution to the needs of the moment. No matter how exquisitely you have designed your worksheet, some students will become stranded in irrelevant details, while others will skim over all that is interesting. Still other students will approach the problem from a point of view you never imagined. All of these students, and many others as well, will benefit from direct interaction with you. As you engage them, getting them started again, deepening their approach or leading them to a new angle of attack, you will feel the most immediate gratification of the sharing of intellectual experiences.

To summarize, the six principles of design are the following:

Environment:

1. The shared event must be specific, concrete, and present.
2. Specific questions and instructions must be written in advance and given to each student.
3. The teacher should exploit the potential of the group.

Activities

4. The worksheet must have within it an underlying problem to be solved. To make the problem genuine and solvable requires activities which:
    (a) elicit current mental structures;
    (b) point to the inadequacy of present structures;
    (c) lead to intellectual restructuring.
5. The workshop must have the texture of a genuine experience.

Teacher:

6. The teacher is there, but out of the middle.

DIVERSE APPLICATIONS

We cannot convey in this brief article the variety of forms that workshops and worksheets may take. The interested reader should refer to our more complete treatment of the subject[1] where numerous examples are given, as well as more detailed guidelines for designing workshops. To suggest this variety, we present here several examples of workshops written by us and our colleagues. Many of these have been composed in collaboration, because we have found that the most effective method of converting intellectual products into activities is for an expert in the subject to join forces with an intellectually inquisitive but naive partner.

---

[1]Finkel, D. L., and Monk, G. S. (1978) *Contexts for learning: A teacher's guide to the intellectual experience.* Olympia, WA: The Evergreen State College.

1.   *Hot Tips*: An exercise that starts with graphs of the prices of four stocks and moves toward an understanding of rate of change at a point—used in a calculus course for social science majors.

2.   *The Ideal Gas Law*: A reconstruction of the Ideal Gas Law in chemistry, which starts with questions about balloons and pistons, and progressively builds toward an understanding of the regularities stated mathematically in the law—used in an introductory chemistry course.

3.   *Examination of Assumptions*: An exercise in philosophical analysis, based on the extraction of assumptions in a fellow student's written argument, and using several written exchanges between the two partners—used in an introductory philosophy course.

4   *How Children Form Mathematical Concepts*: A set of questions used to help students digest a *Scientific American* article read prior to the workshop and brought with them to class—used in an advanced developmental psychology course

5.   *The Problem of Identity in "A View From the Bridge."* An exercise in applying to the characters in a play a psychological concept previously studied, based on the students re-creation of each character's point of view in a closing monologue—used in an interdisciplinary social science and humanities course.

Workshops can fulfill quite a variety of functions within a course. The following is a partial list:[2]

1.   Have students parallel the work of an author before reading about that work.

2.   Help students gather and organize a wealth of detailed and confusing information.

3.   Articulate an intellectual structure by providing a shift of context.

4.   Give practice translating between languages within a discipline to show the power of a new language.

5.   Help students crystallize their knowledge in preparation for a test.

6.   Let students experience physically something they have studied or will study more abstractly.

---

[2]See Finkel & Monk, *Contexts for learning*, pp. 38-43, for amplification.

CONCLUSION

We began by addressing a question all teachers must eventually face: Why teach? We have ended with a proposal for improving instruction, a response to the question: How can I improve the learning that takes place in my class? We believe that these two questions are inextricably linked. Many teachers are quick to make superficial changes in their courses, employing new curricular packages, new kinds of tests, and new texts, in the hope of improving their students' education. We are proposing an alteration in the very structure of the teacher's experience with students. To suggest such a step would be futile without addressing a teacher's most basic needs and hopes. We focused on the goal of sharing intellectual experiences because we have found in our own collaboration with numerous teachers that it is precisely this consequence of designing and running workshops that is so gratifying and sustaining. Calling for such broad and unspecified goals as "significant educational change" or "faculty development" strikes us as unproductive because such sweeping appeals do not address teachers' immediate desires. Teachers don't want to "develop": they want to have intellectual exchanges with their students in a way that lets them see their students' progressive understanding We have proposed one way of creating such exchanges, one that we believe is a significant educational innovation, and one that does result in development—for students and for teachers, too.

We have listed elsewhere[3] the detailed benefits to students and teachers of this workshop approach. Here we can only summarize by saying that virtually all students with whom we have worked have thrived in workshops. Because their teachers have removed themselves from "the middle," they have been able to apply their own intellectual powers to concrete problems, thus gaining an awareness of and a confidence in their own intelligence. Moreover, because their teacher's expertise has not been withheld, the students have felt neither abandoned nor manipulated. Able to interact with an environment constructed by their teacher and to work together in a collaborative atmosphere with their peers, they have made conceptual advances that have altered their mental landscape.

One of the dramatic consequences for teachers who write worksheets first and run workshops based on them is their strikingly sharper view of the effects of their pedagogical thinking on students. Having completed the intellectual work before the workshop, teachers can then see more clearly the quality of their students' thinking. Such a vantage leads to a ready understanding of how better to design the next workshop. Moreover, in having to work backwards from the intellectual products

---

[3]Finkel & Monk, *Contexts for learning*, pp. 99-108.

of their discipline to the activities that lead to them, teachers find they have to rethink many fundamental questions in their field. Their own intellectual excitement in this process parallels the students' enthusiasm in accomplishing the workshops. And within this interactive cycle occurs the genuine sharing of intellectual experience.

27

When We Want to Empower as Well as Teach

Lorraine Wilson

Getting their group over the "nitro crossing" (group initiative) hadn't been too hard for them. Kristen had trouble lifting her feet when she swung across. And no one could carry the bucket of water over without falling off the rope. But after several attempts, they figured out the problem we'd given them.

Then my co-leader and I shifted things around. "Okay, let's use the same equipment: the ropes, the buckets of water, and the tree. But this time, let's *make up* our own problem to solve.

"Huh?"

An hour later, the seven junior high students had conceived and solved a truly unique initiative problem. It didn't just happen . . . we had trouble getting started. Then Tara remembered something her teacher once explained about "brainstorming." They liked the idea of consensus, so we designed a final problem which incorporated everyone's original ideas. And when it proved to be easier than we wanted, we made it harder. After all, it was our problem.

Before we broke up, I asked the group if they were usually asked to come up with their own problems.

They all agreed. "No."

I've gotten excited all over again about teaching experientially. I always knew it was an effective way to involve the learner; I knew it was fun. But I've also discovered that within experiential education, there is a tremendous potential for *empowering* the learner.

This is important for me because learner empowerment is an essential component of the work I do—teaching early adolescents the skills and attitudes of peacemaking and nonviolence.

My working definition for "empowerment," in relation to peacemaking, is "acting on belief or hope." There are two components to that definition, and both relate to experiential teaching.

The first part is the ACTING. To feel empowered, knowing HOW to act is perhaps not as important as knowing IT IS POSSIBLE TO ACT—though knowing how surely helps us feel we can.

When I began teaching nonviolence, I designed these theory courses to cover the skills I thought were important: conflict resolution, problem solving, communication, etc. I was on the right track, those are the important skills. But my students weren't hooked. It seems that middle school students (fifth-, sixth-, seventh-, and eighth-graders) prefer to actually do something rather than talk about what we might do if something were to happen. And there wasn't much happening in these classes.

Rather than keep fighting that energy, I started working with it. Now I offer opportunities for the students to act. In the doing, they discover what skills are needed; we recognize the ones they already have and make plans to learn the ones we need.

The second part of the definition implies that our actions are derived from our hopes and beliefs. It recognizes that the caring, feeling, responsive part of ourselves has hopes, dreams, and visions. It is this part of our being that impels us to be active.

Stephanie Judson, author of *A Manual on Nonviolence and Children*, believes that children have an innate sense of justice, but since children are so often made to feel powerless, they may not feel capable of acting on that sense.

My objective is to help children develop a sense of their own power to be involved in peacemaking. That means I want them to feel they can respond to their issues and concerns related to their sense of justice or injustice. Just as in other experiential programs where the emphasis may be on leadership or risk taking or problem solving, I am looking for more than the students being able to tell me what these skills are. I want them to actually *see themselves* as peacemakers (as leaders, risk takers, etc.).

An experienced-based approach affirmed the children's desire to "do something," but was it necessarily empowering them to see themselves as peacemakers—to make that transference from the curriculum to their own lives?

Ron Gager, of the Colorado Outward Bound School, wrote an informative paper entitled "Experiential Education: Strengthening the Learning Process." He advocates that the inductive nature of experiential learning (observation following activity) is the "basis for a level of intrinsical motivation and learner-centered responsibility difficult to achieve through traditional methods." But he goes on to caution that "to simply include an experiential component is not enough and to believe that it is simply sets in motion program flaws which will ultimately cause it (exp. ed.) to disappear." His point is that we must fully understand how and why experiential education works, in order for it to live up to its ability to be a powerful educational vehicle.

I am asking a similar question. I knew from my own experience that experiential education had the potential to be a very empowering process. But some programs lived up to that and some didn't. I wanted to identify what the keys were—what elements made the difference.

For the past two years, I concentrated on that question in my work with early adolescents. They taught me a great deal that I will try to compress into this paper.

"Make It Real"

One of the important things to remember for making an experience empowering is to make it as real as possible. Effecting the transfer of skills from the (curricular) experience to the student's life is one of the hardest parts of experiential teaching. It requires our best expertise at processing. In my case, I needed to effect a transfer of attitudes as well. Why not make that transfer easier by already letting the group act on their own issues?

It was the students who told us about this desire for realness. We often used group initiatives/challenge events on a ropes course when the sixth grade went to camp. Instead of just saying, "Get your group across these swinging tires," we would enhance it with a dramatic story: "These tires are hanging over a raging river and you have to get some medicine across to a dying heart patient on the other side."

Some groups totally immersed themselves into the fantasy crisis. They told us how much more compelling it was to feel there was meaning in the game. Some groups did not buy into the fantasy but said that if it *was* real, they would have focused more on the problem and less on who went first. At other times, they told how they wished there was more meaning to the things they did in school. It should be noted that "meaning" was explicitly related to the idea of being needed.

There are two ways to make things more real for the participants. The first is to use real problems or situations. Here are some examples:

The traditional model for Friends Day (a middle school, student conference at Friends Select School, Philadelphia) was to enlist a host of resource people to come in and give workshops for the students. It was a good plan, but last year we committed ourselves to making it more real. Six students planned the event, with our guidance.

Tim Foley, a seventh-grader, proposed a title, "Stop, Look, and Listen to What's Really Going On." Then they surveyed the four grades to determine what their peers wanted to know about. The choices ranged from birth control to prisons, but the majority were in the realm of social problems (the homeless, drug abuse, nuclear war). Those interest groups met once to set their goals. Then on Friends Day, they actually went out to visit places and meet people. The experiences they had that day were with real people with names and stories. They shared from these experiences in a concluding meeting for worship. For some of them it was a risk they took, for some an adventure, for others an inspiration.

Those who work in wilderness programs know the value of using real events as the learning medium. Two of my colleagues ran a summer program, "Select Your Own Adventure," which combined adventure and environmental studies. They sloshed through bogs together, crawled through caves, and orienteered their way out of the New Jersey Pine Barrens. The program was a complete joy for all of them, due greatly to the real experiences they shared.

When the event is real, it's easy for participants to recognize what they have accomplished: "We helped these people at the shelter" or "I was afraid to talk to them but I did it."

"What If It Can't Be Real?"

It's not always possible to use a real event. Sometimes we use simulations or role plays. In those cases, it helps to create a larger context in which to view the event. By this I mean that we relate the particular skills and behaviors needed to accomplish this simulated task with ones that are needed in outside real situations. Sometimes you have to point out the realities within the simulation.

We designed a simulation of the Underground Railroad for sixth-graders (and now used for families!). It consists of a series of small group challenges—physical obstacles, moral dilemmas, unusual problems, encounters with strangers—done at night in the woods. Though a dramatic simulation of a historical event, the challenges facing the group are in themselves real. For instance, they must come up with a way to convince the ferryman to take them across the river or they will never reach the end. They have to ask the doctor for help or one of their members will not be able to continue with them.

Over and over again, the students exclaimed that the Underground Railroad "seemed so real." What did they mean? Granted, our volunteer actors did an excellent job of portraying historical characters, but what they were talking about was the fact that they were challenged to respond to these situations. In a later processing session, they told us that it was so exciting because there was no adult to tell them how to do it. They had to figure it out for themselves. That reminded them of times when they had been caught in an emergency and there was no adult around to tell them what to do. They discovered one "larger context"—and apparently a very empowering one for them.

In this case, there was an even larger context to look at. I didn't create the Underground Railroad so much to teach about the historical event as I did to teach about the skills that are needed to deal with situations of justice and injustice. The Underground Railroad is a recurring event in our history. There are always people who must take extraordinary risks to pursue their dreams for a more just life. But these are rarely extraordinary people; they are people like ourselves. I wanted the students to recognize the strengths and the fears they would have, that these were very much like the strengths and fears real people would have in that situation (though our lives were never really in danger).

I have met several high school students who have actually fled from such countries as Cambodia, Laos, El Salvador, and Guatemala. They were children impelled by a dream.

I wanted my sixth-graders to recognize what they were capable of if they were motivated to reach for it.

In both the real experience and the simulation, the facilitator's role is to help the group identify the skills they used, to give them the names, to make sure to affirm their accomplishments. In the paper's opening scenario, somewhere a teacher must have said, "This is a problem-solving technique known as brainstorming" so Tara could own it and use it again.

We need to say something like "That was a peacemaking skill" or "That was very good use of a leadership skill known as . . . ." Sometimes these acts slip by us unaffirmed. For years, I had trouble seeing myself as being the kind of person who takes charge and makes decisions. Then one week I was setting up my first vacation in the Northwest; it was centered around visiting some friends. At the last minute, the friends pulled out of the plan. But I really wanted to make that trip. So I quickly set up some alternatives. And then it dawned on me that I had acted like someone who makes decisions and handles problems. Maybe I was that kind of person.

Ashley Montague once said that the way you become a loving person is to start acting like one!

The opportunity to see ourselves acting in real situations, and to recognize those behaviors and skills when we're using them can develop our sense of our own empowerment.

GIVE THEM A CHOICE

I remember when I thought I'd reached a plateau in teaching when I could set a goal for the group, design a structured activity to "teach" that lesson, and finally process it all to make sure they got the point. There wasn't anything reprehensible about that, because I chose important skills: cooperation, communication, leadership.

But it wasn't very empowering for the group because *I* was deciding what they needed to learn.

Students caught on and gave me the answers that they thought I wanted to hear. We talked ad infinitum about the need for cooperation, but their voices lacked conviction. They weren't interested in this.

I examined my own learning responses and came up with some observations: 1) I really only (willingly) learn what I want to. As an adult, I have autonomy over most of my learning, but as a child, that was rarely true. 2) There's a lot I want to learn, and I'll work very hard to do so. 3) When it comes to my own behaviors, I know better than anyone else what I need to learn, or at least I know what I'm ready to learn. So maybe the kids were the same as me. Maybe they didn't know how to articulate what they wanted to learn—I think that's a skill—but they'll be pursuing their own goals just the same.

The second issue to remember when working toward empowerment is to provide choices for the participants.

WHAT ARE THEIR GOALS?

One of the most significant ways we can offer choice is in the area of goal setting.

At the beginning of the week-long training on Adventure-Based Counseling with Project Adventure in Hamilton, Massachusetts, we were asked to identify our personal goal for the week, leaders included. That process let us see that not only were we all there for a different professional purpose, but for a different internal purpose as well. The workshop belonged to each of us and we were responsible for our experience. My journal entry from that week read:

> "I think this individual goal setting is a giant step toward making sense out of these activities . . . a leap toward ownership . . . a tool for the group to help each other. I can't wait to try it out."

Providing that space for individuals or groups to set their own goals is one of the most important keys to making the event empowering. It sets into motion that vehicle for "intrinsic motivation" that really lets the experience belong to the learner.

I signed up for this climbing course last spring. Climbing had always been a painful metaphor for me—it represented all my needs to perform well. I often left the rocks in tears, but I kept going back. Not because I wanted to become a class 10 climber, I just wanted to be at ease with myself on the rocks—to bring a more playful spirit to this activity.

For this class, I wanted to relearn the set-up skills and have fun with my friends. After making the first two climbs, the 90%, nine-hour day wore me down and I mentioned that I wasn't going to make the last climb.

The instructor didn't know anything about me. But he was sure that I needed a lecture about pushing myself farther and living up to my potential. He played on the spectre of self-doubt that remained. Was I really afraid?

I made the third climb and he probably felt like he'd accomplished something. But I certainly didn't make it with any spirit of empowerment. Instead, I felt like my own goals had been devalued.

I didn't return for the second class. But I do go climbing with my friends.

INTERPRETING THE GROUP'S THEMES

There's another way to let a group set its own goals, and it's a bit more complex. Sometimes, particularly with children, it isn't so easy a thing to say, "Oh, peacemaking, well here's what's holding us back from doing that; we're stuck, so could you design some activities for us that will let us work through that issue?"

But as we become very skilled observers, we begin to see that that is what they're saying. Whatever issues are important for a group, either as stumbling blocks, concerns, or strengths, will emerge in their experience. That's how we were able to discover how important it was for our students to feel they were needed—by watching and listening to what they were responding to on the ropes course I mentioned earlier.

I encourage you to listen more to your students. When I was taught about developmental stage characteristics for adolescents, they didn't say anything about their strengths, their concerns, their issues, their dreams. Whenever a group engages in an experience, they will reveal clues about these things. And those themes should be given a place in the program. Where? First in the processing. In Larry Quinsland's article for the AEE *Journal*, "How to Process Experience," he tells us to prepare ourselves for leading the processing by asking the following questions:

1.   What are the most important questions to which I want to respond?

2.   At what level are these questions (referring to the hierarchy of thinking skills)?

3.   What questions should I use to lay the foundation for the important questions to be answered more easily?

This is a good plan to follow but I would encourage us to think about the first step differently and ask, "What are the most important questions to which my participants seem to want to respond?"

The other way to respond is to design future experiences based on the information you've received (if you have access to that group over time). We intuitively know that we can better plan for a group once we know them. Once we knew that our students wanted to find meaning and purpose in their curriculum, all our future plans were altered to reflect that need.

OTHER TYPES OF CHOICES

Another way to provide choice for participants is to offer a *choice of activities*.

My committee put this type of choice into practice at an intergenerational conference one spring. We wanted the participants to come away feeling more empowered as peacemakers. Each participant chose to be in a workshop which reflected some particular aspect of peacemaking: problem solving, risk taking, envisioning, playfulness, or creative expression.

Initially the facilitators led the activities, to build up the sense of community in the group and to deepen the group's perspective toward the skill. But then the learning focus was shifted back to the group. They were invited to "Choose a risk for yourselves that you will take together" or "Choose a problem you want to work on now," and so on in each group.

I could never have foreseen what kind of risk was important to my group; it was so different from my own choice.

Sometimes we can *choose how we will respond* to the task. I once led a children's program that was part of an adult conference. The kids ranged in age from 6-13. After we talked about why their parents were there (and most of them didn't know), I invited them to make a video about something that seemed important to them. They first chose a format that allowed them a great deal of freedom—a "60 Minutes"-type thing. Some of them wanted to interview their peers about their feelings about Quakerism. Some made news flashes about nuclear weapons. There were mystery stories and sports. We showed this tape to their families.

With some trust, some structure, and some choice, those 30 kids put together a complete video production in one day!

Sometimes we can choose *when* we will undertake an experience. You could offer both climbing and hiking (and the option to do neither) on several days so the student can match their moods with the activity. We're used to doing this in our lives; for children it is not so much an option. Classes run on schedules.

I think choice is inherently affirming and empowering for several reasons. Being given a choice implies that I am capable of thinking seriously about the subject, and making a sound decision. It says that what I care about is important. It says that there is more than one way to do something and that maybe I know just the best way for me. Choice says the leader is not holding all the power or all the answers.

Becoming a Co-Learner

The final key I have so far observed is for the leader to become a co-learner with the group. This involves sharing the power, in ways we have looked at so far. It means revealing some of your own hopes and dreams, some of your own questions, and perhaps some of your own vulnerabilities.

I have pondered some of my deepest spiritual questions with twelve-year-olds who were more than pleased to share their insights. My students have advised me on my problems with my housemates; they have escorted me out of caves when I was disoriented. They have watched me tremble with fear on the high ropes and shiver with joy at the sight of a wild bird.

At first I wasn't sure about it all, if it meant giving up control. If I was going to let the group set its own goals, I could no longer predict how things would turn out—I could no longer take all the credit for what they learned! But in exchange for whatever loss of power or prestige I thought I would incur, I have been more than compensated by the excitement of watching a group discover something for themselves, and feeling their own sense of purpose and importance. And I don't think my "leadership" has ever been forfeited, though I now define my task as that of observing, interpreting, enabling, and connecting.

One of my favorite passages to quote is from Elliot Wigginton's introduction to the second *Foxfire*, where he talks about pushing back the chairs, sitting down on the floor, and finding out what teachers and students can come up with—together.

Summary

When we used an experiential approach to empower groups, there are several important guidelines to keep in front of us: the realness or significance of the experience; individual choice; and leader "vulnerability" (or shared power). I have found these themes to be very valuable in the area of peacemaking. And as many of the skills which are woven into the fabric of peacemaking are also woven into the other types of experiential programs where empowerment is a goal, I hope they are useful to others.

28

A Group Development Model for Adventure Education

Pamela J. Kerr and Michael A. Gass

THE USE OF SMALL-GROUP DEVELOPMENT HAS OFTEN BEEN RECOGNIZED AS ONE of the cornerstones of adventure education programs (e.g., Walsh & Golins, 1976; Jensen, 1979; Kalisch, 1979; Buell, 1983; Landry, 1986). Central to this development, whether the goals of the adventure experience focus on the acquisition of skills, social growth, or therapy, are the various stages each group encounters as it develops. The purpose of this article is to apply a conceptual model of group development theory with the goals of three types of adventure education programs. The focus of such a model builds upon the past successes and techniques of leaders in the field and provides practitioners with a framework to enhance the structured and intuitive strategies currently used in their programs.

USE OF MODELS IN GROUP DEVELOPMENT

It is commonly accepted that as individuals work in groups they progress through a series of developmental stages. As the group evolves in each stage, unique characteristics arise that indicate the group's progress. Awareness of these stages provides leaders with a framework to judge when actions are needed to help a group confront or overcome an obstacle.

In viewing fields that utilize small-group development, the theory that offers the most assistance for the formation of a model in adventure education is the one proposed by Garland, Jones, and Kolodny (1973). This framework identifies five central themes that focus on the stages through which groups progress as they develop. These stages are: 1) pre-affiliation, 2) power and control, 3) intimacy, 4) differentiation, and 5) separation.

1.   *Pre-affiliation.* During this initial period of association, group members strive to become familiar with one another and their environment. Close and efficient associations have not developed and relationships among individuals tend to be superficial and stereotypic. Members are generally ambivalent toward involvement and often experience some kind of anxiety about participating in the group. Individuals' past experiences with other groups (e.g., classrooms, churches, clubs, sports teams) influence how they view this new, small-group environment. Members also attempt to utilize these past experiences to help them in the processes of group exploration and affiliation.

2.   *Power and Control.* Once it has been established that the group is potentially safe and worth emotional investment, members begin testing group power and control issues. Issues can include, but are not limited to, problems of status, communication, and defining group values. It is at this stage in the group's development that familiar frames of reference may not be satisfactory for governing current behaviors, and new behaviors are often implemented in their place. In developing these new behaviors, issues concerning the balance of individual versus group needs occur. The amount of control members have on deciding and planning group activities is also a central issue of this stage.

3.   *Intimacy.* In this stage, members have decided to "affiliate" with one another and must contend with "sibling-like" rivalries and deeper emotions that are characteristic of close relationships. Members are more invested in the group and there tends to be a greater proficiency in planning and conducting projects as a group. There is also a greater desire to immerse oneself in group life and to share emotions arising from common experiences.

4.   *Differentiation.* At this point in the group's development, roles and status of group members tend to be less rigid. Individual differences and personal needs are accepted more freely, and the group becomes more functionally autonomous from the leader(s). The group has created its own identity and members often compare themselves to other groups and previous social situations. The group is seen as being cohesive, yet is able to identify both individual and group needs.

5.   *Separation.* The final stage represents the conclusion of the group experience and members are placed in a situation where they must find new resources for meeting their needs. The task of separation can be accomplished in a positive manner (e.g., reviewing experiences to analyze benefits of the group, incorporating growth of group experiences into future interactions) or a negative one (e.g., denying that the experience is

over, regressing to previous negative behaviors as the experience draws to a conclusion).

The main strengths of the Garland theory lie in its applicability to different types of group development and its ability to provide useful information concerning the progress of the group for the facilitator. Because of these strengths and the structure of the five stages, this model has been chosen to provide a framework that will illustrate small-group development in adventure experiences.

It is important to note that, depending on the goals of the adventure experience, the structure of the stages, style of instructor intervention, and types of participant development will be different for each group. Participants in adventure programs all progress through the five stages outlined by Garland, yet the practices utilized with these groups vary according to the goals set for the particular population.

Based on the need to be flexible yet specific, the authors have constructed a model where the five stages represented by Garland are applied to three central focuses of adventure education. While other focuses exist, these areas represent the intent of most adventure education/therapeutic programs currently being conducted. These three areas include:

1) *Skill Development Program* — Experiences where the focus for the participant is to obtain or improve technical skills, such as students on a semester wilderness-skills course or individuals involved in a whitewater kayaking workshop.

2) *Social Development Programs* — Endeavors that center on the social growth or development of individuals. Examples of this type of program are programs for married couples or programs involved in personal growth experiences.

3) *Therapeutic Programs* — Programs that focus on changing specific behaviors in order to remedy a social dysfunction, such as a course for juvenile delinquents or programs for individuals suffering from drug dependency.

In viewing these three areas, elements from two or three areas often exist in one program. But the main intent of an adventure education program generally focuses on just one of these areas.

GROUP DEVELOPMENT MODELS FOR ADVENTURE EDUCATION

Given these group development stages, how can they be applied to the various goals of skill, social, and therapeutic programs in adventure education? This section of the paper: 1) provides a further description of these areas, 2) shows the application of group development for each area as a group passes through the various stages of growth, and 3) outlines a model for each area summarizing group interaction and instructor roles for each stage.

SKILL DEVELOPMENT

Description

The primary focus of a skill group is the acquisition, maintenance, or improvement of cognitive and/or psychomotor skills. Social focuses exist, yet generally center on interpersonal relationships among group members rather than specific social or therapeutic goals. A group atmosphere of synergy exists and individuals often combine and complement personal strengths to increase the growth of the group and one another.

The instructors of skill development groups often find their responsibilities centering on the organization and preparation of educational activities. The leader often acts as a resource, assessing individual strengths and needs and adapting the learning environment accordingly.

Stages of Skill Group Development

1. *Pre-affiliation.* The leader clearly specifies program goals and objectives and what is expected of group members. The leader also allows for member participation whenever appropriate, and encourages individuals to relate to other group members. For example, in the beginning of a course focusing on backcountry skiing techniques, an instructor would take the time to describe course goals and activities. With the assistance of the participants, the instructor should determine if these goals and activities meet their needs and how changes can be made to help them individualize their learning.

2. *Power and Control.* The leader structures activities so that individuals are able to express themselves. It is important, however, to remain clear as to which decisions can be made by the group and which can be made by the leader. In permitting these group decisions, it is essential that the leader not intercede in the progress unless necessary. A leader overruling group decisions can result in members lowering or invalidating opinions of their decision-making abilities. This discounting often creates an atmosphere where members are less willing to express themselves. For example, students are given the opportunity to select the best possible route through a dense forest. Given that the instructor has ensured that the group can make this decision in an appropriate manner, he/she must allow the group to work through this process, interceding only when necessary.

SKILL GROUP DEVELOPMENT MODEL (FIGURE 1)

	Group Indicators	Instructor's Role
1) PRE-AFFILIATION	1) searching for stability; superficial conversations and interactions 2) unclear expectations 3) insecure feelings; adrift from social and personal anchors 4) questions of role within the group	1) define preliminary goal and objectives of course 2) identify the expectations of group members 3) provide a medium for group interaction 4) encourage member participation in tasks
2) POWER AND CONTROL	1) need to know instructor's role in leadership positions 2) need to identify authority structure of the group 3) need to determine the methods of making decisions	1) maintain clarity of group and leader roles in decision-making processes 2) structure activities to increase the expression of the participants 3) allow for positive group conflict
3) INTIMACY	1) focus on achieving goals 2) sense of cohesiveness occurs 3) sharing of strengths to benefit group	1) allow for member to reassess goals 2) encourage group interaction 3) help members focus on present tasks
4) DIFFERENTIATION	1) acknowledgement of individual strengths and weaknesses 2) further development of work independent of the leader 3) members take on increasing amounts of responsibility	1) encourage acceptance of everyone's role in the group 2) help members to work independently of the leader 3) monitor group support and progress toward constructive goals
5) SEPARATION	1) members reflect on material 2) look for methods of future application	1) encourage reflection and evaluation of learning 2) focus on the transfer and application of material to the future of the group member

Figure 1. Skill Development Model — A Model Depicting the Stages for the Development of Skills in Adventure Education. The model above illustrates the stages of development a group progresses through when involved in learning a skill in an adventure education activity.

3. *Intimacy.* At this point, members either become a group or remain a collection of individuals. For the group to attain intimacy, a sense of cohesiveness must occur among members. During this process, individuals generally experience the benefits of each other's talents as they work together to achieve pre-established goals. The leader should strive to assist the group in seeing that common goals are well defined and can meet the skill development of each individual in the group. For example, if a group involved in learning whitewater canoeing skills had decided to canoe down a Class III rapids, the instructor should continue working with each individual on techniques helping them further their own personal skills.

4. *Differentiation.* The leader helps the group to achieve its own goals. During this stage, there is often a great development of trust among group members. Individuals should be encouraged to take increasing initiative and responsibility in the group's functions. The leader monitors the group and supports its inclination to work independently. For example, as the whitewater canoeing group described above continues to develop, the instructor should encourage members to take on an increasing number of responsibilities involved in conducting the experience, such as checking out the safety systems or taking responsibility for previewing sections of whitewater before entering with a canoe.

5. *Separation.* At this point, the group has achieved the ability to work independently from the leader. Participants should be encouraged to consolidate their individual gains from the group and to apply skills they have learned to other situations after the course.

SOCIAL DEVELOPMENT

Description

The focus for participants in this group is the examination, reform, or enhancement of existing values or beliefs. Group change or growth generally occurs from the support and confrontation by group members and instructors. The leader often takes the role of a facilitator and supports the responsible involvement of group members. This facilitation often includes the development of new perspectives on social functioning by creating situations that challenge previously held ideas.

Stages of Social Group Development

1. *Pre-affiliation.* In this initial stage, the leader encourages exploration, involvement, and trust. In doing so, the leader should be clear about the goals and expectations of the group. While highly structured activities are

used, the importance of these experiences is to foster the involvement of participants. Members are encouraged to participate, but individual differences should be permitted. For example, suppose one member of the group has stated that he has an extremely strong fear of heights. During an initial Trust Fall activity, the exercise should then be adapted to respect his individual needs.

2. *Power and Control.* Though it is important for the leader to allow potential individual power struggles to occur within the group, it must not be done at the expense of other members. Leaders must not permit subgroups to jeopardize the goals of the whole group. The leader's role at this stage is to ensure that the group atmosphere remains open and safe. For example, three members of the group might be continually late to activities. The leader initiates a group discussion as to how this affects the group and encourages participants to generate possible solutions to the problem.

3. *Intimacy.* The leader encourages members to accept greater amounts of responsibility. The program should be flexible in allowing participants to adapt goals and activities to their needs. The leader should help facilitate increased dependency among group members. It is also important for the group leader to be a resource person helping to clarify the group's identity, as well as its relationship to other groups. For example, if the group has agreed for its goal to be climbing a particular mountain, the leader should help participants take ownership of their behavior by providing feedback and clarity when needed.

4. *Differentiation.* Here the leader encourages members to take responsibility for the group's actions, assisting them in achieving complete independence from the leader. Once the group understands its unique identity, the leader encourages members to become involved with other groups without feeling threatened. For example, in climbing the mountain in the situation represented above, suppose two group members fall far behind; the leader helps the group clarify the purpose of the activity in terms of safety and individual needs and encourages group problem solving.

5. *Separation.* The leader helps members by encouraging evaluation and review of the group's exercises. It is important that the group has the opportunity to reflect on what they have learned and then transfer this knowledge to other situations in their lives. Leaders should also discuss ways in which members can specifically enhance this transfer during the "debriefing" of the activity.

SOCIAL GROUP DEVELOPMENT MODEL (FIGURE 2)

	Group Indicators	Instructor's Role
1) PRE-AFFILIATION	1) individuals are unsure of what is expected of them 2) questions concerning group purpose 3) questions of "How do I fit into this group?"	1) clearly represent goals and expectations of group 2) encourage individuals to discuss their expectations 3) encourage trust, exploration, and involvement with group members
2) POWER AND CONTROL	1) individuals seek out others with commonalities 2) development of the norms and boundaries of the group 3) focus on leader for support and the setting of limits	1) monitor role of subgroups in terms of group development 2) allow power struggles but not at the expense of others 3) ensure atmosphere of openness and safety for ideas
3) INTIMACY	1) members look to one another for solutions 2) participants understand where they fit within the group	1) encourage members to accept greater amounts of responsibility 2) adapt goals and activities to group needs 3) act as a resource for group issues, but not as a "resolver" of issues
4) DIFFERENTIATION	1) understand the characteristics of this group and how it is different from others 2) members understand their role and purpose in the group	1) encourage members to take responsibility for the group 2) encourage transfer of developing group behaviors to other situations
5) SEPARATION	1) members may regress back to a previous stage or deny that the group was important to them 2) members may understand more about themselves and begin to apply this to other areas of their life	1) encourage reflection of group experiences 2) focus on the transfer of learning to other situations

Figure 2 Social Development Model — A Model Depicting the Stages for the Development of Social Growth in Adventure Education. The model above illustrates the stages of development a group progresses through when involved in an adventure education program focusing on social growth.

THERAPEUTIC DEVELOPMENT

Description

The main focus in the therapeutic group is the purposeful changing or directing of behaviors to create a healthier social structure for an individual. Specific behavior changes and treatment plans are implemented to remedy inappropriate behaviors. The group often forms an entity where individuals are held accountable for their behavior and its effect on others.

The instructor often utilizes the strength of the group to help create behavior changes in individuals. The direction of this change is often determined with the help of a medical or therapeutic model.

Stages of Therapeutic Group Development

1. *Pre-affiliation*. The leader and the group begin this stage by examining goals and expectations of group members. During this process, individual similarities and differences are explored in conjunction with directions the group can take. Through this process of clarification, the leader helps the group understand the needs of individuals and the expectations of the organization of which they are a part. For example, the judicial system conducting the wilderness program for juvenile offenders expects certain standards to be followed during the course to help in the therapeutic process of each individual.

2. *Power and Control*. The leader attempts to clarify the issue of "power and control" and relate it to the purpose of the group. Rules and requirements are again agreed upon by members. Shulman (1984) stresses that any group rules should emerge from the function of the group, rather than from the authority of the leader. For example, a rule of no physical contact might be imposed because if people get hurt in the backcountry, the group must carry them out. This rationale is apt to be more effective than a rule based upon no fighting because it will be considered an assault and you will be punished.

3. *Intimacy*. In this stage, the leader attempts to diagnose problem areas and present them so that new perspectives may be seen. By using clarification and confrontation, the leader and group explore possible ways in which individuals can meet their needs without compromising the rights of others. For example, if Joe hits Sam, a series of questions might be asked: "Joe, what did you want when you hit him?" "What is another way of getting Sam's attention?" "Which method would get you Sam's attention and still maintain your friendship?" "Why is it hard for you to ask to be noticed?" "What can the group do to help you feel like you belong?"

THERAPEUTIC GROUP DEVELOPMENT MODEL (FIGURE 3)

	Group Indicators	Instructor's Role
1) PRE-AFFILIATION	1) anxiety 2) fear of expectations	1) clearly define program goals and expectations 2) solicit individuals' fears and hopes
2) POWER AND CONTROL	1) individuals seek boundaries and affirmation for their behavior 2) ambivalence to joining the group—"What will I get out of it?"	1) relate issues of power and control to the purpose of the group 2) help clarify what is appropriate and acceptable behavior 3) enforce limits when needed
3) INTIMACY	1) individuals have formed a group and have established norms and values 2) begin to question the role of the leader	1) leader supports positive achievements 2) suggest areas where growth is needed 3) help clarify the function of the group
4) DIFFERENTIATION	1) individuals understand the different roles each plays 2) individuals understand how the group is different from other groups	1) leader begins to relate the new behaviors to situations outside of the group 2) encourages individuals to be flexible in their roles 3) is supportive yet begins to represent more societal views
5) SEPARATION	1) individuals may feel lost without the group 2) individuals may regress or flee in attempts to deny the emotional impact of the group 3) members often review their experiences in a comparative manner	1) leader helps to clarify gains that have been made 2) helps to prepare individuals on how to meet their needs without the group 3) encourages individuals to continue the gains they've already made

Figure 3. A Model Depicting the Stages for the Development of Therapeutic Goals in Adventure Education. The model above illustrates the stages of development a group progresses through when involved in an adventure education program focusing on therapeutic growth. This model does not include specific treatment plans—it is assumed that the instructors will include those that are relevant to the particular population.

4.   *Differentiation*. The leader clarifies what progress has been made in the group and helps individuals transfer this knowledge to other situations outside of the group. The leader remains supportive yet begins to represent the point of view of others outside of the group. An example might be, "We've agreed that it's all right to swear while we are in this group, but if I were a potential employer and heard you using that kind of language, what do you think I would think of you?"

5.   *Separation*. The leader helps to clarify the gains that have been made and encourages members to transfer these methods to other situations. The leader also provides members with alternative methods besides the group to meet the needs that have been fulfilled by the group, such as a student who is leaving a therapeutic wilderness course for alcoholics, being integrated into a local group of Alcoholics Anonymous.

CONSIDERATIONS AND CONCLUSIONS

Adventure education has grown to include a variety of applications and mediums. Central to the value of these programs is the use of a small-group environment to aid in the acquisition of educational or therapeutic goals. As members participate in these programs, they progress through definitive stages of group development. This progression occurs whether the group is involved in learning technical skills, enhancing social behaviors, or rehabilitating social dysfunctions. Given knowledge of group development stages, instructors of adventure programs are provided with valuable information to assist the participants in reaching their desired goals.

In using the information provided by the group development models, it is important for leaders to be aware of several other factors:

1.   *Individual Development* — While the model focuses on the group's development, the instructor must also be aware of the unique needs of each participant. The model presented here focuses on the development of an individual as a group member. Participants may have goals separate from the group that need to be considered.

2.   *Rate and Direction of Growth* — It is important to remember that groups will progress through the stages of development at different rates and individual members within the same group grow at different speeds. This variation in development often makes it important to allow for different individual outcomes to occur for an activity. For example, some participants may progress to a point in a group where they feel comfortable, whereas others may still be questioning whether they are willing to make a commitment to the group.

It is also important to recognize that group members can regress as well as advance through these stages. For example, regression to earlier stages is often evident in therapeutic programs as participants approach the end of the experience.

3.   *Adding and Removing Group Members* — Inserting or removing members from a group will affect its development. Every participant plays a role within the group and when someone is added or removed, a restructuring of the group will occur. This will often result in the group regressing to an earlier stage of development.

4.   *Characteristics of the Members* — Other characteristics such as the age of group members or the cognitive and integration abilities of group members will also affect group development. It is imperative to take into consideration all of these factors when implementing this model for group development.

In the past, leaders have often relied on "what our program has done in the past" and the "magic" of groups to reach their intended goals. By understanding the five-stage model of group development, it is hoped that instructors will choose activities that are appropriate for the needs of the group at that particular stage. When this is done, the program "flows" or has a sense of natural timing, allowing the participants to get the most from the experience. Groups develop regardless of instructor involvement; knowledge of how the instructor can affect this growth is often the difference between providing a valuable education/therapeutic experience and just "surviving" an outdoor program.

29

From Theory to Practice for College Student Interns: A Stage Theory Approach

Dan Garvey and Anna Catherine Vorsteg

The interns slowly shuffled into the staff meeting. Each looked slightly slightly more tired and frazzled than the one before. It was time to debrief the program we had just completed. As we heard the last bus driving away full of happy students singing and talking, we settled into what had become nearly assigned seats in our staff room. The staff had found this program to be particularly difficult to run. The logistics were sloppy, meals were barely acceptable, the participants themselves seemed to require more supervision and direction than usual. Informal discussion was more focused on the upcoming day off than on the next group which would be arriving in less than twenty-four hours.

M ANY PEOPLE WHO HAVE HAD SUPERVISORY RESPONSIBILITY IN AN EXPERIENTIAL education organization may recognize the above scenario. Some who have worked with new groups of interns each year may have even come to expect this dreaded staff gathering, when the "wheels seem to fall off." Everything was going so well. No task was too bothersome or difficult for the interns. They seemed to take pride in demonstrating their level of commitment to the program and each other. And yet, at almost the same time in each program cycle, they get into this "funk." But this is not the only predictable scenario which could have been written. We could have picked a different point in the program cycle and written a description of a scene which might also be familiar to many of those working with interns.

Why is each year with new staff and interns a roller coaster of ups and downs? Possibly personal development theory (i.e., Maslow, 1970; Piaget, 1965; Kohlberg, 1969) could help explain some of the changes that are taking place as interns live and learn in a new environment. Theories of group dynamics—storming, norming, conforming, etc.—may also be helpful as interns work and often live together (Kerr & Gass, 1987). However, the primary expectation of all staff—interns included—is that they meet the needs of the clients. We believe there are unique and important aspects and roles to the internship experience which should be examined more closely. Interns are exposed to a tremendous amount of information as they work to address clients' needs. They must contemplate learning theory, memorize safety systems, and learn a wide variety of both simple and complex tasks. The process through which they come to understand their new roles seems to be a key to interpreting the emotional roller coaster.

Patterns have emerged as interns attempt to balance their own individual needs with the requirements of being a staff member. These patterns appear to be closely related to the ways in which interns operationalize the theories of experiential education. Almost without exception, those interns that have the most successful experience, are also highly successful with their clients. We have always attempted to create a group situation which is a supportive and nurturing environment for new staff. But it is becoming apparent that no amount of peer support can compensate for repeated bad experiences with clients. As supervisors interested in helping to create the best possible internship experience for new staff, we now realize that how we help them integrate theory and practice is at least as important to their ultimate success as is the general group atmosphere.

The purpose of this article is to examine the cognitive process used by college student interns as they attempt to combine theory with practice to fulfill requirements of a class in outdoor adventure education. It is hoped that a careful examination of how a group of students integrates theory with practice will illuminate how those newly initiated to the field interpret theory, and the effects their understanding has on their total learning during the internship.

THE CONTEXT

Providing college students with an appropriate setting for the study of experiential education has been, and continues to be, a challenge for educators. Given the academic requirements of most colleges and universities, frequently students learn theory in a class setting one semester, and are later required to gain practical experience in the application of these theories during an internship or field placement. Because of general education requirements, major requirements, and other educational and social activities sponsored by colleges, it is rare that students have the time to engage in a substantial internship while in residence at the college. However, through the cooperative efforts of the American Youth Foundation's Merrowvista Education Center, and the University of New Hampshire's Outdoor Education Program, a unique opportunity was available for a small group of students enrolled in a course entitled, "Theory and Practice in Outdoor Adventure Education." During the Fall semester of 1991, a group of students enrolled in this course lived and worked at the Merrowvista Education Center, in Ossipee, New Hampshire. The students had their class meetings at Merrowvista and were required to apply their theoretical understandings to a wide variety of client groups whom they worked with during their semester-long internship.

This intense internship experience, coupled with the coursework and class discussions, provided the opportunity to understand how students studying experiential education apply the theories they are learning in class to the leadership positions they are required to fulfill by virtue of their staff responsibilities.

STAGE THEORY

Our observations of this group, and our experiences with previous groups of interns lead us to conceptualize a four-stage developmental process through which students put their new theories into practice. But before proceeding to discuss this developmental process, a few words of explanation about stage theories may be helpful. Social scientists have found some comfort in describing different facets of human behavior and development through the use of a progressive series of levels, which are often clearly recognizable, one from the other. In the area of cognitive development, Piaget (1965) hypothesized a logical sequence of thought that young people use as they begin to make sense of their world. Kohlberg (1969), Gilligan (1977), and Rest (1979), have each offered stage theories attempting to explain moral and ethical development. In psychology, Maslow (1970) detailed psychological development using a pattern of stages and conflict resolution.

The authors' use of a stage theory framework to explain the intellectual process used by student interns is not intended to be a rigid, formal progression of concrete levels of understanding, but rather a possible recognizable pattern that may exist. In this way, our stage theory is more similar to the works of Fox (1991) and Whitehead (1929) who suggested fluid evolutionary phases of development and understanding, rather than a fixed overlay which can be applied to human behavior.

This group of student interns conformed across a semester to a rather predictable pattern of development as they attempted to put their newly learned theory into practice. Our belief is based on the oral and written accounts of the students from this semester, and our accumulated experience working with other student interns in past semesters.

THE FOUR PHASES OF THEORY INTEGRATION

From the accounts furnished by students, and our observations, we have concluded there are four phases as students attempt to move from theory to practice: Exhilaration, Rejection, Integration, and Transformation.

Exhilaration

The students entered the internship experience excited about the potential power of an educational approach they knew little about. Through the class section of the internship, they were exposed to the writings of John Dewey (1938), Richard Kraft (1987), Stephen Bacon (1983), and the works of others which could help the students gain insight into the philosophical underpinnings of experiential education. The new students were often intoxicated by what they understood to be experiential education. They read of the Progressive Education Movement and were exposed through the readings and class lectures to a new and fascinating portrait of what "school" could be. The seduction became almost complete as they read countless testimonials from students who had taken part in experiential programs. Study after study describes how the experiential education process changes the learners and empowers them to take control of their lives.

During this phase, it is natural for the student intern to view "traditional" education with disdain. All that is not experiential may be viewed as worthless and a threat to the experiential principles which must be embraced in the schools. Experiential education becomes a panacea for all that ails schools. Teachers are often seen as falling into one of two distinct groups: they are either experiential educators, or they aren't. If the student intern has been a participant in an experiential program, this further increases the dedication and commitment to this educational approach.

Rejection

Armed with these "new" theories, it is predictable that student interns would want to have leadership and teaching opportunities in which they could try these theories out. During the semester, each of the interns was able to work with a wide range of participant groups. In all cases, the intern came to temporarily reject or seriously modify their previously held belief regarding the efficacy of experiential education. Usually this rejection was not immediate. The intern was often successful with her or his first few programs. This success was due in part to their own modest expectations, and the scheduling design which allowed interns to work with progressively more difficult client groups.

Despite the temporary successes, it is inevitable that not all groups respond equally well to experiential education methods. This fact was made clear to our interns when a group of sixth-grade students from an urban area arrived at

Merrowvista for a three-day program. These "city kids" were not particularly responsive to the introspective questioning techniques of interns attempting to facilitate group development through open discussion. Participants of this program often were hostile toward the staff, and disregarded even the most reasonable rules for safety and respectful behavior.

Faced with this apparent crisis, the interns began to question the vigor with which they had embraced experiential education. The "panacea" was proving ineffective in this situation. Interns expressed intense frustration and a sense of betrayal. They appeared to blame the participants for the bad behavior, and themselves for being gullible in their belief that something other then strong discipline would work with this group. Where once experiential education was the remedy to educational problems, it was now a contributing factor to the lack of control in this program. In the conversations with and between interns, and in their writings, it became clear there was a crisis of confidence and a rejection of the belief that experiential education was universally applicable in all situations.

Integration

Despite the initial exhilaration and rejection, the interns still had to reconcile the fact that experiential techniques did work with many of the earlier groups. It is at this point that the students were most befuddled. If experiential education worked for some of the groups and under some conditions, could one predict which groups would be successful, and under what conditions? O'Reilly (1989) writes of the need to allow students to be "incoherent" in their learning. He reasons that one should not demand totally logical and reasoned answers from students. If students are not allowed to appear disoriented in their learning, they soon learn that the appearance of understanding is more highly rewarded than the struggle to understand. Interns were deeply involved in the struggle to integrate theory and practice. The open nature of the class discussion allowed this struggle to become obvious to each of them.

No theory can be universally applied within the social sciences. Faced with this realization, the interns began to re-examine and re-think the original theories they had studied in light of the experiences they were having. Several questions emerged: Under what circumstances do experiential techniques appear to have the greatest results? What background information does the intern need in order to design experiential activities for the client group? This realization of the need for background information about the client groups was mentioned by several of the interns. One student clearly connects the theories of Dewey, regarding the teacher's obligation to learn about the students, with her experiences during the internship:

> Programs at Merrowvista will not be as productive if the staff are not clued into the backgrounds of the incoming participants. As Dewey has stated in *Experience and*

Education, " . . . the teacher should become intimately acquainted with the conditions of the local community, physical, historical, economic, occupational, etc., in order to utilize them as educational resources" (Dewey, 1938, p. 40). I didn't actually realize how relevant this theory was to the livelihood of programs at Merrowvista until the group from the city came for a three-day program. As a facilitator of the program I was given information regarding the city, though at the time I thought it was for cocktail party conversation. It wasn't until the participants arrived that I realized that the knowledge I was given was pertinent. (Bedford, 1991)

This re-examination of theory based on the students' experiences, forms the crucial link in the ultimate integration of the classroom activities with the leadership opportunities.

Transformation

If the students are successful during the integration stage in connecting a classroom theory with experiences in the field, they are then ready to begin fashioning their own theories. Bacon (1983), Gass (1985), and Kolb (1976), have each described some of the necessary ingredients for the transfer of learning to occur. Students in the transformation stage are attempting to enter new leadership experiences with a set of beliefs and methods which they have transferred from prior experiences. Without the ability to transform past theory and practice into a coherent new or amended theory, the students would always be limited by their need for the theories of others to understand and act on their world.

During the transformation stage, the students attempted to make broader statements regarding their learning:

I was able to learn from each group specific areas in which they needed to work, thus allowing me to intentionally pick which activities I wanted to use. I gained a better understanding of what it is like for a newcomer in the field to try to understand experiential education. And most importantly, I learned first hand that the best way to learn to facilitate experiential education programs is simply to experience it. (Tucker, 1991)

The above quote provides a clear example of the intern's attempt at theory development. This student may not have authored the most exhaustive treatise on the value of experience in the learning process, but she has created a solid theory of learning based on her internship. During the transformation stage, the interns often became excited by their ability to connect seemingly unrelated experiences to help form a clearer picture of what they had learned. Rather than a series of random events, the interns began to recognize that there were often patterned responses by participants to changes in style and activity by the leader. Perhaps the most important element of the internship is the opportunity it provides for interns to recognize these subtle patterns of cause and effect.

Implications

If student interns' understanding of theory and practice is viewed using these four stages, then there are some implications for the way one would work with students during each of these stages. Certainly, alerting interns to these stages would be a possible first step. If students could be encouraged to chronicle their developmental process using diaries or journals, important information could be gathered concerning factors which cause or retard the process of moving from theory to practice.

This stage theory also suggests that there are critical periods for those supervising student interns to be particularly attentive to the interns' educational needs. If supervisors can anticipate and expect a period of rejection, they are in a better position to help the student gain deeper meaning from the experiences that have contributed to this rejection. Likewise, as the student gains seemingly unconnected internship experiences, the supervisor may be able to help in the integration process of these experiences into a more coherent pattern of understanding. Perhaps one of the more important implications of this stage approach is the recognition that each student intern on a staff may be at a different stage of understanding. This is important to recognize because it forces the supervisor to view the interns as a collection of individual learners, each of whom has a unique perspective on the internship. This individual approach will discourage the natural tendency for supervisors to view students as "the interns," as if their group affiliation was more powerful than their individuality. Staff training for interns can take on a new focus if one attempts to meet the individual stage needs of interns, while also addressing the needs of the group.

Educators must also help create internship experiences where students are allowed to fail, and where supervisors are themselves periodically befuddled. Those designing internship experiences should consider ways in which interns and supervisors can work on problems together. Each of the stages of development—exhilaration, rejection, integration, and transformation—provides an opportunity for interns to positively affect the organization with which they are connected, because each individual will resolve these stages differently.

Section VI

Ethics

30

Justifying the Risk to Others: The Real Razor's Edge

Simon Priest and Rusty Baillie

ADVENTURES ARE A RICH BLEND OF JOY AND SORROW. ON ONE SIDE, THERE LIES the exquisite beauty of the outdoors and the exhilaration of facing or overcoming challenges. On the other, there lies the ever-present threat of injury or even death. As common adventurers, with equal rights and responsibilities, we are free to accept these risks and rewards. As facilitators, using adventure as a tool to achieve educational objectives, we are responsible for our charges and to their rights as mandated by law. For us, the professional approach is apparent: we wish to share the benefits of an adventure experience with others. The public, however, has greater concerns. It considers such adventures foolhardy and dangerous and is less likely to agree with us when something goes wrong.

The question clearly becomes, *How can we justify putting the lives of others at risk*? This article discusses the above question through the use of two models: The Adventure Experience Paradigm and Normal Life Risk.

THE ADVENTURE EXPERIENCE

To be an adventure, an experience must have an element of uncertainty about it. Either the outcome should be unknown or the setting unfamiliar. Yet to the adventurer, it must appear possible to influence the circumstances in a manner that provides hope of resolving the uncertainty. Herein lies the challenge associated with adventures. The adventure experience is a state of mind. It is a function of inherent risks, an individual's competence, and changing time. An adventure in time and place may be experienced by one individual, but not by another. Moments later,

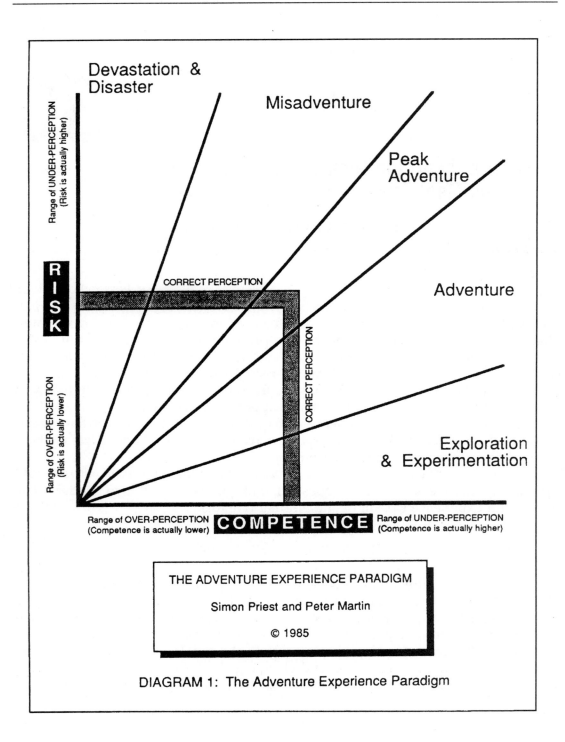

DIAGRAM 1: The Adventure Experience Paradigm

the spirit of adventure may have departed. In another setting, it may not be present at all.

Mitchell (1983) believes people are motivated to undertake adventures because their lives are rationalized, controlled, packaged, and extrinsically rewarding. Their everyday existence lacks the benefits of intrinsic rewards and freedom of choice provided by an adventure experience. Researchers such as Ellis (1973) and Zuckerman (1974) have cited a search for optimal arousal, and the resultant peak performances which arise under such conditions, as probable motivation for people to seek such sensations.

A MODEL

Martin and Priest (1986) have recently proposed "The Adventure Experience Paradigm" as a tool to explain what takes place from moment to moment during an adventure experience. This model is presented in Diagram 1.

The axes of this model are termed *Risk* and *Competence* loosely based on Csikszentmihalyi's Flow Model (1975). Risk is defined as the potential to lose something of value. In the case of a negative adventure experience, this loss may take the form of a physical, mental, or social injury. Competence is the ability of individuals to deal effectively with the demands placed on them by the surrounding environment. In any adventure situation, this ability relates directly to skill, knowledge, attitude, behavior, confidence, and experience aimed at solving problems and avoiding the negative consequences of risk.

Five conditions are identified in the model and are named after Mortlock's (1984) four stages of the outdoor journey. *Exploration and Experimentation* is a condition where risk is low and competence high. Under these circumstances participants are in a setting appropriate to learning skills, such as flatwater paddling and low-angle slab climbing. *Adventure* is the next condition where the risk is slightly greater and where participants are affectively engaged whilst putting their new-found skills to the test.

Peak Adventure is the middle ground where risk and competence are perfectly balanced. This is the setting known as the "razor's edge" (Williamson & Mobley, 1984), where an intense internal concentration is apparent and where "euphoric highs" are achieved. Here, peak experiences or peak performances are possible when risk and competence are matched at their absolute limits. According to theorists of optimal arousal, this is the condition which self-motivated adventurers will seek out most often.

Misadventure is the nearby condition where competence is less than what the situation calls for and where participants are learning experientially from a tipped canoe or a slight fall on a vertical crack.

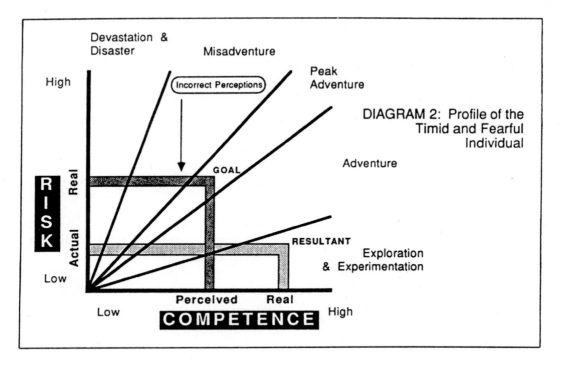

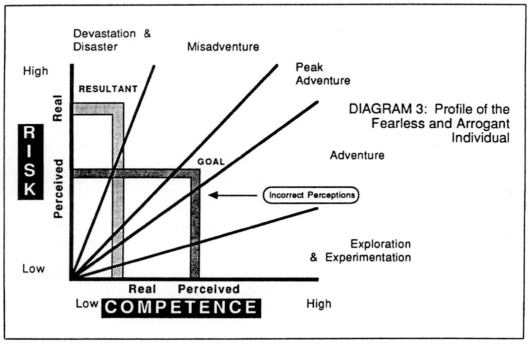

Devastation and Disaster is the logical extension of misadventure where things have gone wrong to the point of injury or perhaps even death. Here, participants lack the competence to match the risks.

There are three possible values for risk and competence: absolute, perceived, and real. *Absolute Risk* and *Absolute Competence* are the uppermost limits of the risk inherent in a situation and the greatest competence the individual could possibly muster in response. From moment to moment, no one can tell with certainty where these values of risk and competence will lie. At best, these values can be estimated by the participants involved in the adventure experience and *Perceived Risk* and *Perceived Competence* refer to those assessments. These values are based upon subjective judgments of the absolute values. *Real Risk* and *Real Competence* represent the amounts of risk and competence which actually occur at a given moment in time. These values arise from the interaction of individual and setting, as a manifestation of the absolute values.

To summarize, absolute is the most extreme value possible, perceived is the participant's best judgment of the probability of such values occurring, and real is the value that actually takes place. Using the example of crossing a potential snow avalanche slope: absolute might be the worst possible scenario of a total slope collapse, perceived might be the concern that a minor slab avalanche is judged as probable, and real might be that nothing at all happens.

Absolute values are of lesser importance in an adventure; the perceived and real values play more important roles. The goal or expected condition for the adventure experience is set by the adventurer and is based on perceived values. Left to their own accord, self-motivated adventurers will seek out levels of risk that appropriately balance with levels of competence in an effort to achieve a peak adventure. Rock climbers capable of a 5.9 lead will choose routes close to their ability and grade IV paddlers will select rapids with a similar range. However, the expectant condition of a peak adventure will only occur for the astute adventure, one who correctly perceives the real levels of risk and competence. If misperceptions occur, as is often the case, then although the individual sought one condition, another is likely to happen. The outcome or resultant condition arises from the interplay of real values.

AN APPLICATION

Take, for example, two types of self-motivated individuals seeking the goal condition of peak adventure. One type is considered to be timid and fearful: they suffer from underperceived competence and overperceived risk. The other type is fearless and arrogant: having underperceived risk and overperceived competence. In Diagram 2, the timid and fearful enter into adventure experiences with peak adventure as their desired goal. The resultant experience is merely one of exploration and experimentation, because their real competence and the real risk dictate the outcome. In Diagram 3, the fearless and arrogant also enter into adventure experiences expecting peak adventures. The condition of devastation and disaster results for these people because conditions are such that they do not have the competence to deal with the risks at hand.

Ethically speaking, adventure educators are charged with seeing that neither of these two scenarios occur. The people described as timid and fearful are destined never to reach their full potential, and the arrogant and fearless folks are likely to injure themselves or others in their quest for adventure. The aim of adventure education is to create astute adventurers: people who are correct in their perceptions of individual competence and situational risk. The aim is ultimately achieved through facilitated adventure experiences.

THE PROCEDURE

The facilitated adventure experience is founded on the premise that expert facilitators will be able to assess the values of risk and competence to a more accurate degree than will novice adventurers. However, the possibility of misperception still exists and hence the importance of sound judgment on the part of both facilitators and participants is critical.

The facilitated experience takes place in two distinct phases. First, the participants' perceptions of risk and competence are made congruent with real values through experiences where only the perceived risk is elevated. Second, competence is improved by exposure to increased real risks. This two-phase procedure is described below and brings up ethical questions related to the manipulation of risk and the justification of exposing people's lives to hazards, whether true or imagined.

Consider timid and fearful individuals: they overperceive the risk and underperceive their competence. The role of the facilitators is to build confidence by increasing the perceived risk of an activity until these participants are expecting a condition of misadventure to ensue. Then, after successfully coaxing the participants through to a condition of adventure, the facilitators further aid them by reflecting back on the experience and drawing out the key points of learning.

Before the experience, the participants are expecting a misadventure, yet an adventure results! They have realized that the activity was not so dangerous and that they really were skilled enough to deal with the circumstances. They have taken a large first step toward becoming astute, and the facilitators have begun to close the gap between real and perceived values.

Next, consider fearless and arrogant individuals: they underperceive the risks and overperceive their competence. Here the role of the facilitators is to gently knock the participants down a notch or two! Structuring for a failure, the facilitators select a more difficult activity, which the participants fully expect to complete as an adventure. A purposely prepared misadventure occurs, and again the facilitators debrief the experience, concentrating on learning from minor mistakes.

Before the experience, participants are expecting an adventure, yet a misadventure results! The participants have realized that the activity was more hazardous than previously expected and that they really were not skilled enough to deal with the circumstances. They, too, have taken a large first step toward becoming astute, and the facilitators have begun to close the gap in the other direction.

Both these facilitated experiences merely represent the first phase of the procedure. The second phase applies only to individuals who are fully astute: correct in perceptions of risk and competence. Once astute for an adventure activity, participants will seek increased real risks in order to balance their increased real competence and thus achieve peak adventures.

SOME ETHICAL QUESTIONS

The initial question of ethics here relates to precisely how the risks are manipulated. In the first phase, it is critical for the facilitators to select activities where the change in risk is strictly a perceived one. It is the participants who must ultimately perceive the risk to be great or minimal. The facilitators must be certain that the real risks remain unchanged and that these are kept to reasonable levels. Most adventure educators would argue that Phase One is ethically acceptable. This phase is the common mainstay of our educative process. Phase Two, however, is a different story.

In the second phase, the concern of raising real risks comes to the forefront of discussion. In order for the participants to increase their competence (especially skill and confidence), greater risks are necessary. Because these people are astute, they will not be fooled by changes in perception. They desire, and will ultimately seek, the real thing! There is one group of educators who see nothing inappropriate with manipulating the real risks, while there are similar numbers of other educators who claim this approach may result in unreasonable consequences.

Ultimately, the decision to utilize the second phase is made by individual facilitators. On our own, seeking common adventure, we are responsible for the ramifications of the risks we assume. Working with others in an educative setting, things are a bit different. Hopefully, the choice to encounter greater real risks is made in consultation with both the participants and the sponsoring program agency. Nonetheless, as each of us makes this educational choice, there is a process of identification, assessment, calculation, and modification which we follow to decide if the risk is worth taking.

First, in an adventure, one identifies the potential dangers of the activity and setting. Dangers are of two types: perils and hazards. Recalling that risk is defined as the potential to lose something of value, perils are sources of the loss, and hazards are conditions affecting the likelihood of a loss occurring. These "give rise to risk, but are not risks themselves" (Williamson & Mobley, 1984, p. 5). Source perils might be a lightning bolt, damaged equipment, and polluted drinking water. Conditional hazards might include a storm, an avalanche slope, and an outdoor leader's poor judgment. The prime difference between the two is shown by the example of the effect a storm (hazard) has on the generation of lightning bolts (perils). The latter causes the loss, while the former alters the probability of such loss taking place.

Any such identification must also consider both environmental and human dangers. Environmental dangers are those which originate outside the participants, arising from within the natural surroundings. Mortlock (1984) termed these objective dangers, beyond control of the facilitator. Examples of environmental dangers are loose rockfall, poisonous animals, and extreme temperatures. Human dangers are within the participants, arising from their individual makeup and group interactions and are more subjective, at least somewhat controllable. Helms (1984) further divides this category into psychological (individual) and sociological (group) phenomena. Examples of human dangers are lack of skill, a large personal ego, and peer pressure from the group as a whole.

Second, whether identified as peril or hazard, environmental or human, these dangers need to be assessed by the facilitators. This requires foresight into not only the inherent dangers, but also into those that are not so immediately obvious. Facilitators must imagine the absolute risks by constantly considering "what if" scenarios. They must be alert at all times and must clearly identify and assess all dangers. They cannot afford to overlook a peril or underestimate a hazard.

Third, after the potential dangers are assessed, a calculation of the probability that risk will arise from these is necessary. Here, not all the information is available to the facilitators. Therefore, the transition from assessment to calculation requires sound judgment on the part of the facilitators. Such judgment comes from a strong base of experiences, to which much personal speculation and reflection has been given by facilitators who are astute.

Fourth, in making the decision to continue with an adventure experience, or perhaps to abort or adapt it, facilitators call on their best judgment at every stage of the problem-solving process. Based on previous experience, they substitute estimated values for the many unknowns and determine the probability of a risk arising from the dangers. If the possible consequence is deemed unreasonable by the facilitators, then countermeasure strategies may be employed to prevent risks from arising. Meier (1985) suggests several such strategies to avoid or control the dangers. Once these countermeasures are executed, the process of identifying, assessing, and calculating is repeated until the possible consequence is deemed reasonable by the facilitators.

Herein lies the crux of the facilitated adventure experience involving real risks. The problem-solving process considers reasonable consequences as the standard by which success and safety are measured. These are closely related to individual facilitators' concepts of reasonable. To one, a fracture may not be reasonable, to another it may!

Returning to the Adventure Experience Paradigm, the authors contend that the real razor's edge for facilitators lies between the conditions of misadventure, and devastation and disaster. Here the difference is set by acceptable and unacceptable outcomes. Obviously, unacceptable outcomes are not desired as part of the adventure education domain. The potential for these is frequently left to common adventurers.

Baillie (1986) describes acceptable outcomes as temporary physical or mental damage, where a minor disruption of lifestyles takes place. Unacceptable outcomes would include permanent physical disability or psychological trauma, coupled with a major disruption of lifestyle. For a whitewater adventure activity, acceptable outcomes (arising within a condition of misadventure) might be minor cuts, bruises, strains, and wet clothing. Unacceptable ones (occurring in devastation and disaster) might be extreme hypothermia, spinal injury, heavy arterial bleeding, and drowning. Drawing the line between major and minor injuries is a personal choice, often made by the facilitators. How often do we ask the participants for their opinions of acceptable and unacceptable outcomes?

Lastly, from this most complex process arises a penultimate decision: to "go for it" or not. However, given our modern times and a litigation-sensitive culture, an ultimate decision, (founded legally as well as morally) becomes necessary. The facilitators are finally faced with justifying their choices. Baillie (1986) proposes the model of "Normal Life Risk" as a means to justify endangering lives of others.

The premise of the model lies in comparing accident data of outdoor adventure-based programs with data from everyday, normal-life activities. Some examples follow. Higgins (1981) found that Outward Bound courses had a lower ratio of disabling injuries than either automobile driving or college football. Meyer (1979) reported fewer deaths due to outdoor adventures than due to automobile accidents.

From this comparison is expected the statement that *adventure experiences are no more risky than everyday living*. However, for the most part, the sources are brief and dated. More work in this area is desperately called for. Collection of current accident data from outdoor adventure-based programs, such as the work being done by Alan Hale's National Safety Network (1985) and as proposed by Williamson and Mobley (1984) for AEE, is critical to the process of justifying the risk to others.

This article has reviewed the bi-phasic Adventure Experience Paradigm for facilitating change. It has presented some thoughts on the ethical question of placing people at risk in order to bring about such changes, and has discussed the process by which facilitators might answer this question. Lastly, the model of Normal Life Risk was suggested as a common means to justify the levels of risk used in adventure education circumstances.

If we wish to win the trust of society, and establish our credibility as a profession, we must establish and follow clear and responsible risk-management procedures supported by stringent accident data collection. It is the authors' desire that this be accomplished without the loss of the experiential essence which is such an integral part of adventure education.

31

Connecting Ethics and Group Leadership: A Case Study

Kate Lehmann

A GROUP OF NINE WOMEN AND I EMBARKED ON A WEEK-LONG CANOE TRIP INTO the Boundary Waters Canoe Area with the outdoor adventure organization, Woodswomen. According to one guide, it was a representative Woodswomen gathering in that the group included women with diverse skills and experiences who came together and evolved in a typical way. After returning home, I began to try to analyze the events and activities of that trip. How was it possible that Woodswomen was able to deliver on their promise that each participant would learn, grow, and have fun on a trip when the individuals came with vastly different experiences? Why did it seem that the group was not being guided and yet the guides had a very strong presence? It is my belief that the effectiveness of Woodswomen's approach is related to the integration of ethical principles with a strong leadership model.

This microcosm of experience involving a small group in an outdoor setting during a finite period is illustrative of the wider and deeper connection between effective leadership and ethics. While there is substantial work which explores this connection on a theoretical level, there is little material that gives concrete examples of how ethics can be a foundation for group leadership models. Woodswomen provides a case study which demonstrates this profound connection as it is actualized in an outdoor group setting.

The theoretical principles for this study come from the work of Robert Terry, an ethicist at the Reflective Leadership Institute at the University of Minnesota, and from the group development and leadership model defined and used by Woodswomen. This research about Woodswomen is not intended as an organizational assessment. Rather, it is a means to explore the connections between ethics and leadership, using a leadership model that seems to be ethical, effective, and adaptable to other organizations or group situations. My conclusions are based on lengthy personal interviews with several Woodswomen guides[1] and Executive Director Denise Mitten. Training materials and personal experiences with Woodswomen also contributed to the study.

ETHICAL PRINCIPLES

In a recent lecture at St. Cloud University, Robert Terry (1991) outlined six basic ethical principles that provide the foundation for effective leadership. Rather than focus on a single principle, such as justice or love, as the basis for a model of ethical leadership, Terry seeks to weave the six principles into a whole cloth. Terry maintains these principles are universal in nature but responsive to situations. Each principle is equally important in building an ethical framework. They are interrelated and interdependent, building on each other but also referring back to each other.

At the root, this is a model of leadership grounded in the concept of authenticity. Terry (1991) explains, "What I mean by authenticity is being true and real in yourself and in the world . . . . True is abstract, real is concrete and so we have to get together what we think is true, in terms of patterns, and the embodiment of that. That is 'live it,' walk your talk." Terry maintains that authenticity is a fundamental condition of being human, it is "presupposed in every human act," even in lying. When we lie, we attempt to convince someone else of something that is not true, all the while knowing what the truth really is. To be inauthentic, or to experience inauthenticity, is to sever or experience a disconnection between appearance and reality. This is the deliberate separation of truth from reality, the ultimate form of dissonance.

Terry (1991) maintains that authenticity is something that we struggle to achieve, calling the experience of authenticity "a liberation . . . when you feel the alignment of who you are and what you're about." He recognizes, however, that this is a process rather than an achievement in itself. It is impossible to reach the point of perfect alignment because we can never find absolute truth. Rather, "we have got to struggle with what's true . . . we have to explore each other's perspectives" and, in so doing, come as close as we can to authenticity.

From the basis of authenticity, Terry (1991) begins building a foundation for leadership with the following ethical principles:

- *Dwelling*: We each "show up" with our histories and our identities and need to accept and agree that it is all right for each of us to be there. If we ignore or deny a person's experience and history, we have, effectively, denied his or her identity. The principle of dwelling is the foundation for

---

[1]Guides were guaranteed anonymity, so the names used in the text are fictitious.

We each "show up" with our histories and our identities and need to accept
and agree that it is all right for each of us to be there.

embracing and respecting the diversity of people present in our lives.
Leadership, itself a relationship between leader and constituents, seeks to
increase both the leader's and the constituent's ability to be present,
recognizing the diverse perspectives and talents of each individual.

- *Freedom*: The ability to make choices and decisions is integral to being able
  to sustain relationships. Based on personal history and preferences, each
  of us can exercise options. This, however, is predicated on the assumption
  that we have chosen to "show up" and participate in the social
  conversation.

- *Justice*: Once we are present and have the ability to make choices, we must
  agree on how we relate to each other. Justice is based on a principle of
  fairness that has three aspects: 1) Equality—All who choose to be present
  are equal in their claims; 2) Equity—The idea that initial inadequacy or
  unfairness can be addressed; and 3) Adequacy—The methods for

addressing issues of equality and equity must be adjusted to consider changes.

- *Participation*: Having determined that we wish to be present and have the ability to make choices within the bounds of justice, we take action to engage, we make a "claim" for our own personal power and take part in the world as ourselves and for ourselves.

- *Love*: Love is the principle that turns people toward each other; it is the recognition that, in our journey, in our conversation, we are in a relationship with each other and that participation is not only for our own sake. The principal aspect of love with which leadership is concerned is caring. This is the notion of "standing with people in their duress, not fixing them."

- *Responsibility*: This clarifies love and maintains adequate boundaries between people by "owning up" to who we are and what we are doing.

Leadership, says Terry (1986), is the "courage to call forth authentic action" in oneself and in others, to increase dwelling, freedom, justice, participation, love, and responsibility. I would add that not only do leaders put forth that call, to be effective on a sustained basis, they must live and encourage others to live according to the principles Terry has outlined. It is through living out the principles that leaders can model a way of being that is an authentic and ethical engagement with the world.

PUTTING ETHICAL PRINCIPLES INTO PRACTICE

Woodswomen advocates leadership that is solidly grounded in these particular ethical principles. Leadership style is based on the personal style of the guide and the level of direction is based on the requirements of the situation, thus resulting in an approach that is flexible and adaptive. The role of the guide is to provide an environment in which constituents discover their own power, their own resources, and exercise their own leadership abilities.

The Woodswomen leadership training process relies on an understanding of group formation and development that aligns with the progression of Terry's principles (see Table).

The tasks of leadership relate to the principles as the experience unfolds. The concept of authenticity provides the basis from which the expedition is launched. The initial stages of group formation relate to dwelling and the establishment of freedom and justice as operative ethical principles. If authenticity is the point of departure, then this part of the adventure is analogous to deciding to go on the trip, becoming familiar with gear and with one's traveling companions.

The Progression of Ethical Principles with Leader Tasks

Ethical Principles for Leadership		Leader Tasks
	First Phases of the Journey	
Dwelling	——————————>	Encourage openness and honesty, determine expectations, concerns
Freedom	——————————>	Foster participation in decision making
Justice	——————————>	Reinforce positive group norms, recognize appropriate contributions
	Later Stages of the Journey	
Participation	——————————>	Involve each person, moderate level of direction according to circumstance
Love	——————————>	Value each person, help each to achieve personal goals
Responsibility	——————————>	Encourage individual responsibility, recognize the power of influence

Mid-trip stages of group development relate to participation, love, and responsibility. The adventure is under way as the group travels and each person interacts with others, as well as seeking personal fulfillment. As ethical principles are integrated, the travelers move toward greater authenticity. Thus, authenticity is both the starting point and the destination sought, while the journey is the process of integration and transformation.

AUTHENTICITY

Authenticity, the alignment and integration of truth and reality, is where the journey begins. Woodswomen's approach is to create an atmosphere in which each participant is encouraged to discover her own intrinsic worth and abilities, and to acknowledge her accomplishments. The truth is that, given the knowledge and the skills, women are capable of having a safe, comfortable, challenging but non-stressful, outdoor experience. The reality is that many women have not been able to do that or believe that they aren't capable of it. One guide addressed this when asked about what difference having an all-women's group made in the experience of being in the outdoors. She said:

> . . . If there are only women there, we do everything. Then we realize that women can do everything . . . it's real powerful. Who's going to carry the canoe? We will. Who's going to use that axe? We will. Who's going to cook? We will. Who's going to drag the canoe up on shore? We will. It's all those little pieces. If it's just us, we will do everything. And that changes their lives because, "If they can do that, what else can they do!"

The search for authenticity is the general goal of this trip, as it is the goal of integrated, ethical leadership. To enhance people's ability to experience authenticity, leaders can promote values that set the stage or provide the tools for constituents to use on their trip.

Dwelling

Terry's first principle, that of "dwelling," is one of the most significant factors in the Woodswomen model. Dwelling means "showing up," and in that, affirming not only one's own history and values but also being prepared to acknowledge the presence and legitimacy of others.

One task of leadership is to encourage and model the idea that it is all right to "show up" as you are, that the first step toward fully participating in the world is to be present, with all our personal histories, both good and not so good.

Woodswomen programs consistently begin not only with traditional introductions of guides and participants, but also with discussion about participants' expectations and concerns. Guides encourage candor but lead the discussion in a way that avoids extensive or inappropriate personal disclosure.

Understanding and accepting a participant's level of skill, her beliefs and values, also contributes to the group process. Encouraging and supporting members of the group in their efforts to be open about their desires and concerns is critical to the guide being able to conduct a safe and satisfying trip. In addition, determining expectations allows the guide to consider the various individual needs and desires. From this, the guides can then respond by designing a trip experience, in concert with the group, which will attempt to address those wants.

The next step is to recognize that participants are able to make decisions about where they wish to go and how they want to get there.

FREEDOM

The ability to make choices, freedom, is another building block of the Woodswomen approach to increasing an individual's ownership and involvement in the group experience. Executive Director Denise Mitten has dubbed the process an "affirming-collective process of decision-making" (Mitten, undated).

The guide's role in decision-making can be central or peripheral, depending on the decision being made and how long the group has been together. The process of decision making seeks to maximize each individual's freedom to choose within the context of the experience. Initially, the leader will identify that a decision needs to be made and is responsible for providing information about the options available to the group. Group members then can add their information, concerns, and desires. The guide then can discern whether there is a general, common interest or groupings of interest that could be accommodated by breaking into smaller subgroups. The guide also might suggest an alternative way to accommodate varying desires. Even if the resulting decision does not completely fit all individual desires, each person has had an opportunity to be heard.

The affirming-collective decision-making process acknowledges that the guide or leader has information that needs to be shared and has the responsibility to put forth options that meet the criteria of safety. By listening to each of the group members, she can voice what action is to be taken based on the information that has come from the members themselves.

One guide related an anecdote that illustrates that, even in the face of having to go along with a decision that she flatly opposed, she felt her opinion was acknowledged and validated. In this situation, Julia was a participant, rather than a guide. During the trip, a decision had to be made about what route to take: one choice would result in an extremely long day and bring them to the site of ancient pictographs; the other choice would be to forego the pictographs and have a shorter day on the water. Julia was one of only a couple of women who opposed the longer day. She told me:

> It was real clear that I was either going to have to choose to paddle with one of the other women alone [and leave the large group] . . . or I was going to have to change my mind. Denise said, "Since that seems to be where we are," recognizing the impasse, "what can you get out of the day? What do you want so that you'll feel like you've gotten something important too because you're having to give a tremendous amount?" . . . Now first of all, I didn't even think I was giving that much which was a real key piece and then I got to choose whatever I wanted. Well, I'm not greedy. I thought about it . . . and said "What I really want is to bear no responsibility for this decision" . . . And it was a wonderful day! . . .

Since then, Julia has used this approach both in leading group trips and in her work and family life. She said:

> We try never to sacrifice individual goals to group goals . . . . I think that's a key to empowerment, that you don't have to just cave in to somebody else's needs, that you can get your needs met while giving up a piece of what you want. But it recognizes [your] generosity instead of saying, of course you ought to do what other people want.

Shared decision making also contributes to encouraging leadership among participants and creates a situation in which group members can exercise their freedom.

JUSTICE

The affirming-collective decision-making process and program activities are also based on the principle of justice. Justice, says Terry, is the concept of fairness with its subsets of equality, equity, and adequacy.

Equality is demonstrated in the thinking that each participant has equal claim to receiving the benefits promised to her, namely a trip that is safe and fun, and through which she can acquire additional knowledge and skills.

Another aspect of justice is equity. This is operative in two ways: skills training, and individual contributions to the tasks of the group. Since there are varying skill levels represented among group members, instruction is available to those who desire to advance their level. Guides provide training to the extent that an individual wishes it. Contributions to the group tasks are also done in an equitable manner based on how an individual wishes and is able to contribute. Tasks are not assigned or rotated. Each person is encouraged to contribute in ways that are appropriate for them. This, in turn, acknowledges the diverse interests and talents available in the group. Denise Mitten has written:

> Delighting in group diversity is important. Recognize differences . . . . We look for cues from participants, and when they are extended, we accept them . . . . Reinforce that a "sunset watcher" can be as important as a "fire builder." Equal is not that we each carry 55 pounds, but rather that we contribute appropriately. One woman may carry a limited amount due to a weak back, but she may cook a little more often, or sing wonderful songs as the group portages. Often, given the space and support, participants will equal out the tasks. (Mitten, 1985)

Finally, the third subprinciple of justice is adequacy. Equality and equity need to be responsive to changes in the situation. As skill levels increase or individual interests and abilities change, new situations may arise. The guide must respond appropriately by altering the amount of direction given to individuals or the group.

For instance, a group that has been together for a few days will need little or no direction in how to set up tents or prepare a meal.

Having acknowledged the right of each person to be present and to make choices, and having established the norms of equality, equity, and adequacy, the group members can now move into interaction and relationship building. This is the journey toward each other as well as farther into themselves.

Participation

Participation is the principle of claiming and exercising power. Participation suggests that, once a person is present (dwelling), accepts their ability to make choices (freedom), and agrees that interaction will be on a playing field leveled by the concept of justice, then they must act. Leaders, says Terry (1991), "act in concert with followers." Followers, or constituents, also must exercise their power; otherwise, lack of participation will result in oppression.

Participation is tied to the stage of group formation and process known as "performing." At this stage, participants are familiar enough with task requirements, such as setting up camp and loading canoes, so that the work gets done smoothly and without much discussion. They have acquired more skills and feel more comfortable with their surroundings. The trust that has been engendered previously allows participants to reach this comfort level. Because of the trust level, more personal information may be shared and friendships begin to form. Mary stressed that once a group has full participation and has reached the performing stage, the guide needs to moderate her behavior accordingly:

> You have to look at what information they do need but not be really directive because people don't need that any more. One of the things we talk about is how, if you're a good guide, you basically get yourself out of the role. You're less and less of that central directive person.

The level of participation of any individual is still a personal decision. Again, Woodswomen stresses that each participant needs to assess her needs and desires and figure out her limits. Neither the organization nor the guide predetermine standards or goals for the participant. Rather, each woman is encouraged to choose her own level of challenge. Julia maintains that:

> . . . given the choice, most people will stretch more . . . . In my experience people will choose stuff that is amazing to me, that's really out there on the outer edge of what they can do . . . . Since you have permission to quit whenever you want, then you can push yourself further.

Mary concurred, saying:

> It's not assuming that we know what they need to do to build their characters. We don't think they need to climb to the top of the rock to build their characters. For some women just being there is building their characters incredibly, or going part way up the rock. People come from different places and they are their own best judge of where they're coming from and what they need to do.

There is a critical distinction between creating a situation in which individuals find and exercise their own power, and sharing or giving away power. Power is not a commodity in this model. The guide is not in a position to broker it away. Instead, in fact, the guide is always in a position, vis-à-vis the group, to exercise power as it is appropriate to the situation.

LOVE

Recognition of one's own power and the move to act is not done in isolation. Participation means that there is interaction and relationship with others. Terry (1991) says that love is the act of attending to one another, of "discovering the we-ness of our relationship." It is finding our similarities and differences. Love tempers power and participation by acknowledging that there are others involved in this interaction.

One guide, when asked about what an appropriate name for this philosophy of leadership might be, suggested that it is based on unconditional love. It is apparent that caring, as a principle of love, is of great importance to the success of the Woodswomen group experience.

> I think people want to be respectful, I think people want to love each other [and] want to be loved, and we often don't know how to do it. So one of the things that I teach and our model embodies is how to do what we want to do anyway. (Mitten, personal interview)

With the onus on the individual to take responsibility for herself, caring is emphasized that is affirming of the value of the individual rather than "caretaking" or "curing."

On the group interaction level, enabled by genuine care, individuals can begin to differentiate themselves from the group. Differentiation is the healthy expression of oneself through the sharing of personal information, needs, and desires (Mitten, undated). It is all right for a participant to risk being or doing something different. Personal goals become as important as group goals and subgroups may form around a particular interest or activity. The fear of being different has been mitigated by the expression of genuine care by the guide and by other group members.

Woodswomen maintains that achieving differentiation is critical to reaching the goal of helping women to discover their own power:

> Often in a group where things are assigned all the time and everybody does their own piece, the whole group depends on everybody doing his or her piece at the right time and so there's no room for individuals to say "I am good at that but I don't want to do it any more, I want to do something else." . . . We, from the first, talk about having options—all of us can do this or some of us can do that. Right from the beginning we try to instill that sense. Again this goes back to our empowering philosophy, it's not only okay to make a choice different from the group but it will be supported and encouraged if that's what a woman wants to do. So you see how that differentiating stage is really critical to our philosophy. (guide interview)

RESPONSIBILITY

Robert Terry tells us, "Love needs to be clarified by responsibility . . . that is, as long as I don't own up to my piece of the action, love is going to blur what's going on." Each person is responsible for who she is, how she behaves, and what she contributes. This is particularly important in the relationship of guides and participants because of the power difference between them.

Responsibility is a key value in this model. It is fostered by allowing participants to design what they want into the activities. Responsibility is also stressed in relation to how the guide models behavior, leads the group through the experience, and brings it to a close. It is central to the affirming-collective decision-making process and is apparent in the attitude that there is no single right way to do something. A guide told me:

> Everything is a possibility so I think that initially women respond to that by feeling a little cast adrift. They're not going to be told what to do all the time . . . . We're really reinforcing that women can do things already. They don't have to have instruction about every single thing in order to be able to operate in the woods. So they feel just a little bit like we're not guiding them but they come to realize, and they've commented on that too, that by the middle or end of the trip they've been talking among each other rather than just having participant-guide, guide-participant communication going on.

While there is a focus on participants learning to take responsibility for themselves, there is an equally strong emphasis on the guide's responsibility for her own actions and conducting herself in a manner that is appropriate to the situation. The key component in the leader taking responsibility is the recognition of how powerful a position she is in and the amount of influence a leader can have over members of the group.

One example of how influential the guide can be is in the use of language. Language sets the tone of the trip and influences how participants view their environment and how they react to situations. In essence, language shapes experience.

Since participants are encouraged to choose what constitutes their own challenge, success/failure language is avoided. Mary described an example related to a hiking trip:

> Language is critical. On the North Shore hiking trip, on Saturday, you have three options for hikes. There's a longer hike, a medium hike and a shorter hike. It's really important that when you describe the advantages and disadvantages of each you don't say there's an easy hike and a hard hike because then all of a sudden there's all this value judgement attached to the easy hike like it's taking the easy way out.

In addition, humor is used to try to counteract the use of negative terminology by participants. Mary related to me:

> You know there are some people who are always dumping on themselves and we can contradict that in a real gentle way. Women learn about being wimps. That's a real common word . . . so we say, "Yeah, you know that stands for Women Improving Muscular Prowess." That just sort of diffuses that as a derogatory term.

The power of language is one example of the influence a guide can have on the atmosphere and tone of the trip. Responsibility then, for the guide, is acknowledging how influential her behavior can be and exercising that power in a manner that promotes individual choice, growth, and responsibility.

At the end of the trip experience, guides have a significant responsibility to perform closure on the trip in some way that is appropriate to that particular group: outright recognition and discussion of the fact that this adventure has come to an end, introducing the topic of returning home, and/or helping to integrate the experience into the guide's and participant's life by seeing the experience in context. The memory of the trip and the skills gained, both technical and personal, can be integrated into the person's life rather than the trip existing in memory as a circumscribed event. This integration is crucial to the development of authenticity, the alignment of truth and reality.

CONCLUSION

The journey with Woodswomen took us along a route that began and ended with the search for authenticity. Along the way, members of the group underwent various transformations as did the nature of group interaction. At each stage, the guide adapted her leadership style to the circumstance and, on each leg of the journey, ethical principles guided both the leader and the constituent interactions. These principles, upon which Woodswomen has based its program philosophy and approach to group leadership, provide the foundation for a successful group experience.

32

Ethics and Experiential Education as Professional Practice

Jasper S. Hunt, Jr.

THIS ARTICLE WILL ARGUE FOR GIVING ETHICS A CENTRAL ROLE WITHIN THE emerging profession of experiential education. I hope to accomplish this by connecting the ethical thought of Alasdair MacIntyre and Aristotle to issues in experiential education in general and the adventure-based wing of experiential education in particular. The danger of allowing experiential education to become a set of techniques devoid of ethical control by practitioners will be outlined. Finally, some thoughts on avoiding this danger will be offered.

Two scenarios will serve to present the type of issues central to this paper:

You are working as an adventure therapist at a psychiatric hospital. You have a group of patients on the high ropes course. The staff psychiatrist is out with the group, watching as they go through the course. A young man, high up on the course, demands to be lowered to the ground immediately. You work with him psychologically, yet he continues his insistence that he be lowered. You have been trained in the "challenge by choice" method of experiential education (developed by Project Adventure) and you agree to lower the young man. The psychiatrist looks at you and tells you that the young man is at the point of a great psychological breakthrough but that it will be missed if you lower him to the ground. The psychiatrist tells you not to lower the man. You object to the psychiatrist's order. He looks at you and reminds you that he is a psychiatrist and that you are merely an employee of the hospital, acting as a technician under his direction, and that, as with all technicians employed by the hospital, you are to follow physician's orders.

The A.B.C. Acme Toy Corporation has contracted with your experiential education program to develop teamwork and group cooperation utilizing adventure-based activities. All employees are told to participate in this new and wonderful event. They show up. One of the initiatives being used is the Trust Fall, starting out with low falls and ending with a high fall back into the arms of one's fellow employees. One woman refuses to do any of the Trust Falls arguing that these activities have nothing to do with making quality toys. The C.E.O. of the corporation steps in and tells the woman that she needs to display her loyalty to the corporation and that if she will not participate in the exercises, her commitment to the A.B.C. Acme corporation will be called into question. The C.E.O. then strongly urges the woman to attempt the falls. The instructor on the spot, although nervous about the coercion of the C.E.O., feels strongly that the C.E.O. is ultimately in charge of his employees and that whether or not coercion is justified with the woman is the C.E.O.'s decision, not the instructor's.

Both of these examples represent an issue of growing importance and controversy in experiential education. At first glance, the ethical issue may appear to be whether it is morally permissible to use coercion in experiential education, and if so, then when. However, there is a deeper, more profound issue in these two situations. It is whether experiential educators are autonomous professional practitioners or technicians operating under the orders of others. Whether the others are psychiatrists, corporate executives, school teachers, or principals, does not matter.

There is no doubt that one of the biggest growth areas for experiential education lies in its potential benefits for executives and business managers, psychiatric patients, public school employees and students, and other groups or organizations with some control over the fates of their members. The ethical issue that is relevant here is what special moral obligations do practitioners have to screen the participants in programs and to *set the moral standards* which govern activities.

One logical possibility is to take the position that experiential educators (I include adventure therapists and other specialists using experiential activities under the heading "educator") are merely technicians providing a service to an organization. It could be argued that it was not within the ropes course instructor's role and responsibility in the psychiatric example to interfere with the psychiatrist and the patient in ethical matters. It is possible that the instructor ought to defer to the judgment of the psychiatrist in all matters involving the welfare of patients. The same logic could be used in the situation involving the C.E.O. and the employee.

An alternative possibility would be to argue that the experiential educator is an independent practitioner who is not only *permitted* to intervene in the relationship between the organization and its members, but *is morally obligated* to intervene in that relationship if it is professionally relevant to the experiential educator. Note that in both the psychiatric and corporate situations, there exists an unequal power relationship between the person who sent the group for the experiential activities (C.E.O. or psychiatrist) and the group members (employees or patients). The question then becomes, Do experiential educators have, in matters involving ethical judgment, a foundation upon which to base a countervailing power relationship against the organization on behalf of participants? If the answer is no, then experiential educators are not really autonomous *professional practitioners* but are, instead, *technicians* providing a service at the command or contract of others. If the answer is yes, then experiential educators become morally obligated to protect the best interests of participants against possible moral harm by others, including C.E.O.s, psychiatrists, and other leading authorities within organizations.

EXPERIENTIAL EDUCATION AS A PRACTICE

Before proceeding with the issue of coercion further, it is important to this topic to discuss the issue of a practice in some detail. It is my contention that only if experiential education is understood as an autonomous professional practice does it make sense to argue morally for or against the use of coercion. Otherwise, experiential educators may be required to defer to the wishes of others in moral matters like coercion.

The term "practice" is a technical one. It is one of the words which connects all of the ideas in this article together. Philosopher Alasdair MacIntyre (1984) has defined a practice in terms that are useful for the topic at hand:

> By "practice" I am going to mean any coherent and complex form of socially established cooperative human activity through which goods internal to that form of activity are realized in the course of trying to achieve those standards of excellence which are appropriate to, and partially definitive of, that form of activity, with the result that human powers to achieve excellence, and human conceptions of the ends and goods involved are systematically extended. Tic-tac-toe is not an example of a practice in this sense, nor is throwing a football with skill; but the game of football is and so is chess. (p. 187)

Belaying a ropes course is not a practice in MacIntyre's sense, but using a ropes course as an educational or therapeutic modality is. Just as I can be an excellent surgeon or a poor surgeon, so too can I be an excellent experiential educator or a poor one. The goods or "standards of excellence" which are achievable by a surgeon, a football player, or an experiential educator are goods attainable only by those who participate in the practice of medicine, football, or experiential education. Participating in a practice presents the practitioner with the potential of achieving various standards of excellence which are inherent in the specific practices.

The use of the term "goods" is open to a confusion that should be mentioned. MacIntyre makes a distinction between goods which are *internal* to a practice, and goods which are *external* to a practice. Suppose, for illustration, that an experiential education program was to hire an instructor who was primarily seeking employment in order to finance his or her latest mountaineering expedition. The instructor does an adequate job, receives the appropriate pay, and uses the money to go on the expedition. The good which this hypothetical instructor receives is the money. There is no reason for this instructor to do more than the minimum required in order to be paid for the job. Indeed, if the instructor can do less than is called for, and not get caught, then the person still receives the pay and can be called successful. This sort of good achieved by the instructor is what MacIntyre calls a good external to a practice.

Internal goods, on the other hand, are goods which are attained purely because of the excellence achieved by participating in a well-executed practice. An experiential educator pursuing internal goods will receive satisfaction by being recognized as achieving a level of excellence only attainable by participating in the practice. Thus, instructing a ropes course with style and care reaps rewards to the instructor which are not identical to the pay received for the work completed. This does not mean that internal and external goods are mutually exclusive. An experiential educator who is well paid may, at the same time, receive internal goods from a job well done.

Thus, it makes sense to talk about a good or a bad experiential educator. Presumably, what is desired are good educators rather than bad ones. This is where ethics emerges as inherent to the very core of what it means to participate in the practice of experiential education. Practices logically imply standards of excellence for practitioners to measure themselves against. As MacIntyre (1984) argues:

> A practice involves standards of excellence and obedience to rules as well as the achievement of goods. To enter into a practice is to accept the authority of those standards and the inadequacy of my own performance as judged by them. It is to subject my own attitudes, choices, preferences and tastes to the standards which currently and partially define the practices. (p. 190)

I may aspire to achieve excellence as a baseball player, but I do not achieve it if I am only able to hit the ball given five strikes, instead of three. The point of MacIntyre's quote immediately above is that inherent to achieving the label of "a good baseball player" is the idea that I am only allowed three strikes at bat. Any more than three strikes and I am no longer playing baseball. The three-strike rule provides a standard of excellence by which my performance is judged. If I am to achieve excellence as a baseball player, it will only be possible insofar as I conform to the standards set by the practice of baseball. The goods that I achieve by meeting these standards are the goods internal to the practice of baseball.

The end result of someone who achieves levels of excellence set by a practice is to refer to that individual as a virtuous person. In formulating the definition of virtue, MacIntyre (1984) writes:

But what does all or any of this have to do with the concept of the virtues? It turns out that we are now in a position to formulate a first, even if partial and tentative definition of a virtue. *A virtue is an acquired human quality, the possession and exercise of which tends to enable us to achieve those goods which are internal to practices and the lack of which effectively prevents us from achieving any such goods.* (p. 191)

The first step, then, in formulating a conception of a virtuous experiential educator is to look at the practices which make experiential education what it is. For a person can only attain the status of a virtuous experiential educator through his or her functioning within the practice. The achievement of goods internal to the practice of experiential education is the key to achieving virtue in this context.

There is often a tendency to restrict discussion of practices to purely technical activities. In other words, a practice could be limited to articulating the standards of excellence purely in terms of such things as the technical and interpersonal skills needed to function as an experiential educator. If this were the case, then virtue in experiential education would reduce to the mastery of purely technical and interpersonal skills, and the issue of ethics would, therefore, convert to discussion of those matters. One could argue that: I have mastered these skills; therefore, I am a virtuous experiential educator. This argument would be valid as far as it goes. Certainly mastering the technical, internal goods of the practice of experiential education is a vital part of the virtues of the practice. But there is more to virtue than just technical and interpersonal activities.

Aristotle (McKeon, 1941) discusses two kinds of virtue that are very helpful:

Virtue too is distinguished into kinds in accordance with this difference; for we say that some of the virtues are intellectual and others moral, philosophic wisdom and understanding and practical wisdom being intellectual, liberality and temperance moral . . . . Virtue, then, being of two kinds, intellectual and moral, intellectual virtue in the main owes both its birth and its growth to teaching (for which reason it requires experience and time), while moral virtue comes about as a result of habit whence also its name *ethike is* one that is formed by a slight variation from the word *ethos* (habit). (p. 952)

Aristotle makes the distinction between an intellectual and a moral virtue. Knowing how to perform the technical and interpersonal activities of experiential education falls under the umbrella of an intellectual virtue. The intellectual virtues, however, cover only part of the territory of virtue. *A moral virtue is one which must be developed in order that the intellectual virtues be guided and controlled toward their proper ends.* For example, I may achieve the excellence of making good safety judgments about the appropriate use of ropes-course belay techniques when working with various student populations. Suppose, however, that I am lazy and I, therefore, do not use these techniques because they make my job more difficult. My laziness becomes a character flaw within me that gets in the way of my exercising the intellectual (technical) virtue of being a good ropes course facilitator. Unless I develop the moral virtue of industriousness as well as the intellectual virtue of good technical skills, I will never achieve the internal goods of being an experiential educator who utilizes ropes courses. *Without moral virtue I could become an experiential educator, but I could not become a good experiential educator.*

According to Aristotle (McKeon, 1941), therefore, ethics becomes the formation of the right habits needed to guide the intellectual virtues:

> This, then, is the case with the virtues also; by doing the acts that we do in our transactions with other men [humans], we become just or unjust, and by doing the acts that we do in the presence of danger, and being habituated to feel fear or confidence, we become brave or cowardly . . . . Thus, in one word, states of character arise out of like activities. This is why the activities we exhibit must be of a certain kind; it is because the states of character correspond to the differences between these. It makes no small difference, then, whether we form habits of one kind or another from our very youth; it makes a very great difference, or rather all the difference. (p. 953)

If MacIntyre is right about virtue being a necessary ingredient for achieving goods internal to practices, then the virtues become essential for practitioners to achieve their ends. If Aristotle is right that ethics is the development of right habits needed to guide the intellectual virtues, then it seems reasonable to conclude that in order to have a practice of *good* experiential education, ethics and virtue are needed as inherent to the practice.

This leads into a pivotal question: Is experiential education a practice? Does experiential education at its current state of development meet the definition of a practice articulated by MacIntyre, or is it merely a set of techniques blowing in the wind, to be grabbed and used in any way that an individual or group chooses? One can think of a practice as either a static, completed final product, or one can think of a practice as an emergent element within a larger social context. If one takes the static, final completion route, then it seems clear that experiential education is not a practice. But I will argue that no practice is final and complete. Whether the practice is medicine or baseball or law, they all are changing as appropriate to fit new situations and contexts.

Therefore, my position is that experiential education is on the way to becoming a practice, but that it is not fully there yet. Clearly, most existing programs realize internal goods by adhering to standards of excellence. Experiential educators measure themselves against the rules and standards of the programs in which they operate. The attitudes, choices, preferences, and tastes of individual experiential educators are held in check by the contexts in which they work. For instance, an Outward Bound instructor who engages in sexual relations with his or her students will be censured by Outward Bound. A Project Adventure instructor who coerces and forces unwilling participants into doing activities would also be censured. Every program that I am aware of has standards of excellence which partially define the bounds of acceptable behavior to which educators must adhere.

A critical issue facing experiential educators is whether or not there are universal standards of excellence which are not program specific and which all experiential educators measure themselves against. This issue is extremely controversial. Although controversial, nevertheless, it must be faced. Unless there are standards of moral excellence to which all practitioners must adhere, experiential education cannot be called a practice and the whole argument of this paper collapses. My view is that there are de facto universal moral standards but that these have not been made as explicit as they could be. If the profession is to measure up to MacIntyre's criteria of a practice, then the moral standards must be as clear for experiential educators as they are for physicians, baseball players, and lawyers.

By implication, therefore, if I am correct that experiential education is an emerging professional practice, then the issue of coercion of students is of professional concern to practitioners. This gets the argument going, but it does not resolve it.

Just as there can be disagreement within the practice of experiential education about the details of the technical issues, so, too, can there be disagreement about the moral virtues. It is beyond the scope of this paper to resolve the specifics of coercion as a virtuous or a vicious act. However, the implication of the philosophical argument is that this issue should be dealt with from *within the profession* and that the ethical resolution not be handed over to those who contract for services. It is enough, at this point, if I have convinced readers that the complete welfare of participants is of concern to the professional experiential education practitioner, and that this concern includes both moral as well as technical issues.

Psychiatrists or corporate executives may have the power to order people to show up at an experiential education site in the first place, but that power ends the moment the participant "steps off the bus" and enters into the professional realm of the experiential educator. If coercion of participants, whether under psychiatric care or corporate edict or whatever, is ethically problematic, then the practitioner had better tread very carefully before coercing his or her students into doing experiential activities. Whether the coercion comes from the experiential educator or from some other source, it is still under the professional ethical purview of the practitioner. Failure to recognize this fact could well result in the practitioner not achieving the internal goods open to him or her by participating in the practice of experiential education.

I want to argue that a central new direction must be to scrutinize the virtues necessary for achieving the ends of experiential education in general and the adventure-based wing in particular. This scrutiny can only be accomplished by practitioners being willing to submit themselves to the scrutiny of the community of fellow practitioners.

Experiential educators are notoriously individualistic, and the idea of submitting oneself in one's professional life to the scrutiny of other practitioners' views on professional ethics may be troubling for some. However, MacIntyre is very clear about this necessity. A collegial relationship between practitioners is a special relationship. MacIntyre (1984) writes:

> It belongs to the concept of a practice as I have outlined it—and as we are all familiar with it already in our actual lives, whether we are painters or physicists or quarterbacks or indeed just lovers of good painting or first-rate experiments or a well-thrown pass—*that its goods can only be achieved by subordinating ourselves within the practice in our relationship to other practitioners.* We have to learn to recognize what is due to whom; we have to be prepared to take whatever self-endangering risks are demanded along the way; and we have to listen carefully to what we are told about our own inadequacies and to reply with the same carefulness for the facts. In other words we have to accept as necessary components of any practice with internal goods and standards of excellence the virtues of justice, courage and honesty. For not to accept these . . . so far bars us from achieving the standards of excellence or the goods internal to the practice that it renders the practice pointless *except as a device for achieving external goods.* (emphasis added) (p. 191)

To paraphrase, colleagues in a professional practice are part of the fabric which defines what the practice is and, therefore, colleagues are partially definitive of each participant in the practice. This means there is a built-in moral obligation to share one's technical and ethical ideas with one's colleagues in a professional practice. This is in contradistinction to the society at large, where no such obligation exists.

The alternative to practitioners establishing their own ethical parameters is for others, possibly in other professions or government, to establish them. As experiential education becomes more sophisticated in its technical dimensions, so, too, must it become more sophisticated and accountable in the ethical dimension. If MacIntyre is correct about the moral virtues being essential for the achievement of excellence within a practice, then professional experiential education practitioners are obligated to begin to define what is virtuous and what is vicious within the practice. Failure to do this would be to engage in an absurd enterprise. Success in defining virtues and vices will help in the development of experiential education as a sophisticated professional practice.

Notes

The author wishes to express his gratitude to the Editor of the *Journal* and the two reviewers for their helpful critiques and criticisms of an earlier version of this paper.

33

Understanding Moral Development and Environmental Values Through Experience

Almut Beringer

$\mathbf{M}$ANY EXPERIENTIAL EDUCATORS AIM TO DEVELOP ENVIRONMENTAL VALUES IN students which support a sustainable planet in which humans and non-humans live together in dignity. Activities and programs often take place in the outdoors because it is felt that teaching environmental values is most effective in the setting to which those values are geared. Many experiential educators attest to the power of the natural environment in changing individual behaviors and group dynamics. However, until recently, psychologists have overlooked the impact of the natural environment on human experience (see Kaplan & Kaplan, 1989). The sociocultural environment is accepted as a factor influencing childhood maturation, yet the impact of the natural environment is not well documented in the scientific literature.

Despite the limited work in this area, experiential educators need skills and tools to help students acquire appropriate value positions and moral perspectives. How do individuals develop environmental values, and what factors influence this development? How do children learn to care for the environment and what factors contribute to that learning? How is responsibility toward the natural environment expressed behaviorally across the life span and across cultures? These questions are waiting to be addressed. This paper will provide a brief overview of two prominent theories of moral development in order to identify the theoretical concepts which seem valuable for understanding the development of environmental values. It will then describe the *narrative technique* in detail, one approach which seems to hold particular promise for educators interested in environmental moral development, particularly those with an experiential orientation.

MORAL DEVELOPMENT AND ENVIRONMENTAL VALUES

From a psychological perspective, morality is three-dimensional, consisting of moral thoughts (cognition), feelings (emotion), and behaviors. The dynamic interplay of the cognitive, affective, and behavioral aspects of morality constitutes moral experience.

Moral psychologists who work on understanding moral experience have formulated theories that describe how individuals come to understand concepts of justice (Levine et al., 1985), care (Gilligan, 1982), and responsibility toward other people. These concepts are applied to the context of human relationships alone. Moral psychologists have overlooked the notion that morality and ethics extend to the natural environment, which can be labeled "environmental morality." This disregard may partly be due to the fact that traditionally in Western culture, ethical considerations have not included the environment (see Passmore, 1974), and partly because the natural environment has been taken for granted until its value was recognized in the face of the ecological crises.

Lawrence Kohlberg's theory of moral development is the most prominent one in the field, yet it makes no reference to the environment. Kohlberg equates morality with the concept of justice. His theory is based on the premise that moral development means learning to act on principles of fairness, equality, and reciprocity. This learning, Kohlberg argues, is closely linked to an individual's cognitive development and takes place in a series of stages (Levine et al., 1985).

Kohlberg's stage model of moral reasoning states that an individual's morality can extend to all humankind. Although Kohlberg himself limits morality to the human community, Partridge (1982) suggests that Kohlberg's highest stage of moral reasoning includes a capacity for an "ecological morality." Research has shown that most of society functions at the lower egocentric stages and very few people achieve the highest stage of moral reasoning (cited in Iozzi, 1989), a discovery that must be alarming for environmental educators.

Similarly, in Carol Gilligan's model (Gilligan, 1982), humans at the highest level of moral reasoning include self as well as others in considering responsible conduct and extending care. Her model fails to state that this "other" may be nonhuman beings, a place, or the natural environment.

Very little empirical work has been done in environmental moral development. Iozzi (1976) took Kohlberg's model and applied it to environmental issues. His research demonstrated that people who are more knowledgeable about environmental problems reason at higher levels on moral issues dealing with the environment than those who are not so knowledgeable. This finding implies that it may be important to teach natural science concepts and information from fields such as biology, ecology, and geography, in addition to highlighting the sociocultural, economic, and ethical parameters involved in environmental issues. Only then might it be possible to challenge students to think about environmental matters from a moral/ethical perspective and promote students' moral development.

There are dangers in applying existing models of interpersonal moral development to research in environmental morality. One must assume that the acquisition of environmental values proceeds in the same way as the acquisition of interpersonal values. The more fundamental question is whether the stage model even applies to environmental morality.

Furthermore, many moral philosophers who wish to make a contribution to environmental morality follow a deductive approach: they aim at developing an environmental ethics theory and then teach the public moral principles to make appropriate environmental decisions (see Hargrove, 1989). However, research has shown that people's moral actions are not based on philosophical analysis but upon human response to a situation, i.e., moral action is rooted in a sense of self rather than in a knowledge of rights and rules (Mergendoller, 1989, p. 137). The philosophers' approach, like Kohlberg's, fails to recognize that moral experience includes emotions and behaviors as well as cognitions.

Gilligan's framework of moral development, although an interpersonally-based theory, is more appealing as it avoids the pitfalls of both a stage model and a cognitive environmental ethics approach. In the following paragraphs, I elaborate on Gilligan and her colleagues' research technique—the narrative approach—for environmental-values education and research.

NARRATIVES IN MORAL DEVELOPMENT RESEARCH

The narrative approach to understanding moral development is inductive. Researchers analyze and interpret retrospective accounts of people's moral experiences. The informants are asked to recall a situation in which they encountered a personal moral dilemma in which they were unable to decide on right and wrong. This technique allows for an understanding of morality to emerge from the richness and uniqueness of people's life experiences.

Gilligan (1982) presents empirical data concerning the moral decision making of women. This research leads her to state that there are two different moral voices which reveal different themes—the ethic of care and the ethic of justice. These moral voices are gender-related in that girls and women tend to reason in terms of sustaining relationships and avoiding harm (ethic of care), while boys and men tend to make decisions based upon principles of fairness and reciprocity (ethic of justice). Consequently, women's moral development is distinct from, but parallel to, that of men. These findings are intriguing to environmental educators, especially if one argues that the ethic of care may be more suitable than the concept of justice to protect the diversity of life on this planet (see Caduto, 1985, p. 13).

Gilligan's investigation not only identifies the effects of gender on moral development, but also, indirectly, opens up the consideration of the interrelationships between morality and other human characteristics such as race, class, and culture. In the context of environmental morality, systematic analyses and interpretations of narrative accounts of moral dilemmas might reveal if and how gender, culture, race, and socioeconomic background affect moral development and the acquisition of environmental values.

A NARRATIVE EXAMPLE

Researchers have used a formal, semi-clinical interview in order to elicit narratives of people's moral experiences. The Real Life Moral Conflict and Choice Interview (Brown et al., 1989) invites people to tell their stories of real-life conflict and choice in depth. These formal interviews are transcribed and subjected to an interpretive analysis that is sensitive to the subtle nuances of language, moral voice, and perspective.

For example, Mary, a 47-year-old participant in a wilderness leadership training program, was asked to recount a moral conflict in her life in which she knew the natural environment was going to be affected in a negative way by her behavior, a situation where she did not know what was the "right" or "moral" thing to do. She replied:

> I'm a bird lover. I've had a cat for years that my children acquired. Cats and I don't get along too well. I'm more a bird lover and I've learned over the years from watching birds that even a presence of a cat in the neighborhood—even if the cat does not catch birds, even if the cat does not kill animals—will discourage the birds from hanging out in the area, from nesting there, from coming around to eat. Just knowing there's a danger in the area [the birds] will stay away. So in the summer and spring time—this has happened for ten years now—I put my cat inside; it has to stay in the house. And that's my rule. I just need to compromise. That's the only thing I could think of short of getting rid of the cat. I can't really get rid of it, because it has become such a part of the family now. I have considered many times of doing him in, but each time I think about it, I think I just can't do it. So I compromise: the cat can roam all winter and late fall, but in the spring time and in the summer he has to stay indoors.

The interviewer then asks her to specifically identify the conflict in the situation:

> I really want the birds outside. The cat is a domestic animal, sort of a human-raised creature, and I feel he has lower priority than the birds to me. The birds have greater priority to me . . . to nest in freedom and to raise their little babies, and to be.

Later in the conversation, Mary mentions another moral dilemma:

When I was a kid, my mom would shoot the hawk or the owl that raided the chicken house so there's another good example of "Do you save the chickens or do you get rid of the hawk or owl?" and I used to be of the school where we would shoot the owl or the hawk. But then I noticed that it didn't really do that much good either, I mean, there's always some animal that would get in and get the chickens sooner or later. What I do now is when a hawk or owl comes around to get the chickens I just figure, well, that's how it goes. I side with the owl or the hawk. I might try to protect the chickens better, but I figure the owl or the hawk has a much more precarious existence and more rights than the chickens.

In line with Gilligan et al.'s approach, Mary recalls these particular experiences in her life by telling a story about them; she constructs a narrative to represent them. Moreover, Mary's narrative is about a real-life moral conflict. In both incidences, her story involves the actual or potential killing of an animal (cat, hawk, chicken). Mary's story also exposes an important lesson she learned from her experience ("I just need to compromise . . . I can't really get rid of it"). Consequently, a critical aspect of her own moral development is expressed in the story she tells.

By telling a story, Mary is forced to reflect on the past events. The process of constructing a narrative about a moral dilemma gives her the opportunity to consider the consequences of her thoughts, feelings, and actions. Moral development can occur through reflection (Tappan & Brown, 1989, p. 192).

Narrating one's story about a moral conflict is valuable because it asserts one's own particular moral perspective, one's moral authority. Claiming authorship means honoring what one thinks, feels, and does with respect to right and wrong (Tappan & Brown, 1989, p. 190). The interview excerpt shows evidence that Mary assumes responsibility for her moral thoughts, feelings, and actions ("I side with the owl or the hawk").

Mary's narrative account illustrates the complicated and complex interactions of the cognitive (what she thought), affective (how she felt), and behavioral (what she did) elements that constitute her moral experience. She *thought* that "the presence of a cat in the neighborhood . . . will discourage the birds from hanging out in the area," and "that's the only thing I could think of short of getting rid of the cat." She *felt* the cat "has become such a part of the family now," and decided to *act* by putting the cat in the house. Her thoughts and feelings influenced her action, yet her behavior also influenced how she thought and felt ("he has a lower priority than the birds"). In Mary's story, we can see the fundamental interconnection between the three psychological dimensions of morality. Without focusing simultaneously on the three dimensions of Mary's moral conflict, one runs the risk of misunderstanding her story, her reasoning and behavior, and environmental morality in general.

The narratives reveal some insights into what constitutes environmental moral conflicts for Mary and how she resolves them. In both situations, the existence of a domestic animal and a wild animal is at stake (cat vs. birds, owl/hawk vs. chicken). Mary decides the conflicts in favor of the wild creatures, although she admits it more directly in the second incident ("the cat has lower priority," "I figure the owl has a much more precarious existence . . ."). Mary's process of moral decision-making indicates a hierarchy of rights and value based upon the "wildness" of the animal. The animal's degree of wildness serves as a source of her moral standards. From preliminary analyses of other narratives, this scale of rights and value rooted in the degree of naturalness of animals, plants, and landscapes emerges as well and may constitute an important insight into how people make environmental decisions when parts of the natural environment are at stake.

Lastly, Mary expresses her current values and contrasts them with her mother's values. Her statement is significant in that it demonstrates the role of ecological knowledge in changing her values. Her knowledge of the precarious existence of many birds of prey has encouraged her to reflect on the values she was taught as a child, and subsequently, she discards those values and acts on new values which she considers more appropriate.

NARRATIVES AS AN EDUCATIONAL TOOL

Many environmental educators use stories and other written works regularly in their teaching. Case studies of environmental conflicts and decision making (a form of narrative) can be valuable educational tools in the classroom (Monroe & Kaplan, 1988). Storytelling has been a means of transmitting values in many cultures. What is new or different about Gilligan et al.'s narrative approach?

It is unique in inspiring students to tell their own moral stories. The objective is to enable students to develop cognitive, emotional, and behavioral capabilities that strengthen environmental values and moral positions. On the basis of knowledge of individual students, the instructor may then decide which features of moral conduct need to be encouraged or discouraged in each student.

The narrative technique has a number of educational advantages: 1) storytelling in moral education encourages individuals to appraise moral situations and claim responsibility for their own moral stance: 2) it is based on a model of moral development that does not concentrate on issues of justice and fairness, but one that is sensitive to various moral voices and perspectives of race, class, and gender; 3) the technique honors each student's particular experiences; and 4) it acknowledges the unbreakable bond between thinking, feeling, and doing when trying to understand and cultivate morality. Values education that emphasizes moral thinking is insufficient. Students also need to be sensitized to moral emotions and guided in constructive conduct.

Educators can provide various opportunities for students to author their own moral stories (see Tappan & Brown, 1989, pp. 194-196):

- The instructor can elicit stories one-on-one, so that students can tell their stories of real-life conflict and choice in depth. This narrative can be a starting point for further discussion, debate, elaboration, and clarification. This one-on-one interaction can give the instructor valuable insights into the student's moral reasoning and provide a starting point for individualized moral education.

- Students can share their stories in a group of peers, e.g., around a campfire. A responsive peer audience may provide the opportunity for students to learn important lessons from each others' stories. Through mutual inquiry, students may understand why their peers considered a particular situation to be a moral dilemma They can become sensitized to the values and moral positions of others. In the process of social reflection, important issues can be discussed, alternative solutions to the dilemma proposed, and answers to questions of values approached.

- Journals or essay assignments that focus on students' moral conflicts and decisions can give them the chance to voice their own moral stories. The instructor can promote students' authorship and moral development if he or she can respond to each narrative with sensitive and astute comments. In a case where the instructor judges the solution to be destructive, there may be a need to point out the deficiencies and encourage the consideration of alternatives.

Educators should carefully consider the following points when employing the narrative technique (see Tappan & Brown, 1989, pp. 193-197):

- The success of this approach depends on peer and instructor rapport. One of the powerful ingredients of the narrative approach is the audience, either an individual or a group of active and empathetic listeners. Unless an environment is created that is conducive to mutual trust and respect for each individual, the effects of sharing moral experiences may be detrimental.

- The narrative technique can be dangerous: students (and teachers) become vulnerable by sharing difficult, painful, and perhaps even tragic experiences. Teachers and peers must anticipate and be briefed about the opportunities and risks inherent in this approach and must be ready to respond appropriately in each individual case.

- Moral experience is affected by gender, socio-economic background, and other factors. The way a story is understood is equally affected by the same factors. Stories are open to multiple interpretations which depend in same factors. Stories are open to multiple interpretations which depend in part on who interprets them and on the listener's own moral experience. There is no single, right way to understand a story. Consequently, the instructor cannot readily assume that he or she knows what a student's story means, and must exhibit care in judging a particular story as "inappropriate," "immoral," or "wrong."

CONCLUDING THOUGHTS

Western societies are finally recognizing and reappreciating the impact nature has on the quality of our lives. We are rediscovering the ancient wisdom of including animals, plants, and the inanimate environment in our ethical system. While some moral principles are shared across cultures, this does not characteristically lead to similar judgments about what is right and wrong. A culture's ideology and worldview have a significant bearing on how the natural environment is treated ethically. In turn, human interactions with nature and the landscape shape cultural and ethical systems. Both the interactions with other people and with nature have an impact on the development of moral understandings in the individual as well as the culture, and the task remains to uncover these influences and then to use them effectively.

REFLECTIONS ON RESEARCH IN ENVIRONMENTAL MORALITY
AN ADDENDUM

The need for quality research in environmental morality stands in stark contrast to available theories and methods which may support such research. Progress in illuminating the question of how people acquire an "ecological conscience"—i.e., into the process and dynamics of moral development where the object of moral concern is nature, not the human community—is hindered by conceptual as well as methodological difficulties. In environmental philosophy, it is the focus on justice conceptions of morality and the "rational man" model of human functioning which impedes the development of theory. In psychology, it is the neglect of nature in human development research which calls for revisions of existing theory. The basis of research in environmental morality must be "practical morality," i.e., morality which expresses itself in people's deliberations and actions (Haan et al., 1985; Packer, 1989); the goal of research in environmental morality must be correct theory—correct because it illuminates real life (Haan et al., 1985).

Experiential educators interested in contributing to the development of correct environmental moral development theory should take into consideration the following three points:

1) Studying environmental moral development requires specifying the goal or telos of moral development; this telos serves as the end point against which development can be assessed empirically. However, the twenty-year-old debate in environmental philosophy has not yielded a conclusive definition of environmental morality which could be translated into a developmental telos for the purpose of psychological research. Consequently, the researcher needs to find other ways to define and justify a telos (or teloi). One avenue could be to precede developmental inquiry with a Delphi study which defines environmental morality and determines appropriate developmental telos (or teloi). An alternative, participatory approach—one which reflects the philosophical foundations of experiential education—is to ask the research participants to define their own development (Tappan, 1987). In practice, this translates into extracting from the narratives of moral conflict and choice the research participants' moral ideals, i.e., their conceptions of environmental morality, which govern thought and action. This approach has the advantage of including the public in the debate of what environmental morality may be; on the other hand, it does not negate expert knowledge as ethicists are called upon to philosophically justify or reject the proposed moral ideals in light of the goal of global environmental sustainability. In addition, educational psychologists are needed to decide whether and which educational measures need to be taken to promote or thwart the student's environmental moral development along her/his particular path.

2) Environmental morality research grounded in interpersonal morality theory runs the risk of misunderstanding rather than illuminating the phenomenon of environmental morality. Theories of social moral development are built on certain assumptions; assumptions which might not hold or are counterintuitive for environmental morality. For instance, many theories of human development (including Kohlberg's theory of moral development) chart a path of maturation from a state of psychological connection to separation. But is it not the task of experiential and environmental educators to guide students from feeling separated to feeling connected with nature? Hence, must not the reverse developmental progression—from separation to connection—be reflected in environmental moral development theory?

3) My experience with the experiential approach suggests that the research participants need to be led into the task of providing narratives of real-life moral conflict and choice by giving them examples of what environmental moral conflicts may be. For many of my research participants, the task of reflecting on environmental issues from a moral/ethical perspective

seemed difficult. This is not surprising, considering that neither Western philosophy nor our society provides us with rich and precise language to voice our moral intuitions with regard to nature. Actual or hypothetical dilemmas, selected by the researcher, are adequate stimuli to trigger moral reflection on environmental issues.

The experiential approach and the narrative technique described in the 1990 article above, and in greater detail in Beringer (1992) circumvent the conceptual and methodological problems outlined above. A study with 31 high school juniors, students in a semester-long experiential/environmental education program, yielded the moral ideals of care and respect, ideals which further question the appropriateness of Kohlberg's justice conception for environmental morality as well as the adequacy of the environmental philosophy debate. The environmental moral ideal of care, delineated independently of Gilligan (1982), nevertheless shows much accord with the interpersonal "ethic of care." Whether an environmental moral ideal of care and a social moral ideal of care are merely aspects of one moral orientation and whether these "care" ideals develop autonomously or together remains subject to further research.

ACKNOWLEDGMENTS

I am grateful to Alaska Women of the Wilderness and NOLS Alaska for providing me the opportunity to interview students and instructors. Thanks are also extended to Dr. Mark Tappan for his encouragement, and Karin Gunkel, Dr. Alan Warner, and anonymous reviewers for helpful comments on an earlier version of this paper.

Section VII

Research and Evaluation

34

Research in Experiential Education: An Overview

Alan Ewert

To me truth is precious . . . . I should rather be right and stand alone than run with the multitude and be wrong . . . . The holding of my beliefs has already won me the scorn and ridicule of some of my fellow scholars . . . . But truth is truth, and though all the world reject it and turn against me, I will cling to truth still.

Charles deFord, 1931

FOR THE EXPERIENTIAL EDUCATOR, DEALING WITH COLLEAGUES, PEERS, AND THE public can often be described by the above quote. Experiential educators know the "truth" that combining experience with education is an effective way to learn. The problem lies in convincing other professionals and lay people. Before we move too far into the realm of self-righteousness, we would do well to remind ourselves that the above quote was from a booklet written by Charles de Ford in 1931 (Gardner, 1951, p. 12) in which he attempted to prove that the earth was FLAT.

In order to reach the "truth" and better understand experiential education, research and evaluation become very useful tools. More specifically, these tools help us explore the questions of *what* happened in an experiential education program, *how* it happened, and how the program can be altered to make "it" happen again, only *better*. While the terms "research" and "evaluation" are similar, research is generally associated with theory testing and evaluation is more directly linked to information-gathering for decision making in programs (Weiss, 1972). Both are vital links in the information chain of experiential education between the practitioner and researcher.

The purpose of this introduction is to outline some of the major issues surrounding research and evaluation in experiential education. These issues include the gap between the researcher and practitioner and current directions in research. Finally, some suggestions for addressing these and other concerns are provided so that future research efforts in experiential education might avoid the pursuit of a "FLAT" earth.

THE RESEARCHER/PRACTITIONER GAP

. . . a tale told by an idiot, full of sound and fury, signifying nothing.

Shakespeare

As illustrated by Shakespeare, one concern in experiential education is the separation of fact and fiction in examining research findings. Of equal concern is the distance between the researcher and practitioner with respect to areas of interest and types of information considered useful or valuable. Moreover, information that is acquired either by the practitioner or researcher is often not fully integrated into the other group. Reinharz (1979, p. 95) suggests that research is frequently conducted on the "rape model," where researchers take, hit, and run away with the information. All too often research in experiential education becomes an exercise in data generation rather than the production of meaningful findings.

Part of this problem is structural in that practitioners and researchers are often faced with different concerns. For example, the practitioner may be interested in getting information in order to facilitate making decisions about a program. Conversely, the researcher may be more concerned with theoretical relationships of little relevance to the practitioner. A sample of possible differences which can lead to misunderstandings is provided in Table 1.

Table 1. Differences Between Researchers and Practitioners	
Researchers	**Practitioners**
Obligation to be critical	Don't like to criticize
Searching for truth	Need to make decisions
Emotionally neutral	Emotionally involved
Information for theory development	Information for decisions
Limited by research design	Limited by cost
Working toward a perfect world	Making an imperfect world work
Modified from Ewert (1986)	

Table 2. Criticisms Between Researchers and Practitioners	
Criticisms Of Practitioners By Researchers	**Criticisms Of Researchers By Practitioners**
Never ask the right questions	Never get a straight answer
Pay little attention to advice	Too cautious, can never make generalizations
Want easy black-and-white answers	Never have enough data or information
Not interested in objective truths	Retreat into research jargon
Reactive rather than proactive	"Could be" instead of "will be"
Looking for bargains	Crackpots versus capable—who can tell?
Do not comprehend the term "reliability"	Do not comprehend the term "meaningful"

Modified from Ewert (1986).

These differences often result in criticism between practitioners and researchers which is often justified and contributes to a lack of understanding and communication between the two groups. A portion of these criticisms is listed in Table 2.

This is not just a dilemma for the researcher. If practitioners want information which is both useful and specific, they must open their programs up to research and evaluation. A program with no allowance made for permitting research or evaluation will yield little in the way of new theoretical or developmental knowledge which could help the practitioner deliver a better product. While there are no repair manuals for fixing this situation, Hamilton (1979) suggests research and evaluation efforts that are cooperatively designed by researchers and practitioners. Practitioners should be afforded the opportunity for professional development in areas such as program evaluation or understanding research findings. These opportunities should be located at the workplace rather than the classroom and should focus on how-to's rather than strictly on theory. Lawson (1985) refers to this as recipe-knowledge and believes that it is an important part in the development of a profession.

CURRENT RESEARCH DIRECTIONS

One swallow does not make a summer; nor do two "strongly agrees," one "disagree" and an "I don't know" make an attitude or social value.

(Webb, et al., 1966, p. 172)

Experiential education is concerned with a variety of behavioral, educational, and affective components. These components are often complex, multifaceted, and difficult to observe. The issue is to determine what the researcher should study and how to study it. Too much of the research currently being done in experiential education is concerned with the outcome of the program (Shore, 1977; Burton, 1981). This is a problem, for while outcomes are often the sine qua non of experiential education, this type of research often does not provide an understanding as to *why* it happened or *how* it can be made to happen again. Without the ability to explain how and why an outcome (e.g., enhanced learning) is realized, we lose our ability to predict that outcome in different situations or with different participants. Moreover, being able to explain how something works implies that it can be modified to become a better product. However, it should be remembered that this method of education places a strong emphasis on action and direct participation rather than passive verbalization. Not addressing the impact and effect of direct experience on an individual would ultimately do a disservice to the profession. A balance is needed, with research devoted to both outcomes and process.

Another research area which has been neglected is program issues, such as the optimal mix of activities to place in a course and the most efficacious ways to market the activities and programs. Heath (1985) indicates that there is often too much concentration on statistical technique at the expense of conceptualizing a clear purpose or interpretation of the findings.

Obtaining these findings can involve using *qualitative* and *quantitative* research methods. Quantitative research is often associated with model testing, statistical treatments, prediction, and relationships between variables. Qualitative research has been termed naturalistic inquiry, participant observation, or ethnographic research, and involves phenomenology, field notes, self-descriptions, and open-ended interviewing. Both forms of research have an important role to play in experiential education with no one method being intrinsically "better" than the other. The proper use of qualitative and quantitative research has always included the process of hypothesis testing, sound reasoning, and theory formation (Kirk & Miller, 1986). Qualitative work can provide theoretical insight, validate survey data, and help in the interpretive portion of a quantitative study. Quantitative research can be used to identify individuals or cases for further qualitative work (Fielding & Fielding, 1986).

Whatever style is used, any research and evaluation effort should be systematic, based on measurement and/or observation, explanatory as well as descriptive, replicable and explicit about the limitations. The importance of this research should not be underestimated as the future quality of our programs is dependent on the information presently being gained—or lost.

IMPLICATIONS AND SUGGESTIONS

Wisdom came to earth and could find no dwelling place.

Enoch

Ultimately, the most important question asked of a research or evaluation study is, What does it all mean? This is the critical link in the chain of knowledge in experiential education. A growing number of experiential educators have the statistical and research/evaluation design skills to conduct a variety of data collection projects. Research, however, is more than statistical analysis for it implies "meaning making" out of collected data. Finding relevant meaning out of a collection of information involves an interpretation of those data that often moves beyond the circumstances of their origin. Johnston and Pennypacker (1980, p. 395) refer to this as generality and suggest that generalizing research findings involves prediction with different subjects, settings, methods, and processes. What is suggested here is a refocusing of attention on the *interpretation phase* of research and evaluation. There may be some danger in this approach as researchers might formulate the wrong interpretations or draw incorrect pictures of reality. These errors can arise from inaccurate observation, illogical reasoning, ego-involvement, and premature closure of inquiry (Babbie, 1983, pp. 10-15). While all these concerns are justified, to err is human and often worth the risk. By intensifying the interpretation phase of research, experiential education will gain valuable insight into the processes it promotes and the impact these methods might have on individuals.

What is needed is a *multimethod, multivariable approach* in which a number of variables are combined with a variety of methods. Research in experiential education is still too truncated, focusing mainly in the outdoor area. Work needs to be done in other arenas such as cross-cultural analysis, traditional education, and other social institutions that incorporate learning. Moreover, life is not so episodic that one event, even in experiential education, is unrelated to the other aspects of one's existence. There is a bonding between events and experiences which serves to provide a backdrop for the attitudes, behaviors, and abilities of an individual. Exploring this multivariable concept involves much more sophisticated research methods than are currently used in experiential education.

As research and evaluation in experiential education develop, the concern for ethical practices also increases. Bachrach (1981, p. 123) indicates that ethical research must contain the elements of informed consent, confidentiality, and acceptable procedures. With the increased emphasis on qualitative research methods, a number of ethical issues will develop. These issues include: role conflict between the participant and observer, observing people without their knowledge, and reporting on participants who are violating program policy. In addition, using research and evaluation to hide the reality of an ineffective program continues to plague this and other fields.

In sum, when compared to the more established disciplines of education or psychology, research in experiential education is still in an early stage of development. After all, it was only 13 years ago when experiential education became represented by a formal organization. Since that time, a substantial amount of research has been undertaken. Much of this research has pointed to the effectiveness and power of combining experience with education. To date, there are no indications that this trend will diminish, with research and evaluation continuing to play an important role in that process.

Our research base is still very much focused on widely divergent outcomes, with little in the way of building on the past work of others. Moreover, the research has consistently offered scant tidbits of practical information for people trying to make their programs work. What practical, usable advice the research community in experiential education can give the practitioner still remains an elusive mystery. Solving that mystery must remain one of the goals of future dialogues within the experiential education community.

35

Anxiety and the Outward Bound Process

Charles E. Drebing, Scott Cabot Willis, and Brad Genet

Since the creation of the first Outward Bound School by Kurt Hahn in 1941, wilderness trips that emphasize learning through stressful situations have grown in their popularity and diversity of application (Wade, 1983). There are a vast number of programs employing the original principles of self-improvement through challenging experiences. Many of these have remained surprisingly faithful to the structure and philosophy of the Outward Bound School and Hahn's educational principles. They can, therefore, be profitably discussed as a whole under the rubric described by Walsh and Gollins (1975) as the "Outward Bound Process" (OBP).

Over the past fifteen years, a number of studies have been done examining the efficacy of the OBP in producing positive change in participants. A wide variety of potential therapeutic benefits have been examined, with the most common factors being self-concept (Ewert, 1983), personality change (Drebing & Willis, 1987), and behavior change (Baer, Jacobs, & Carr, 1975). Despite the inadequacies of many studies on efficacy, most reviewers of the research conclude that experiential education programs employing the OBP have a positive impact on participants (Burton, 1981; Shore, 1977).

There continues to be a lack of a clearly articulated theory of how the OBP works. Wichmann (1983), in reviewing past research, states that it is important that future research be more *theory-based*, investigating the questions of *how* and *why* wilderness programs work effectively. This study is an attempt to utilize a *theory-based* procedure to examine one factor, anxiety, which has been identified as playing an important role in the OBP (Ewert, 1987a; Ewert, 1987b).

Figure 1

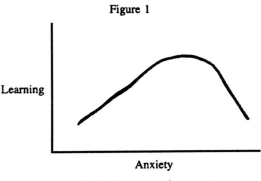

Learning

Anxiety

Yerkes-Dodson Learning Curve

Anxiety is a central part of any student's experience during the OBP. Unfamiliar settings and activities, challenging and stressful tasks, and emphases on introspection and self-evaluation, are all anxiety-producing aspects of the OBP. Kalisch, in *The Role of the Instructor in Outward Bound Educational Process*, describes anxiety as a critical factor in the OBP, determining whether successful learning will or will not occur. "Unless a student experiences enough anxiety to put his confidence in doubt, he will probably not put forth much energy to make any changes in himself" (1979, p. 53).

In the *Leadership Manual of the Vanguard Wilderness Courses*, Williams states:

> Psychologists have found that unless people are anxious and afraid about the life situation they are in they probably will not put forth effort to change and grow . . . the fact that it is anxiety producing makes the participants more ready to try out new behaviors and methods of problem-solving. This can be overdone, however. An excessive amount of anxiety causes a person to come apart at the seams and the situation becomes destructive. (1975, p. 31)

This description, from the experiential education literature, of the role that anxiety plays in the learning process is better known in theoretical psychology as the Yerkes-Dodson Law (1980). This paradigm of learning-theory is illustrated in Figure 1. According to this principle, maximum learning is promoted when the student's anxiety is at a moderate level. When anxiety is too low, learning is inhibited by poor motivation, and inhibited again if the anxiety level is raised too high. It appears that the Yerkes-Dodson Law is ideally suited to help answer the question of how and why experiential education programs that utilize the OBP are able to have beneficial outcomes for the participants.

Thus, using this learning-theory principle from psychology, the present study was designed to examine the way in which the anxiety level of the student is related to his or her performance and experience in the OBP. Since the theory articulates a *curvilinear* relationship between anxiety and learning, each of the first three hypotheses presented below is operationally defined to be curvilinear in nature. The fourth is included to investigate a related, though different, aspect of the important relationship of anxiety to prior experience with OBP activities and with the wilderness environment in general.

HYPOTHESES

The following hypotheses were put forth to be tested in accordance with the Yerkes-Dodson Law relating anxiety to learning:

Hypothesis 1 — Those students with a moderate level of anxiety will have learned the most during the course and will report the highest degree of satisfaction from the trip, while those students with low or high levels of anxiety will have learned the least during the trip and will report the least amount of satisfaction. Those with a moderate level of anxiety will experience sufficient stress such that the course is challenging, and yet the stress will not be so high that it is overwhelming nor so low that they are bored (i.e., under-motivated). This first hypothesis assumes students enroll in experiential education programs for some purpose related to learning (e.g., learning about themselves, learning about others, etc.). Thus, their satisfaction with the course will be dependent upon whether they perceive themselves to have achieved some degree of learning.

Hypothesis 2 — Student understanding during the course and directly after the course will be related to anxiety in the same curvilinear manner as satisfaction, described in Hypothesis 1 above. Student understanding is crucial to a successful experiential or adventure education program. Along with the emphasis on the experiential, there is a matching emphasis on reflection and introspection. This is necessary in order to promote or facilitate the students' learning from their experience. The degree to which the students are able to understand their experiences is very much related to the degree to which they benefit from the course.

Hypothesis 3 — Students with moderate levels of anxiety are hypothesized to be more involved in the learning process, and, therefore, will have an enhanced relationship with the leaders; while those students with low or high levels of anxiety will not be as involved in the learning process, and so will not be as involved with the leaders. It is through this relationship with the leader that student learning is developed and enriched. In students with low levels of anxiety, the leaders are likely to note a lack of involvement in the learning process as lack of involvement in their relationship. In a similar manner, students with high levels of anxiety are likely to be expending energy in merely coping with the experience. Thus, they are also likely to be less involved in the student-leader relationship. This will be measured by feedback both from the students and the leaders.

Hypothesis 4 — The more experience the student has with the wilderness environment and with OBP activities, the lower their level of anxiety prior to beginning the experiential education program. As OBP activities (e.g., rock climbing and rappelling, backpacking, endurance running, etc.) become more popular in our culture, more students will have been exposed to them as well as to the wilderness environment. Thus, the degree to which these students have "experienced" the wilderness environment and OBP activities will serve to lower their anxiety prior to the onset of the course or program. This is a separate hypothesis from the first three as it predicts a linear relationship rather than the curvilinear relationship of the Yerkes-Dodson Law.

METHOD

Subjects

The 39 subjects were incoming freshman at Wheaton College who signed up to participate in the High Road program, which is based at Honey Rock Camp in northern Wisconsin. The High Road program was developed directly from Outward Bound and utilizes the OBP. There were 27 males and 13 females, each assigned to one of five groups with two experienced leaders. This was a three-week course, which included a variety of activities such as a major expedition, a three-day solo experience, rock climbing, and rappelling. For a more detailed description, the reader is referred to the leaders' manual for the Vanguard program (Williams, 1975) or the Outward Bound programs (i.e., Wade, 1983; Walsh & Gollins, 1975).

Procedure

All participants were administered the State-Trait Anxiety Inventory (STAI) (Spielberber, Gorsuch, Lushene, Vagg, & Jacobs, 1977) as a measure of their general level of trait anxiety at the beginning of the course. Both state anxiety (situational) and trait anxiety (a characteristic of one's personality) are pertinent factors in the Outward Bound Process. Trait anxiety was chosen as the independent variable for determining the low-, medium-, moderate-, and high-anxiety groups, as the focus is upon the OBP as a whole and how a person typically responds to it (Ewert, 1987b) rather than being upon individual situations within the OBP. The STAI has been widely used in research and in clinical settings, has good reliability and validity, and is administered quickly (20 items).

After the course was completed, they were also administered a student questionnaire (SQ) which examined various aspects of their experience, including satisfaction with the course, perceived stressfulness of the course, understanding during and after the course, and relationship with the leader. All these items utilized a seven-point Likert scale. The SQ also contained ten statements pertaining to experience in a wilderness setting and experience in OBP activities. Students were asked to indicate how much they had participated in these ten activities prior to the course. Group leaders were also asked to fill out a questionnaire (LQ) ranking their students on factors regarding performance, learning, and relationship with the leader.

RESULTS

For the first three hypotheses, the statistics require that the anxiety scores be converted to four nominal categories (low 0-28, medium 29-33, moderate 34-39, high anxiety 40+) with an equal number of students in each category. The scores obtained from the students showed a normal distribution and covered the entire range measured by the STAI. These were then tested using a trend analysis (Keppel, 1982).

Hypothesis 1 — The hypothesis that anxiety and students' reported overall satisfaction would exhibit the same curved relationship that is seen in the Yerkes-Dodson Law was not supported. A comparison of the mean satisfaction scores shows only a trend (i.e., not significant at the accepted $p < .05$ level) toward a positive linear relationship between level of anxiety and satisfaction ($r = .25$, $F = 2.40$, $p < .10$).

Hypothesis 2 — The hypothesis that anxiety and understanding relate in a way similar to the learning curve found mixed results. Understanding *during* the trip was found to relate in the hypothesized manner to anxiety ($F = 3.41$, $p < .05$). However, after the course was over, with two days of debriefing, the relationship had changed considerably (see Figure 2). There was no longer a significant curvilinear relationship ($F = 0.42$, n.s.).

Hypothesis 3 — The hypothesis that anxiety and the student-leader relationship also resemble the Yerkes-Dodson learning curve was supported with the data from the leaders but not with the data from the students. The leaders' general evaluation of the relationship was found to relate significantly ($F = 5.23$, $p < .05$) to anxiety in this curved manner (see Figure 3).

However, when anxiety scores are related to the students' evaluation of the relationship, the curvilinear pattern was not found to occur, but a positive linear relationship did emerge ($r = .37$, $F = 5.77$, $p < .05$). This indicates the higher the level of anxiety, the more positively the students rated the relationship with the leaders. Therefore, according to the leaders, they had the best relationships with students with moderate anxiety, but from the students' perspective, it was the students with higher anxiety who reported having a more significant relationship with the leader.

Hypothesis 4 — This hypothesis, that the more experience the student has with the wilderness environment and with OBP activities, the lower their level of anxiety prior to beginning the experiential education program, was supported. Anxiety was found to have a significant negative linear relationship ($r = -.36$, $p < .05$) to the

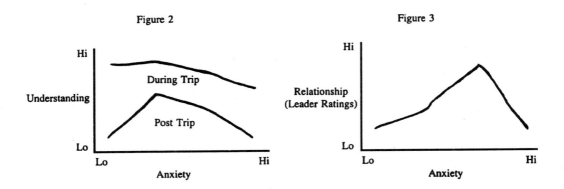

Figure 2 — Understanding vs. Anxiety (During Trip, Post Trip)

Figure 3 — Relationship (Leader Ratings) vs. Anxiety

students' experience in the wilderness and in OBP activities. Those with little prior experience tended to have higher anxiety than those who had already participated in many OBP activities or who were familiar with the wilderness environment.

DISCUSSION

The value of doing theory-based research, as opposed to testing intuitive hunches or exploratory investigations in search of empirical truth, is that the theory is the reference against which the results are understood and interpreted. Though not all of the results obtained in this study supported the hypotheses, the results can all be interpreted in light of the underlying theory.

Support was not found for Hypothesis 1. If anything, the numbers suggest that the more anxious the students, the less satisfied they will feel with their experience. Possibly this is due to a difference between learning and satisfaction, pointing to an error in the assumption underlying this hypothesis—i.e., a greater amount of learning leads to a greater degree of satisfaction. Further investigation is warranted here since both student learning and satisfaction are central goals of any wilderness program.

Hypothesis 2 was supported with regards to understanding *during* the course but not afterwards. During the course, students with high levels of anxiety and students with low levels of anxiety find it harder to understand their experience than those students with a moderate level of anxiety. As already stated, students with very low levels of anxiety may not be motivated toward understanding and those with very high anxiety are more distracted with coping with the stress and less able to attend to the learning process. However, it is vitally important to note that students in both the high and low groups quickly made up lost ground when they were out of the stressful environment and deeply involved in debriefing and reflection. This would then suggest the importance of a debriefing time and a time for personal reflection at the end of a course in order to facilitate understanding in those students who were either underanxious or overanxious. It should also be noted that the particular wilderness course used in this study follows the standard OBP which includes debriefing and group interaction sessions during the trip as well as after. This result also suggests that if anxiety levels during the course can be kept at a moderate level, then greater student understanding may be facilitated at that time. This would require that leaders be sensitive to individual levels of anxiety for each participant and find ways to moderate it, either by increasing the level of stress for those individuals who do not appear challenged or by reducing the stress for those who appear overwhelmed (Ewert, 1987a; Ewert, 1987b).

Hypothesis 3, regarding anxiety and the student-leader relationship, was supported in the evaluations from the leaders but not from the students. The results show the students with the highest anxiety reported having a more significant relationship with the leaders than did others.

From the leaders' point of view, those students with moderate anxiety were the ones with whom they developed the most satisfying relationships. This might suggest that those students who were more involved in the learning process and understanding what was going on at the time would be the ones with whom the leaders felt most involved. Those students who appeared to understand the process less, i.e., those with very high and very low anxiety, may have been seen as less involved, and were therefore less attractive.

From the students' point of view, it appears that as anxiety increases, so does the importance of the relationship with the leader. Clearly, the most natural response when stress or anxiety is overwhelming is to seek a refuge or source of security. In the wilderness, there is a noticeable absence of sources of safety and security for those unfamiliar with the wilderness environment. The only options available in this regard are the group of fellow students and the leaders. It is not unreasonable to think that the leaders become the primary source of security as it is they who have the training and experience to get them safely through the program and out of the wilderness. Alternatively, this may also suggest that the leader is seen as a source of learning, making him/her of more importance to those with the felt sense of needing to learn more in order to survive the program. This latter explanation seems less parsimonious than the clear impetus to satisfy security needs in the face of high anxiety. Both measures of the relationship are subjective and need to be interpreted in this fashion.

Finally, the fourth hypothesis found support, confirming that previous experience in wilderness is related to lower initial anxiety at the start of the OBP course. It remains to be investigated as to how this prior experience with the wilderness environment relates to learning and satisfaction. It does suggest, though, a few words of caution for leaders. If both low and high levels of anxiety are associated with lower levels of understanding, then students with both low and high levels of experience may need special consideration to optimize their learning. Experienced students may need extra support. Also, as wilderness activities such as rock climbing and backpacking become increasingly popular in our culture, it may be profitable for wilderness programs to find new activities and alternatives to add to their repertoire in order to maintain an optimal level of anxiety.

Overall, the present study is an important step in theory-based research investigating the role of anxiety in the OBP. Certainly, further research is needed in this area and in all areas concerning how the OBP works. Issues such as how anxiety changes over the course of a program, and how it relates to perceived stressfulness, are important aspects warranting future research. Eventually, there may be sufficient information to warrant the assessment of anxiety in participants prior to the course as a means of improving their experience.

36

The Effects of a Wilderness Orientation Program on College Students

Michael A. Gass

OVERVIEW OF THE STUDY AND ITS CONCLUSIONS

SINCE THE ESTABLISHMENT OF THE FIRST ORIENTATION PROGRAM IN 1888 AT Boston University, colleges and universities have been interested in providing programs that assist in the adjustment of first-year students. While the focus of some orientation programs has been to combat the variety of factors which lead students to drop out, the goals of other programs have been the intellectual, moral, identity, and interpersonal development of students while they are at school.

In addition to the establishment of traditional programs, alternative methods of student orientation have been utilized. One such adaptation has been the development of wilderness orientation programs. Since the inception of the Dartmouth College program in 1935 and the Prescott College program in 1968, over forty institutions of higher learning have established wilderness orientation programs for first-year students (Gass, 1984). While their goals vary, some of these programs have been developed with the same purposes as traditional programs—to ease the transition of students to college, to reduce the attrition of students, and/or to provide a means of facilitating student developmental growth.

The purpose of this study was to examine the effects of a wilderness orientation program specifically designed to reduce student attrition and assist in the development of first-year students at a university. Another intention of the study was to illustrate the use of multiple covariates and similar comparison groups as methods of reducing the internal and external validity threats that can limit interpretations of quasi-experimental design research.

DISCUSSION

While the goals of some wilderness orientation programs are limited in scope (e.g., serving as an introduction to the college outing club), others focus on providing variable curricula that assist students in adjusting to and developing in the college/university environment. In striving for recognition and inclusion in higher education, such programs find themselves evaluated in the same manner as traditional orientation programs: Does the program assist in the incoming or ongoing orientation of students? Does it aid in the intellectual, moral, identity, or interpersonal development of students? Does it increase the retention of undergraduate students?

The results of the study showed that the Wilderness Orientation Program positively influenced the retention of first-year students at the University of New Hampshire. Factors that contributed to this retention that were also evident in the study were higher first-year grade point averages and greater levels of student development. Table 1 illustrates these areas of student development and their identifying characteristics.

One of the central reasons for the gains seen in the participants was the focus of the program on goals that related specifically to the area of undergraduate student development. The focus on these factors, the positive benefits of learning experientially in an outdoor environment, and the ability to transfer the learning and successes from the wilderness orientation experience into the university environment all played pivotal roles in the accomplishments of the program.

It is important to note that the Wilderness Orientation Program had no significant effect on students in the area of developing purpose (i.e., influences in the areas of appropriate educational plans, mature career plans, and mature lifestyle plans). It was felt that many of these characteristics remained unaffected since they represent focuses of development achieved during a student's junior or senior year in school. Other researchers (e.g., Hood, 1982) have found these characteristics to develop later in a student's career or even following their undergraduate education.

One important factor of the study was the effect that time had on the variables of student retention and grade point average. While changes in student development behaviors were evident seven weeks after the initial five-day program, statistical differences between the groups in retention and grades were not present until the end of the student's second semester of school. As potent as the initial experience was, it seems that the success of such a program was partially dependent upon the transfer and follow-up experiences that occurred throughout the participants' first year of school. It is recommended that colleges and universities view wilderness orientation programs as a year-long process. This is particularly true if these programs are implemented as a strategy to reduce attrition.

Table 1. Descriptive Characteristics for the Task and Subtask Areas Found to be Significant

*1.   Task Area: Developing Autonomy

A. Emotional Autonomy	B. Instrumental Autonomy	*C. Interdependence
• self-concept • self-directed • self-motivated • self-reliant • manages emotions in appropriate ways	• self-sufficient • self-supporting • problem-solver • geographically mobile • manages time, money, and other resources well • brings about desired changes when needed	• supportive • good citizen • cooperative • does own share • collaborates effectively with others

*2.   Task Area: Developing Interpersonal Relationships

**A. Appropriate Relationships with Opposite Sex	B. Mature Relationships with Peers	**C. Tolerance
• honest • caring • concerned about partner • supportive • aware of and expressive of feelings • sensitive to the needs and well-being of the relationship	• trusting • dependable • supporting • accepting of differences • warm • open • aware of the needs of others	• respectful • understanding • flexible • accepting of diversity • able to effectively and objectively interact with many different kinds of people

* $P < .05$ ** $p < .01$

It is obvious that future research needs to be done in this area. While the evaluation of such efforts is not an easy task, it is imperative that it be conducted if wilderness orientation programs are to achieve a stronger role in the areas of incoming and ongoing student orientation.

METHOD

Subjects

Three groups of incoming freshman (September 1984) at the University of New Hampshire (UNH) participated in the study: 1) the Summer Fireside Experience Program (SFEP) group (N = 32; 19 females and 13 males); 2) the Freshmen Camp (FC) group (N = 64; 38 females and 26 males); and 3) the control (CG) group (N = 64; 38 females and 26 males). The FC and CG samples were randomly selected from their larger populations. Sample populations of 64 were utilized by the researcher to achieve a proportional research design. Participants of the SFEP and FC groups were recruited for these two programs by brochures mailed to incoming freshmen and a ten-minute slide presentation given during a two-day orientation for incoming freshmen during the summer of 1984.

Procedures

Students in the SFEP group participated in one of three identically structured five-day programs prior to beginning school at UNH. Activities during each five-day program included initiatives, orienteering, rock climbing and rappelling, backpacking, a "solo" experience, service projects, and a long-distance run. Structured follow-up experiences also occurred for this group throughout their first year at school. These experiences included a rock climbing reunion trip with faculty two weeks after the beginning of the Fall semester, letters from the program director consisting of related materials from the initial five-day program, an adventure weekend program during the beginning of the Spring semester, and one day of low- and high-ropes course activities in the middle of the Spring semester.

Students in the Freshmen Camp (FC) group participated in a four-day session at a residential camp setting prior to the beginning of school. Activities during this time period included small group discussions with upperclassmen, skits about campus life, a "faculty-student day," and cheers/songs to increase interaction. Structured follow-up activities included letters from upperclass counselors. The FC group was utilized as a non-equivalent comparison group since it matched many of the same selection characteristics as the SFEP group (e.g., a voluntary program prior to the students' freshmen year, a program lasting four days where students must pay for their experience).

Students in the Control Group were members of the incoming class that did not participate in either the SFEP or FC programs.

Instrumentation

The three groups were compared on attrition/retention rates, grade point averages, and task and subtask areas from a shortened version of the Student Developmental Task Inventory (SDTI-2) (Winston, Prince, & Miller, 1982). The reliability of the shortened inventory was .79. Task and subtask areas measured by the SDTI-2 are shown in Table 2.

Table 2. The Developmental Tasks and their Corresponding Subtasks Measured by the Student Development Task Inventory (SDTI-2).			
	Tasks		
	Developing Autonomy	Developing Purpose	Developing Mature Interpersonal Relationships
	Emotional Autonomy	Appropriate Educational Plans	Appropriate Relationships with Opposite Sex
SUBTASKS	Instrumental Autonomy	Mature Career Plans	Mature Relationships with Peers
	Interdependence	Mature Lifestyle Plans	Tolerance

Data Collection

After a comprehensive review of the literature on factors related to student retention and development, five variables were selected for use as covariates in the study.

Five covariates were utilized since there was little change in the reduction of variance when more pre-study variables were incorporated into the analysis. The five selected were:

1.   In-state/out-of-state classification.

2.   Academic profile (the combination of college aptitude test scores and adjusted high school rank).

3.   The need for financial aid assistance.

4.   The goal of career development for the student.

5.   The choice of UNH as the school they wanted to attend (i.e., 1st, 2nd, other).

Outcome measures were collected during three periods of the 1984-85 academic year. Seven weeks after the initial treatment of the SFEP and FC programs, each member of the three groups was sent the SDTI-2 Inventory and a participant release form.

After the completion of the first semester (January 1985), the second data collection began. The final collection of data occurred in June 1985 and was conducted in the same manner as the second collection of data

Data Analysis

The statistical analysis of the data was a 3 x 2 Treatment by Sex design. ANOVA and ANCOVA analyses of other secondary factors (i.e., the interaction of sex with treatment, the effect of different instructors in the SFEP program, methods of solicitation used to facilitate questionnaire response, methods of subject recruitment) were also conducted to determine their relationship to the outcomes of the study.

RESULTS

Attrition/Retention

Attrition/Retention was measured following the first and second semesters of the students' freshmen year. While there was no significant difference among the groups after one semester, there was a significant difference among groups after two semesters ($F2, 157 = 3.38, p < .05$). The adjusted means for the three groups are found in Table 3.

To determine where the differences occurred among the three groups in attrition (as well as for all other significant findings with the dependent variables), the Newman-Keuls (N-K) multiple-comparison procedure was utilized. Results of this test revealed that the SFEP group experienced a significantly greater retention rate than both the FC and the CG groups ($p < .05$). From these statistical data, it can be seen that SFEP participants were more likely to stay at the University after one year of school.

Table 3. Adjusted Means for Those Dependent Variables That Achieved a Level of Statistical Difference in the Study.

	SFEP Adj. Mean	FC Adj. Mean	CG Adj. Mean
Rate of Retention	.94	.79	.69
Cumulative 1st Year GPA	2.74	2.44	2.49
SDTI-2 Task Areas:			
• Developing Autonomy	15.58	13.98	13.01
• Developing Interpersonal Relationships	17.18	15.00	14.69
SDTI-2 Subtask Areas:			
• Interdependence	5.82	5.11	4.68
• Appropriate Relationships with Opposite Sex	5.81	4.22	4.39
• Tolerance	5.49	4.63	4.31

Grade Point Average (GPA)

First-semester and cumulative first-year grade point averages (GPA) were also measured in the study. No significant differences were found between the groups in first semester GPAs, but there was a significant difference among groups after two semesters (F 2, 129 = 3.55, $p < .05$). The adjusted means for the three groups are found in Table 3.

In examining the differences among groups with the N-K multiple-comparison procedure, it was found that the SFEP group mean was significantly greater than both the means of the FC and CG groups ($p < .05$). From these results, it can be observed the SFEP participants attained a significantly higher GPA than the FC and CG members.

Student Development Behaviors (SDTI-2)

Investigation of the SDTI-2 results revealed a significant difference among groups on the task areas of Developing Autonomy (F 2, 96 = 4.05, $p < .05$) and Developing Interpersonal Relationships (F 2, 96 = 3.50, $p < .05$), and the subtask areas of Interdependence (F 2, 96 = 3.81, $p < .05$), Tolerance (F 2, 96 = 5.17, $p < .01$), and Developing Appropriate Relationships with the Opposite Sex (F 2, 96 = 18.31,

$p < .001$). There was no significant difference among the groups on the task area of Developing Purpose or the subtask areas of developing emotional autonomy, instrumental autonomy, appropriate educational plans, mature career plans, mature lifestyle plans, and mature relationships with peers.

Inspection of the significant task and subtask scores (using the N-K multiple-comparison procedure) revealed that the SFEP group was significantly superior to the FC and CG groups in the task area of Developing Interpersonal Relationships ($p < .01$). For the task area of Developing Autonomy, the SFEP group was found to be significantly greater than the FC ($p < .05$) and CG ($p < .01$) groups. (See Table 3.) Table 1 identifies the descriptive characteristics associated with those task/subtask areas found to be significant.

37

An International Survey of Outdoor Leadership Preparation

Simon Priest

OVERVIEW OF THE STUDY

LEISURE SERVICE AGENCIES REPORT A GROWING INTEREST IN THE PROVISION OF "risk-related" activities (Dunn & Gublis, 1976). With increasing numbers of people going outdoors for their recreation, there is a corresponding increase in accidents, environmental impact, and negative experiences (Nash, 1982; Ford & Blanchard, 1985). One suggested solution to this problem has been the education of the user by competent outdoor leaders. To develop a pool of such outdoor leaders, outdoor leadership preparation programs have been created in the five nations of Australia, Canada, Great Britain, New Zealand, and the United States of America (Ford & Blanchard, 1985). A close examination of these programs, and the opportunity to share the ideas of experts from these nations, may bring about improvements in outdoor leadership preparation in North America. Thus, this study was undertaken to shed international light on this topic.

The primary concern of this study was to seek out differences and similarities in the attitudes and approaches of experts from five related nations concerning outdoor leadership preparation. A secondary concern was to identify national characteristics, unique to each nation, and to use those characteristics to explain the differences and similarities which arose. Accomplishing the study required that the experts from each nation be surveyed on: 1) their attitude as to what is required to create a competent outdoor leader; 2) their approach as to how outdoor leaders are prepared; and 3) national characteristics which might explain why the countries apply different techniques in their preparation of outdoor leaders.

Fifty experts from each of the five nations, (Australia, Canada, Great Britain, New Zealand, and the United States of America) were selected on the basis of their current expertise in outdoor leadership preparation. The study was limited to these five nations for several reasons, among which were common languages, common educational systems, and common legal systems. However, the most important reason was the existence of outdoor leadership preparation programs with common roots traceable to the original British Mountain Leadership Certificate Scheme. The premise of the study was founded on the assumption that since these programs began with similar roots, any differences in attitudes or approaches to outdoor leadership preparation were likely caused by circumstances specific to the nation. By controlling for these and other commonalities, singling out fundamental differences, and identifying unique national characteristics, an explanation of why the experts of each nation might differ in their attitudes and approaches to outdoor leadership preparation would be possible.

The survey was modeled after those of earlier researchers (Buell, 1981; Green, 1981; Swiderski, 1981; Priest, 1984) and was pilot tested twice. Twenty survey questions were founded on fourteen components of effective outdoor leadership. These fourteen components (seven skills and seven attributes) were synthesized from a review of the five nations' literature on outdoor leadership:

Skills	Attributes
Technical activity skills	Motivational philosophy and interest
Safety skills	Physical fitness
Organizational skills	Healthy self-concept and ego
Environmental skills	Awareness and empathy for others
Instructional skills	Personable traits and behavior
Group management skills	Flexible leadership style
Problem-solving skills	Judgment based on experience

The final coded survey was mailed to 250 selected experts. One month after the initial mailing, a follow-up postcard was sent to all non-respondents encouraging completion of the survey.

GENERAL FINDINGS

Several differences regarding the importance of the fourteen outdoor leadership components and their inclusion in a preparation program were noted among nations. Extensive comments provided by the experts, in answer to questions regarding national characteristics, helped greatly with explaining these results.

In terms of rating and ranking the components, only four components showed differences: problem-solving skills, safety skills, technical skills, and organizational skills. These differences may be due to several reasons. Of paramount explanatory power would be the concern for litigation, which was a major concern in North America, although there existed a positive safety attitude among all responding experts. Because of their concern for litigation, Canadian experts considered safety skills to be of the utmost importance. On the other hand, problem-solving skills were not as important to the British as to the North American experts. The British have yet to experience liability problems like those in North America, and hence, considered problem-solving skills to be less important. Also, some experts commented that the nation of Great Britain was extremely slow at accepting the importance of such "soft" skills to outdoor leadership preparation.

In terms of training, field trips were considered to be the most important method and were allotted the greatest amount of time. The British experts placed more emphasis on the time allotment for field trips than did the Americans. Additionally, the American experts had a preference for simulation exercises which the British experts did not. This difference between the British and Americans can be accounted for by the high number of outdoor pursuits centers in Great Britain. The opportunities for access to the adventure environments are greater and more common for this nation. On the other hand, the United States is a land of technological extremes, where simulations are a cultural norm. For example, respondents pointed out that they perceived the United States as the world leader in simulation training for aircraft pilots, automobile drivers, and the militia. Americans, in some parts of their nation, cannot get easy access to adventure environments and hence, have highly developed such artificial challenges as ropes courses to simulate the "real" adventure experience. Americans are more accepting and more promoting of simulation than the British for these reasons. The British prefer to "do the real thing—what it's really all about" as several experts related in their comments.

In terms of assessment, the evaluations of program trainers were thought to be the most desirable method by most respondents. The British and Australian experts preferred to use outside experts for the second assessment. Americans and Canadians preferred to consider the assessments of peer leaders and group followers, while the New Zealand experts emphasized a preference for candidates assessing themselves. The British and Australian preferences can be explained by the structure of their outdoor leadership programs. These nations have programs which frequently assess candidates by using observers from outside the particular program, but from within the formal structure. The North American nations do not have formally structured programs and, according to some respondents, are reluctant to share evaluations with outside professionals for fear of criticism. Lastly, the New Zealand preference for self-assessment is easily explained by the "do-it-yourself" attitude that was so often mentioned by responding experts.

The desire on the part of Australian and New Zealand experts to increase public participation is not present in the experts of Great Britain and the United States. These latter two nations contain heavy population densities by comparison to the former. The natural resources of Great Britain and the United States do not have the carrying capacity to support the additional impact of more users. Australia and New Zealand, on the other hand, have much greater opportunity for people to recreate outdoors. Adventure tourism for overseas visitors was mentioned as a major drawing card for these countries.

The experts from New Zealand, Australia, and Great Britain were more interested in creating a professional outdoor leadership association, and in maintaining positive relations among users, than were the North American experts. This desire for a professional association comes from experts wanting to have control over their own interests. Currently in these three nations, outdoor leadership preparation is controlled by bureaucratic agencies with close connections to the government sector. The experts commented many times that there was a need for developing an alternative system to standardize training and assessment as well as to do away with the "red tape which makes outdoor programs as institutionalized as indoor ones."

DETAILED RESULTS

Of two hundred fifty surveys, 170 were returned for a return rate of 68.0% proportionate across all five nations. Of these, only one return was considered to be unusable. There were no indications of a time-ordered trend in the responses and hence, no evidence was available to support a concern for bias on the part of the 32% of non-respondents.

Thirteen (7.7%) of the total respondents were female. A total of 21 (8.4%) female subjects were sampled, indicating that return rates among genders were comparable, indicating no gender bias present in the data. The low number of female experts is due to the field of outdoor leadership preparation being heavily dominated by males, as several experts were quick to point out and desired to change.

The youngest respondent was 28 and the oldest 78, with a mean age of 43.1 years. The group reported a range of from 1 to 60 years' experience preparing outdoor leaders (mean = 10.3 years) and a range of from 8 to 73 years doing outdoor pursuits and adventure activities (mean = 26.3 years). When broken down by nation, these reported lengths of experience differed only slightly, indicating that the responding sample was comprised of experienced experts.

Time taken to complete the survey ranged from ten minutes to fourteen hours! A majority (81.1%) took between one and two hours, with the average time taken being 81.5 minutes. Despite this rather long completion time, internal consistency (as

Diagram 1: The Experts' Relative Ratings and Rankings of the Fourteen Components of Outdoor Leadership.						
Components	Rating 6-1	Ranking 1-7		Summary of Differences		
Skills and Attributes	Mean (S.D.)	Mean	Median	High Nations	Low Nations	F-H
Safety	5.68 (0.48)	2.50*	2	Canada	Australia	H = 12.3
Judgment	5.55 (0.55)	2.19	1			
Awareness/Empathy	5.51 (0.58)	2.47	2			
Group Management	5.33 (0.62)	3.60	3			
Problem Solving	5.25 (0.81)*	3.91*	4	Canada/USA	UK	F = 7.5
						H = 32.3
Instructional	5.20 (0.62)	3.94	4			
Technical Activity	5.15 (0.71)	3.94*	4	New Zealand	Canada	H = 10.1
Flexible Style	5.10 (0.74)	4.28	4			
Philosophy/Interest	5.07 (0.79)	4.33	4			
Environmental	5.06 (0.76)	5.04	5			
Organizational	5.06 (0.68)*	5.06*	5	Australia	USA	F = 2.8
						H = 12.3
Traits/Behaviors	5.00 (0.74)	4.68	5			
Self-Concept/Ego	4.88 (0.83)	4.64	5			
Physical Fitness	4.68 (0.74)	5.42	6			

*indicates whether the difference was found for rating and/or ranking of importance ($p < 0.05$)

demonstrated by cross-correlation of associated responses) was found to be sound. This result suggests that respondents were consistent in their answers and did not select them randomly.

The data arising from the experts' responses were treated by distinct statistical procedures depending on the type of response given. One type of response involved a simple, yes-or-no answer, and was described by using frequencies (percentages). Another type involved placing a mark on a continuous Likert scale from 1 to 6, and mean (average) values were used to describe these responses. The third type involved rank-ordering a list of statements from 1 to 7, and these were described using the mean and the median (middle choice) values.

Differences were sought among nations using statistical procedures which were dependent upon the type of response given. Chi Square (X^2) was used to seek differences among nations for yes-or-no answers. Analysis of variance (ANOVA, F-test) was used for the continuous Likert scale answers. Kruskal-Wallis nonparametric tests (H-test) were used on the rank-ordered answers. A probability criteria of 0.05 was set for all tests. Due to the large number of tests performed, only the outcomes exceeding this criteria are presented. The high and low differences on values are summarized in each of the five diagrams. On an item where two or more nations are

Diagram 2: A Comparison of the Experts' Preferences for Selecting and Preparing Outdoor Leaders on the Basis of the Fourteen Components.

Components Skills and Attributes	Select Yes-%	Select Order	Prepare Yes-%	Prepare Order	Summary of differences High Nations	Summary of differences Low Nations	Chi-Sq
Physical Fitness	85.6%	1	58.4%	12			
Philosophy/Interest	84.5%	2	60.2%	11			
Awareness/Empathy	83.9%	3	75.8%	9			
Traits/Behaviors	81.7%	4	51.5%	13			
Self-Concept/Ego	81.7%	5	47.9%	14*	All Other	Australia	$X^2 = 11.2$
Technical Activity	77.4%	6	95.8%	4			
Safety	73.8%	7*	99.4%	1	Canada	Australia	$X^2 = 9.6$
Judgment	65.7%	8	73.9%	10			
Environmental	60.7%	9*	94.5%	5	Canada	All Other	$X^2 = 15.1$
Organizational	59.3%	10	92.2%	6			
Problem Solving	57.4%	11*	89.8%	7	Canada/USA	All Other	$X^2 = 19.7$
Flexible style	53.3%	12*	88.6%	8	Canada	Australia	$X^2 = 12.7$
Instructional	53.0%	13*	96.4%	3	Canada/USA	All Other	$X^2 = 20.8$
Group Management	47.6%	14*	97.0%	2	Canada/USA	All Other	$X^2 = 20.3$

*indicates whether the difference was found for selection or preparation ($p < 0.05$)

listed together (as being either high or low), these nations may also be considered as drawn from the same population, and for all intents and purposes may be thought of as holding to the same higher or lower value for that item.

Experts were requested to rate the importance of the fourteen components to a practicing outdoor leader on a Likert scale ranging from extremely important (value of 6) to extremely *un*important (value of 1). They were also asked to separately rank the same seven skills and seven attributes from most important (1st) to least important (7th). A summary of the averages and the differences among nations can be found in Diagram 1.

The position of awareness and empathy, group management, and problem-solving skills near the top of the list is indicative of a growing interest in the field to inject more "soft" components into the preparation of outdoor leaders. Several experts, commenting on improvements they would make to the current programs, stated an immediate need to cut down on the "hard" components, especially technical ones, and to replace these with more people-oriented training.

Experts gave their preferences for selecting outdoor leadership candidates on the basis of the candidate possessing fourteen components. They also listed which of the fourteen components they would choose to include in an outdoor leadership preparation program designed to train and assess candidates. Diagram 2 summarizes the outcomes and highlights the national differences.

Method	Favored	Time Allotment		Summary of Differences		
Training	Yes—%	Order	Yes—%	High Nations	Low Nations	F-ratio
Field Trips	98.8%	1	49.4%	UK	USA	F = 3.0
Discussions	97.0%	2	15.2%			
Lectures	95.8%	3	14.7%			
Simulations	88.6%	4	11.4%	Canada/USA	UK/Aust.	F = 3.7
Role Playing	74.9%	5	8.1%			
METHOD	**FAVORED**	**WEIGHTING**		**SUMMARY OF DIFFERENCES**		
	Yes—%	Order	Yes—%	High Nations	Low Nations	F-ratio
Program Trainers	95.2%	1	38.4%			
Candidate's Self	89.3%	2	21.7%	New Zealand	All Others	F = 6.7
Outside Experts	76.8%	3	18.5%	UK/Aust.	All Others	F = 3.5
Peer Leaders	70.8%	4	12.3%	Canada/USA	All Others	F = 6.9
Group Followers	69.0%	5	8.5%	ALL Others	UK/Aust.	F = 3.2

Diagram 3: The Experts' Preferences for Training and Assessment Methods During an Outdoor Leadership Preparation Program.

*indicates whether the difference was found for favored preference, allotment, and/or weighting ($p < 0.05$)

In terms of selecting outdoor leadership candidates on the basis of the fourteen components, several related differences were apparent. Canadian experts preferred to select for flexible leadership style, safety skills, environmental skills, group management skills, problem-solving skills, and instructional skills in greater numbers than the experts from Australia. Furthermore, experts from the United States preferred selection of the latter three components in greater numbers than the experts from Australia, Great Britain, or New Zealand.

Despite the fact that physical fitness, healthy self-concept and ego, personable traits, and behaviors were all low on the list of importance, these same components were found to be high on the list of selection criteria. In addition to the attributes, the experts preferred outdoor leadership candidates to have a solid base of technical activity and safety skills. It was suggested by a few experts that the way to improve current programs is to do away with the training of technical and safety skills, and instead, require that these components be obtained prior to enrollment in a preparation program. This would allow the program to merely reinforce these components and to concentrate on training other components.

The interesting occurrence with regard to the experts' opinions on an outdoor leadership program curriculum is that all the skills were perceived as important content. Except for awareness and empathy, the attributes which were previously high on the list for selection were now low on the list for preparation. Many experts

Diagram 4: A Comparison of the Experts' Preferences for Preparing and Certifying Outdoor Leaders on the Basis of the Fourteen Components.

Components	Prepare		Certify		Summary of Differences		
Skills and Attributes	Yes-%	Order	Yes-%	Order	High Nations	Low Nations	Chi-Sq
Safety	99.4%	1	69.6%	2			
Group Management	97.0%	2	38.2%	6*	Aust/UK	New Zealand	$X^2 = 16.3$
Instructional	96.4%	3	52.9%	3			
Technical Activity	95.8%	4	72.8%	1			
Environmental	94.5%	5	44.2%	4*	All Other	Australia	$X^2 = 9.8$
Organizational	92.2%	6	39.5%	5			
Problem Solving	89.8%	7	26.9%	7			
Flexible Style	88.6%	8	20.5%	10			
Awareness/Empathy	75.8%	9	17.6%	11			
Judgment	73.9%	10	26.3%	8	A statistical majority existed ONLY for		
Philosophy/Interest	60.2%	11	15.3%	12	certifying the first two components: safety		
Physical Fitness	58.4%	12	21.0%	9	skills and technical activity skills.		
Traits/ Behaviors	51.5%	13	14.0%	13			
Self-Concept/Ego	47.9%	14	13.4%	14			

*indicates whether the difference was found for preparation or certification ($p < 0.05$)

explained this in their comments by stating that the skills, mostly "hard" components, were more easily trained and assessed. Improvements in the attributes, although highly desirable during selection, were not to be easily gained during preparation and, for that reason, were excluded by some experts. The inclusion of judgment based on experience, and awareness and empathy for others were seen to be useful strictly from a perspective of the overall importance of these components to aspiring outdoor leaders. The trend overall appeared to allow for candidate selection based on desirable attributes and a few core skills, and then prepare those core skills and the remaining other skills with little concern for the attributes.

Experts ranked the methods of training and assessment they would use in an outdoor leadership program. They also stated the amount of time they would allot to each training method and the weighting they would place on each assessment method. Summaries are presented in Diagram 3.

In general, experience and the opportunity to gain experience were both considered extremely important by a great majority of the experts. This concept was reinforced by most experts' comments in favor of practicum opportunities for outdoor leadership candidates. In terms of the preparation process, however, the experts presented diverse opinions on the training and assessment of outdoor leaders.

Agreement among experts was present both in the order of preference for using a method and in the percentages to be devoted to each method. Experts preferred field trips as a primary method of training outdoor leaders. Many experts mentioned a need in preparing outdoor leaders to provide plenty of opportunity for the candidate to gain experiences and to reflect on those experiences with a practicing outdoor leader. This was confirmed by a near consensus from the experts on the option to include a practicum experience in the preparation process, and by their comments on the role of experience in outdoor leadership preparation.

All experts agreed that program trainers are the best qualified to assess the outdoor leadership candidates, because the trainers have had the closest contact with the candidates throughout the preparation process. Mixed responses were obtained for the other assessment methods. Many experts relied on outside experts as a second opinion of a candidate's leadership ability. Some thought that the followers in the group led by candidates and other candidates acting as peer leaders would be most likely to obtain accurate assessments. Others felt that the candidates themselves should be responsible for knowing when they were ready to be outdoor leaders.

Experts established their preferences for outdoor leadership certification and for certification by components. A summary is presented in Diagram 4.

Although experts remained divided on the issue of outdoor leadership certification, agreement was reached on certifying technical activity and safety skills. In fact, many commenting experts mentioned that they only considered outdoor leadership certification to represent the certification of these two components. Certification of some of the other components, such as instructional and environmental skills, received mixed opinions. Further analysis showed that for some skills, agreement among the experts to certify might be possible. The experts were not interested in certifying any of the attributes, especially judgment based upon experience. With regard to judgment, they felt that since training and assessment of this component was so difficult, no certification process could possibly assure sound judgment in outdoor leaders.

Experts were requested to rate their concerns by agreeing with thirteen purposes for preparing outdoor leaders on a Likert scale ranging from strongly agree (6) to strongly *dis*agree (1). They were also asked to rank seven concerns from greatest (1) to least (7). A summary of the averages and the differences among nations can be found in Diagram 5.

In responding to the items on purposes for preparing outdoor leaders and greatest current concerns, experts from the nations agreed on the top reasons: ensure positive experiences, teach outdoor skills, reduce accidents, reduce environmental damage, and ensure objectives are met. National disagreements did occur however. The Canadian and American experts had higher concerns for avoiding litigation, and lowering insurance premiums than did the New Zealand and British experts. Australian and New Zealand experts seemed more in favor of increasing

Diagram 5: The Experts' Relative Ratings and Rankings of Thirteen Concerns or Purposes for Preparing Outdoor Leaders.

Concerns Purposes for preparing	Rating 6-1 Mean (S.D.)	Ranking 1-7 Mean	Median	Summary of Differences High Nations	Low Nations	F-H
Positive Experience	5.48 (0.67)	1.85	2			
Teach Outdoor Skills	5.09 (0.80)*			New Zealand	Aust./US	F = 2.6
Reduce Accidents	5.04 (0.97)	1.85	2			
Reduce Env. Damage	4.78 (0.99)	2.92	3			
Learning Objectives	4.65 (1.14)					F = 4.2
Positive Relations	4.21 (1.08)*	4.83*	5	New Zealand	USA →	H = 16.3
Prof. Standards	4.12 (1.36)	5.77*	6	NZ/Aust.	Canada/USA	H = 19.1
Public Attitude	4.03 (1.17)				→	F = 7.2
Litigation Protection	3.46 (1.34)*	5.26*	5	Canada/USA	All Others	H = 45.7
Public Participation	3.46 (1.38)*			NZ/Aust.	UK/USA	F = 6.9
Search & Rescue Costs	3.26 (1.37)					
Resource Regulations	3.00 (1.12)				→	F = 6.5
Insurance Premiums	2.54 (1.27)	5.55*	6	Canada/USA	NZ/Aust.	H = 10.7

*indicates whether the difference was found for rating and/or ranking of importance ($p < 0.05$)

participation rates than did the American or British experts. American experts had a lesser concern for maintaining relations with resource users and managers than did other experts. Lastly, experts from Australia, Great Britain, and New Zealand had greater concern for creating a professional association than did Canadian and American experts.

Section VIII

Speeches and Perspectives

38

Excerpts from the First Kurt Hahn Address

Joe Nold

KURT HAHN SAW DECLINE IN THE WEST—AND SPOKE OF THE DECLINE IN FITNESS through the increase in spectator sports, spectatoritis. This was before the era of television. He spoke of the decline in craftsmanship, man's alienation from his work given the monotony of assembly line industrialization. There was the decline in concentration, given the increased use of drugs, and this was before the decade of the sixties. Above all, there was a decline in *compassion*.

This is the diagnosis. The prognosis we know well: adventure training to develop fitness. Not just physical fitness, but the psychological toughness that goes with it—resilience and resolve. Crafts and the arts are to nurture aesthetic sensitivity, but also to foster pride in one's creativity, the defining of oneself through one's works. And finally service—Samaritan service to instill compassion.

This part of Hahn's thought is well documented. But I repeat it not only for emphasis but to point out the difference in intellectual perspective from the great American experiential educator, John Dewey. Hahn's formative life experiences were World War I, the dreadful slaughter and rending of the fabric of European civilization. It is a disaster that cast a depressive pall over European life and thought for two generations. The war was followed by the collapse of Imperial Germany, and then the face of democratic Germany, the rise of Hitler and Nazi barbarism, and the Holocaust. Hahn was a Jew and was left, perhaps, with the guilt so many surviving Jews experience. So "decline" was not merely malaise, or mid-life crisis, but was a

Address given by Joe Nold, October 1983 at the AEE Conference on Kurt Hahn, John Dewey, and William James.

deeply rooted, existential response to his life experience. He viewed the world broodingly, deeply conscious of man's capacity for evil, a Jew's sense of sin and guilt — but also of redemption. Indeed Hahn distrusted the intellectual community, seeing how easily they were cowed by Hitler. He was witness to their failure to resist. To him, the purpose of education is moral, moral and social. Indeed, with Hahn, education is a form of redemption.

How different from Dewey. We tend to seek the commonalities between Hahn and Dewey. The differences are more significant. Dewey has a totally different intellectual perspective and view of human nature. Dewey comes out of the American experience (the naiveté of the American experience, our European colleagues would add) with the optimism, the progressivism, the sense of success in America, the belief in infinite perfectability. Dewey has a belief in democracy—its inherent strength and goodness—and to him, education is the pillar and cornerstone of a free and democratic people. "Democracy and Education" is Dewey's educational testament.

These are two divergent streams of thought that underpin experiential education, or at least experiential education as espoused by AEE. I do not know if Hahn ever read Dewey. He makes no mention of him. Certainly Dewey never read Hahn, for Hahn never wrote much, and he does not read well. But both did read William James. The pragmatism of William James is central to Dewey's thought. The essay James wrote, "On the Moral Equivalent of War," was central to Hahn's educational practice. James points out that aggression is deeply rooted in human nature, imprinted in our genes and lodged in the very marrow of our bones, and that man will always respond to the call of the bugle, and take up the banner of war, because he is drawn to the excitement, to the adrenalin rush. He craves the exhilaration. The pacifist solution will never be successful, the peace will never be secure until mankind finds a substitute, a moral equivalent for war, that stirs his loyalty and galvanizes his energy, that draws on his need for daring and excitement. James saw the answer in hard physical labor of a risk-taking kind, work in the mines, on the fishing boats in winter; he called for a conscription of youth in service of the needy. This idea inspired the CCC (Civilian Conservation Corps of the 1930s), the forerunner of Job Corps, and the Peace Corps in the 1960s. It also inspired Hahn. This was language he understood, and he incorporated it into his educational thought and practice.

ON QUESTIONS OUTWARD BOUND HAS FACED IN THE PAST 22 YEARS

Do You Force All Students Through the Outward Bound Mold or Do You Design a Program That Meets the Needs of Students?

The questions became pressing ones as we were challenged to take more inner-city youth. In the late sixties, cities were burning—Newark, Detroit, Watts—and Outward Bound was seen as a way of keeping the cities cool. Funded by federal grants under the War on Poverty, large numbers arrived on the mountainside with cigarettes, knives, and drugs; ill-informed, unfit, and unprepared for the rigors of the course. While some did not succeed, surprising numbers did. British instructors, many from a working-class background and speaking in broad overseas accents, were particularly effective with their direct, no-nonsense approach. Somehow, they were not seen as "white honkies," a part of the white establishment. But most of all, it forced us to look at the interaction between instructor and student, student and student, and the group process more closely; to examine our assumptions about fitness standards and question what a student was really gaining from the experience. What is the difference between an adventure and an ordeal? Most of all, the approach became more client-centered, and the Outward Bound mystique had to be bent to accommodate new mores.

Is Outward Bound the Custodian of a Program or the Steward of an Idea?

Greg Farrell was the first to insist that the idea of Outward Bound was greater than the Outward Bound organization; that Outward Bound had an opportunity, indeed a responsibility, to apply its technology to new circumstances, to adapt to the urban setting. "What is the moral equivalent of the mountain in the city?" Farrell was director of the War on Poverty community action program in Trenton, New Jersey. He put himself through the Outward Bound program and then sent others—teachers, parole officers, youth workers, street gang leaders—and when they returned, he helped them set up their own programs.

The idea caught on. Outward Bound as an organization began to see itself in a new light. In quick succession, adaptive programs sprang up in the late sixties. The Massachusetts Division of Youth Services set up "Homeward Bound" on Cape Cod, and the Job Corps Centre in Collbran, Colorado, where Murray Durst was director, contracted Outward Bound instructors to develop a program. Prescott College and Dartmouth College both set up programs developed around Outward Bound concepts, and high schools in Denver adapted experiential-based curriculum.

There was much experimentation. Sometimes too much. And, of course, there were skeptics. Within Outward Bound we called adaptive programs "Mainstream." "The only streams I know all run downhill," was the way one crusty trustee expressed his concern.

ON THE DANGERS OF BEING "HOOKED" ON ADVENTURE

It is easy to be hooked on adventure. We have a distorted view of Hahn's vision, given the Outward Bound bias. Hahn valued the adventure ethic for the qualities of character it nurtured: self-reliance, self-sufficiency, endurance in the face of hardship, resilience. But he also harbored an underlying suspicion of Outward Bound. He was concerned lest it become a toughness cult or a haven for the wilderness freak, the social drop-out. Hahn was particularly concerned with the development of responsibility, personal responsibility and social responsibility, and above all, of compassion. He spoke most resoundingly of Samaritan service. The mature Hahn institutions have followed this lead. The Round Square Conference Schools, founded by Kurt Hahn or those influenced by him, sponsor a student-volunteer, village development project in India, building schools in Himalayan villages. The United World College of the American West, in New Mexico, one of six of the Hahn-inspired colleges around the world, requires two afternoons of service training a week. Service is the core of the activities program. All students are trained in basic wilderness skills so the whole college can be called upon for mountain search and rescue. At least half the students are involved in some aspect of community service: working with handicapped and retarded children, visiting old-age homes, organizing community clean-up campaigns, assisting in day-care centers. At Pearson College, the United World College of the Pacific in British Columbia, marine biology students taught deaf and dumb students scuba diving, who in turn taught them a sign language shorthand that has become the standard language of underwater communication. It is no longer necessary to surface to give instructions. Schools wishing to be serious about service as a program requirement have proven precedents. "There is the need to be needed," says Alec Dickson, the founder of VSO (Voluntary Service Overseas), the model and precedent for the Peace Corps. Hahn's answer to the alienation of youth is to "help them overcome the misery of unimportance."

39

Education At Its Peak

Jolene Unsoeld

You can't see my knees knock.

You can't feel my stomach churn and flutter.

Why am I afraid?

For the last several weeks—no, months—I've been asking myself, "Why am I going to Colorado? What in the world am I going to do?"

Why *am* I here?

If Willi had been here he would have sauntered up, stroking his chin, looking for all the world like an incompetent prospector, and then he would have picked you up and taken you on a wilderness search to encounter your spiritual roots.

That would have been Willi.

I have so many drawbacks to speaking here today.

I don't have any lyrical metaphorical subject and I'm hopelessly non-verbal.

I'm a doer, not a speaker. But I'm here to tell you something about Willi and—more important—to try to tell you why you're here.

FIRST, WHO WAS WILLI?

WE WERE JUST A COUPLE OF COLLEGE STUDENTS WHO CLIMBED MOUNTAINS together and fell in love. We met at the base of a mountain—an Oregon State College Mountain Club climb.

He used to say he was smitten because I was wearing G.I. mountain pants.

In fact, he lied. There was another student wearing red shorts. He went out with her first.

But I had an unerring eye for quality. He had the best mountain stove and he was the finest storyteller.

He had hitchhiked around the world and climbed in the Himalayas by the age of 23. He was bitten by the "Why?" of the world. Gave up physics and embarked on his quest. We were married and had 4 kids while he was in graduate school.

Teaching at OSU was all theory.

Peace Corps was all doing.

Outward Bound helped identify some ways of changing people.

TESC provided the opportunity to apply it all—the theories and the doing.

Willi did a lot of public speaking. He would come sauntering up here, stroking his shaggy beard, and tell you that as a species, modern folks have lost touch not only with this earth but also with our fellow humans.

He would take you on a walk through wilderness to encounter the holy. He would use the spirit and magic of wilderness to make you see yourself in a cosmic perspective. And then he would bring you back and tell you that the only thing important in this life is how we treat each other.

As Willi saw it, a major part of any curriculum should be aimed at the moral values within a social context (Alexander Mickeljohn, *Education Between Two Worlds*).

Willi felt that we were alienated from our emotions . . . .

We're alienated from each other . . . .

Alienated from nature . . . .

We're in control and that alienates us.

We don't have to take into account reality.

We're in control and we prefer it that way.

He would suggest that this alienation from nature constitutes *the* key to the other alienations. Nature, which includes us, is a seamless robe which we deny by our process of analysis. We say that we can chop down a tree, pave a valley, dam a river, and it doesn't affect anything else. There's no necessary connection between chopping down a tree and *all* the rest of us in this room.

Willi's assertion was the exact contrary—that nature is a seamless robe to a degree far beyond our awareness. We're *connected* and when you shake any portion of it, the rest trembles. And then he would go on to say that the way we treat things affects how we treat people. And that when we start abusing the physical things of this world, which our culture is *based* on, then the abuse of each other follows as automatically as the day follows the night.

The final product of this whole tendency is not only an alienation from ourselves and from each other and from nature, but a total loss of meaning, a total loss of "at homeness" in the universe. A de-sacrilization of the universe which results from our objectification of our *entire* experience.

This was what made the wilderness experience religious to him. Defining religious as anything having to do with that in which we hold *ultimate* concern. Ultimate concern. What keeps us going? What makes it all worthwhile? The answer to the question, "Why bother . . . at all?" "Why you? Why me? Why anything instead of nothing?"

And *that's* where he used nature—the beauty and the risk of wilderness—to provide that *other* dimension.

His approach to the beauty, and hence the meaning, was always keyed to the risk that's present in nature. The riskiness of climbing or kayaking. The willingness to take a risk of being wrong, of having people jeer at you. The risk of riding your first bicycle or going skiing. That little inner quiver that alerts you and mobilizes your whole resources. And for him, that was critical. One of his more profound philosophical observations was . . . life is tough.

And students got madder'n hops at that at Evergreen. Some of them didn't want it to be tough. They wanted it to be beautiful and painless. He saw our youth being conditioned on the other side of the track too much. Being warped over here to the conviction that if it's risky, it's bad. And besides, it's your right, your birthright, to have it all laid out for you.

"You aren't going to have to work as hard as I did, kid." Well, we know all about that now—the indulgent parent murdering the soul of the child who is fighting for a suffocating breath of air to try to get out with a chance to do his or her own thing. And it's latched onto a self-concept which arises from meeting risk and learning you can cope with it.

"We pay too great a price when we excise risk from our total economy," he used to tell them in Outward Bound when parents came round to ask, "Can you guarantee the safety of our son Johnny?" (No daughters in early O.B. programs.) He said they finally decided to meet the question head on.

"No, we certainly can't, ma'am. We guarantee you the genuine chance of his death. And if we could guarantee his safety, the program would not be worth running."

"Well! If that's all you have to say . . . ."

"No, I have one more thing to say. We do make one guarantee as one parent to another. If you succeed in protecting your boy as you're doing now and as it's your parental duty to do . . . you know we applaud your watchdog tenacity. But if you succeed, we guarantee you the death of your child's soul."

He felt there was a mystery in nature which is one of its great attractions for us. There's the hiddenness of organic growth, of how a seed decides to be an oak tree. No matter how much reference we have to the genetic coding of RNA and DNA, somehow it doesn't come out totally explained. There is a mystery there in which we are engulfed.

He was, of course, greatly impressed with the mystery of mountaineering. The very mundane question, "Will it go?" "Well, will it?" "I don't know." "What are you doing here if YOU don't know." But that is the fascination. You have to find out. So you go a little farther and you never know until finally you reach the summit and then you know. Except, "How about getting down?"

And his final test of this wilderness experience that we all have known, his final test of its efficacy—because having been there in the mountains, alone, in the midst of solitude, and this feeling, this mystical feeling if you will, of the ultimacy of joy or whatever there is—the question is, "Why not stay out there in the wilderness the rest of your days and just live in the lap of satori or whatever you want to call it?"

And the answer—his answer—to that was, "Because that's not where people are." And the final test for him of the legitimacy of the experience was "how well it enables you to cope with the problems of mankind when you come back to the city."

And so he saw it as a renewal exercise leading to a process of alternation. You go to the wilderness for your metaphysical fix—your reassurance that the world makes sense. It's a reassurance many of us don't get in the city. But with that excess of confidence, of reassurance, that there's something behind it all and it's good, you come back to where humans are, to where humans are messing things up, 'cause they tend to, and you come back with a new ability to relate to yourself and to your fellow humans and to help them relate to each other. And that's the kind of alternation which he saw crucial for experiential education.

And that's the peak of education for which he was reaching.

That was until one stormy Sunday in March.

Suddenly a test of our own theories of risk and the purpose of our lives and the meaning of mountains to me.

I lost a daughter in the mountains. I lost my husband and partner. I nearly lost a son. One could say the mountains have been cruel to me.

And I've known those who have turned away from the mountains after losing loved ones there. I'm lucky. I responded to and understood what mountains are before I met Willi, and that understanding and love for the high places was constant throughout our lives together and today remains unchanged.

But there is no easy way to handle death. The days and weeks and months pass, but the pain lingers and sometimes still, it leaps out to grab me most unexpectedly.

For a long, long time—3 years in fact—there were things of beauty such as a crimson sunset, a full moon, certain pieces of music, and other things that could bring back an agonizing, overwhelming sense of loss. I would find myself driving down the highway in the late afternoon and becoming aware of the glorious sky and clouds as the sun touched the horizon. Suddenly, I would be overcome with excruciating pain at the reminder of Devi's death and then Bill's death.

And then one day, I became aware that I was looking at this glorious sunset and it was not the sense of loss that was overwhelming me. Rather, I was aware of the beauty that was their lives and I could feel that beauty as very much a part of this universe. I could feel all that Willi was on this earth, all that we were together and it was all very much a precious part of me.

I still know the loss, but I have found strength from what we *were* together and what we still are.

Now I want to switch gears and pull a "Willi."

He'd use his family in any way imaginable to illustrate what he wanted to talk about. He'd do it with or without permission and with or without accuracy. One of our kids would come innocently hitching into town, totally unsuspecting, and be accosted by someone they'd never seen before. This stranger would come up to gush over the graphic details of the latest "affair of the heart" and the *cosmic* overtones with which Willi had invested it. What may have really happened was of no importance. Willi would simply glom onto whatever flimsy shred of truth could be used to illustrate his latest moral imperative.

And so . . . I have a son who is surviving his first year of teaching high school. Two of the subjects he's never even been exposed to: consumer economics and law. It is the freshmen in his law class who captured my imagination: they say the only reason they don't go out and steal a car or knock off a 7-11 store has nothing to do with right or wrong or moral conscience. Rather, their choice of action is determined by whether it is legal or illegal and their chances of getting caught and their fear of punishment.

A 1981 survey showed only 13% of the Class of 1980 felt that "working to correct social and economic inequalities" is very important. Some 31% rated "having lots of money" as very important.

This is precisely the challenge that all of you practicing "education at its peak" find yourselves up against.

Success is not a destination—it's the quality of everything you do.

It's how you respond to those things that are going on around you—and the example you set for others.

You are educators not only for what you tell your students, and what you get them to experience, but, probably more importantly, for the example—the role model—you provide.

Most of us want to shut out the world and what is happening. When approached with a petition to get an initiative on the ballot, a young professional woman said,

"Oh, no, I never sign petitions."

She never asked what the issue was. Never asked how it affected her.

A recent letter to the editor described the scene of an Olympia intersection one Friday afternoon. The writer was a witness to a collision and stopped to help. One man stumbled out of his truck and lay motionless on the road.

The other man was gushing blood from his head, and she ran to give him assistance. As she was trying to stop his bleeding, *other cars* drove by—*respectable people—my age*. She made eye contact with them and yelled, "Help me!" They looked away and continued driving.

We have a strong desire to have government—and other unpleasantries—just leave us alone.

But the world can't be shut out.

Tear down the walls and have a look.

You will see examples of inspiration—the two guys spinning through Olympia recently—paralyzed from the waist down—wheelchairing from Spokane and back to collect money for Handicapped Unlimited.

The 10-year-old who pulled her grandparents to safety when their car plunged off a highway and was submerged in eight feet of water.

When the family car stopped at a busy intersection and burst into flame, and while her mother and older brother were struggling to get a baby out of a jammed car seat, nine-year-old Karen got her three younger sisters out of the back seat as smoke and flames poured from the hood and underneath the car. "I was very scared," Karen admitted. "Other drivers, who had to stop because of the car fire, were angry and yelling at us and I was trying to comfort my sisters. I got them onto a nearby safety island, then when the light changed to walk, I led them across the street to a gas station."

Sarah Doherty (25), a physical therapist and rehabilitation expert from Seattle, was struck by a car while riding her bicycle to a junior high track meet in 1973. She lost a leg and part of her hip. An artificial leg can't be fitted to her. She must travel on one leg and two crutches, one in each hand. Despite her handicap she climbed Mt. Rainier and then Mt. McKinley this last spring. Now she's looking for a higher mountain.

But in spite of these stellar examples of human behavior, there is some pretty horrible stuff going on in this world, too.

The White House has decided that the United States will formally cease to recognize the authority of the World Court except in nonpolitical cases. We are afraid we'll be found guilty for our actions such as in Nicaragua so we're picking up our marbles and going home.

Never mind that our participation in the World Court is needed. It is a matter of principle to our government that we not be accountable for our actions.

While our economy is still ravaged from the last undeclared war, we now have an administration that says:

"Social expenditures are inflationary, *but the same expenditures to rearm an American empire are necessary for this country's welfare and security.*"

Without the social security trust included in the budget, the U.S. spends 50% for military, 25% for servicing the national debt, and the remaining 25% has to pay for everything else.

In the mid '50s, corporations paid 25% of the national taxes. It is now about 6%. Boeing was refunded $267 million and Weyerhauser $139 million.

And some of those same military contractors who don't pay their share of taxes are charging thousands and thousands of dollars for gifts, ship cruises, and entertainment, private club dues and then, in some cases, charging $99 to $340 per-hour labor costs for $750 pliers.

I'm known as an "activist." How did it come about?

Married young, didn't finish college. Four kids during 7 years of grad school. Stayed home until we went to Nepal with Peace Corps and youngest in kindergarten.

When we came back from Nepal in 1967, I had cultural shock.

Compared to the Nepali people we had so much—and yet we had so little.

I didn't know how to translate my own desire to make this world better into action. Things were just too complicated. I didn't know how to make a difference, so I shut out the world for a year and baked cookies or some darn thing.

We had never had television . . . starving Biafrans.

TV brought automated warfare and assassinations into our living room and a kid who said to his parents, "Well, what'cha goin' to do about it?"

Wow! You either abdicate parenthood or you start examining your own image as a role model for your kids.

And so now I'm trying to get industry in Washington State to help pay for their share of protecting our environment. I happen to think they ought to share in the cost of keeping our Puget Sound sparkling and vibrant, healthy and productive. I'm working to try to get industry to participate in keeping our groundwater free of pollutants.

90% and 10%. 50% get their drinking water. Organic toxics.

Industry is fighting me. The AWB says there is no *proof* that there is a problem, and they put tens of thousands of dollars against me in my election campaign. I imagine they'll put more in this time.

But those are some of the battles worth fighting. And it's exciting and challenging. When you lose, you go back to your cave and lick your wounds and start plotting how to whip them next time. And, oh golly, when you have a victory, it's the sweetest nectar.

Read the newspapers and what do you find?

The head of OSHA *re*called a brochure on occupational safety because he was "offended" by a picture on its cover—of a brown lung victim—*not by brown lung disease.*

Suspicious burglaries in a Seattle sanctuary-supporting church. The only things taken were membership information and notes of telephone calls to a pastor in San Salvador.

And now the administration wants to have the legal authority to examine your private tax and insurance records.

You'll read about corporations who—as a matter of lofty principle—insist on their right to pollute, to avoid taxes, and to endanger the health of their workers and their communities.

Who can forget the 2,000 people who were poisoned when gas leaked from the Union Carbide Corporation pesticide plant in Bhopal, India?

Asbestos—and asbestosis . . . .

Agent Orange . . . .

Dumping pesticides . . . .

Love Canal . . . .

PCBs, EDBs, nitrates, drinking water contaminated . . . .

16 million kids in the U.S. have *no* health care.

Canada spends 8% of its GNP—everyone is covered.

The U.S. spends 11%—20% of our people are not covered.

I'm asking you to read the newspapers and weep.

Read the newspapers and vomit.

Once you get over vomiting, do something about it!

These are the battles that have to be fought for social justice. These are the battles that have to be fought to keep our earth a living place—*as a participant.*

Staying on the sidelines is deceiving yourself into believing it doesn't make any difference, that you don't make any difference.

These are times filled with battles worthy of your skills.

I was really tickled to read last month about a citizen effort to keep a hydro project off the North Branch River and to read that Susan and Richard Herman were in the thick of the battle.

And recently Tom Herbert was selected by *USA Today* as one of the top 10 teachers.

I would hope no member of AEE would turn away from someone bleeding in the street.

I would hope no AEEer would refuse to enter that gaping maw of bureaucratic battle.

I would hope no AEEer would flinch at speaking out against "official" injustice—even when it's unpopular.

That is the beginning: the example you set for your students.

And that's why you're here. That's the summit of educational experience.

You *can* change things—*you* can make a difference. It is your example, the way you approach an injustice, and what you do to make this world a better place that may make that bigger difference in the lives of your students.

Yeah, the earth will continue to spin if you turn away—the world will go on.

You can't do everything. But you must do something.

And you were made for challenge.

So bring on the giants!

    Bring on the dragons!

You can handle them!

40

Habits of the Heart

Robert S. MacArthur

Ethics can be reduced to the question: "How *ought* we to live?" The question applies not only to individuals but to groups as well, and part of what I have been asked to do is to reflect on the major ethical issues that have faced experiential education as a profession.

You will be relieved to know that I won't try to do that. It would take us too long to define who would be included and to determine whether or not we constitute a profession. Instead, I will try to do four things.

1. First, I will try to prime the pump, so to speak, by offering a few definitions, descriptions, and quandaries that may orient your minds to the central theme of the Conference.

2. Second, since I am more familiar with AEE than the field of experiential education as a whole, and I am acquainted with some of the issues the organization has faced or avoided since it began, I will offer my perception of the significant dilemmas we have been wrestling with in AEE.

3. Third, I will raise what I think is the major ethical issue today confronting us as individuals and AEE as an organization.

4. Fourth, I will conclude with a set of questions for all of us to consider.

Adapted from the Keynote Address presented at the 14th Annual Conference of the Association for Experiential Education, Moodus, Connecticut, September 25, 1986.

I want to begin by telling you how I am defining ethics. The word goes back to its Greek root, *ethos*, and referred initially to the "dwelling" or "stall" where men put animals for shelter and protection. When applied to the way human beings live, the word became associated with the stability and security which are necessary if one is going to act at all (Lehman, 1963, p. 24). Ethics provide a guiding framework, a dwelling place of our aspirations that informs how we behave. Nice to know that all this lofty business really gets down to basics like straw and manure! If this seems a bit far-fetched, remember that the ethics of at least one of the world's religions were born in a stable.

When the Romans took over from the Greeks, they translated the word *ethos*, to the Latin word *mos*, *mores*, from which we get our word "morality." Over the years, a distinction evolved between the two words which I think is worth noting. According to theologian Paul Lehman, "'morality' came gradually to be reserved for behavior according to custom, and the word 'ethics' for behavior according to reason, that is, reflection upon the foundations and principles of behavior" (Lehman, 1963, pp. 24-25).

Action and reflection! Where have we heard that before? Experiential learning depends on *action* and *reflection*. We do something, step back in order to interpret it, and then return to the arena of action better informed and able to act again in a new way. Another way to state this simply is to say that if the question of ethics is, "How *ought* we to live?", the question of morality is, "How *do* we live?"

Let's take an example from AEE. As an analogy to an individual's ethical framework, an organization's mission statement which expresses its *purpose*, describes its key *values*, and determines its *audience*, should convey its collective ethics—the dwelling place that provides definition and stability for its activity. The current statement reads:

> *The mission of AEE is to support and promote the process of learning through direct experience.*

Does this statement truly convey our collective purpose, our central values, and the groups we serve? If it does not, what will we put in its place? The question of morality becomes, "Do we practice what we preach?" Have we achieved what we aspire to? Although they are intimately related, ethics and morality are distinct.

In the next few minutes, I want to present a profile of the behavior and customs of AEE that will lead us into our ethics. This exercise will reveal some historic dilemmas. Dilemmas indicate that we are torn between alternatives. Since we are unstable when we're in the midst of making choices, we turn to a reference that will inform our situation. This reference is our ethical framework.

A Profile of AEE and Its Implications for Ethics

First Of All, Who Are We?

1. We are predominantly outdoor or adventure oriented. That's not altogether surprising, since our first two gatherings were sponsored in large part by Outward Bound. We began with a modest gathering in Boone, North Carolina, as people engaged in Outdoor Pursuits in Higher Education. Later, we reconvened at Estes Park with a much larger conference, broadening the group from higher education but affirming the adventure orientation. A few conferences later, we began to diversify, which meant for us, recognizing that experiential activity can occur in settings other than the wilderness—opened ourselves to cultural journalism, apprenticeships in crafting, classroom learning, service learning, and finally, a nod to the arts.

2. We are predominantly white and middle class. In the middle years of our history, we began to realize that we were shortchanging ourselves and grossly undervaluing a large contingent of experiential educators from diverse racial and cultural backgrounds. We passed a resolution in Portsmouth and took modest steps at Sante Fe, Toronto, and Lake Junaluska to involve people from cultures other than our own. Where are we today? Skin color is surely not necessarily an indicator of cultural diversity, but as we look around us tonight, it is clear that the prevailing color is white.

3. We are, for the most part, fringe types. We're by no means radical, because basically, we believe enough in institutions to want to reform them, create them, or at least tap into their resources. Let's call it, "mainstream fringe." We hang around the edge of the mainstream, putting up with the problems of interpreting why we do what we do, hoping that others will see the light. We are very critical, because we see a better way, and we keep our distance, not wanting to risk the compromises we see that others have made. When we tire, we have a ready-made platform for venting criticism or playing the victim. However, there is enough security there to appeal to us, enough to support our habits.

One of the key values of being on the fringe is that we keep our options open. We are not really willing to make the full commitment to mainstream ways. As a survival technique, this probably makes a lot of sense, and our training to carry our home on our back may serve us well. However, this may also mean that we are not committed enough to effect change politically. We are too transient in life to commit to one community, too concerned about our own freedom to invest in one place or one group of people for very long. And there are some of us who find politics and administration distasteful. Hence, we cannot sustain the momentum for significant change in our communities.

Dilemmas About Who We Are

We are torn, because in our hearts we really dig what we do, and we enjoy doing it with those who share our feelings and interests. Intellectually, we know that experiential education embraces many forms other than adventure, and that the majority of the world (and increasingly of our own country) is comprised of people of races and cultures other than our own.

We hold keenly to our sense of freedom and our unconventional lifestyles. This is the triumph of our individualism. Yet we are torn by a desire to be legitimized by the mainstream—we are trying to establish AEE as our professional organization—and the knowledge that if we really wanted to change education or society, we would have to commit ourselves to more sustained commerce with the mainstream or move to the radical-fringe, neither of which we seem anxious to do. This is the failure of our individualism.

What Is It That We Do?

1. For one thing, most of us do our own thing. That's a positive attribute, because we enjoy our work, despite low pay, the lack of professional status, and few mainstream benefits. We have fewer ties than most, and our flexible schedules permit the variety of fun and adventure that we enjoy.

2. Most of us are involved in risk-oriented activities. Some of these risks are associated with outdoor challenges—weather, heights, difficult terrain, heavy packs, remote communication, and portable support systems. Some of these are risks associated with emotional vulnerability—being asked to try new things and risking failure or awkwardness in front of peers; being thrown together in a small group with strangers, some of whom may come from very different backgrounds; being expected to be open and supportive in ways that would be socially suicidal back home.

3. What we do is related to where we do it, and for many of us, that environment is the outdoors. There has been a constant theme relating to the environment, first articulated by Willi Unsoeld at Estes Park when he inspired us with a talk on the Spiritual Uses of the Wilderness. It appears in the issue of limited access to the wilderness, which led to the adoption of *Common Practices in Adventure Programming,* and in the choice of our conference locations, all but two of which have been in non-urban areas. But, there have been dilemmas. Is our interest in the environment for the environment's sake or for its utility to our educational process? And, is it really the bottom line of economics that drives our interest—no wilderness access - no program - no clients - no revenue - no way to support our habits?

Dilemmas about What We Do

First, we acknowledge the need for standards of managing risks, and we have done a laudable service to ourselves and others in drafting *Common Practices*. On the other hand, we are reluctant to hold each other accountable for compliance to those standards. Second, we join ranks with the mainstream forces that are besieged by the insurance industry to argue that it is our inalienable right to take risks and to expose others to them, and, at the same time, be protected from indemnity if we screw up. Third, I wonder how willing we are to take the risk of compromising our individuality for making common cause with other networks engaged in experiential education.

Whom Do We Serve?

1. An expanding continuum of age and sex. In the early '60s, *Life* published an account of the first Outward Bound program in Colorado, entitled, "Marshmallow becomes a Man." The protagonist was an average, middle-class, overweight, white male, for whom the course was a civilian version of military training; a softie learned toughness in a rite of passage for boys only. Over the years, that profile has changed somewhat. We accepted that girls could do the things boys could do. The Women's Special Interest Group is now one of the most active in AEE. We found our programs appealed to the adolescent in each of us, no matter that we were between 21 and 65. The adventure of the rite of passage of youth gave way to the challenges of the mid-life passage. Personal growth activities and therapy for adults have mushroomed under the umbrella of professional development and career counseling. I don't know whether that's because we are maturing in our understanding of the breadth of experiential education, or because we are all growing older and taking the movement with us as we go to serve our own needs.

2. A growing number of special populations. We soon found that the action programs appealed to young people at risk socially, or at least it appealed to those responsible for administering programs treating them. Adventure therapy was more engaging and more cost-effective than incarceration. The need to develop the sense of self-worth and social skills through the experience of participating in the community of the teen-group has been compelling. Work with youth at-risk has expanded from juvenile delinquents to alcoholics, drug dependents, and those under the umbrella of mental health care.

3. We are involved with more racially and culturally diverse participants in our programs than in the membership or leadership of our Association. I dare say the most racially and culturally diverse programs are those under the umbrella of special populations, and most of them are captive audiences. Let's face it, rising early in the morning to abuse your body by immersing it in a freezing cold lake, masticating the soggy product of your efforts to cook a meal in the rain, and spending your waking hours lugging your seventy-pound, portable home up a mountain is an appealing regimen to a limited number of the world's cultures. Our inability to attract a more diverse membership may be related to a morality that recognizes intellectually that diversity is desirable educationally (and inevitably from the perspective of global survival), but that practically, it takes a lot of effort to which we have just not committed ourselves.

4. Finally, we have attempted to serve those in mainstream education. Our earliest attempts to incorporate adventure training in teacher education and the various experimental curricula in schools and colleges were aimed primarily at taking students outdoors. In the next stage, when we had isolated a process of experiential learning that we thought was applicable to many settings, we began to emphasize what could be done *in* the classroom. However, there is an overall lack of resolve to meet mainstream education at the centers of power. Our research library is embarrassingly thin, our networking with other education associations is limited, and our attempts to hold conferences in cities or other population centers to attract more teachers have met with mixed results.

Dilemmas about Whom We Serve

The first is, to what extent do our programs reflect the product we believe in, and to what extent do we adapt our program to the forces of the marketplace? "Guts! It takes them to sign up and it takes them to complete the course." This was the way Leo Burnett marketed Outward Bound some years ago. Their market research said that this slogan with its accompanying picture of a person on a Tyrolean Traverse high above a huge waterfall, was what the public wanted to see. For a short time, it did bring in a lot of inquiries. It also brought a lot of people to Outward Bound who had no idea of the program, only a fantasy image of themselves. It's hard to leave Outward Bound without mentioning the standard course. Can you really do it in less than 26 days? Of course, the original 26 days was an adaptation by Kurt Hahn to the British pay period of World War II. Initial results from a longitudinal study of Outward Bound participants, conducted by Chris Jernstedt at Dartmouth, indicates that the short-term outcomes are the same, regardless of the length of the course. So, perhaps the marketers are correct. Go with the flow. The growth of programs with special populations is due as much to the available funds as it is to our mission.

The second dilemma also relates to marketing. If the length of program is related more to audience than outcome, why are we not putting more emphasis on designing curricula, conducting research, and campaigning with Boards, superintendents, and principals for 45-minute blocks of time, afternoon periods, and weekends, in order to reach one of our largest markets, kids in schools?

These are certainly not the only dilemmas that have faced us in AEE, but they provide some examples that indicate we have reason to examine our practices and our ideals and to take steps to bridge any gaps that we perceive.

FRAMEWORK FOR CHOICE

How ought we to deal with dilemmas? What are our points of reference? Fortunately, Jasper Hunt and the AEE Board have done us the service of providing such a reference in the book that he has just published called *Ethical Issues in Experiential Education*.

In his concluding chapter on "Methodology," Jasper offers us a framework for approaching our dilemmas. Not surprisingly, it sounds very much like the way we are involved in learning anything experientially. I think it is a useful guideline to follow in our discussions this conference.

1) Step One is to recognize and anticipate what some of the major ethical issues are *before you find yourself in the situation.*

2) Step Two is to distinguish between facts in a situation and the values that are competing.

3) Step Three is to understand what the reference points are from history, religion, or philosophy; the sources that will inform your response.

4) Step Four is to act on the basis of your best judgment, and

5) Step Five would be to evaluate how you did.

What I would like to do is complete my talk by using this framework for looking at an ethical issue that weaves itself through many I have summarized about AEE.

INDIVIDUALISM

Let me now assert that I think the major ethical dilemma facing us is the ethics of individualism. In the historical dialectic between the individual and the group, be it family, community, nation, or global village, the pendulum swings back and forth. Today, I fear that we put too much stock in individual rights rather than obligations;

in self-actualization rather than the welfare of the community: in the enclaves of our private life rather than public service.

Following Jasper's scheme, let's look at some of the facts and the values that might be competing.

1) In its December 9, 1984 issue, *US News & World Report* cited a recent study showing that young people "believe their right to be tried by a jury is critical to a free society but practically none of them said they would serve on a jury. Also, they said they want to be defended, but they don't want to serve in the armed forces."

2) In the Carnegie Foundation's report, "Higher Education and the American Resurgence," author Frank Newman reports that the annual surveys of 250,000 incoming freshmen show

> . . . a 15-year decline in expectation of participation in the political life of the country, in any form of altruism, or of concern for the interest of others. Over the same time, there has been a steady rise in student interest in those values associated with money, status, and power . . . . The values which show the largest decline are: 1) developing a philosophy of life, 2) participating in community affairs, 3) cleaning up the environment, and 4) promoting racial understanding. (Ende, 1985)

3) Darryl Brown, editor of *Youth Policy*, cites journalist Susan Littwin, who writes of today's college students in *The Postponed Generation*: "This is not a generation of pioneers. They are just kids with a high sense of entitlement and a not so high sense of reality." The older generation gave the young their high expectations with little mention of what might be asked in return. There was no mention of the social contract put succinctly by John Gardner: "Freedom and responsibility. Liberty and duty. That's the deal" (Brown, 1986).

The predicament is perhaps best described by Robert Bellah and his associates in their book, *Habits of the Heart, Individualism and Commitment in American Life*. The book is based on research on white, middle-class Americans and takes for its major reference point Tocqueville's analysis of American society, written in the mid-19th century. Tocqueville was interested in assessing whether democratic societies would be able to maintain free political institutions or whether they might slip into some new kind of despotism. He looked to the mores of America, the practices of family life, religion, and political participation, which he called "habits of the heart," as the key to establishing and maintaining a free republic. He is attributed with coining the word "individualism."

> "'Individualism' is a word recently coined to express a new idea," he wrote . . . . "Individualism is a calm and considered feeling which disposes each citizen to isolate himself from the mass of his fellows and withdraw into the circle of family and friends; with this little society formed to his taste, he gladly leaves the greater society to look after itself." (Bellah, 1985, p. 37)

Tocqueville admired American individualism as the heart of our character. He also feared it. Isolated from their contemporaries, such people, he claimed, come to "forget their ancestors" and also their descendants. Written 150 years ago, this description sounds uncannily modern.

What are the values at work in this dilemma? Obviously, there are those values associated with the rights of the individual to make choices regarding his or her life. In contrast, there are values which the society claims to have over individuals in order to maintain itself, protect individuals from each other, and mediate justice. Both of these ethics are deeply embedded in the American psyche.

This is the dilemma: the threat that the very individualism which we value so highly will isolate us from those collective forces that will ultimately destroy individualism. [A summary of major points in *Habits of the Heart* was given at this point in the speech.]

If we believe that individualism, the trend toward privacy and isolationism, is a serious issue, then what are the consequences for our failure to act? There is a subtlety about our situation, an irony, which leads us to realize that unless we become more public minded, more involved in communities and politics and global citizenship, the very rights and freedoms we enjoy will be obliterated. To cite some obvious examples:

1) The superpowers are poised on the brink of destroying the planet. Unless the planet survives, there will be no human beings to be individuals.

2) Decisions that affect the world are increasingly concentrated in the hands of fewer people, including multinational corporate heads, specialists in technology, and those who underwrite liability insurance.

3) The middle-class, industrialized, Western minority are consuming a disproportionate amount of the planet's non-renewable resources. Are we surprised or outraged that growing numbers of the world's population are staking claim to their share of those resources under the banner of holy war or basic human rights?

4)   The world is gravitating increasingly toward two societies, those with and those without. It is incumbent on those of us who are in-between, the middle class, despite being drawn into increasingly private lives, to reconnect with a sense of future history and our descendants.

In a report released last fall called "Reconnecting Youth," president of the Education Commission of the States, Frank Newman, stated that about 14 million children—one in five—live in poverty in this country, and that stark figure has been accompanied in recent decades by skyrocketing rates of teenage drug abuse, suicide, unwed pregnancy, and unemployment. Newman's vision is that the United States is moving toward a two-tiered society—a smaller, affluent, and educated class with little sense of social or civic responsibility, and a much bigger, impoverished class of Americans, largely locked out of society's benefits because they lack basic education, employment skills, and job opportunities (Brown, 1986, p. 12).

One implication for us middle-class folks has to do with the costs now and in the future for our republic to sustain those who are locked out. Harold Hodgkinson of the Institute for Educational Leadership forecasts the following on the basis of demographics. By 2020, most of the Baby Boomers will be retired; their retirement income will be provided largely by the smaller age-group to follow. "For example, in 1950 seventeen workers paid the benefits of each retiree. By 1992, only three workers will provide the funds for each retiree, and one of the three workers will be minority." One interpretation would be that it is in our own self-interest to ensure that jobs exist and well-paying jobs at that, and that young people are better prepared to hold those jobs in order to pay for the benefits that will support us in our habits when we retire.

CONCLUSION

What can we do about the trend toward individual privacy and lack of involvement in civic obligations? Let me close with some questions, because change can only begin with a change of resolve, a change in the heart of each of us.

Let us begin with ourselves. Examining our own lives and our own values, where do we fall on the spectrum of private and public involvement? Do we believe our actions make a difference, that what we do or do not do now affects the next generation? How many volunteer organizations do we belong to, contributing our time and talents? Are we active in local politics? Do we vote in national elections? What is the level of our knowledge of world geography? Current events? Who are the people we associate with most—are they like us or do they challenge us because they are different?

Let us look at our programs. Do we define personal growth primarily in terms of individual achievement and self-esteem?? Are our groups comprised of people from diverse backgrounds? Do our programs provide skills in managing differences—learning about and celebrating different cultural customs and events; understanding how to manage conflicts? Do our programs include those from other generations? Do our programs provide hands-on experiences in government? Is service a key practice to raising consciousness and contributing labor or problem-solving expertise for a community? Are we looking to develop incentives to draw people out of themselves, such as expecting community service involvement as part of the admissions process at schools or as a component of financial aid?

Finally, let us ask some questions about AEE. Does our current mission statement embody the guiding principles of the organization? Are we content to remain as we have been pretty much since the beginning: a friendly, outdoor adventure-oriented enclave, isolated from other groups and larger issues? Do we reach out as effectively as we can to others who are involved in experiential education or to those in mainstream education? Do we really want to take the personal empowerment we see transforming individuals in the field, and incorporate it within a larger strategy for social change?

Certainly, we all need enclaves to return to, special friends and relationships that know, understand, and support us. AEE serves us well in that regard. But, if we are to become more than a haven for hikers, we must shift our sights. In doing so, we must examine that set of propositions that has become the ethical framework of our behavior. In my mind, that will involve a significant shift from the emphasis on personal growth alone to one which reinforces personal growth *and* civic responsibility.

I dare the Board to continue the process begun by the theme of this conference and the pre-conference workshop on the future of AEE, and to reexamine the ethical basis for who we are and where we are headed as an Association. From that leadership, our behavior should follow. I dare each of us to do the same in our own lives and with the people whom we service in our programs.

41

Reflections on Living with Respect: The 1991 Kurt Hahn Address

Dan Conrad

Note: This is the edited written text of an address given by Dan Conrad, in accepting the Kurt Hahn Award for his wife, Diane Hedin. It was given at the Association for Experiential Education's 19th Annual International Conference at Lake Junaluska, North Carolina, October 25, 1991. The emotions and words of a specific moment and place usually do not translate well into the two-column format of a journal article—much less an address reflecting on one person's life, a person whom readers may not have known. But increasingly, many philosophers and educators examining the relationship between theory and practice are arguing that good theory comes out of reflective practice rather than vice versa. It is in this way that the address is so pertinent to the theme—it reflects on the lessons and gifts of one life as a means to ask questions of each of us and promote our reflection on our theories and practices of education and, for that matter, of living. These words express the power and importance of examining our theories in practice.

This article was originally published in the *Journal of Experiential Education*, Vol. 15, #2, August 1992.

INTRODUCTION

Thank you. I am proud to accept this year's Kurt Hahn Award in my wife's name. Diane earned a lot of awards and accolades in her life—I'm still running across little plaques and certificates stashed in odd places all over the house. She never paid much attention to them, not out of some sense of being "above it all," but more because she never turned over to others the role of judging whether or not she was living well or accomplishing anything of value.

But this recognition was different, and I can vividly picture how moved she was when she got the call informing her of it. We talked about it for some time, and why it was special. Part of it, I guess, was the time in her life when she received it, when it was getting harder to envision getting well again, when one can't avoid assessing the difference one's life has made. Part of it stems from the nature of the person in whose name the award is given. A good part of it stems from the mission and special integrity of AEE, and part of it from the company a Kurt Hahn Award Winner keeps: Jim Kielsmeier, Alec Dickson, and Joe Nold, for example, have been friends and respected colleagues for a long time. Others have inspired us by their life's work and writing. Others—well, I can't help recalling the very first AEE convention Diane and I attended in Monterey-By-The-Sea. We "happened" into a speech by Willi Unsoeld and experienced a "happening" of the most profound and moving sort.

This is also a moment of profound sadness for me. I'm sure you can well imagine there has never been any speech to any group that I have been less happy to be delivering. When the award was announced, we had reason to expect she would he here to receive it and be talking to you herself, but fate determined otherwise. She died, with me, and in our home at about 10:30 p.m. on the night of August 11th. This followed two-and-one-half years of living with cancer and about ten days of dying from it.

I don't guarantee I'll make it through these remarks without incident, but should I falter and there are momentary pauses, you needn't be embarrassed for me, and I will not be either.

For there's a lot of sadness in this world, and my own is but one instance of that experienced by countless others—including, I'm well aware, many of you in this room tonight. And before I launch into the main body of these remarks, I want to say a word or two about that as well.

ON SUFFERING AND LOSS

Throughout the period of Diane's illness, there were many times when our 6½-year-old Jeremy would skin his knee or bump his head, and I would say something to the effect that "it doesn't hurt any less just because his mom has a bigger hurt."

But I'm seeing now I wasn't entirely correct, for since Diane died, it has mattered to me to realize that the tragedy I've experienced is matched and exceeded by the tragedies and horrors felt by so many others.

Some of you may recall the story of the mustard seed, which concerns a woman in India whose little boy had died and how she took her dead son in her arms and went from place to place asking for medicine for him. Many scoffed and laughed at her, but one man took pity and advised her to seek the assistance of the wisest teacher in the land. Taking her son with her, she asked the great teacher for medicine for her son. The teacher told her that she had done well in coming to him but that before he could do anything, she must go throughout the city and, in whatever house no one had suffered or died, from that house to gather a grain of mustard seed. So she went from house, to house, to house, but never succeeded in finding a home where no one had suffered. And learning this, of course, was the very medicine prescribed.

So, we are never alone in our sadness. Suffering is a common experience of all humankind. It binds us together. For we are one species, not several, sharing with all others the same sources of laughter and hope and tears and the same need for love, respect, and compassion.

In the days immediately following Diane's death, I often thought about how the sun and moon and stars that filled my sky were the same as shone down on others who were grieving a wife, mother, father, child, sister, or friend. Some from disease, some from accident, some from hunger, from murder . . . or even from war.

And somehow I kept coming back to those 50 to 100,000 Iraqi dead who were being mourned as deeply as I mourned Diane—with the difference that they were dead on purpose. They were killed by high-tech weaponry, systematically employed by persons whom we afterward celebrated as heroes with songs and fireworks and jubilant ticker-tape parades. And the destruction they wrought, and the suffering and tears that resulted, were pointed to as igniting a great new spirit in America, a resurgence of national pride and a renewed sense of confidence and dignity. It was said we could hold our heads high once more. It's a strange world.

But I don't bring this up to make a political statement. I'm no expert in foreign affairs or on how to deal with other militaristic nations and aggressive leaders. But I do know something about individual suffering and loss, and about motherless children—and wish profoundly that our decisions to go to war and our celebrations following would take the whole story into account.

Would it be less patriotic to feel as much compassion and regret as joy and pride over what occurred in that, and all other wars? In America we have so many better things to be joyful and prideful about.

Just the other night, I had this wonderful idea about that New York City ticker-tape parade. Remember it? Well, just imagine this for a moment: What if right in the middle of that parade everything had just stopped, all of a sudden Schwartzkopf, the patriot missiles, everything stopped—just for a moment—and all the people stood silently together while a thousand or more runners came weaving their way through the floats, convertibles, battalions of soldiers, and marching bands, with each runner carrying a banner inscribed with the names of a hundred persons who had died: American, Israeli, Saudi, Egyptian, Kuwaiti, Iraqi, Turk. And as the runners passed these silent watchers, everyone (as is the custom in some synagogues on Yom Kippur) turned to the person next to them and said, "I'm sorry," "I'm so very sorry." And when the runners had passed, the parade and music and storm of ticker tape continued on once more.

Well, it's just an idea, and time, right now, for me to continue on. It is not my intention to use this as a forum for my ideas about politics or education, or to run out some reassuring platitudes about the need for experience or the importance of informal education. We all know and agree on most of those things anyway.

The Lessons and Implications of Diane's Life

In accepting this assignment, the only thing I could think of that would be appropriate and authentic for me to do would be to acquaint you a little with Diane, in order to consider what we may learn from her life and work for how we might live our lives and conduct our work—wherever that may take us. So that's what I'll begin to do right now.

The Need Not to Be Perfect to Be Good

The first lesson I'll draw from Diane's life may seem an odd place to start, but it is that you don't have to be perfect to be good, or flawless to merit emulation. It's a great temptation to mythologize our heroes and heroines, but we do so at the risk of losing touch with the fullness of who they were, and of creating an unwarranted distance between their lives and our own—with our own too-apparent foibles and flaws.

Diane was a truly remarkable woman—but could be a bundle of trouble as well, with a flashing temper and acerbic tongue who could holler at you louder than an outraged umpire. A few years ago, she taught for most of the academic year at the University of Haifa. It was a time of deep meaning for her, but when quizzed about it, she didn't talk about connecting with her ethnic and spiritual roots so much as how Israel was the kind of place where if someone offended you, say, by cutting in front of you at a bus stop, you could scream any invectives you could think of at any decibel level you could attain and no one would think any worse of you for it. That was Diane's kind of place.

In a play by Ignazio Silone, entitled "A Poor and Humble Christian," he has one character say: "Saints, my boys, are all right on altars, after their death, but while they're alive they mean nothing but trouble." This statement is more than just a left-handed compliment about their being a pain to the establishment. It also implies they were regular people who could screw up, just like you and me. Our greatest heroes were a bunch of irritating bumblers a lot of the time, but they could also rise to greatness when the occasion demanded. And so can we, and so can even the most exasperating of the young people with whom we work. I teach a community service class at my high school which is not, I assure you, an assemblage of adolescent Albert Schweitzers and teenage Mother Theresas. Their primary motivation is to get out of the damn school building—but they sometimes rise to greatness and do some pretty extraordinary things. Many of you have seen this yourself in your own students.

So people need not be perfect to be good; institutions do not have to be perfect to be worth working in, or on; and relationships do not have to be perfect to be satisfying and worth the effort to make more fulfilling. We're imperfect beings in an imperfect world, and just gotta do the best we can with what we have, as our heroines did with what they had.

Our Attitudes Toward Life

What we can do is quite a lot, which sort of leads into the next implication I wish to draw which is that the value and importance of an activity, event, or encounter are not inherent in those things themselves, but are a consequence of the value we endow them with and the level of energy and attention we bring to them.

A little information on Diane may be required here if this is to be more than a hollow platitude. I realize that many of you did not know her, and others only through her writing or research. But you don't need a vita summary or publications list, for the people she affected most profoundly usually didn't know (or care) about these any more than the people we meet care about our professional histories. What made encounters with her extraordinary was not what she had done in the past—but the immediate power of her presence, the genuineness of the attention she paid to you, and the energy she infused into any setting she was in.

Some years ago, Colin Wilson wrote a novel he called *The Space Vampires* in which he came up with a fanciful but weirdly plausible explanation of why some people just seem to drain us of energy, why their very entrance into a staff meeting could put the entire group into a catatonic state . . . you know the type. Just thinking you might run into them makes you tired. Now, Wilson's idea was that these people have been taken over by creatures from outer space who are making a kind of lunch stop here on earth in order to suck not blood but energy—until they have gained sufficient life force to enable them to continue their celestial voyage.

Now that's sort of an odd way of arriving at no more than a description of what Diane was not—but it's hard to describe in words that aren't simply sappy and sentimental. People said a lot of things to me about Diane after she died but what was noted most often was the power of her personality, her energy, and how she was fully engaged in whatever she was doing, and fully present to whomever she was with: When planting bulbs, she really planted them; when walking in the woods or baking a spinach pie or teaching a class, she was totally engaged; and whether meeting the mayor or a little neighborhood child, she was as fully present for either. She lived attentively and mindfully. I sometimes thought of her as a Zen Buddhist without the calm serenity. When Diane was around, something interesting was always happening, or just about to happen.

We talk glibly about living life to the fullest, and many may even envy a person like Diane whose life seems so full of interesting and extraordinary events. But what we really ought to envy (or emulate) is their power to find or create, out of even the most common occurrences of life, something marvelous and beautiful.

It is our attitude to life that we can be in charge of, and maybe it's only that—but that gets me into my next point which has to do with choice, chance, and control.

Choice, Chance, and Control

When Diane and I first learned she had cancer, we scoured the literature on its causes, on appropriate diet and other curative and preventive measures we could take, on things we could do to stimulate the immune system, techniques to heighten our bodies' healing powers after we become sick. The irony was that Diane's personality, lifestyle, eating habits, and the rest virtually defined what we are supposed to do and be like to avoid cancer. But she got it anyway and died at age forty-seven.

The day following her return home from the first operation and original diagnosis of cancer, we were visited by a physician friend, an oncologist, who himself had colon cancer. Diane's first question was "Joe, why did this happen to us?" And Joe, digging deeply into his personal experience as well as years of medical training and practice, said: "Who the hell knows?"

"Who the hell knows?" It is the only honest answer to a lot of questions of life—and death, of sickness and health, intelligence and stupidity, wealth and poverty, success and failure. There are so many things that seem to be ruled by luck, chance, and forces we cannot control. Admonitions to be choice-makers and to take control of our lives diminish their impact by inflating the possibilities. It is not the abundance of choice and power, but their very scarcity that should compel us to make the most of those opportunities we do have. Rare resources must not be squandered.

Diane outlived the original projections for how much time she had by over two years. She couldn't choose whether or not to have cancer, but she could choose whether or not to let the cancer control and define her. She tried every avenue of cure: from operations, chemotherapy, imaging, meditation, seeking out the newest practices, and the most ancient—even consulting an exiled Tibetan physician. But it was none of these, I believe, that kept her alive so long as it was the spirit that inspired their pursuit, the spirit that kept her running and swimming, that got her to tuck her chemo pump into a belly pack and climb up and paint the highest peaks of our house that I hadn't the nerve to tackle. It kept her pulling weeds in her garden only days before she died, and empowered her to make cupcakes for Jeremy's party on the very morning of her final admittance to the hospital.

Machines and medical technology can do some wonderful things for those parts of us that are like a machine. There is no medicine, no technology, for that in us which is not machine: the mind and the spirit. We can choose: to curse the universe, or plant a flower—and Diane was always planting flowers.

Doing What Matters Now

The next implication I want to pursue is a kind of extension of the last. To make it, I need to return to the conversation between Diane and our oncologist friend when it moved from why it happened to what do we do now. Asked this, Joe reflected a moment on all the times he'd had to tell people they had cancer and then said: "You know, it's a funny thing, no one, not one person, ever, has reacted to the news by saying 'Doc, my only regret is that I didn't spend just a little more time at the office.'"

The point is obvious, I guess, and I wouldn't even bother to bring it up except that it is truly one of the most peculiar characteristics of human life that we spend so little of it doing what we claim we enjoy most, or believe is most important. Mostly we wait—as if an infinity were available to us to do what matters, go to the places we wish to go, become the person or parent we want to be, or repair the relationship that is slipping away. And even if there were a lot of time, what exactly are we waiting for?

I don't have the foggiest notion about any form of life we may have had before or will have after this one, but I sometimes think, "What if it were neither blind chance nor an act of God that tossed me up here on this shore? What if I'd been lolling about some other realm of existence and decided, quite on my own, to enter into human form again, had spent a century or two pulling strings to get the chance, the time finally came to be born—and then I spent the next fifty or sixty years just sort of sitting around, or worrying about whether people liked me, or getting myself into a little routine that I could replay every twenty-four hours, eventually forgetting why I'd bothered to come here at all (except through some weird and bizarre dreams that I could never remember or make any sense of in the morning). "Living," as Ionesco put it, "like someone hoping to win first prize in the lottery without even buying a ticket."

Doing Things Because They Are The Right Thing To Do

Now don't get me wrong, and this is my next point, life isn't a sort of game with a big scoreboard in the sky, recording our deeds and accomplishments. It's tempting to imagine that this is so, and then sell our souls to whomever we imagine the scorekeepers to be—waiting on their approval, or thank you, or recommendation.

The value of our efforts, in the important things of life, ought not be determined by the judgment of others or even by whether we succeed or fail—but in doing them at all, just because it is the right thing for us to do.

Diane fought hard against cancer. Finally, she died from it. Does that mean she lost and the effort was in vain? Not in the slightest. I said at the outset that Diane lived with cancer for two-and-one-half years and only died from it for a few days. That was the triumph—and her pushing back against pain and potential despair stands as a metaphor for how we must also push back against the frustrations and evils we confront—and why we must do so.

Take the evils of war and senseless violence that are everywhere. If to work for peace I must believe, in the words of that song we used to sing, I'll "see that day come round," then I either have to live some kind of fantasy—or quit in despair and discouragement. For the fighting always continues. The same if our aim is to eradicate hunger, poverty, injustice, suffering, or loneliness.

Rather, I believe, we fight these things simply because it is the right thing to do, and do them we must to remain fully alive and true to our humanity.

Camus wrote about this in *The Rebel* and painted a picture of each of us as besieged, all around, pressed in upon by hatred, injustice, bigotry, and despair—and that we have the choice to acquiesce, become a part of it, or to push back, and that it is in the act of pushing back that we assert our humanity—that we define ourselves, that we affirm we are not bystanders, or collaborators, but active agents who, if not exactly conquerors, are still champions of the ideals we strive to live by.

Diane pushed back—against the ill-treatment of kids, against injustice, against stupidity and lethargy, against poverty and hunger, against the violence she met as a child and the cancer she faced as an adult. And it was this pushing back that defined her, refined her, made her someone we rightly honor and from whose life we can learn.

Explore, Experience, and Explain

There's much more I could say about these things, but I need to switch now from the implications of Diane's life for how we live our own, to the implications for how we live with others—particularly those whom it is our calling to lead and teach.

A day or two after Diane was informed of the Kurt Hahn Award—and of the opportunity to address this Conference—we talked for a while about what she would say to you this evening. It was only once—but I remember it well.

We talked for a time about education, about experience, about the needs and also the great power that kids have, and something she said prompted me to say, "Wait, I have just the thing. A paper by one of my students is just perfect." And I ran and got it, and read it to her. It was written by one of my twelfth-grade philosophy students last spring, whose assignment was to describe his personal philosophy of life. When I finished she said, "That's fabulous; get me a copy, I'm going to read it in North Carolina." I got her a copy. In fact, here it is right now, and I'm going to read it as she would have.

THE MEANING OF LIFE

Well, here I am, a Tuesday, it's about 8 o'clock p.m. and I, Josef Antonio Enrique Barela have to write my own opinion on what the meaning of life is (Shit!). Lord knows this won't be the easiest paper I've wrote. But here it go's.

To me the meaning of life is to explore, to experience and then try to explain. By explore, I mean to try to go out and see as much as your eyes let you. By experience I mean to try not to let a day go by without trying to do something different. By explain, I mean after you have either explored or experienced, you should think and debate about what you did, saw, heard, smelt, felt and tasted (I will go into further details later).

Now, let me try to explain myself a little bit more clearly here on what I mean by exploring. By exploring I don't think you should run away or become a nomad (although you would see a lot more that way). What I mean is you should maybe sometime or other, just go out for a drive sometime or even a walk. But don't just walk around the block. Hell, run if you want. All I'm saying is go some place new, like go to Nebraska, Iraq, Vietnam, Mars, hell, and if you want, crawl under your bed. As long as you're someplace that's different to you.

Don't let society put your life into a program by making you feel trapped or swindled into being the traditional—go to school—get a job—have a family—retire—buy a condo in Florida, etc. BE FREE!!!! SEE THINGS IN A NEW PERSPECTIVE!!

Okay, let me try to explain myself on Experiencing! I think this is one of the keys to finding out the most about yourself. Have you ever said to yourself? "Only if I didn't do that" or, even worse, "Only if I did do that?"

When I grow up I want to he able to say. I've had a very eventful childhood. When I'm on my death-bed I don't want to say "God don't take me now. There is so much I haven't done. In a nutshell, I'm saying; DON'T EVER SAY I CAN'T!!"

When I say Explain myself, I mean let me try to rationalize myself to you. Don't ever get me wrong, Anthony Barela has had his share of screw ups. But I do my best to get over them. We all have done something we regret. And we all sooner or later can understand why we did them.

If we never thought about what we did we would be perpetual numbskulls. All of us should be as free-spirited as each individual possibly can. But we should always find a reason as to why we're doing what we're doing.

Have you ever caught yourself in the middle of something and said "What in the hell am I doing??" In my mind I'm always saying that. I'm not saying I'm always insecure. I just have to know why a lot of things are the way they are.

In summary, I truly believe that none of us will find our own true meaning of life until we die. But until then I'm going with this theory I just wrote.

If you have any questions, please ask.

I swear that's the best brief description of experiential education I've read by anyone, any time, and I don't think I need elaborate on that aspect of it for this audience.

But beside its being a profound statement of what we believe about life and learning, it is a remarkable description of the way Diane lived her life: Explore, Experience, and Explain—a briefer and more alliterative way of saying that we should live life to its fullest demands: being fully present, engaged, and energized, being in control of one's life, not missing opportunities for choice, acting on the values and ideals we hold, and acting now, not waiting for a more propitious time. This doesn't even get to the "explain" part which deals with Diane's work as a writer, teacher, researcher, and speaker and such, which I've chosen to not say much about tonight.

INTERPERSONAL RESPECT

But it's a funny thing, when I finished reading Tony's paper, she had a rather different point she wanted to make and typically, one that went beyond what I had seen in it. "Look." she said, "that illustrates exactly what I've been talking about.

Kids have a lot of important things to say, and important things they can do. We've just got to give them a chance, we've got to pay attention to them, listen to them, not out of some patronizing politeness, but seriously, and accord them dignity and respect—yes, respect them. In fact that's it, that's what I will talk about: Respect."

She went on to say that people can talk all they want about this reform or that, this curriculum or that, this institutional arrangement or that, gifted programs, remedial programs, discipline, length of school day, time on task, ad infinitum and ad nauseam. We fiddle with these things endlessly, but the only thing we can be absolutely sure of is that most people will consider that whatever we're doing now is wrong, representing some inexplicable (or even demon-inspired) drift from the practices and high standards that prevailed in some prior golden era—when, of course, the very same critique was being made. (In this regard, I can't resist recalling a study, from the 1930s no less, that derailed the appalling ignorance of college freshmen only about half of whom, as I recall, could identify Abraham Lincoln as being President during the Civil War.)

Anyway, the big point she planned to make is that the central dynamic of education is not institutional or structural but is interpersonal. How adults and young people relate to one another as human beings makes more difference than any formal framework they operate within. Just ask the kids, as Diane did, by the thousands, in polls and interviews conducted over years and years. "Who are the good teachers?" "The ones who listen to us, take us seriously, respect us." What makes a school a good or bad place to be?" Well, let me actually quote Diane from an article summarizing several years of poll-taking:

> The quality of personal relationships is the most important criterion for judging organizations or institutions in which adolescents participate . . . . While students say having a wide and varied curriculum, a good physical plant, a variety of extracurricular activities, etc., are important, they were not sufficient to make a school exemplary! The quality of personal relationships, however, was.

It's remarkably simple, isn't it? And should be so simple to do. Being a good teacher or youth worker is not all that mysterious or hard, if we just listen to what kids tell us they want—which is to be respected—which means . . . well, I've neither the time nor inclination to present an exegesis on the term. You folks don't need it anyway. Let me instead just illustrate its dynamics, first from Diane's life, and then your own.

The theme of respecting kids, taking them seriously, believing in their capacity to succeed—and challenging them to do it—was unquestionably the thread that ran through everything she taught and wrote, every program she designed, and every encounter she had with young people. I've thought about where that came from, and wondered if it didn't grow as much from memories of her own experience as from what young people would tell her about theirs.

Diane knew only too well what it meant not to be respected as a child. She grew up in the rural fringes of the Twin City metro area. (That Garrison Keillor was her high school classmate, gives you some sense of this.) She attended a classic, one-room school (1st row, 1st grade, 2nd row, 2nd grade, etc.) in which she and her brother were not only the only Jews, but the poorest of the many poor kids in the school. I don't believe that either of her parents finished high school. But I do know that her father was abusive in as many ways as you wish to imagine, and that her mother was no buffer or comfort, being more often in mental institutions than out, and that her home was ramshackle without, and considered by the neighbors, to this day, as a "garbage house within." Diane was, in today's parlance, very much "at risk" (to employ a phrase I never recall her using, except in derision). At the same time, there was no idea she hated more than the one that all youth are equally "at risk"—whatever their circumstances. Some kids just plain do have it tougher than others—as her own experience, and just plain common sense, clearly show.

At the same time, there is, in every child, the wherewithal to succeed, at something, if someone just *respects* them, believes in them, encourages them, challenges them, gives them a chance—and if they are able to believe this themselves. Her own life proved it. Her work with young people demonstrated it.

Diane was never one to bemoan her troubled childhood. To be honest, even this bare sketch had to be gleaned from relatives and friends. Diane never talked about it. Not from shame, I don't think, but from irrelevance. It was past and gone, and better to think about now and the future. She didn't "stuff it" exactly, more just let it go. Not surprisingly, she could never get into things like "victimization" and the need to "heal the inner child" or that we have to take care of ourselves before we can care for others, and that sort of thing that is so popular now. In jargon words, she was into the developmental rather than therapeutic model, and liked to focus on power and possibility, and just getting on with life. You could call it the "Respectful Model."

But don't take it from me or Diane. Just reflect on your own experience and it will reveal that *respect* is not just a nice social ideal, but the key to exceptional performance in any endeavor, academic and intellectual included. Think about how you perform with different people. Are there not some you can think of with whom you are exceptionally bright, witty, insightful, and clever? And is there not at least someone you can think of who treats you like you're some sort of idiot and, with them, you consequently are? I know I can.

I'm reminded of the British socialite who reported on her experience with two prominent British artist/intellectuals, and of one, she said, "When he left, I was convinced he was the cleverest person in all of England," and of the other, she said, "When he left, I thought I was."

Now just think of it, what if we could create, among the people with whom we work, the kind of relationship that we experience when we feel most witty, profound, and capable. Why, it would amount to some kind of revolution, including an intellectual and academic one. The Japanese would come and study us! Well, that was to be Diane's principal message to you tonight: Respect. Respect yourself, the people you teach or lead—and each other. She could not be here to say that, but her life said it, both loud and clear.

She lived well: fully engaged in life, to energize others, to control what she could and ignore what she couldn't, to figure out what she wanted to do, and be, and not wait until tomorrow to work on it.

CONCLUSIONS

That almost wraps it up, except for one final thing that's haunted me all the while I prepared these remarks and even while I've been delivering them to you. In a way, it negates almost everything I've said. That one thing more is that talk is cheap. I've tried to draw some lessons from Diane's life that could guide us as we live, or teach, or lead adventure groups, or administer programs, or whatever we do.

Any of you could have stood up here and offered similarly good advice. Because, you see, it's not knowing what to do that's hard, it's doing it! Kierkegaard said it well when he wrote, "Everyone knows what ought to be done, but no one is willing to act." The Apostle Paul said, "The good I would do I do not, and that which I would not do is what I practice." Perhaps the best way to learn from the life and work of Diane is to just forget it, forget about her wisdom and example, and look instead to our own.

"When I get to heaven," said Rabbi Susya shortly before his death, "they will not ask me, 'Why were you not Moses,' but 'Why were you not Susya? Why did you not become what only you could become?'" I don't have the formula for how you do that, but I think I know where to look. Browning wrote:

Truth is within ourselves; it takes no rise
From outward things, whate'er you may believe
There is an inmost center in us all,
Where truth abides in fullness; and around,
Wall upon wall, the gross flesh hems it in,
This perfect, clear perception—which is truth.
A baffling and perverting carnal mesh
Binds it, and makes all error; and to know,
Rather consists in opening out a way
Whence the imprisoned splendor may escape,
Than in effecting entry for a light
Supposed to be without.

Perhaps that is Diane's greatest legacy, that she lived by her own wisdom, her own light, and showed us that we both must, and can, do so as well.

But there are a couple of things we could do, right away, to carry on the legacy that Diane has left us, and even begin to open a way to that light within ourselves. One thing I've talked to you about already. Respect. Can you imagine the effect on each of us, throughout the rest of this conference, if we were to truly respect one another, if we could be confident that those around us would take us seriously, listen to us, accord us dignity, care about us, see (as Santayana put it) "beyond the surface encrustations to the god within," and that we did likewise for each that we meet? This would be a gathering like none before.

Let me add one other thing I've not mentioned before. Diane had an eye for beauty, and a love of the beautiful. She found it everywhere. No one appreciated the beauty of a flower, or the glory of a sunset, or the majesty of a mountain, or the serenity of a tree more than she. And when it was not there, she created it—in her exquisite gardens, in her painting and needlepoint, in the setting of a table, in the art with which she filled our home.

There's an old piece of advice that her life suggests, that to stay really alive we must, each and every day, experience, really experience, something of beauty—be it a poem, or a flower, or piece of music, or sunrise, or painting—and each day we should ask ourselves: "What thing of beauty did I take time to enjoy today?" I couldn't think of anything more important to do, or any place where it would be easier to accomplish than this place of extraordinary loveliness.

So let the legacy of Diane's exceptional life live on in you, and me, in respect for one another and in our attention to the beauty of the stars tonight and the mountains and streams tomorrow, and in the beauty of the people we encounter in our life and work from this day on.

42

My Breakfast with André: A Discourse on the Intent of Experiential Educators

Mitchell Sakofs and David L. Burger

ANDRÉ IS A PARADOX: A JOVIAL SORT WITH GRACIOUS GREETINGS AND KIND words for all, yet with a serious side which compels him to challenge people to reflect on their lives. He always said, "An unexamined life is not worth living" (he borrowed that from some philosopher whose name currently eludes me), then always added "and an unlived life is not worth examining." He had always been one to think "out of the box." He was a mountaineer, rock climber, academician, and an all-round trouble maker.

We were to meet at a steak house on the hill, and I enjoyed the cute little Irish green umbrellas over the table . . . sort of an existence-proving paradox for André—a vegetarian who would rather run in the morning than eat. I dreaded this meeting as I was not in the mood to be challenged on my ideas and purposes in life at 7:30 A.M.: for at 7:30 in the morning, it takes all the energy I can muster to simply sit erect in a chair. André selected this quaint, if not tacky, coffee shop for our meeting. The booths were well equipped with salt, pepper, hot sauce, ketchup, flies, and a napkin dispenser. While the overhead ceiling fans whirled, and the sounds and smells of eggs, hash browns, and bacon filled the air, I sat and watched the parade of early morning eaters eating. As I sipped my coffee, I marveled at how they could get that stuff down so early in the morning; I also wondered where André was since he was now 30 minutes late.

While the waitress was pouring my third cup-of-joe, André walked in and briskly made his way to the booth where I sat. I stood and greeted him, we shook hands, smiled, and exchanged pleasantries. Yet by the look in his eyes I could tell that he was ready to get down to business. He began much as I might have expected, and much as I may have wanted to resist, i.e., in the cosmos . . . .

André: Well, I think we should promote a new way of thinking in experiential education. WE ARE THE MOON!

Wally: Ahuhhhh, André, what-da-ya-wanna-eat-for breakfast? I'm a little hungry.

André: The great Sufi saint, Nasrudin, once stood up in a tea house and said. "The moon is a more important source of illumination than the sun." A devotee soon gathered his strength to question the saint and stood up saying, "Why is that Mulla?" The Mulla smiled and said, "It is because the moon is out when we need it most!"

Wally: Well, mooo-lla, why do you say that? Do you drink coffee?

André: I think that true experiential educators are ministers of the Light of Understanding. They are not the sun, yet they reflect it. They are not the dark, yet they live in it. Ask yourself, what is the difference between an experiential educator and a teacher? A true experiential educator, to me, is one who has experienced a higher truth and is actively involved in liberating others. True experiential educators choose not to work for institutions that offer facts and skills, but work for groups that seek knowledge and wisdom. Now, there are inherent ethical issues worth discussing here. For example, one issue is that when such ministers are not clear about their purpose, or a group or school is not clear about their intent, the resulting outcomes may have little power and thus the outcomes are mediocre. That is unethical and damaging to experiential education as a School of Thought. A second issue concerns representation. If they represent themselves inaccurately to the public and to their students as disseminators of information and skills and not ministers of transformation, then they are being deceptive and unethical.

Wally: André, before we talk about ethics or transformation, explain to me what you mean by ministers.

André: What gets a person into the role of an experiential educator, Wally? I think it is a desire to be a secular minister. I don't mean a minister of secular humanism, as that movement is mainly concerned with the individual and not an "Other." I do mean, however, a minister, religious or not, interested in the individual being involved mutually with the "Other." In experiential education, and especially adventure-based education, there are many experiences likened to conversion experiences. However people define a higher truth, be it "the Other," "the Numinus," "The Great Spirit," "God," "Cosmic Consciousness," there is power related to that concept, and anything that brings human *consciousness* closer to that is a conversion experience.

An experiential educator who is getting those profound conversion experiences is somehow connected to that power, and thus, they are in fact ministers thereof. These ministers are often people who cannot stand rigidly organized religions or institutions. They have left them because they are too tight with form and absolute, stagnated rules. They tend to prefer the freedom of thought and action found outside such institutions. These same ministers may, however, also be insecure with a formless walk, and so experiential education has provided a middle ground, a home for those perpetual seekers. So, it is more than a mind set, it is a set of operating premises based on one's intellect and soul: premises created in relationship, in a conversion experience.

Wally: (*to the waitress*) I'll have the scrambled eggs, hash browns, pancakes, and more coffee, please. Thank you. (*to André, stroking his chin*) That is interesting, but don't you think that to call these educators ministers is a bit too strong? For the most part, experiential educators are just young, idealistic kids who choose a romantic lifestyle which they soon realize barely enables them to pay the bills, and so they soon grow bored and leave the job. Somehow, I don't link this all-too-common phenomena with a ministry. And those who stay in experiential education find their lives caught up in routine, planning for lessons which they have taught countless times. They habituate to the lesson and thus, the essence of anything profound is lost to them and they become cynics.

André: Just as an educator is different from a teacher, so is there a dichotomy in preaching. Some preachers preach at people and some draw on what is within people. Isn't that the point anyway? Are people using the umbrella of experiential education to help others expand the consciousness that is already within them, or are they pushing their own personal definitions of truth? That is why I use the word minister and not preacher.

But to respond to your question, I see two points. One, is that the true minister who walks into experiential education does in fact maintain that connection with the "Other." It may be through the wilderness, but more likely through the relationship with students who are having intangible experiences. Which means that those ministers can leave the wilderness and go anywhere that they can share those intangible experiences. They could go to Xerox and become a corporate trainer, or to a college and become a professor, or to a public school. In short, they could go anywhere and have those intangible experiences with students, because that is where the power is. That is where the art is. When you see those people go into the corporate world, for example, they do not become merely trainers. They are people interested in the transformation of companies, creating corporate cultures or an ethos for a company that is transforming for all the members, that really makes a difference in the personal lives of people. Experiential educators, being pragmatists, do not believe in absolutes. However, that may only mean empirically measurable absolutes. They may consider non-tangible absolutes such as Love. An infinite, metaphysical light leads those few.

The others, I would suggest, probably never had a calling to the ministry. They stumbled into experiential education because they loved climbing or teaching outside of the classroom or teaching beyond worksheets. It is like the difference between managers and leaders. They are more interested in doing the right thing, than doing the thing right. Some seek security in rules and power in holding the right answers or in using a novel set of techniques. Some use those novel techniques and do not observe any transforming experiences.

In a way, there is no experiential education. Everything is an experience. Maybe we should not be calling "it" experiential education, but then again, what is in a name?

Wally: I don't know, André. It seems to me that you're making a bigger deal out of this than is warranted. Most experiential educators are not ministers at all, but simply educators who embrace more alternative forms of teaching than do most teachers: that's it; that's all.

André: You think that is all they do, do you? They teach science, or math, or literature experientially, and thus improve their student's content knowledge by making it more relevant through context. Well, I don't think that is it at all. You are certainly right when you say concrete experiences can improve on the quality of information assimilation and retention enjoyed by learners over traditional didactic models of teaching. Didactic models often present lessons in an "experiential void" or in a context which is out of context with the content. However, if you think of it, experiential models do much more. Experiential models have as their goal the assimilation of information at a level which transforms the individual in two ways. The first transformation is the incorporation of information at the level which Spinoza felt resulted in intuitive understandings and which Piaget might have argued promotes a schematic shift in the individual's conception and thus interaction with the world. Piaget was a realist, so I would add interaction with the innerworld as well. The second kind of transformation I think experience-based learning promotes concerns the role the individual plays in his/her own education.

Learners discover that they need not be passive; rather, they have choice over what they learn and a clear vision of how knowledge can be used in the world. Most traditional educational or instructional formats do not demand that the learner be engaged in the process in this way, nor do they tend to result in a Piagetian schematic shift. Those demands are linked to Freire's sense of the praxis, which he spoke of in his book, *The Pedagogy of the Oppressed*—that dynamic balance between action in the world and reflection upon the world. In other words, as one lives, one interacts with the world. Knowledge guides these actions, and in turn, with the acquisition of knowledge, demands are made on the individual that old actions be assessed in terms of their functionality, and if found lacking, be modified. Thus, true learning requires that the individual be transformed intellectually which in turn transforms the way in which s/he interacts with the world.

Wally: (*to the waitress*) May I have some more coffee, please? (*to André*) So what you are talking about is the transformational power of true learning, are you not? And are you saying that experiential educators who promote transformation are in fact ministers, for the religious experience is, by definition, transformational? If I understand you correctly, you are arguing that experiential educators are more than teachers, for teachers, in general, have limited views of what they teach. Math teachers teach math, whereas educators seek to transform people and thus, they are ministers who empower, who encourage transformation in their students through self-discovery.

André: Exactly. I would capitalize Self-discovery to push it beyond individualism. Remember Wally, it is experience in a social context that the forefathers pushed. And that is where the ethical question arises. Is it ethical to call yourself an experiential educator, and be only interested in slick techniques for learning skills or information, or for an end that may exclude a larger reality? Or even worse, an End? The important question is, What is the purpose behind education? *Thehowandwhatthatgoonaredirectedbythewhy behindthem.* A person could use experiential techniques, include the learner, have them reflect on actions—and still not be powered by deeper purposes.

Here is an interesting difference. Teaching is very polarized. There are clear poles that keep coming up, like the-wilderness-speaks-for-itself versus you-can-learn-anything-in-a-classroom; or clean-scientific-linear-approach is most effective (objectivity) versus those who believe that a so-called "holistic" or multilinear approach is the most effective (subjectivity). In order to grasp the arguments, I especially like Foucault's model of the pendulum. Have you ever seen one?

Wally: No, what is it? (*then to the waitress*) More coffee?

André: It is a pendulum that spins from a single point, rather than a shaft. This configuration allows the pendulum to not only go from side to side, but also swing to many points. Have you been to the Smithsonian in Washington? They have one there. As the pendulum swings, the centripetal force of the earth has the pendulum complete a full circle of opposites. It is still an imperfect model, yet it is more like life. Every pole that the pendulum swings to could be considered truth. We land on those poles and, for a moment, see things clearly. People begin to fight for that temporary clarity as if it were the only truth. Those people begin to think in a digital fashion of black and white, right and wrong. Some people can see a few points at a time and have an expanded view of truth. Yet conscious people have had the ability to see things from the position of the axis, and see that all the points are only true for awhile. No absolutes, merely temporarily tenable positions. Such a transcendent view has synergistic power in it. Those more conscious people don't argue if education should be rooted in Idealism or Realism, or even Pragmatism. They say it could be one, or all, or none of the above. The transcendent view rises above defending a limited temporal view, and artfully provides an intangible view. That is what conversion experiences are about, and that is what true ministries are all about.

Furthermore, it is like most religions where, after the originator goes, the masses begin to debate individual value issues and forget the basic axial experience that holds them together in the first place. A lot of defense builds up, and instead of expanding and liberating each other, there is a state of rigid polarization. There are often mystical traditions within a religion that hold on to the axial experience. For example, some born-again Christians, some Hasidic Jews, some Sufis in Islam, and other subgroups of major religions demonstrate a view of the axis and not toward defending the lower arguments. Experiential educators have been the mystical tradition in education, and now these educational mystics face the ethical issue of selling out to the professional world, or to a Realism camp, or to any singular popular point of view in order to be heard and have status. Our culture has developed a strong pressure to conform with its present measurement-mindedness. The mystical walk is very demanding for it asks not that we have answers, but that we live co-creatively in each moment with the "Other." That is more than conforming to non-conformity, as there is no norm. There is little that can be done as a lesson plan for such an orientation: it is very insecure, and those who cannot do it well are always trying to get people to conform to the security of some limited world view. *Iftrueexperientialeducatorsarenotconscioustheywillsellouttothepowerfulpullofthetruly darkside* and that is an ethical issue. Perhaps some just see this as a question of purity, for example, one believing in anti-materialism can now rationalize owning a BMW, but I see it as an ethical issue. No amount of argument seems to change a weakness into a strength. Anti-materialists look bad and lose power, while the world has one more argument in support of conforming. The ethical question is, "Are we congruent with our beliefs?" It is not, "Can we be consistent?" That may result in being consistently bad. The anti-materialist in the BMW can come up with a very creative, well-handled rhetoric that looks consistent, but cannot make the act congruent with the belief system. Without seeking the congruency of conscious education, experiential education is doomed to become another religiously dogmatic sect, void of spirituality.

Wally: Don't you think that is a little too spiritual? I mean, you can take people into the wilderness, or process them through some experience, and not everyone will have a conversion experience. In fact, there is invariably a portion of any group that will refuse to let down their guard. Not everyone shares that transcendental experience: in fact, they may continue to polarize.

André: But isn't that a different issue? That issue may be that those people did not have a conversion experience. Are we arguing the details or the poles and missing the point? The question is, What is central about that conversion experience? What is it about that memory, that re-cognition of something deeper that can tie us all together, that cannot be argued. What a minister in our trade would call a success is a time when people have a nonrational experience, a magic moment where people experience some sort of oneness. Yes, they are very spiritual moments, and are defined in non-absolute terms by those people in that moment. And what is nice about experiential education is that participants are not tied to a dogma. They are free to define the conversion experience in the moment, and evolve as they experience more.

Remember Wally, what happens in ordinary life is the pendulum and polarization. It just so happens that everyone is stopping at different poles at different times and seeing truth differently. When we argue for those singular perspectives, truth is missed. A final definition of experiential education would be a lie that a conscious minister would not support. The conscious secular minister in experiential education senses or knows these things, and teaches them consciously. They draw people, impel people into experiences where they have a connection to something transcendent. They see it as a step in a process of becoming. They see it as all true, for a while. They pose the questions that are not answered with tangible responses. They respect both the tangible and the intangible and are not dissuaded by that paradox. Not being aware of the difference between the poles and the axis unethically clouds the purpose of education, and turns it into schooling. We begin to train one another in limited perspectives. We jail ourselves with those self-conceived limits.

Wally: How enlightened do these ministers have to be, André? Because I get a sense that it is not tied to the ministry, it is tied to the individual. Your original question may be a moot point, because it is not the minister who provides the insight, it is the individual.

André: We are the moon—it is a simple religious teaching that says we need a teacher. The sun is too bright. To receive the light straight is more than most of us can comprehend or bear, for we live in the dark. We need some reflection, some mirror that is not the light, but is somehow a reflection of the light. Now, it is clear that some experiential educators may not provide a very clear reflection—it may just be the timing and openness of the participant that is reflecting their own light from within. Or, in some cases, it may just be the reflection provided by the context. One point is that education is a relationship. It needs three members in the relationship to complete an educative moment: 1) The teacher must be an educator, meaning that there is some connection to the "Otherness." Sometimes the context is the educator, like the wilderness, and not a person. The learner alone may be the context. 2) There needs to be the learner in a state of readiness. And 3) there needs to be this "Otherness." If there were no "Otherness," there would be no conversion experience. What I am suggesting is that with all three, we have experiential education, and that the experience to have is a nonrational one. Otherwise, we are only teachers—trainers involved with transmitting facts. Merely keepers of a temporal truth.

Wally: I disagree. I think that it happens independently of the instructor, completely. For example, take a rock-climbing class. The instructor may not have any interest in spirituality, and only be interested in setting up a good safe climb. The instructor may only delight in the students' confrontation with fear. The instructor may have no interest in this transcendental experience. Yet the student may come away with a spiritual experience. The mission statement of some adventure-based schools does not include personal growth, but students certainly have such experiences. An IBM employee or a military person may have the spiritual experience independent of the organization's primary purpose.

André: I think the learner is not dependent on the instructor, yet the point is that a transcendental experience is an interdependent experience. The educator can be the context, instead of a person, but there is still an interdependence.

If we did not sometimes need the moon, we could all go straight from the dark to the light. Remember Plato's analogy of the cave—without someone going up to the light, the people would seldom have the impetus to seek. And, if we had to depend only on people to educate us, we might be left wanting. Isn't learning done in relationship?

Wally: So, what are you arguing for André—disclosure? That experiential educators more formally explain to their students their intent so as to not confuse them, and more importantly, to be ethical in terms of their professional objectives? Moreover, for experiential educators who are employed by school systems which claim to be content-oriented, it is critically important that experiential educators disclose their intent and curricular objectives to parents, for they are bound by professional ethical considerations to do so. Are you saying that experiential educators, or Ministers of the Secular Light, or whatever you want to call them, should have a warning sign posted on the doors to their classrooms: "Warning—experiential education may transform you, make you dissatisfied with the world as you know it, and make you long for the Light of Understanding. Warning—experiential education may make you a revolutionary, a heretic to the social order; make you an outcast who will seek more experiences just as junkies seek drugs. Warning—experiential learning may be a hazard to your health, for it may transform you and thus, make you dissatisfied with the world: you may become unhappy and an outcast from the mainstream. Thus, you may become like many of the great prophets, enlightened, and thus, a liability in the world, a threat to the world social order." Is that what you are saying?

André: Yep.

Wally: What do you mean by "Yep?"

André: I am simply saying that it is critically important when one considers the role of an educator, and the ethics of education, that students, educators, and the world at large be properly informed of the potential for transformation inherent in experiential programming. Experiential programs are potentially different from traditional teaching with regard to both form and outcome, and thus, as ministers/educators, we are bound by a code of ethics to inform our students and the public of that potential. Further, if a person is in the ministry, regardless of whether it is in instruction, administration, marketing, or whatever, they must be aware of their purpose. If one is not aware of it, and does not remain in concert with its deeper purposes, they work against their purpose and peddle a more mediocre outcome under the name of experiential education. The power of the relationship is diminished, and the name of experiential education falls into the ranks of hypocritical organizations weakly missing the points of their own originators. Are we resting on half-conceived notions of Pragmatism, while slipping into a Realist interpretation of experience? Have our scientists and thinkers given up basic science and research for applied science?

For now, I am not interested in debating efficacy of techniques—consciousness of and congruence with clear deep purpose is the issue. Those in experiential education with lower purposes, or a notion that techniques make the difference, do an ethical disservice to an otherwise powerful purpose. We must ask ourselves, "Are we seeking power, control, fame, acceptance, security, or for the anguish of paradox and ambiguity to go away? Are we seeking only answers, only answers for ourselves? Or are we engaged in an ever deeper metaphysical inquiry, in transcending limits, in trusting the process and the very spirit in ourselves and within others?" Those that live in fear of the darkness become dark by thinking only of the dark. An experiential group that seeks acceptance by the dark side is like those who sell wares in the synagogue. If we sell ourselves as the sun, or the darkness, we are lying. We must consciously remain marginal members of the mainstream, lest we become the mainstream. We must keep our eyes focused on the light, and live by it congruently. We are the moon! The next time we talk, Wally, we should consider pushing the philosophy of experiential education and Pragmatism to new insights. We should ask ourselves if the axis is absolute, and are there other non-things to learn via new ways of learning. For now, we are the moon . . . .

André and I talked for a while longer, until I glanced down at my watch and saw that the hour was getting late. Time seemed to mean little to André, as did my subtle yet persistent exclamations about the time. While he talked, I gestured to the waitress to bring the check. When the check came, he snatched it away from me, dropped a ten-dollar bill on the table, rose from his seat, and made his way to the door. I followed behind, thanking him for breakfast.

When we were outside, André turned to me and asked if I wanted to go for a hike in the mountains on this glorious day. I, of course, had to go to work. Upon hearing my dilemma, André turned to me, smiled, and said, "Give 'em heaven." He then winked and walked off around the corner without so much as a good-bye. When he was out of sight, I went to the pay phone which was located just outside of the coffee shop, called my boss, and told her that I would not be working today as I was not feeling well. She told me she hoped I would feel better soon and hung up. I, then, hopped in my car, and headed for the mountains.

43

Using Experiential Principles to Encourage Reform: An Interview with Peggy Walker Stevens

Joyce Hankey

Note: Peggy Walker Stevens is a past president of the Association for Experiential Education and former editor of the *Journal of Experiential Education*. She has worked for the past seventeen years as a teacher and program director in schools and universities. She currently works as a program director for the Education Development Center in Newton, Massachusetts, a nonprofit organization which is engaged in over seventy projects throughout the world in the areas of health, human development, curriculum development, and educational improvement.

Joyce: The proponents of educational reform in the 1960s and 1970s had a limited, long-term impact on mainstream education. What do you think might be effective strategies in the 1990s which build upon past experiences?

Peggy: It's a little hard for me to say, in that I was a teacher in the 1970s and early 1980s, and what one can do as a teacher, relative to my present role as an outside facilitator, is a bit different. I used to think that as long as my teaching techniques were exciting and educationally and philosophically sound, people would see the merits of them and would rush to embrace them. What I've learned is that the culture of any institution, the norms that govern its day-to-day operations, are very strong. Schools have essentially been operating in the same way for the past ninety years, so they are very resistant to change. One has to go about improving schools through involving everyone and slowly changing the culture. Much as one plans a wilderness trip by starting with the needs and perspectives of the students, you have to start to work with schools based on where the participants are—the principals and teachers—and work with what they do.

I'm working right now in Lawrence, Massachusetts, an old mill town which is a very poor, largely Hispanic community. My role is to design and implement a drug prevention program through meeting the needs of students, beginning in one middle school and then spreading the model to other schools. When I started working in the one school, I didn't go in talking about experiential education or adventure, the particular skills I had, or the programs I knew about. Instead, I simply spent time getting to know the school, from the secretaries to the teachers, and tried to help out wherever I could. If a teacher wanted some information about how to teach writing better, I would help out there; when the guidance counselor was working with a leadership program, I began to help her by doing games and initiative problems with the kids, encouraging the group to begin to try to solve problems in the school. Gradually, I became a part of the school and they began to see me as someone who had lots of ideas and resources. That was the first step—just to be known by the school, to help them with their interests in change or reform.

Joyce: It doesn't sound like there was a lot of resistance to your work initially. Did they accept you as an outside consultant?

Peggy: It wasn't quite so smooth. For the first several months, the principal didn't want me working with anyone, even though the school system had agreed to this drug prevention grant. I think he was uncertain as to what I was going to do and how much trouble I might cause, So I moved very gradually, and I took the first opportunity he gave me to help. The staff slowly came to know and trust me, and saw that I was just trying to help them do whatever they wanted to do. I didn't come in with a fixed agenda as the big advocate of experiential education—although I certainly am; my role was to try to help them make the school a better place. So, they developed trust in me and one thing led to another, and we've been able to do a lot of positive things. In Lawrence, many of the teachers are veteran teachers who have been working there for twenty years. They've seen endless education programs come and go, endless promises of people who had the answer to improving the school. So, if you come in thinking you have the answers, they would be pretty resistant.

Joyce: Do you think your experience as a teacher helped you to understand their concerns and where there might be resistance?

Peggy: Yes, and I think my teaching experience gave me some credibility. They would see me at one of the programs we started with the youth leaders. I might be out at recess doing activities with one hundred kids to help cut down on the fighting. They would see me handle these kids and see the kids' excitement about doing the programs, so they respected me as a teacher. I also went in and did some demonstration lessons in classrooms for teachers with whom I was friendly. They realized I could teach and handle city kids, which increased my credibility.

My teaching experience also included implementing a range of alternative programs over ten years, so I was used to figuring out where the resistance would be and possible ways to overcome it. I think the keys are to figure out what you can do to help people, and what you can do to make other people look good, especially the principal. You do not have to jump up and down taking credit for your programs. You figure out what they need and want in the school and you go from there. It comes from the philosophical assumption that you don't have the answers either, but that maybe you have some additional resources, some skills that they haven't yet acquired, that you can pass on.

Joyce: So, you tried to work with the strengths of the teachers, supporting them as professionals, and not as teachers who couldn't teach in a school which was failing. Is this similar to how experiential educators approach helping individuals to grow and learn?

Peggy: I think we do very well with individuals—looking for their strengths and building on them. On the other hand, I think what we sometimes do less well and can be very judgmental about is encouraging changes in institutions. We may decide that a school is lousy because it doesn't espouse our philosophy or is not serving its students well. Yet we have to remember that there are some very well-intentioned people in the school who like children, and who want the children to succeed. There are always a few exceptions to that, but I've never been in a school where that wasn't generally the case. One assumes good will, one assumes that people can improve and be competent. It's the very thing we would think about if we were on a wilderness adventure with those individuals, but we have to take this perspective of the institution. I think a lot of experiential educators are suspicious of traditional institutions and that gets in the way of their being effective.

Joyce: Do you feel experiential educators tend to be impatient and want quick, overall change, rather than working through an evolutionary change process?

Peggy: Yes. Change is evolutionary and that's very frustrating. When I was in my early twenties and first teaching, people said it took seven years to bring about an effective change in a school. I was just aghast. There was no way I could wait seven years to have that happen. I didn't even have two or three years to wait. Over time, I've realized that it is a slow process. At the school in Lawrence, I picture that a significant change process will take four to five years. There are certainly changes after a year, but they are just a start and the old culture would reassert itself quickly were it all to stop now.

Joyce: So you see the value of outside agents in school change, not so much as reformers, but as facilitators who help the evolutionary process whereby schools keep up with social changes?

Peggy: I think it's always true that someone from the outside of an organization can have a perspective that's hard to see when you're in the middle of it. When you're on the inside, you're very involved in the personalities, strengths, and limitations, and you do not have the same overall picture. You occupy a position in the hierarchy. As a teacher, I was in an odd position when I talked to the principal about what he or she might do differently to bring about change in the school. As a consultant, I can move more freely because I have no particular role in the school and do not have to fight turf issues. People know I'm not after their job or their power.

Joyce: How do you envision the future of schools? You must have a vision for the direction of mainstream education? Let's say you're in the year 2000.

Peggy: Well, that's such a big question—it reminds me of when I was in college and my goal in life was to do something significant to reform American education. Now my goal is to do something significant to change one school and that seems sometimes almost more than I can manage. If I can put it a little less ambitiously, I would like to envision that the school that I'm in would be a place where teachers as well as students see themselves as continual learners. They would be excited about learning and happy about themselves. I think that many of the teachers in the schools in which I work have low self-esteem, just like the kids. Their position isn't valued. They are underpaid and have low prestige in our society. They are frustrated with difficult demands. There are estimates, and I think they're low, that 50% of the children in their classrooms are children of alcohol or drug abusers. They're surrounded with poverty and more than half of their classes have English as a second language. There are a tremendous number of factors working against their success and they are not rewarded for what they do.

I would want to see the teachers be people who are excited and interested in doing new things. They would have high expectations of their students and a wide repertoire of skills they could utilize to help children succeed. They would understand child development; they would understand how people learn and would do a lot of hands-on, experiential learning. They would be adventurers of one sort or another. They would be models of risk taking, personal growth, and curiosity. The schools would be very nurturing and supportive places for children, where everyone would value diversity.

Joyce: Let's say experiential educators can develop effective ways to influence mainstream schools. Do you think the time is right? Is there more interest in experiential education than there used to be?

Peggy: One of the interesting things is that a lot of the present reform efforts are related to experiential education. For example, cooperative learning is a very hot topic, getting kids to work together in interdependent groups. You hear a lot about "process" approaches to learning, the whole language movement, integrating thinking and problem-solving skills into the curriculum, "hands on" science and math, etc. Service programs are springing up everywhere, often in the guise of teaching citizenship and imparting values. Peer leadership programs in almost every community prepare youth to help others with the many problems facing young people today, such as substance abuse.

What this means for experiential educators is that there are many opportunities to link with the mainstream, particularly if we understand that adventure is just one of the many effective activities through which people learn from experience. There is a general recognition that "Back to the Basics" failed and people are looking for ideas which do work. I have been amazed at the number of times I now hear the term "experiential" learning—at conferences, in the media, from administrators. In the previous ten years, I had seen the word only once outside of the context of AEE and a few related organizations. Many people read or heard the word as "experimental" education and I was constantly correcting them.

Joyce: So what are the challenges for our field if we are to have an impact in the coming years?

Peggy: Our challenge is to broaden our efforts to include effective work within traditional institutions as well as creating alternative programs. We must be sensitive to the local audience and be willing to look for the common ground we share with them. We need to create not only "pull out" programs where we take people out of schools and other institutions, but also "put in" programs where we add to and improve the institutions. To accomplish this goal we will need to take all our well-honed skills with individuals—communication, collaboration, trust, teamwork—and apply them to institutions. There are some fine examples of experiential educators who have combined these skills with patience, tolerance, and a persistent commitment to their ideals in order to change institutions. It is an adventure to attempt change in institutions, an adventure which I hope more experiential educators will embark upon.

44

Opinion:
Opportunity and Adversity

Mitchell Sakofs

THE TERM "EXPERIENTIAL EDUCATION" IS A TOUGH ONE TO DEFINE. FOR MANY people, it is most easily conceptualized as a philosophy of education which embraces the notion that one learns through action, i.e., one learns by doing. This conceptualization is neat, clean, and fundamentally accurate.

Few experiential educators of whom I am aware would argue that experiential education is one and only one kind of activity, e.g., wilderness adventures, team building, service learning, or internships. Clearly these activities are conceptually in the realm of experiential education. However, they exist as subsets within the broader framework of experiential education which includes these elements as well as school-based learning and a broad range of other possibilities. No one group has a lock on experiential education; no one perspective is the only true form of experiential education. Thus, I have come to the conclusion that experiential education can be best understood as action which is accompanied by an attitude which embraces the adventure of learning, regardless of the format or environment in which learning occurs. Attitude and action are key elements of true experiential learning.

It is this attitude toward learning, which is complemented by a willingness to risk in the learning process (or at least a post hoc realization of the value of risk in learning), which has propelled experiential educational strategies into mainstream academic, therapeutic, and recreational arenas. By propelled, I mean that experiential strategies, in each of these fields, has received quite a bit of attention from more traditional practitioners in such fields, for these traditional practitioners sense the power and efficacy of experiential education in promoting learning and growth within people. As a result of this growing interest in and acceptance of experiential education on the part of mainstream educators, therapists, and other professionals, experiential educators, in all their diversity, have been called upon to bring the spirit of adventure, risk, and challenge to the mainstream, i.e., the mainstream markets.

Clearly there are many ways in which this last sentence could have been phrased. However, I chose the imagery of markets for I think it best characterizes the opportunities which present themselves to experiential educators as well as the concomitant adversity which I sense accompanies this opportunity.

The imagery of markets, in my mind, has many faces. For example, one face which shines through is that of economic opportunity. There are jobs out there for experiential educators in traditional educational institutions, businesses, corporations, and service organizations. Another face which presents itself is that of impact. The power of experiential programming is being brought to and having an impact on the lives of more and more people. Finally, and this is the issue which most concerns me, there is the face of complacency, a sense of satisfaction with what is, and thus, a loss of the spirit to grow. I feel this last face of opportunity is a very real threat to the spirit and vitality of experiential education. More specifically, I fear that this spirit and vitality, which has kept experiential educators searching for new and better methodologies, will be supplanted by a satisfaction with simply broadening and expanding established experiential program ideas into new markets, rather than broadening and expanding the boundaries of experiential education itself.

Clearly, there is a place for individuals in experiential education who have as their mission the broadening of the marketplace in which experiential programming occurs. And people who engage in this kind of activity provide the needed and profound service for experiential educators of creating jobs. Additionally, these individuals accomplish a clear service for people who comprise the "mainstream" by bringing experiential programming to heretofore unserved populations. In and of themselves, these are noble endeavors with great benefit. With this in mind, however, I feel obliged to warn experiential educators that there is also a downside to the opportunities which expanding markets present. More specifically, this downside, or adversity, is related to complacency—the complacency which constitutes a level of contentedness with what is, a level of contentedness with simply adapting programs to new populations with the result that efforts to explore new territories, new ideas, and new and deeper elements of experiential education are left unrealized.

Conceptually, I have always viewed experiential educators as the pioneers of education. In my mind, experiential educators were never simply program delivery people, but rather explorers of ideas and concepts which hold progressive value in education and society. In my mind, experiential educators have always been pioneers, not settlers, and thus I view the growth market and subsequent opportunity which the field of experiential education is now experiencing as a potential adversity. It is an adversity which may distract us from our mission of conceptualizing meaningful educational programs, to one of simply marketing those programs which have already been conceptualized. Let us not make our opportunity an adversity which co-opts the spirit of experiential education; rather, let us remain true to our calling and transform not only our adversity into opportunity, but our opportunity into opportunity as well.

45

Adventure and Education

Erik Leroy

SEVERAL YEARS AGO, I INSTRUCTED MY FIRST OUTWARD BOUND COURSE IN THE Three Sisters Wilderness of Oregon. During that course, a very simple but enlightening experience became the catalyst that since then has sent me puzzling along the paths of adventurers, comparing their experiences in pursuit of their peaks, their poles, their transoceanic crossings, with the more humble (but not less significant) adventures of students at Outward Bound and programs like it.

My experience went something like this: In the mist and clouds of a typical Oregon day, surrounded by quite wet and very cold Outward Bound students, I was joyfully lost in the preparation of prusiks, butterfly knots, and other essentials that a beginning group makes before a siege of the formidable bergschrund on the Prouty Glacier, much too lost in the minutiae of the impending climb to sense the growing consternation of my group.

My ignorance, however, ended quite abruptly when Priscilla, in the vernacular of her Bronx origins, and in a voice full of anger, anticipation, and fear, blurted out that she did not then, or at any moment for the duration of the course, want to "take any more risks." Initially I was flabbergasted, then hurt—and then angered. After all, this woman before me on the Prouty Glacier was from New York City. Now I knew about New York City. I had ridden the subways there and knew quite well how slight the risks were for her on the Prouty compared to her daily menu back home! Or did I? Or could I? Or *should* I?

In spite of her very forcefully articulated concern that she not be subjected to any more risks, Priscilla did walk out onto the glacier that day, and after two whizzing falls, each caught by an equally terrified compatriot, she climbed the bergschrund. Every day thereafter until and including the marathon, she analyzed each boulder, stream, hill, and cloud for its danger-dealing potential. She never flinched for long, though, and in retrospect, she loved every minute of it.

Priscilla begat my interest in the nature of adventure by teaching me a valuable lesson. Back on the glacier, what I perceived as a simple exercise, a Saturday stroll, Priscilla perceived as high adventure, full of danger, difficulty, and the unknown. Priscilla taught me that when we try to understand "adventure," the physical magnitude of the peak, pole, lake, or trail is no more important than the emotional response the task elicits.

In our programs at Outward Bound, the magnitude of the thing is much less important. Certainly Priscilla's psychological adventure was monumental, just as deserving of acclaim as anything Amundsen did at the South Pole or Hillary did on Everest. And, in turn, what those elicited emotions of Priscilla the conqueror (of herself) might in turn create are monumental in possibility. In fact, the creation of those emotions and all the potential for self-knowledge and growth that accompanies them are the reasons for any adventure program's existence: the accompanying possibilities and sense of one's own capacity and self-confidence are major steps to promoting the ideal of an individual with a sense of responsibility toward humanity, which was a very explicit goal of Outward Bound's founder, Kurt Hahn.

Because we should be primarily concerned with the subjective adventure experience, we should look with great interest and familiarity to the experiences of some of the Arctic explorers and their mountaineering counterparts. The adventure experiences of these explorers are different from Priscilla's only in magnitude, and magnitude is an unimportant criterion. In character and psychological ramifications, the similarity is striking.

There is one characteristic that sets apart Fridtjof Nansen's account of his struggle with fear and the unknown as he set out to winter-over on drift ice near the North Pole from that of a novice in the wilds on a first adventure course, and that is the revealing eloquence with which the former writes. As Vilhjalmur Stefansson, preeminent Arctic explorer, noted: "The explorer is the poet of action and exploring is the poetry of deeds." What Stefansson urges us to do, if we are committed to action and deeds, is to pay heed to adventures and adventurers; they not only will speak of adventure, they will, in their poetry, illuminate adventure. By introducing some of the literature and personalities of our adventuring tradition, I hope to approach more precisely what it is we do with adventure in an Outward Bound setting, as well as perhaps cast the seeds of literary friendships that might prove as fruitful to others as they have to me.

Defining "adventure" is not an easy task. Wilfred Noyce, in prefacing *The Springs of Adventure*, felt it best to eliminate the element of risk, and called adventure, ". . . a novel enterprise undertaken for its own sake." A more traditional definition, found in the dictionary as well as in literature, includes the risk element as well as "an undertaking of uncertain outcome, a hazardous enterprise; an exciting or very unusual experience." Stefansson being a bit obdurate, offered a more pejorative definition: "Adventure is the result of past mistakes." When Peter Freuchen, renowned Danish explorer who lived as an Eskimo for many seasons, was asked to define "adventure," he answered, a bit equivocally, "Adventure is not an act in the line of duty. It is not something done for science either. Adventure is a strange experience for its own sake."

Peter Freuchen was a wise man. He knew there was no ultimate definition to be had. We who are the conjurers of adventure for hundreds of seekers each year, are we anymore prepared to define the phenomenon than Peter Freuchen was? I contend we are not, nor should we be. An adventuresome experience has a mystery about it that cannot be violated. The twinkle in our own eyes should tell us this when we describe a forthcoming trip as an adventure. Certainly adventure would fascinate us less if it did not contain such a substantial element of the unknown.

Adventure's elusiveness should not, however, preclude us from talking about it. There are things we do, characteristics of the experiences we orchestrate, that are but attempts at replication of the experiences more noted explorers than ourselves and our students have had. Specifically, I can identify four characteristics common to all adventure, and particularly present within our courses, that should be expanded upon: difficulty, danger, commitment, and stress—or the need to choose wisely under pressure.

THE DEGREE OF DIFFICULTY

What we do in a program or on a course should be difficult for our students. Men and women who have sailed, climbed, and skied have always understood the challenge and difficulty of their enterprise as an aspect of the adventure they sought. Fridtjof Nansen, writing of his impending sledge trip from his ice-shrouded ship *Fram* in search of Franz Josef Land to the north, wrote:

> H'm! as if dissatisfaction, longing and suffering were not the very basis of life. Without privation there would be no struggle, and without struggle no life—that is as certain as that two and two makes four. And now the struggle is to begin, it is looming in the north.

Knud Rasmussen, on his sledge journey across Arctic America, found, to his surprise, an Eskimo witch doctor who thought much as Nansen did about these matters:

> All true wisdom is only to be learned far from the dwellings of men, out in the great solitudes; and is only to be attained through suffering. Privation and suffering are the only things that can open the mind of man to those things which are hidden from others.

Though the thoughts are similar, the difference between the two is obvious: Nansen chose the ice, the Eskimo was born upon it. Nevertheless, the lesson here is a valuable one. What Nansen would tell us is that if our path is free of privation, we cannot know the meaning of life; whether one is born to it or must seek it out, privation is an explicating element in the experience of life. George Mallory, possibly the first to climb Everest, wrote upon his return from his first traverse of Mont Blanc, "to struggle and to understand. Never the last without the first. That is the law."

THE ELEMENT OF DANGER

Another characteristic which we hold in common with more renowned expeditions is physical risk: what outdoor challenge programs offer is dangerous. "Just by going into the mountains we invite disaster," we are told somewhat quizzically by those "outsiders" who do not understand our purposes. Yet they are correct, I think. Mountains move and snow slides. We subject ourselves to these perils and there is, to some significant degree, no escaping them. When we enter these realms, the possibility of injury or death is present for the instructors to a bearably small degree. However, the apparent possibility of the same catastrophes is present for many students to an excruciatingly large degree.

Of course, instructors have a refined understanding of the objective dangers, and the consternation of students is more than three-quarters ignorance. That distinction means nothing and it means everything. It means nothing because even though the danger is really quite slight, the feeling of being *subjected* to danger is overwhelming, and it is the feeling that is important. It means everything because the feeling of danger that the experience elicits is, in a sense, a spiritual preparation for self-growth. We could not in good conscience run our program if the dangers were as great as our students sometimes insist they are. Yet those feelings that lead to students' insistences are filled with growth potential and are actually what we seek. We succeed when what we do is reasonably safe for us but seems horribly dangerous to students. Priscilla's decision to venture out onto the Prouty Glacier was just as significant as Hermann Buhl's decision to attempt the summit of 26,000-foot Nanga Parbet by himself. Both thought they were chancing a great deal.

I can be a bit more specific about the value risk bears. Herman Rohrs, who wrote a biography of Kurt Hahn, said, "the sharp felt impact of an event or a deeply felt personal experience can rouse a man from complacency, and the taking of a risk can have a similar result." Nansen, writing in his journal after months locked in the ice, was just as much to the point:

Oh! at times this inactivity crushes one's very soul; one's life seems as dark as the winter night outside: there is sunlight upon no part of it except the past and the far distant future. I feel as if I *must* break through this deadness, this inertia and find some outlet for my energies. Can't something happen? Could not a hurricane come and tear up this ice and set it rolling in higher waves like the sea? Welcome danger, if it only brings us the chance of fighting for our lives—only let us move onward!

Months later, Nansen again wrote, "What I would not give for a single day of struggle—for even a moment of danger."

COMMITMENT TO PERSIST

Commitment is another characteristic all adventure holds in common. The demand that an extended course of risk and difficulty makes requires a mental commitment to persist: likewise with the commitment to the unknown that forces a shaky rock climber out onto the very first nubbin that will turn the trick and unravel the climb. Though there is a subtle difference between these two shades of commitment, there is also a commonality that ties these and all other acts of commitment in adventure together: The eventual outcome is unknown. When a group finally stops talking and starts walking, there is an omnipresent question: "Did we choose right?" Of course, they will only find out by seeing their choice through, and that act demands commitment. One of the remarkable characteristics of the Willi Unsoeld/Tam Hornbein first account of the West Ridge of Mt. Everest in 1963 was the commitment it demanded. Once through the rock band, there was no turning back; it was up and over the top or perish.

Similarly, Nansen, embarking upon his sledge journey, wrote:

I cannot deny that it is a long journey and scarcely has anyone more effectively burned his boats behind him. If we wished to turn back we have absolutely nothing to return to, not even a bare coast. It will be impossible to find the ship, and before us lies the great unknown. But there is only one road, and that lies straight ahead, right through . . . .

"By endurance, we conquer" was the Shackleton family motto, and there is scarcely a better example of perseverance than Ernest Shackleton's 1913 sledge journey to the South Pole.

UNDERSTANDABLE STRESS

Commitment, difficulty, and risk in combination are the components of an experience as familiar to our students as to a leader of a polar expedition. Presence of mind under fire or under stress is not a trait we necessarily cultivate in our everyday lives as I suspect our forebears did. It may not even be a trait to which many of us aspire. However, subjection to stress, "understandable stress," can be a highly educative experience and not one to avoid.

The difference between stress and "understandable stress" is the knowledge with the latter that certain correct responses will resolve the crisis. I think Justice Oliver Wendell Holmes spoke as clearly as anyone about the value of the stressful experience when he wrote, "To make up your mind at your peril upon a living question, for purposes of action, calls upon your whole nature." To be able to choose at peril is a sign of a "person complete in all her or his powers." Really quite seldom is our "whole nature" called upon. Yet in our various programs we ask (or at least we should ask) for complete efforts. When all of the elements already discussed combine in a moment of crisis, a complete effort is demanded.

In the famous accidents of mountaineering, we find examples of the most complete efforts. While we do not lay in wait for such moments so we may prove our worth, reading of the events on the 1953 accident on K-2, or of Maurice Herzog's descent from the summit of Annapurna in 1951, or of the incredible self-rescue by Doug Scott who crawled from 24,000 to 18,000 feet down The Ogre in 1977, buoys our faith in our own and generally in our species' ability to survive. Upon a smaller scale, the demand for decisiveness "upon a living question" evokes what capacities our students have and may help create, in Holmes's words, "persons complete in all their powers."

FINAL QUESTIONS

All of these characteristics—difficulty, danger, stress, and commitment to the unknown—define the adventure we orchestrate in an adumbrated fashion. Much more can be said about adventure; however, I don't think we can hope for more clarity. Adventure, after all bears a fascination and a mystery that make it in definition somewhat inviolable. Furthermore we've no need to probe deeper. But there are some questions we should ask: for what purpose does this adventure experience exist? What does the experience mean for our species or civilization? And finally and perhaps most importantly for the purpose of this paper, why do we foster adventure experiences in our programs? For the latter, I believe a clear answer exists, but for the previous two, all I can do is suggest possible answers.

To assume in the first place that adventuring such as is found in mountaineering is purposeful could be a step in the wrong direction. Many have said that it is not purposeful. For example, Lionel Terray, a well known French climber, titled one of his books, *Conquistadors of the Useless*. H. W. Tillman, member of several pioneering attempts on Everest, may have had a similar outlook to Terray's when he prefaced his account of the 1938 Everest attempt with G. K. Chesterton's now famous piece of puzzlement:

> . . . I think the immense act has something about it human and excusable and when I endeavor to analyze the reason for this feeling I find it to lie, not in the fact

that the thing was big or bold or successful; but in the fact that the thing was perfectly useless to everybody, including the person who did it.

But some answer does lie within this paradox. The immense act is useless in one sense: useless in terms of most characteristics that our culture places value upon; useless in a materialistic sense. Adventure is not a materialistic experience; rather, it is a spiritual or perhaps a humanistic experience. Is there any use in our civilization for materially useless, spiritually rich experiences? The question, I am sure, need only be asked rhetorically, particularly when the audience is a crowd of mountaineers.

Ours is a society ruled by scientific process. Explanation, logical and derivable, is expected and usually obtained. The adventure experience doesn't fit this mold. As we have seen, there is a considerable array of questions about adventure that have not been answered, nor are they going to be. Most, if not all, of the things adventures do are useless in the materialistic sense. Yet there are many who very definitely see it as purposeful endeavor. Sir George Trevelyan commented during the christening of the Aberdovey Outward Bound School's first schooner that, "If youth ever loses the thirst for adventure, any civilization, however enlightened, and any state, however well ordered, must wither and dry up." J. R. L. Anderson, in a book entitled *The Ulysses Factor*, postulated "some factor in man, some form of special adaptation which promotes a few individuals to exploits which, however purposeless they may seem, are of value to the survival of the race."

Now, how can such spacious generalizations as these be defended? In part, defense is best left to each of our own perspectives on the world, each of our own opinions regarding the efficacy of our civilization. There are some characteristics that adventurous experiences infuse that are, in my opinion, essential for our species' survival. Several, if not all, are held in common with those possible values we all hope to instill: perseverance, strength in individuality, compassion in the multiplicity of group experience, the ability to use one's mind, and to think—or perhaps the reason to think. If we value these attributes and if we believe that they are not handed out at birth or in school or in work within our society, then I think we must agree that the vehicle through which they are offered—adventure—is a very purposeful endeavor, particularly if the spirit of mankind is to persevere.

Kurt Hahn had the negative tendencies of civilization in mind when he first toyed with the idea that would become the underlying principle of his educational philosophy. From Rohrs's biography:

In its fully developed form, Hahn's answer to the problem is, as we have seen, "experience therapy"—a form of fresh youthful experience which makes it possible for young people once again to feel wonder and astonishment, and so, contemplating, to look outward and upward to new horizons. The experience itself has no more than an ancillary function—namely, to uncover the deeper layers of human personality, which in everyday life have all too often been overlaid by conventions of civilization.

Kurt Hahn recognized the alienating character of a materialistic civilization. His purpose, very specifically and concretely, was to reunite us, one with another, through the instillation of self-knowledge that would allow, finally, "a sense of responsibility towards humanity." That final sense was for Hahn, as I believe it should be for us, the harbinger of unalienated existence.

It is particularly important for us now to remember Hahn's purpose. If we forget it, we also lose track of any purpose we as professionals of his tutelage now have. We are engaged in a purposeful enterprise with clear goals, not a miasma of uncollected and unarticulated reasons for being. And we are not, or should not be, merely a collection of climbers and kayakists who have found in the program for which we work a means of supporting our habits.

Adventure is a purposeful enterprise. It instills characteristics found in few other places of our civilization. Some of those characteristics will, hopefully, break through the alienation accompanying technological life. When one is no longer stranger to another, then "a sense of responsibility to humanity" is not only possible, but nearly assured.

The Risk of Freedom

Steve Simpson

I'LL TELL YOU STRAIGHT OFF THAT THIS STORY HAS A SAD ENDING. THERE IS JOY in it, satisfaction in it, and a few exciting ideas in it, but the end of this story is a sad one. Perhaps the next story I tell will be different.

This story is about my first try at using experiential education in the public school system. The story takes place in a high school in Olympia, Washington. Before I tell you what happened, I should explain what my idea of experiential education is. Unlike most of the experientially based programs with which I am familiar, my methods did not involve wilderness, mountaineering, whitewater, or any other physical action beyond moving chairs around and talking. The most dangerous things we did were saying and writing what we thought. Despite the lack of scenery, I believe our experience was as profound and powerful as anything we could have accomplished on a glacier or in an alpine meadow.

I understand experiential education to be education gained from something personally encountered, undergone, or lived through. It can be more simply stated as being what you learn from what you do. What we did was an attempt to learn as much of the standard curriculum as possible while letting the students do most of what teachers normally do in the public school system. What we learned may surprise you.

One of my fundamental beliefs is that no one really understands how the human animal learns things. I believe that people are too complex and subtle to be boxed or labeled or fed some learning system recently thought up by one educator or another. The human animal can grasp an idea intuitively or after painfully rational analysis or by osmosis after reading the back of a cereal box. Learning is in the same ballpark as artistry. If someone were able to define the ingredients that produce artistic ability, then they could gather them up and mix us an artist. The same is true of learning. If we really knew how people learn, we could gather all of those ingredients and whammo, everyone could learn everything. But we can't, and they can't, and this is why I decided to try experiential methods in my classes

Whatever it is that we humans have inside us which enables us to learn, it is there when we are born and from Day One, we kick it into gear in order to survive. A mother may teach her child love by keeping it warm or feeding it or petting it or any of the thousand other things mothers consciously do for their children. But that mystical bond that exists between a mother and child cannot be solely attributed to those actions. There is more to it. Somewhere in the womb listening to her heartbeat, or somewhere in her smell or in her voice or in the look in her eye at two in the morning, the child learns things about mother that mother does not consciously teach. The child learns by experience. I believe that students learn by a process based on the whole of an experience and which none of us really understands.

Because there is a dimension of learning gained from doing which simply cannot be gained any other way, I decided to start by letting the students do as much as possible in my classes. I would let the students decide what learning methods they preferred, and we would use those methods. They would decide how they wanted their work to be evaluated and what they felt was appropriate behavior in the classroom. My function as the teacher was to be their guide. Like a guide, I knew the dangers because I had climbed the peak many times. I knew the subject matter. I knew the restrictions enforced by the administration and legislators and parents. I had the ultimate authority in the classroom because I had the ultimate responsibility. My job was to use my skill as a guide and allow the students enough freedom to take risks and yet not allow so much freedom that they climbed a foolish route and got badly hurt. It was a fine line, but I used the simple rule of letting the students do everything I possibly could. If my experiment resulted in failure of the students to learn enough of the standard curriculum, then I would lose my job. On the other hand, if we could pull it off, the students would not only learn the standard curriculum, but they would learn a thousand more subtle, more important, more useful things that can only be gained experientially.

The classes with whom I tried this method were studying sociology. Sociology is supposed to be the study of human groups and of human institutions, so I decided to let the students create a classroom society, do something with it, and learn from the experience what they could.

The first discussions we had were on the purpose of being in school. They talked about the reasons they needed an education, what an education is, and how difficult it is to learn about life when we are literally boxed off from life by the four walls of the classroom and the laws which force us to stay there.

After we had talked about why we were in school and in a general way, what we planned to accomplish, we began to discuss some of the details of learning. We began with a discussion of what behavior would be acceptable during the class. This was an area which made me particularly nervous. One of the classes consisted of roughly 75% behavior-problem students, including six or seven drug abusers who came to class loaded and often nodded off during class, two or three loud, disruptive types, and one who had a history of beating up teachers. I was told before the quarter began that most of the students were slow learners and/or behavior problems. Most had failed the class before and were only taking it again because they had to pass the class in order to graduate. I was to be considered successful if only 10 or 15 percent failed the class and no one got hurt. You can understand why I was hesitant to experiment with new techniques.

I gave you more details about this particular class than were necessary because I want to emphasize their success. I believe that no one can simply move from childhood to adulthood and, by some magic of modem body chemistry, wake up one morning as a responsible citizen. I don't believe that you become familiar with self-control, group behavior, or the restrictions of our society by passing a lot of tests. I believe that students learn these social skills through practice. I decided to give the students the freedom to decide what kind of behavior would result in the learning environment they needed. They would create the laws under which their classroom society would agree to live.

I found that when given the freedom to decide what kind of behavior they wanted in the class, virtually every student voted for a system which would be most teachers' dream. Our rules were simple and everyone understood them. The students had to bring their books, paper, and writing materials to class every day. Every student had to attempt every assignment. They had to be in class and on time every day. No student had to talk during class unless he wanted to, but each student had to listen when someone else was talking. No student was allowed to come to class loaded, sleep during class, or disrupt class in any way. Our class rules were based on the principle that every student has the right to learn and if another student (or teacher) disrupts class in any way, they are stealing from the others their right to learn.

Like any system of law which involves less-than-perfect humans, our system required reinforcement. We developed a grade system which rewarded positive behavior, and we included in our ethical system the principle that if someone has a problem, they need help rather than punishment.

In our class, we discussed the idea of rehabilitation versus the idea of punishment. The result of our discussions was a fairly clear understanding of our penal system and a class decision that punishment may deal temporarily with a symptom, but it does nothing to solve the problem. In our class, we had several students test the rules in one way or another for the first few weeks. In every case, class was immediately stopped and the class tried to find out what was wrong and help if possible.

This could easily have degenerated into a version of pop group psychology. It was my job to avoid that and keep the discussions on the relatively simple turf which included straightforward questions and some basic discussion and suggestions. For instance, when a student put his head down and appeared to be asleep, class was stopped and the student was asked why he was sleeping. About half an hour of discussion revealed that he had a job and worked late, that this was his choice and not required for the welfare of his family, and that after work, he had gone out on a short date. The class discussed again why it was important for everyone to participate in class. Some of the suggestions included having the student figure out his priorities, and adjust his hours and spending habits accordingly. It was not a very deep or philosophical discussion, but it was honest and non-threatening. I said very little. We wasted a class period but since everyone heard the arguments, everyone was able to think about his own priorities and make his own adjustments. There were several situations that came up, but after the class realized that I meant what I said and consistently stopped class while we dealt with problems, the behavior problems disappeared.

The second half of our reinforcement came from the grade system we developed. In our class, we decided that the process of learning was more important than testing. We felt that the skills gained were more important than the grade received. We felt that the general methods used in school involved fear-based learning. You tend to study because you are afraid of failing rather than because you want to learn. For these reasons, we developed a system which rewarded students who tried to do every assignment with full credit, whether the quality of their work was high or low. Before you jump on this, let me explain our thinking a little more clearly.

During our discussions, we decided that everyone is of equal worth as a human being. We accepted as fact that some people know more words or have quicker reflexes or better families or genetic differences. We felt that one of the major problems in our society was that despite what it says in the Declaration of Independence, the Constitution, or the various laws of the United States, all people were definitely not treated equally. It was a fact of life in the public school system that athletes were given special privileges, people who cheated got better grades than people who didn't, and students who were verbally skilled got better grades than students who didn't talk a lot in class.

In order to have our classroom society treat people equally and reward effort rather than results at any cost, we created a system which awarded 30% of the grade for class participation, 30% for homework, 30% for test scores, and 10% for participation in the class project. To earn the 30% class-participation grade, students were required to be in class every day, behave according to the class standards, and participate in all classroom activities, such as role playing, group discussion, free-writing, and sustained silent reading. (Remember, the class rules said the student had to be there, listen, and be alert. The rule did not require students to talk unless they wanted to.) Since we accepted nothing less than full class participation at any time without stopping class, every student could get full credit if they missed no classes. We deducted 5% of this grade for each absence from class. No excuses for absence were accepted because we decided it didn't matter why students were gone.

It was a fact that if they were gone, they didn't participate, and we were simply hard or honest enough to recognize this without making value judgments about reasons for being absent. If you weren't there, you did not get the credit. If you were there, you were participating, and you got credit.

Our homework assignments were based on the methods of learning the students wanted to use. We did things like watching television commercials and writing about what the commercials taught our society about sex roles. We would divide the class into groups and assign each group to prepare a short presentation on a major religion or on different sides of political issues, such as the draft or the justice system. We might have everyone in class produce a list of the ten most important things a person needed to study in a sociology class, and pick the most popular questions for study. We frequently did assignments using dictionary definitions. Whatever we did, if the student made an attempt, the student was given full credit for the assignment. If the student attempted every assignment, they would receive 30% credit. For each assignment missed, a number of percentage points was subtracted. No value judgments were ever made which praised students who thought or spoke or wrote a certain way. Our decision was that everyone had something of worth to say and it was not the job of a teacher to decide which student (which person) was of more worth than another. This appears to fly against the letter grade system, but that was not the truth. The students ended up deciding their own grade (or worth) based on how hard they tried. Their grades were based on the percentage points they earned and the grade was not based on the subjective judgment of the teacher.

The tests we had in class were worth 30% of their grade. The students decided that they wanted tests which included different kinds of questions. They felt that some people did better on true/false and others did better with multiple choice. Others liked the matching questions. They did vote to include one essay question per test, despite the fact that essay questions are open to subjective grading by the teacher. They decided they trusted my ability to grade at least one question fairly and, just in case, we decided all grades were subject to review by a group of peers if there was any problem that could not be worked out between the teacher and the students. No problems ever developed. On tests, students did not get full credit for trying to answer the questions. They had to get the correct answer to get credit.

We stressed the fact that this was a covenant and not a contract. The difference is that a contract is enforceable by law, or from without. Our covenant was a form of moral agreement. It was an agreement relating to principals of right and wrong in behavior and was enforced only from within the group. This made all the difference.

You can see that under our system, a student who tried to do everything and came to class every day could get no lower than a 70% or a grade of C. If they missed a day of class or failed to try an assignment and failed all the tests, their grade would fall below 70% and they would get either a D or an F grade. On the other hand, if the student tried to do everything and missed no classes and got even 30% of the test questions correct, that student would then get 10% for the test grade, 30% for homework, 30% for class participation, and 10% for participation in the class project. The total would be 80% and a grade of B for the class. We were very proud of our system. We felt it allowed for human differences in communication skills, genetic make-up, etc., and still ended up with students earning grades which accurately reflected their abilities. I still like the system and hope to use it again.

I have tried to describe in some detail what we did in our attempt at having a class where the students learned by doing. It was, in my opinion, a classic example of experiential education which was easily applied in a public school situation without any extra cost or problems. I would like to spend a few pages reflecting on the experience and try to draw from the class some ideas which may help other teachers who want to use experiential education in the public school system.

First, I would like to stress the fact that the teaching method I have described is based on trust. I built this trust with the students by the simple means of doing what I said I would do and by holding them to their word as well.

Everything that we decided on in the class was written down in our class covenant. A covenant is a formal, solemn, and binding agreement between people for the performance of some action. Our covenant included a statement of why we were in school, how we would learn, how our learning would be evaluated, and the specifics of what acceptable class behavior was. We all signed the document and many arguments were quickly settled with the words, "Because it's in the covenant." Our covenant was reached by consensus, that is, by unanimous group agreement and not by majority rule. If one person was not satisfied, we hammered it out until we could all agree. Again, we based this on the idea that everyone was of equal worth and in our society, there would be no angry minority. It worked in the class, even though we agreed it could never work with more than a small number of people.

Another important element was that, in my class, students were encouraged to make mistakes. I would tell them over and over that if they were doing or saying something and if they made no mistakes, they already know how to do it. If that is the case, they should be trying to master something else. I tell the students not to be hesitant in class. Class is their opportunity to learn how to be adults. If they try new activities, behaviors, and ideas, if they make their mistakes in the classroom, they may not make the same mistakes in adult life. The older they get, the more responsibility they will have and the more serious will be the repercussions if they make a mistake. I feel it is better to have a little chaos early in the class, rather than people getting hurt or having bad lives because they make mistakes as adults.

My last observation is really a word of caution. We live in an industrial/hierarchical society filled with bosses or government or teachers or television telling our young how to think, what to do, what to eat, what to wear, etc. Then, we come unglued when they make bad judgment calls. Our school system typically consists of a teacher telling students what to memorize, then telling them to spit it out on a test, and then telling them they are an A or an F person. The school system tells them how to act and how to talk and what is okay to think.

If you plan to use a system which lets students think and lets students experience learning firsthand, you must be aware that many of your students will have had no previous experience in the free use of the mind. They may not have even the most rudimentary skill at analysis and abstract thought. I encourage you to be patient. Go slowly. If you give them a lot of thinking in too abstract a way too quickly, they will rebel. Gradually increase the scope of what you give them to think about. It is a skill they are learning, just like rock climbing or ice climbing. It will take some time before they will be graceful doing it. I encourage you to help them because it is the most important skill they can learn.

The sad ending? I tried this method when I was a student teacher. My supervising teacher was what I call a straight-row man. By this, I mean he likes the students in their seats, the seats in straight rows, the knowledge in the notes," the notes memorized, and the answers in the tests. He needs absolute control. This type of teacher is not uncommon in the public school system.

When I first met this man, he told me he was burned out. He said he was sick of teaching and sick of "wise-ass kids." He said that he was glad I had some ideas and that I could do anything I wanted with the class, as long as I had good lesson plans and could tell him what I was going to do before class. He was tired, but he was afraid he would get in trouble with the principal if I made any mistakes.

This man became more and more unstable as the class became more and more self-actualized. As I think back, I suppose he began to wonder what good he was if the students were able to do the thinking and were doing the doing. It was the final breakdown of this man during class that provided the sad ending.

When the class decided to have a free car wash as a class project instead of something like helping old people or the mentally retarded, this man panicked. He was certain that if the class had a free car wash, he would get in trouble with the principal. I tried to calm him down and help him understand that it wasn't all that bad and besides, he had approved the covenant and it was part of the covenant that they could choose their project. That was a major part of our basic trust, and I told him I couldn't break the trust and violate the covenant. He said that he was the supervising teacher and he could and would.

It was a twisted, angry, and confused man who took over the class, vetoed the covenant, and told the students to take their chairs out of the circle and put them back in rows. It was a frightened man who told the class that from now on, he would do the teaching and they had better get used to doing some real work for a change. It was a tired and brutal man who told the class that from now on, there would be no more group discussion, no more sharing of personal experiences, no more voting, no more reading in class, no more free-writing, and they had better score well on his tests or they would fail the class. It was a hard time for me and it was a hard time for the class. I had failed. I had not failed with the students, but I had failed to communicate with and help the one person in the room who apparently had needed it most. It is not a mistake I ever hope to repeat.

So now you know the story and the sad ending. I had to leave that school and finish my student teaching at another school. I did finish, and I got my certification and my paper and my freedom to try again in another class. Working from within the public school system for positive change is a tough game. There is much risk. You will always find a principal or other teachers or parents who really don't feel good about you teaching their children to think freely and trust their own judgment. But, I believe that unless the young in our society learn to think, learn to do, learn to trust their own judgment, we will end up with a society filled with incapable, fear-filled, small-minded human beings. I urge you to take the risk.

— References/Bibliography —

Section I: Philosophical Foundations

3 Dewey's Philosophical Method and Its Influence on His Philosophy of Education ▪ Jasper Hunt, Jr.

Brodsky, G. M. (1976). Recent philosophical work on Dewey. *The Southern Journal of Philosophy.*

Brodsky, G. M. (1978) Dewey's enduring vitality. *Human Studies.*

Conkin, P. K. (1968) *Puritans and pragmatists: Eight eminent American thinkers.* Bloomington, IN: Indiana University Press.

Dewey, J. (1926). *Democracy and education.* New York: Macmillan.

Dewey, J. (1929). *Experience and nature.* Lasalle: The Open Court Publishing Co.

Dewey, J. (1934). *Art as experience.* New York: G. P. Putnam.

Dewey, J. (1938). *Experience and education.* New York: Collier.

Edwards, P. (Ed.). (1967). *The encyclopedia of philosophy.* New York: Macmillan.

White, M. (1972). *Science and sentiment in America: Philosophical thought from Jonathan Edwards to John Dewey.* New York: Oxford University Press.

White, M. (1973). *Pragmatism and the American mind.* New York: Oxford University Press.

4 Kurt Hahn and the Aims of Education ▪ Thomas James

Brereton, H. L. (1968). *Gordonstoun.* London: Ward R. Chambers, Ltd.

Darling, J. (1981). New life and new education: The philosophies of Davidson, Reddie and Hahn. *Scottish Educational Review, 13* (May), 12-24.

James, T. (1980). Sketch of a moving spirit: Kurt Hahn. *Journal of Experiential Education, 3*(1), 17-22.

Miner, J. L., & Boldt, J. (1981). *Outward Bound USA.* New York: William Morrow.

Richards, A. (1981). *Kurt Hahn: The midwife of educational ideas.* Ed.D. dissertation, University of Colorado at Boulder.

Rohrs, H. (1966). The realm of education in the thought of Kurt Hahn. *Comparative Education 3* (November), 21-32.

Rohrs, H., & Turnstall-Behrens, H. (Eds.). (1970). *Kurt Hahn*. London: Routledge & Kegan Paul.

Skidelsky, R. (1969). Hahn of Gordonstoun. *In English Progressive Schools*, London: Penguin Books, 1969, (pp. 181-239).

6   The Need for Something Different: Spirituality and Wilderness Adventure
■ L. Allison Stringer and Leo H. McAvoy

Beck, C. (1986). Education for spirituality. *Interchange, 17*(2), 148-156.

Beck, L. A. (1988). The phenomenology of optimal experiences attained by whitewater river recreationists in Canyonlands National Park. (Doctoral dissertation, University of Minnesota, 1987.) *Dissertation Abstracts International 48*(9), 2451 A.

Brown, M. H. (1989). Transpersonal psychology: Facilitating transformation in outdoor experiential education. *Journal of Experiential Education 12*(3), 47-56.

Chenery, M. F. (1984, September/October). Nurturing the human spirit in camping. *Camping Magazine 57*, 21-27.

Csikszentmihalyi, M. (1975). *Beyond boredom and anxiety*. San Francisco: Jossey-Bass.

Fox, F. E. (1983). The spiritual core of experiential education. *Journal of Experiential Education 6*(3), 3-6.

James, W. (1902/1958). *The varieties of religious experience*. New York: New American Library/Mentor Books.

Kaplan, S., & Talbot, J. F. (1983). Psychological benefits of a wilderness experience. In I. Altman & J. F. Wohlwill (Eds.), *Behavior and the natural environment*, Vol. 6, 163-203. New York: Plenum.

Lincoln, Y. S., & Guba, E. G. (1985). *Naturalistic inquiry*. Beverly Hills: Sage.

Maslow, A. (1968). *Toward a psychology of being* (2nd ed.). Princeton, NJ: Van Nostrand.

Maslow, A. (1970). *Motivation and personality* (2nd ed.). New York: Harper & Row.

Otto, R. (1970). *The idea of the holy* (2nd ed.). (J. W. Harvey, Trans.). New York: Oxford University Press. (The original work was published in 1950.)

Patton, M. Q. (1980). *Qualitative evaluation methods*. Beverly Hills: Sage.

Pendleton. S. (1983). The Norwegian nature life approach. *Journal of Experiential Education 6*(1), 10-14.

Section II: Historical Foundations

7   A History of AEE ■ Dan Garvey

Adams, A., & Reynolds, S. (1985). The long conversation: Tracing the roots of the past. R. Kraft (Ed.), *The theory of experiential education*. Boulder, CO: The Association for Experiential Education.

Association for Experiential Education (1977). Article of incorporation, June 17, 1977, State of Colorado.

Association for Experiential Education (1982). Minutes of Board of Directors meeting, St. Louis, MO.

Association for Experiential Education (1985). Minutes of Board of Directors meeting, September 8, Denver, CO.

Association for Experiential Education (1985). Minutes of Board of Directors meeting, January 31, Boulder, CO.

Boyer, E. (1987). *College: the undergraduate experience in America.* New York: Harper & Row.

Hawkes, G., & Schulze, J. (1969). *Evaluation of Outward Bound teachers practica.* Reston, VA: Outward Bound, Inc.

Minor, J., & Boldt, J. (1981). *Outward Bound, USA: Learning through experience in adventure-based education.* New York: Morrow.

Shore, A., & Greenberg, E. (1978). Challenging the past, present, and future: New directions in education. *Journal of Experiential Education 1*(1), 42-48.

Taft, H. (1974). The value of experience (unpublished address).

10 Babies and Bath Water: Two Experiential Heresies
- **Theodore F. Wichmann**

Bruner, J. S. (1962). *On knowing.* Cambridge: The Belknap Press.

Bruner, J. S. (1966). *Toward a theory of instruction* (pp. 39-72). Cambridge: The Belknap Press.

Counts, G. S. (1932). *Dare the school build a new social order?* London: Feffer & Simons.

Cremin, L. A. (1964). *The transformation of the school: Progressivism in American Education 1876-1957.* New York: Random House.

Dewey, J. (1929) *My pedagogic creed.* Washington: Progressive Education Association.

Dewey, J. (1938). *Experience and education.* New York: Collier.

Gager, R. (1977). As a learning process . . . it's more than just getting your hands dirty. *Voyageur, 1.*

Greenberg, E. (1978). The community as a learning resource. *Journal of Experiential Education, 1,* 22-25.

Hall, E. T. *Beyond culture.* New York: Anchor Press/Doubleday.

Leiweke, T. (1979). Experiential education as a movement. *Journal of Experiential Education, 2,* 4-5.

Levin, H. M. (1975). Education, life chances, and the courts: The role of social science evidence. *Law and Contemporary Problems, 39,* 217-240.

Nold, J. J. (1977). On defining experiential education: John Dewey revisited. *Voyageur, 1.*

Pipho, C. (1978). *State activity related to minimal competency testing.* Unpublished report. Educational Commission of the States, Denver, CO.

Shore A., and Greenberg, E. (1977). Challenging the past, present and future: New directions in education. *Journal of Experiential Education, 1,* 42-46.

Spady, W. G. Competency based education: A bandwagon in search of a definition. *Education Researcher, 6,* 9-14.

Walsh, V., and Golins, G. L. (1976). *The exploration of the Outward Bound process.* Denver: Colorado Outward Bound School.

Section III: Psychological Foundations

12 Programming the Transfer of Learning in Adventure Education
   ▪ **Michael Gass**

*** Bacon, S. (1983). *The conscious use of metaphor in Outward Bound.* Denver, CO: Colorado Outward Bound School.

• Bruner, J. (1960). *The process of education.* New York: Vintage.

• Darnell, D. K. (1983). *On consequences, learning, survival and "the good life."* An unpublished report. Dept. of Communications, University of Colorado.

*** Gass, M. A. (1985). *Strengthening adventure education by increasing the transfer of learning.* Durham, NH: University of New Hampshire.

• Johnson, G., Bird, T., Little, J. W., & Beville, S. L. (Center for Action Research, Inc.). (1981). *Delinquency prevention: Theories and strategies.* U. S. Dept. of Justice: Office of Juvenile and Delinquency Prevention.

*** Kalisch, K. (1979). *The role of the instructor in the Outward Bound process.* Three Lakes, Wisconsin: Honey Lakes Camp.

• MacArthur, R. S. (1982). The changing role of service in Outward Bound. *Journal of Experiential Education, 5*(2).

• Mitzel, H. (Ed.). (1982). *Encyclopedia of Educational Research.* (Vol. 1) (American Educational Research Association) (5th ed.) (pp. 1947-1955). New York: Free Press.

• Rhoades, J. S. (1972). *The problem of individual change in Outward Bound: An application and transfer theory.* Doctoral dissertation. University of Massachusetts.

*** Richardson, B. L. (1978). *The transfer of learning from high-risk activities in adventure-based outdoor education programs.* An unpublished report. Northern Illinois University, p. 22.

14 Piaget — A Psychological Rationale for Experiential Education
   ▪ **Mitchell Sakofs**

Dewey, J. (1963). *Experience and education.* New York: Collier.

Maynard, G. (1975). A middle school identity. *Transescene: The Journal of Emerging Adolescent Education, 3.*

Piaget, J. (1954). *The construction of reality in the child.* New York: Basic Books.

Sund, R. (1976). *Piaget for educators.* Columbus, OH: Merrill.

Section IV: Social Foundations

17 White Awareness and Our Responsibility to End Racism ▪ Karen Fox

Anzaldua, G. (1990). *Making face, making soul—Hacienda caras: Creative and critical perspectives by women of color.* San Francisco, CA: CA: Aunt Lute Foundation.

Gibson, B. (1989). Meeting the interpretive needs of minorities. In the *Proceedings of the 1989 National Interpreters Workshop.* St. Paul, MN: National Association of Interpretation.

Katz, J. H. (1978). *White awareness: Handbook for anti-racism training.* Norman, OK: University of Oklahoma Press.

Kaufman, J. (1989, June 18). The color line: Blacks and whites in a divided America (Part I). *The Boston Globe Magazine,* 16-59.

Kaufman, J. (1989, June 25). The color line: Blacks and whites in a divided America (Part II). *The Boston Globe Magazine,* 18-49.

Klauda, P. (1990, June 14). Dark skin perceived as a crime waiting to happen. *Minneapolis Star Tribune,* pp. 1, 17, and 19 A.

Klauda, P., and St. Anthony. (1990, June 15). N. Minneapolis minority neighborhoods get fewer home loans from banks. *Minneapolis Star Tribune,* pp. 1 and 8A.

Lee, E. (1985). *Letters to Marcia: A teacher's guide to anti-racist education.* Toronto, ONT: Cross Cultural Communication Centre.

McAllister, P. (1991). *This river of courage: Generations of women's resistance and action.* Philadelphia, PA: New Society Publishers.

Mcintosh, P. (1991). White privilege: Unpacking the invisible knapsack. *Matrix,* pp. 5-6.

Robson, B. (1990, January). Pride and prejudice. *Minneapolis St Paul Magazine,* pp. 42-51, and 130.

von Steber, B. (1990, June 15). Minnesota power structure is overwhelmingly white. *Minneapolis Star Tribune,* pp. 1, and 18 and 19 A.

Weiner, J. (1990, June 19). Sports teams slow to reach out to minority fans. *Minneapolis Star Tribune,* pp. 1, 17, and 19 A.

Welch, S. D. (1990). *A feminist ethic of risk.* Minneapolis, MN: Fortress Press.

Young, W. (1970). Exceptional children: Text of a keynote speech. In J. H. Katz (1978), *White awareness: Handbook for anti-racism training.* Norman, OK: University of Oklahoma Press.

19 "Borrowing" Activities From Another Culture: A Native American's Perspective ▪ Gordon W. A. Oles

Bradbury, R. (1953). *Sun and shadow*. New York: The Forthnightly Publishing Company.

Hawk, W. (1990). *Native American religion and New Age cults*. University of Wisconsin. Symposium on Wisconsin Indians.

Linderman, F. B. (1967). *Plenty-Coups, Chief of the Crows*. Lincoln: Bison Books.

Wigginton, E., (Ed.). (1974). *The Foxfire book, vol. 1*. Charlotte: Foxfire.

Wilder, L. I. (1976). *The little house in the big woods*. New York: Scholastic Books.

20 Snips and Snails and Puppy Dog Tails . . . The Use of Gender-Free Language in Experiential Education ▪ Deb Jordan

Berger, J., & Zelditch, M. (Eds.). (1985). *Status, rewards, and influence*. San Francisco, CA: Jossey-Bass.

Connell, R. (1987). *Gender and power*. Stanford, CA: Stanford University Press.

Eagly, A. (1987). *Sex differences in social behavior: A social role interpretation*. Hillsdale, NJ: Lawrence Erlbaum Associates.

Miller, C., & Swift, K. (1988). *The handbook of nonsexist writing* (2nd ed.). NY: Harper & Row.

Pearson, J. (1985). *Gender and communication*, Dubuque: Wm. C Brown Publisher.

Sargent, A. (1984). *Beyond sex roles* (2nd ed.). NY: West Publishers.

Shivers, J. (1986). *Recreational leadership. Group dynamics and interpersonal behavior*. Princeton, NJ: Princeton Book Co.

Swiderski, L. (1987). Soft and conceptual skills: The often overlooked components of outdoor leadership, *The Bradford Papers Annual, 2*, 29-36.

Thorne, B., & Henley, N. (1975). *Language and sex: Difference and dominance*. Rowley, MA: Newbury House.

Time (1989, January 2) Planet of the year: Endangered earth. NY: Time Magazine.

Webster's New World Dictionary (2nd concise edition). (1978). NY: Avenel Books.

Werner & LaRussa (1985). Persistence and change in sex-role stereotypes. *Sex Roles, 12*(9/110), pp. 1089-1100.

Wilkinson, S. (1986). Sighting possibilities: Diversity and commonality in feminist research. In S. Wilkinson (Ed.), *Feminist social psychology*. Philadelphia, PA: Open University Press.

21 Learning to Cross the Street: A Male Perspective on Feminist Theory ▪ Gary Rasberry

Connelly, M., & Clandinin, J. (1988). *Teachers as curriculum planners: Narratives of experience*. New York: Teachers College Press, Columbia University.

Lewis, M. (1990). *Politics, resistance and transformation: The psycho/social/sexual dynamics in the feminist classroom.* Unpublished manuscript, Faculty of Education, Queen's University.

Lyttelton, N. (1987). Men's liberation, men against sexism and major dividing lines. In G. Hofmann-Nemiroff (Ed.), *Women and men: Interdisciplinary readings on gender,* pp. 472-477. Montreal: Fitzhenry and Whiteside.

22 Sharing Lesbian, Gay and Bisexual Life Experiences Face to Face
■ Mary McClintock

Knowles, M. (1980). *The modern practice of adult education.* New York: The Adult Education Company.

Wes. (1992). Quotation used by Wes in her work on AIDS, reprinted on buttons by Tickle Graphics. For more information, contact Wes at Box 383, Southington, CT 06489.

Suggested Readings

Alyson, S. (1991). *Young, gay, and proud!* Boston: Alyson Publications.

Blumenfeld, W. (Ed.). (1992). *Homophobia: How we all pay the price.* Boston: Beacon Press.

Blumenfeld, W. J., and Raymond, D. (1988). *Looking at gay and lesbian life.* Boston: Beacon Press.

Cohen, S., and Cohen D. (1989). *When someone you know is gay: High school help line.* New York: Dell.

Hutchins, L., and Kaahumanu, L. (Eds.). *Bi any other name: Bisexual people speak out.* Boston: Alyson Publications.

23 In Our Own Words: Service Learning in Native Communities
■ McClellan Hall

Wigginton, E. (1986). *Sometimes a shining moment.* New York: Anchor Press/Doubleday.

Section V: Theory and Practice

24 What is Experiential Education? ■ Steve Chapman, Pam McPhee, and Bill Proudman

Dewey, J. (1938). *Experience and education.* New York: Macmillan.

Gass, M. A. (1991). Enhancing metaphor development in adventure therapy programs. *Journal of Experiential Education, 14*(2), 6-13.

Kjol, R., & Weber, J. (1990). The 4th Fire: Adventure based counseling with juvenile sex offenders. *Journal of Experiential Education, 13*(3), 18-22.

Kolb, D. A. (1976). Management and the learning process. *California Management Review*, Spring.

Peters, R. S. (1970). *Education and the educated man*. London: Society of Philosophy on Education.

25 The Student-Directed Classroom: A Model for Teaching Experiential Education Theory ▪ Karen Warren

Auvine, B., et al. (1977). *A manual for group facilitators*. Madison, WI: Center for Conflict Resolution.

Avery, M., et al. (1981). *Building united judgement: A handbook for consensus decision making*. Madison, WI: Center for Conflict Resolution.

Chrislip, D. (1980). *A process guide for teaching*. An unpublished paper of the Colorado Outward Bound School.

Katz, M. S. (1978). Teaching people to think for the future: Some guidelines for teacher education. *Journal of Teacher Education, 29*(4), 57-61.

Lockwood, L. G. (1979). What my students have learned about classroom ecology. *Journal of College Science Teaching, 9*(11), 80-82.

Rich, A. (1979). Claiming an education. In *On lies, secrets and silence*. New York: Norton.

Wigginton, E. (1985). *Sometimes a shining moment: The Foxfire experience*. Garden City, NY: Anchor Press/Doubleday.

26 The Design of Intellectual Experience ▪ Donald L. Finkel and G. Stephen Monk

Finkel, D. L. and Monk, G. S. (1978) *Contexts for learning: A teacher's guide to the design of intellectual experience*. Olympia, WA: The Evergreen State College.

Suggested Reading
Dewey, J. (1966). *Democracy and education*. Free Press.

Kohlberg, L., and Mayer, R. (1972). Development as the aim of education. *Harvard Education Review, 42*, 449-496.

Furth, H. (1970). *Piaget for Teachers*. Prentice Hall.

28 A Group Development Model for Adventure Education ▪ Pamela J. Kerr and Michael A. Gass

Buell, L. (1983). *The 24-hour experience: An outdoor adventure program*. Greenfield, MA: Environmental Awareness Publications.

Garland, J. A., Jones, H. E., & Kolodny, R. L. (1973). A model for stages of development in social work groups. In S. Bernstein, *Explorations in Group Work.* Boston, MA: Milford House.

Jensen, M. (1979). *Application of small group theory to adventure programs. Journal of Experiential Education, 2*(2), 39-42.

Kalisch, K. (1979). *The role of the instructor in the Outward Bound process.* Three Lakes, Wisconsin: Honey Lakes Camp.

Landry, P. (1986). *The instructor's handbook.* Thunder Bay, Ontario: Canadian Outward Bound Wilderness School.

Walsh, V., and Golins, G. (1975). *The exploration of the Outward Bound process.* Denver, CO: Colorado Outward Bound School.

Additional Readings in Small Group Development

Agris, C. (1970). *Intervention theory and method: A behavioral science view.* Reading, MA: Addison-Wesley.

Glasser, P. H., Sarri, R., & Vintner, R. (Eds.). (1974). *Individual change through small groups.* New York: The Free Press.

Liberman, M. A., Yalom, I. D., & Miles, M. B. (1973). *Encounter groups: First facts.*

Napier, R. W. & Gershenfeld, M. K. (1983). *Making groups work: A guide for group leaders.* Boston: Houghton Mifflin.

Rogers, C. R. (1970). *Carl Rogers on encounter groups.* New York: Harper & Row.

29   From Theory to Practice for College Student Interns: A Stage Theory Approach ▪ Dan Garvey and Anna Catherine Vorsteg

Bacon, S. (1983). *The conscious use of metaphor in Outward Bound.* Denver, CO: Colorado Outward Bound School.

Bedford, M. M. (1991). *Moving from practice to theory.* Unpublished paper, University of New Hampshire, Durham, NH.

Dewey, J. (1938). *Experience and education.* New York: MacMillan.

Fox, M. (1991). *Creation spirituality: Liberating gifts for the peoples of the earth.* San Francisco, CA: Harpers.

Gass, M. A. (1985). Programming the transfer of learning. *Journal of Experiential Education, 8*(3), 18-24.

Gilligan, C. (1977). In a different voice: Women's conception of self and of morality. *Harvard Educational Review, 47,* 481-517.

Kerr, P. J., & Gass, M. A. (1987). A group development model for adventure education. *Journal of Experiential Education, 10*(3), 39-46.

Kohlberg, L. (1969). Stages and sequence: The cognitive-developmental approach to socialization. In D. Goslin (Ed.), *Handbook of socialization theory and research* (pp. 347-480). Chicago: Rand McNally.

Kolb, D. (1976). Management and the learning process. *California Management Review,* Spring.

Kraft, R. (1987). Towards a theory of experiential learning. In R. Kraft and M. Sakofs (Eds.), *The theory of experiential education* (2nd edition), (pp. 7-38). Boulder, Colorado: AEE.

Maslow, A. (1970). *Motivation and personality* (revised edition). New York: Harper & Row.

O'Reilly, D. (1989). On being an educational fantasy engineer: Incoherence, the individual and independent study. In S. Warner-Weil and I. McGill (Eds.), *Making sense of experiential learning: Diversity in theory and practice* (pp. 94-100). Stoney Stratford, England: The Society for Research into Higher Education and Open University Press.

Piaget, J. (1965). *The moral judgement of the child*. (M. Gabain, Transl.) New York: The Free Press. Originally published in 1932.

Rest, J. (1979). *Development in judging moral issues*. Minneapolis, MN: University of Minnesota Press, p. 4.

Tucker, J. (1991). *Theory and practice*. Unpublished paper, University of New Hampshire, Durham, NH.

Whitehead, A. N. (1929). *The aims of education and other essays*. New York: Macmillan.

Section VI: Ethics

30 Justifying the Risk to Others: The Real Razor's Edge ▪ Simon Priest and Rusty Baillie

Baillie, R. (September. 1986). *Hazarding the lives of others: How can we justify it?* Paper presented at the AEE Conference, Moodus, CT.

Csikszentmihalyi, M. (1975). *Beyond boredom and anxiety*. San Francisco, CA: Jossey-Bass.

Ellis, M. (1973). *Why people play*. Englewood Cliffs, NJ: Prentice-Hall.

Hale, A. (1985). *1985 Injury Data Base Review*. Bellefontaine, OH: National Safety Network.

Helms, M. (1984), Factors Affecting Evaluations of Risks and Hazards in Mountaineering. *Journal of Experiential Education, 7*(3), 22-4.

Higgins, L. (1981). "Wilderness schools: Risk vs. danger." *The Physician and Sportsmedicine, 9*(3), 133-6.

Martin, P., and Priest, S. (1986). Understanding the adventure experience. *Adventure Education: The Journal of NAOE, 3*(1), 18-21.

Maslow, A. H. (1968). *Towards a psychology of being*. New York: Van Nostrand Reinhold.

Meier, J. F. (1985). Injury countermeasures in outdoor adventure programs. *Parks & Recreation, 20*(4), 70-4.

Meyer, D. (1979). The management of risk. *Journal of Experiential Education, 2*(2), 9-14.

Mitchell, R. G., Jr. (1983). *Mountain experience: The psychology and sociology of adventure*. Chicago, IL: University of Chicago Press.

Mortlock. C. (1984). *The adventure alternative.* Cumbria, UK: Cicerone.

Williamson, J., and Mobley, M. (1984). Editorial: "On the razor's edge . . . ." *Journal of Experiential Education, 7*(3), 5.

Zuckerman, M. (1974). The sensation seeking motive. In B. A. Maher (Ed.), *Progress in Experimental Personality Research, 7.* New York: Academic.

31 Connecting Ethics and Group Leadership: A Case Study ▪ Kate Lehmann

Mitten, D. (1985). A philosophical basis for a women's outdoor adventure program. *Journal of Experiential Education, 8*(2), 20-24.

Mitten, D. (undated). *Meeting the unknown: Women bonding in the wilderness.* Unpublished manuscript.

Terry, R. (1986). *Leadership - A preview of the seventh view.* Hubert Humphrey Institute of Public Affairs.

Terry, R. (1991). *Ethics for the 21st century and beyond.* Lecture broadcast on Minnesota Public Radio.

32 Ethics and Experiential Education as Professional Practice ▪ Jasper S. Hunt, Jr.

Macintyre, A. (1984). *After virtue.* (2nd ed.). Notre Dame: University of Notre Dame Press.

McKeon, R. (Ed.). (1941). *Nicomachean ethics.* From The basic works of Aristotle. New York: Random House.

33 Understanding Moral Development and Environmental Values Through Experience ▪ Almut Beringer

Brown, L. M., Tappan, M. B., Gilligan, C., Miller, B. A., and Argyris, D. E. (1989). Reading for self and moral voice: A method for interpreting narratives of real-life moral conflict and choice. In M. J. Packer & R. B. Addison (Eds.), *Entering the circle: Hermeneutic investigations in psychology.* Albany, NY: State University of New York.

Caduto, M. J. (1985). *A guide on environmental values education.* Paris, France: UNESCO.

Gilligan, C. (1982). *In a different voice: Psychological theory and women's development.* Cambridge, MA: Harvard University Press.

Hargrove, E. C. (1989). *Foundations of environmental ethics.* Englewood Cliffs, NJ: Prentice Hall.

Iozzi, L. (1976). Moral judgment, verbal ability, logical reasoning, and environmental issues. Rutgers University: Unpublished doctoral dissertation.

Iozzi, L. A. (1989). What research says to the educator. *Journal of Environmental Education, 30*(3), 3-9.

Kaplan, R., and Kaplan, S. (1989). *The experience of nature: A psychological perspective.* New York, NY: Cambridge University Press.

Levine, C., Kohlberg, L., and Hewer, A. (1985). The current formulation of Kohlberg's theory and a response to critics. *Human Development, 28,* 94-100.

Mergendoller, J. R. (1989). Good and ill will: War resistance as a context for the study of moral action. In M. J. Packer & R. B. Addison (Eds.), *Entering the circle: Hermeneutic investigations in psychology.* Albany, NY: State University of New York.

Monroe, M. C., and Kaplan, S. (1988). When words speak louder than actions. *Journal of Environmental Education, 19*(3), 38-41.

Partridge, E. (1982). Are we ready for an ecological morality? *Environmental Ethics, 4*(2), 175-190.

Passmore, J. A. (1974). *Man's responsibility for nature: Ecological problems and western traditions.* London, Great Britain: Duckworth.

Tappan, M. B., and Brown, L. M. (1989). Stories told and lessons learned: Toward a narrative approach to moral development and moral education. *Harvard Educational Review, 59*(2), 182-205.

Addendum to article

Beringer, A. (1992). *The moral ideals of care and respect: A hermeneutic inquiry into adolescents' environmental ethics and moral functioning.* University of Michigan, doctoral dissertation.

Gilligan, C. (1982). *In a different voice.* Cambridge, MA: Harvard University Press.

Haan, N., Aerts, E., & Cooper, B. A. B. (1985). *On moral grounds: The search for practical morality.* New York, NY: New York University Press.

Packer, M. J. (1989). Tracing the hermeneutic circle: Articulating an ontical study of moral conflicts. In M. J. Packer & R. B. Addison (Eds.), *Entering the circle: hermeneutic investigations in psychology,* (pp. 95-117). Albany, NY: State University of New York Press.

Tappan, M. B. (1987). *Hermeneutics and moral development: A developmental analysis of short-term change in moral functioning during late adolescence.* Harvard University, doctoral dissertation.

Section VII: Research and Evaluation

34 Research in Experiential Education: An Overview ▪ Alan Ewert

Babbie, E. (1983). *The practice of social research* (3rd ed.). Belmont, CA: Wadsworth Publishing.

Bachrach, A. (1981). *Psychological research: An introduction.* New York: Random House.

Burton, L. (1981). *A critical analysis and review of the research on Outward Bound and related programs.* Doctoral dissertation. Rutgers University, The State University of New Jersey.

Ewert, A. (1986). What research doesn't tell the practitioner. *Parks and Recreation, 21*(3), 46-49.

Fielding, N., & Fielding, J. (1986) *Linking data.* Sage University Paper series on Qualitative Research Methods (Vol. 4). Beverly Hills, CA: Sage.

Gardner, M. (1957). *Fads and fallacies in the name of science.* New York: Dover Publications.

Hamilton, S. (1979, April). *Evaluating experiential learning programs.* Paper presented at the Annual Meeting of the American Educational Research Association.

Heath, D. (1985). Teaching for adult effectiveness. In R. Kraft and M. Sakofs (Eds.), *The theory of experiential education.* Boulder, CO: Association for Experiential Education.

Johnston, J., & Pennypacker, H. (1980). *Strategies and tactics of human behavioral research.* Hillsdale, NJ: Lawrence Erlbaum Associates.

Kirk, J., & Miller, M. (1986). *Reliability and validity in qualitative research.* Sage University Paper series on Qualitative Research Methods (Vol. 1). Beverly Hills, CA: Sage.

Lawson, J. (1985). Challenges to graduate education. *Journal of Physical Education and Recreation, 44,* 23-25.

Reinharz, S. (1979). *Social science.* San Francisco: Jossey-Bass.

Shore, A. (1977). *Outward Bound: A reference volume.* New York: Topp Litho.

Webb, E., Campbell, D., Schwartz, R., & Sechrest, L. (1966). *Unobtrusive measure: Nonreactive research in the social sciences.* Chicago: Rand McNally.

Weiss, C. (1972). *Evaluation research: Methods of assessing program effectiveness.* Englewood Cliffs, NJ: Prentice-Hall.

35 Anxiety and the Outward Bound Process
- Charles E. Drebing, Scott Cabot Willis, and Brad Genet

Baer, D. J., Jacobs, P. J., & Carr, F. E. (1975). Instructors' ratings of delinquents after Outward Bound survival training and their subsequent recidivism. *Psychological Reports, 36,* 547-553.

Burton, L. M. (1981). A critical analysis and review of the research on Outward Bound and related programs. *Dissertation Abstracts International, 42*(4), 1581-B. (University Microfilms No. 8122147)

Drebing, C. E., & Willis, S. C. (1987, April). *Personality change as a result of a wilderness experience.* Paper presentation at the 67th Annual Convention of the Western Psychological Association, Long Beach, California.

Ewert, A. (1983). *Outdoor adventure & self concept: A research analysis.* College of Human Development and Performance; Department of Recreation and Park Management, Center for Leisure Studies, University of Oregon.

Ewert, A. (1987a). Fear and anxiety in environmental education programs. *Journal of Environmental Education, 18*(1), 33-39.

Ewert, A. (1987b). *Reduction of trait anxiety through participation in Outward Bound.* Manuscript submitted for publication.

Kalisch, K. (1979). *The role of the instructor in Outward Bound educational process.* Three Lakes, Wisconsin: Author.

Keppel, G. (1982). *Design and analysis, A researcher's handbook* (2nd ed.). New Jersey: Prentice-Hall.

Shore, A. (1977). *Outward Bound: A reference volume.* New York: Topp Litho.

Spielberber, C., Gorsuch, R., Lushene, R., Vagg, P., & Jacobs, G. (1977). *The State-Trait Anxiety Inventory.* Palo Alto, CA: Consulting Psychology Press.

Wade, I. (1983). *Pacific Crest Outward Bound: Instructor's manual.* Pacific Crest Outward Bound.

Walsh, V. & Golins, G. (1975). *The exploration of the Outward Bound process.* Denver, CO: Colorado Outward Bound.

Wichmann, T. (1983). Evaluating Outward Bound for delinquent youth. *Journal of Experiential Education, 5*(3), 10-16.

Williams, B. (1975). *Leaders' manual for vanguard wilderness courses.* Wheaton, IL: Wheaton College.

Yerkes, R. M., & Dodson, J. D. (1980). The relation of strength of stimulus to rapidity of habit-formation. *Journal of Comparative Neurological Psychology, 18*, 459-482.

36 The Effects of a Wilderness Orientation Program on College Students
- Michael A. Gass

Gass, M. A. (1984). *The value of wilderness orientation programs at colleges and universities in the United States.* Durham, NH: University of New Hampshire, Outdoor Education Program. (ERIC Document Reproduction Service No. ED 242 471)

Gass, M. A., Kerr, P. J., and Garvey, D. (1986). Orientation in wilderness settings. In R. Kraft and M. Sakofs (Eds.) *Experiential education in the schools.* Boulder, CO: Association for Experiential Education.

Hood, A. B., (1982, March). *Student development on three vectors over four years.* Paper presented at the Annual Convention of the American Personnel and Guidance Association, Detroit, MI. (ERIC Document Reproduction Service No. ED 220 736)

Winston, R. B., Miller, T. K., & Prince, J. S. (1982). *Assessing student development.* Athens, GA: Student Development Associates.

37 An International Survey of Outdoor Leadership Preparation ▪ Simon Priest

Buell, L. H. (1981) *The identification of outdoor adventure leadership competencies for entry-level and experience-level personnel.* Unpublished doctoral dissertation, University of Massachusetts.

Dunn, D. R., & Gublis, J. M. (1976) The risk revolution. *Parks and Recreation, 11*(8), 12-17.

Ford, P. M., & Blanchard, J. (1985). *Leadership and administration of outdoor pursuits.* State College, PA: Venture.

Green, P. J. (1981). *The content of a college-level outdoor leadership course for land-based outdoor pursuits in the Pacific Northwest: A Delphi consensus.* Unpublished doctoral dissertation, University of Oregon.

Nash, R. (1982). *Wilderness and the American mind* (3rd ed.). New Haven, CT: Yale University Press.

Priest, S. (1984). Effective outdoor leadership: A survey. *Journal of Experiential Education, 7*(3), 34-36.

Swiderski, M. J. (1981). *Outdoor leadership competencies identified by outdoor leaders in five western regions.* Unpublished doctoral dissertation, University of Oregon.

Section VIII: Speeches and Perspectives

40 Habits of the Heart ▪ Robert S. MacArthur

Bellah, R., et al. (1985). *Habits of the heart: Individualism and commitment in American life.* Harper & Row.

Brown, D. (1986, April). *Youth Policy.*

Ende, A. (1985, October 31). *SPS (Student Press Service).*

Hodgkinson, H. (1985). *All one system: Demographics of education, kindergarten through graduate school.* Institute for Educational Leadership.

Lehman, P. L. (1963). *Ethics in a Christian context.* Harper & Row.